BUDDHIST TRADITION SERIES

General Editor
ERNST STEINKELLNER

Joint General Editor
ALEXANDER VAN ROSPATT

Founder Editor
Late ALEX WAYMAN

Editorial Advisory Board
CHR. LINDTNER
KATSUMI MIMAKI
LOKESH CHANDRA
MICHAEL HAHN

VOLUME 41

STUDIES IN THE LANKĀVATĀRA SŪTRA

BODHIDHARMA (達摩)

Father of Zen Buddhism in China

Painted by Mu-ch'i (牧溪)

Studies in
The Laṅkāvatāra Sūtra

One of the most important texts of Mahayana Buddhism, in which almost all its principal tenets are presented, including the teaching of Zen

D.T. Suzuki

MOTILAL BANARSIDASS PUBLISHERS
PRIVATE LIMITED • DELHI

Reprint : Delhi, 2007
First Indian Edition : Delhi 1999

© MOTILAL BANARSIDASS PUBLISHERS PVT. LTD.
All Rights Reserved

ISBN: 81-208-1656-0

MOTILAL BANARSIDASS
41 U.A. Bungalow Road, Jawahar Nagar, Delhi 110 007
8 Mahalaxmi Chamber, Warden Road, Mumbai 400 026
120 Royapettah High Road, Mylapore, Chennai 600 004
Sanas Plaza, 1302 Baji Rao Road, Pune 411 002
16, St. Mark's Road, Bangalore 560 001
8 Camac Street, Kolkata 700 017
Ashok Rajpath, Patna 800 004
Chowk, Varanasi 221 001

FOR SALE IN SOUTH ASIA ONLY

PRINTED IN INDIA
BY JAINENDRA PRAKASH JAIN AT SHRI JAINENDRA PRESS,
A-45 NARAINA, PHASE-I, NEW DELHI 110 028
AND PUBLISHED BY NARENDRA PRAKASH JAIN FOR
MOTILAL BANARSIDASS PUBLISHERS PRIVATE LIMITED,
BUNGALOW ROAD, DELHI 110 007

FOREWORD

It is a wonderful contribution to this Buddhist Tradition Series to have D.T. Suzuki's important *Studies in the Laṅkāvatāra Sūtra.*

This work discusses such important matters of the basic Sūtra as the theory of the subtle body (*manomaya-kāya*), Bodhisattva Stages, the relation of the mind to the external world, reasons for the evolving of eye-perception, and other theories usually associated with the Mahāyāna school called Yogācāra.

Alex Wayman

PREFACE

While preparing a second series of *Essays in Zen Buddhism,* the author thought it desirable for the reader to know something more about the *Laṅkāvatāra* than had been sketched out in the First Series To do this he had to study the sutra more thoroughly, and as he was doing so, his interest in it grew stronger and wider. Then, he came to the conclusion that his study of the *Laṅkāvatāra* might be published independently and even prior to the second series of Zen Essays. The result is this book now before the reader.

The *Laṅkāvatāra* is a Mahayana text difficult in more than one way to understand perfectly as to its meaning and also in its proper historical setting. But its importance as giving most of the fundamental tenets of Mahayana Buddhism has urged the author to publish whatever results he has gained so far in his study. They are no doubt short of being quite satisfactory from a strictly scholarly point of view, but the author's earnest wish is to open the way, if he could so hope, for further study and more thoroughgoing investigation of the text. Mahayana Buddhism is just beginning to be known in the West As to the appreciation of its full significance we have to wait patiently for some years yet to come.

The first two parts of these *Studies* were already published in *The Eastern Buddhist,* but in the present work they have been revised fully and inaccuracies corrected as far as available. The third part is entirely new. As the *Studies* were not planned out as a whole from the beginning but have grown progressively in the author's mind, some repetitions have become inevitable. The second part dealing with the *Laṅkāvatāra* containing the philosophy of Zen Buddhism was written first. As it was being revised after its publication in *The Eastern Buddhist,* Volume IV, Nos. 3–4, for 1928, the thought suggested itself that the sutra must be studied also textually since there are still three Chinese and one (or two) Tibetan translations. The result was the first part of the present work, which appeared as an independent article in *The Eastern Buddhist,* Volume V, No. 1, for 1929.

The *Laṅkāvatāra* does not belong exclusively to the Zen school of Buddhism, it is also the common property of the Mahayana. When it is studied apart from Zen, some of the important conceptions developed in the sutra, which do not necessarily belong to the philosophy of Zen, are to be expounded, however briefly. Hence the third part of the present *Studies,* entitled "Some of the Important Theories Expounded in the *Laṅkāvatāra.*"

The author has prepared for the benefit principally of his Japanese and Chinese readers a glossary of the Sanskrit technical terms found in the book. This he hopes to be of use in their perusal of Sanskrit Buddhist literature and at the same time illustrative of the methods of the Indian-Chinese translators.

It is the pleasant duty on the part of the author to acknowledge all the help given him in various ways by the following friends: Mr. Dwight Goddard of Vermont, U.S.A., who typed the whole manuscript while he was staying in Japan last winter; Professor Hōkei Idzumi who gave valuable information whenever the author met with grammatical difficulties in reading the Sanskrit text; Mr. Bunkyō Sakurabe who collected facts concerning the Tibetan translations of the *Laṅkāvatāra*; Professor Shizusato Sugihira and Mr. Kensei Yokogawa who read the proofs for typographical errors.

The author further wishes most sincerely to thank Mrs. L. Adams Beck for her critical reading of the proof-sheets and for many valuable suggestions. He appreciates the genuine interest she has taken in his attempt to introduce to the West the Mahayana way of viewing human life and the world.

The work of proof-reading has also fallen to his wife who is always ready to help the author in his literary undertakings, and for which he remains ever thankful.

Finally, the author mentions with gratitude the substantial help and encouragement ungrudgingly rendered by his friend, Mr. Yakichi Ataka, of Osaka, without whom this work would probably never have seen the light so soon and in such favourable conditions. Whatever merit there is, according to Mahayana teaching, in the production of such a work as this, may be transferred over to the further growth of his spiritual welfare and also to that of all the author's other friends and fellow-beings.

DAISETZ TEITARO SUZUKI

Kyoto, September 1929

CONTENTS

ABSTRACTS OF STUDIES

I

AN INTRODUCTION TO THE STUDY OF THE LANKAVATARA SUTRA

II

THE LANKAVATARA SUTRA AND THE TEACHING OF ZEN BUDDHISM

PART ONE

GENERAL SURVEY OF THE PRINCIPAL IDEAS EXPOUNDED IN THE SUTRA 90–153

PART TWO

(A) THE INTELLECTUAL CONTENTS OF THE BUDDHIST EXPERIENCE

PART THREE

LIFE AND WORKS OF THE BODHISATTVA

III

SOME OF THE IMPORTANT THEORIES EXPOUNDED IN THE LANKAVATARA

I

AN INTRODUCTION TO THE STUDY OF THE LANKAVATARA SUTRA

I

AN INTRODUCTION TO THE STUDY OF THE LANKAVATARA SUTRA

1. THE CHINESE AND THE TIBETAN TRANSLATIONS

The *Laṅkāvatāra Sūtra* is one of the nine[1] principal Mahayana texts in Nepalese Buddhism; in China and Japan it also occupies an important position in the philosophy of Mahayana Buddhism as containing the doctrines of Mind-only, Tathāgata-garbha, and Ālayavijñāna, and again in the literature of Zen Buddhism. The study of the sutra, however, owing to various reasons has not been very popular. The publication of the Sanskrit text in 1923 by the late Dr. Bunyū Nanjō has evidently revived the general interest in it though to a limited extent. The full title of the sutra in Sanskrit reads:

॥ आर्यसद्धर्मलङ्कावतारो नाम महायानसूत्रम् ॥

which, liberally translated, means "A Mahayana sutra called *Laṅkāvatāra* containing the noble orthodox teaching of Buddhism." *Laṅkāvatāra* literally is "entering into Laṅkā" while Laṅkā is one of the islands in the south of India. It is popularly identified with Ceylon, but scholars are not quite certain about it. "Entering" probably refers to the Buddha's coming over to the island. The sutra is supposed to have been delivered by the Buddha while staying there. The dialogue takes place between him and Mahāmati who is the chief one of the Bodhisattvas assembled there. It is unusual for a Buddhist sutra to be delivered in such an out-of-the-way place as Laṅkā, a solitary island in the middle of the ocean. Compared, however, with the

[1] The nine are: 1. *Ashṭasāhasrikā-prajñāpāramitā*, 2. *Gaṇḍavyūha*, 3. *Daśabhūmika*, 4. *Samādhirāja*, 5. *Laṅkāvatāra*, 6. *Saddharma-puṇḍarīka*, 7. *Tathāgata-guhyaka*, 8. *Lalita-vistara*, and 9. *Suvarṇa-prabhāsa*.

Avataṁsaka which was given partly in mythical heavens, the Laṅkā has a more earthy foundation even when it is regarded as preached for the benefit of Rāvaṇa, Overlord of the Rakshasas.

Altogether four Chinese translations of the *Laṅkāvatāra Sūtra* were made between about A.D. 420 and 704, of which we have at present three still in existence. The first, in four fasciculi, was by Dharmaraksha, whose title was, "Master of the Law, Teacher of the Tripitaka, of Central India." According to 開元錄,[1] this was done from the same text which was later used by Guṇabhadra, Bodhiruci, and Śikshānanda. But this statement is not quite exact. "The same text" here undoubtedly allows of a wide latitude of interpretation as we shall know below when a comparative study of the different translations is made. He came to China in 412 and settled in Ku-tsang (姑臧), the capital of the Northern Liang. He spent eight years in translating the *Mahāparinirvāṇa-Sūtra* in forty or thirty-six fasciculi, which he revised three times. Though it is not exactly known when the *Laṅkāvatāra* was translated by him, it is likely that the work was taken up after the *Parinirvāṇa-Sūtra,* that is, between 412–433. He was assassinated in 433 when he was forty-nine years old. Roughly speaking, the first Chinese translation of the *Laṅkāvatāra* was produced about fifteen hundred years ago. Unfortunately, this is lost. The title was simply, *The Laṅkā-Sūtra* (楞伽經).

The second translation, also in four fasciculi, which appeared in 443 bears the title, *The Laṅkāvatāra-Treasure-Sūtra* (楞伽阿跋多羅寶經) and the translator is Guṇabhadra, "The Law-teacher of the Tripitaka, of Central India." He came to China by sea in 435. On his way the wind ceased, the ship could not sail on, the supply of fresh water was exhausted, and the sailors did not know what to do.

[1] *Kai-yüan Lu,* Fas. IV, 38a (Kōkyō Shoin edition). This is a catalogue of the Buddhist Tripitaka compiled in the Kai-yüan era (713–741, A.D.), of the T'ang dynasty.

The situation, however, was improved by the mystic rites performed by Guṇabhadra; for the wind began to blow more favourably and a pouring rain saved them from dying of thirst. Among his translations we may mention the *Śrīmāla, Aṅgulimāla, Samyuktāgama,* etc. He died in 468 at the age of seventy-five.[1]

The *Laṅkāvatāra Sūtra* which is recorded as having been handed by Bodhidharma to his disciple Hui-k'ê was probably this Guṇabhadra translation in four fasciculi. It is strange that the first translation was lost so early as 700 when the fourth translation was issued. At the time of Tao-hsüan's *Catalogue of Buddhist Literature in Great T'ang* (大唐内典錄),[2] which was completed in 664, mention is made of the first one. In Fas. VIII of this *Catalogue* under the heading, "Those sutras which have been translated under the former dynasties and at present are kept among the Tripitaka collection" (歷代衆經見入藏錄), he refers to the "*Laṅkāvatāra Sūtra* in ten fasciculi, kept in one case," which is evidently that by Bodhiruci; and a little further down there is another entry: "The *Laṅkāvatāra* in four fasciculi, two sutras in one case." This must be the case for the first and the second translations, as they were both compiled in four fasciculi. In the *Kai-yüan Catalogue,* however, which was finished in 730, Dharmaraksha's *Laṅkāvatāra* is mentioned as lost. The loss must have taken place even earlier as I stated before; for Fa-tsang (法藏) who had much to do with the fourth or T'ang translation (done in the years 700–708) makes no reference whatever to the first. This was only forty years after the compilation of Tao-hsüan's *Catalogue.* It is quite unfortunate that we now have no means of seeing how far the agreements go between the first and the second translations, as they are

[1] *The Kai-yüan Lu,* Fas. V, 45b et seq. (the Kōkyō Shoin edition).

[2] 大唐内典錄, (*Tai-t'ang Nei-tien Lu,* a Catalogue of the Buddhist Books Compiled in the T'ang Dynasty), Fas. III, 64a (the Kōkyō Shoin edition). This is an earlier compilation than the *Kai-yüan Lu,* as the preface is dated the first year of Lin-tê, that is, A.D. 664.

both in four fasciculi and it is likely that they were made from the same original. Fa-tsang[1] criticises the second (or Sung) translation as being not quite good as a translation, for it retains to some extent the original Sanskrit diction which puzzles even the intelligent Chinese reader adequately to understand the text.

The third one (入楞伽經) in ten fasciculi is by Bodhiruci, "the Law Teacher of the Tripitaka, of Northern India." It was finished in 513, about one hundred years after the Sung translation. Fa-tsang's remarks are: "Although this translation is fuller than the preceding one, the original meaning is not fully expressed and errors are more apt to creep in." This may be true to a certain extent, but as we now have no original text of this third, or Wei, translation, there is no way of verifying this criticism of Fa-tsang. There are, however, some points in it which are in

[1] He died in 712, one of the greatest scholars in China and a most eminent figure in the history of the Avataṁsaka school of Buddhism. He was a contemporary of Hsüan-chuang (玄奘), I-tsing (義淨), Hui-nêng (慧能), Shên-hsiu (神秀), Śikshānanda, Dīvākara, Bodhiruci (all of the T'ang dynasty), etc. When Hsüan-chuang came back from India, Fa-tsang was one of the learned scholars chosen by Hsüan-chuang to be his assistants or co-workers in converting the Sanskrit texts into the Chinese language. Fa-tsang, however, disagreed with Hsüan-chuang in the interpretation of the texts and withdrew from the translation bureau. Later, he worked with Sikshānanda in the translation of the *Avataṁsaka Sūtra* and the *Laṅkāvatāra Sūtra*, and illuminating lectures were given by him on the teachings of the *Avataṁsaka* for the edification of the Empress Tsê T'ien (則天), who was one of the great women-rulers of China. His 入楞伽心玄義 (*Ju lêng-chia hsin hsüan-i*) is a short expository treatise on the *Laṅkāvatāra Sūtra* throwing much light on the understanding of the text and its philosophy, and in this he complains of the second translation being difficult even for men of superior intelligence to understand thoroughly, not to say anything about the ignorant and unlearned who are apt to give wrong interpretations to the text. This being really the case, as was confirmed later by Su Tung-pei and Ch'iang Chih-ch'i, noted Chinese scholars of the Sung dynasty, the understanding of the *Laṅkāvatāra* must have caused a great deal of trouble among scholars. So far, however, in China and Japan the four fasciculi one has had a far wider circulation than the ten or the seven fasciculi one.

better agreement with the Nanjo edition than with the others. It may not be quite fair to say that Bodhiruci put in his own words to help the reading of the text; the fact may be, perhaps, that his original was largely mixed with gloss and that he was not discriminating enough to reject it as such. This fact partly shows that the *Laṅkāvatāra Sūtra,* being a difficult text to understand, not only textually but doctrinally as well, was already in bad condition from a literary point of view when it was brought into China by these early Indian missionaries.

The fourth Chinese translation, entitled the *Mahāyāna Laṅkāvatāra Sūtra* (大乘入楞伽經) in seven fasciculi, was produced in 700–704, and the chief translator was Śikshānanda. More details are known of this translation than of all the preceding ones as regards circumstances and persons concerned. The preface by the Empress Tsê-t'ien Wu-hou (則天武后) tells how it came to be translated once more by Śikshānanda and others; and, moreover, Fa-tsang, who was one of the Chinese scholars who were engaged in revising the translation by Śikshānanda, wrote a sort of commentary-introduction in which is given not only an analytical resumé of the *Laṅkāvatāra Sūtra,* but a full account of the work itself. The following is quoted from the book whose Chinese title is 入楞伽心玄義:

"With regard to the translation: the four fasciculi one was done by Guṇabhadra, Master of the Tripitaka, of India, at Chih-huan Ssŭ (祇洹寺), Tang Yang (丹陽), in the Yüan-chia (玄嘉) period (424–453) of Sung; Pao-yün (寶雲) the monk took down the master's dictation and Hui-kuan (慧觀) put it into writing.[1] The ten fasciculi one

[1] 寶雲傳語慧觀筆受. *Chuan-yü* literally means "to transmit words," and *pi-shou* means "to receive with a writing brush." As Guṇabhadra who came from India probably could not speak Chinese well enough to make himself fully understood, Pao-yün acted as a kind of interpreter; or Guṇabhadra gave a literal translation of the original, which was done into literary Chinese by Pao-yün, and this in turn was put into writing by Hui-kuan. When the Indian translators were not complete masters

was done toward the end of Wei by Bodhiruci, Master of the Tripitaka, of India, who was engaged in the work at Yung-nêng Ssŭ (永寧寺), Lo-yang (洛陽).[1]

"As to the present one, [that is, the seven fasciculi one], Śikshānanda, Master of the Tripitaka, of Yü-t'ien (于闐), is the translator, who, after finishing the translation of the *Avataṁsaka* at Fo Shou-chi Ssŭ (佛授記寺), of the Eastern City, in the first year of Chiu-shih (久視, A.D. 700), was ordered by the Empress Tsê-t'ien to take up once more the task of translating the *Laṅkāvatāra*. Before the work was completed, Śikshānanda returned to the Capital and was given residence at the Chin-ch'an Ssŭ (清禪寺). The translation was roughly finished here, but before he had time to revise it he was allowed to return to his native land, by

of the Chinese language, there was always a "transmitter" who acted as a "go-between." In some cases there were other scholars engaged in the work, whose office it was to see if the original meaning was correctly understood, or to put the translation into better classical style, or to see that the translation fully expressed the original ideas. This more or less round-about way was inevitable, seeing that the translator had not a complete command of the two languages, Sanskrit and Chinese. But it was in this way, too, that the Chinese translators so well produced the sense of the original, and it helped a great deal towards making Buddhism strike root firmly in the native soil. From the linguistic point of view, however, there might have been something missed in the Chinese versions which is retained in the Tibetan texts. So we read in the life of Hsüan-chuang as recorded in the *Kai-yüan Catalogue* (fas. VIII, 73a) that "in the former days the sutras were translated in this way: first, the original text was translated literally word by word, and this was turned round to adapt itself to the Chinese style of diction, and finally the words and sentences were rearranged and revised by those especially skilled in writing. Thus, while going through so many hands, the original writing suffered much alteration, sometimes something added, sometimes something taken away. But now in the case of Hsüan-chuang everything was managed single-handed; as words came out of his mouth they were at once written down and made a perfectly readable translation." Literary accuracy was thus gained, but the strange fact is that some of these older translations are still in far better circulation than the newer ones.

[1] According to the *Kai-yüan Catalogue* (fas. VIII, 56a), Sêng-lang (僧朗) and Tao-chan (道湛) put the translation into writing.

Imperial order. In the second year of Chang-an (長安, 702), Mi-t'o-shan (彌陀山), [a Master of] the Tripitaka, came from Tu-huo-lo (吐火羅), who, before coming to China, had spent twenty-five years in India, thoroughly mastering the Tripitaka, and he was especially learned in the *Laṅkāvatāra.* By Imperial order he was requested to revise Śikshānanda's translation, aided by such monk-translators as Fu-li (復禮), Fa-tsang (法藏), etc. Fu-li was engaged in giving a final touch to the revised Chinese version, and an Imperial preface to the sutra was written, in which its merits were extolled.

"As to the four fasciculi translation, the rendering is not perfect, the wording is after the Western grammar (?語順西音), which makes even men of superior intelligence confused, not knowing how to read it, while the ignorant and unlearned are apt to give wrong interpretations.

"The ten fasciculi one is somewhat fuller in paragraphs and chapters [than the preceding one], but the sacred sense is not adequately expressed. When words are added and sentences are mixed in, the meaning grows murky, frequently causing errors, and the result is that the truth, bright and clear, becomes obstructed in its course on account of the local dialect.[1]

"The Empress regretting this inadequacy ordered another translation to be made. The present one was made by comparing in detail five Sanskrit copies, and after examining the two Chinese translations. What was in accordance with [the true sense] was adopted, while what was not properly done was corrected. Many years of labour have thus ended in producing this splendid work, in which it is expected that the [original] sense is accurately repre-

[1] This is the translation of 方言, *fang-yen,* but what it really means is hard to decide; for the ten fasciculi version of the *Laṅkāvatāra* was not surely written in any other language than the Chinese just like the other translations. May it, however, mean that Bodhiruci's original was well mixed up with gloss written in the local dialect of his native Northern India?

sented and scholars may thus be saved from committing further errors."

The preface by the Empress Tsê-t'ien, which is usually found attached to the T'ang edition, generally agrees with the account given by Fa-tsang, but there is one point that is not quite clear and seems to disagree with Fa-tsang. Among other things we have the following in the preface which concerns the translation itself: "Originally this sutra was brought here from the Western country (西國), in the era of Yüan-chia. Guṇabhadra translated it, but it had not a wide circulation. Bodhiruci's version came out in the era of Yen-chang, but it misses the original meaning in many respects. Full of reverential thoughts about the transmission [of the Good Law], I earnestly wished for its prosperous condition. In the first year of Chiu-shih, which corresponds in the cyclical commutation to the year of *kêng-tsŭ,* and in the sixth month of the year, during the summer season, I went to Chi-fêng (箕峯) to escape the heat and enjoy the cool air by the river Ying-shui (潁水), when at the San Yang palace another translation was produced. The essentials of the three copies were inquired into and the perfect teaching was compiled into seven fasciculi. The Very Reverend Śikshānanda of Yü-t'ien who is a learned monk of the Tripitaka, and Fu-li, a priest of Tai-fu-hsien Ssü (大福先寺) and others [partook in the work]; they have all the reputation equal to that of Tao-an (道安) and Hui-yüan (慧遠), and virtues like those of Ma-t'eng (摩騰) and Fa-lan (法蘭); they are again all worthy to succeed in the steps of Nāgārjuna, and have deeply delved into the secrets of Aśvaghosha; they are equally great in the fragrance of their moral conduct and in the flowers of their enlightened minds; the jewel of their intelligence and the moon of their spiritual essence are both perfectly full: therefore, they are capable of thoroughly understanding the mystery [of Buddhism] and manifesting the deepest significance of it. The final copying [of the translation] was completed on the fifteenth day of the first month of the fourth year of Chang-an."

In this flowery composition by the Empress Tsê-t'ien, the phrase "討三本之要詮, to enquire into the essentials of (the) three books (or copies?)," is somewhat ambiguous. Does "*san pên*" refer to the three preceding translations, or to three Sanskrit copies which they utilised? As the first translation was already lost at that time, the "*san pên*" must mean three original Sanskrit copies which they then had at hand. If so, the number does not agree with that mentioned by Fa-tsang as already quoted, for he says distinctly five copies instead of three. Could the character "three" be an error of the scribes? Fa-tsang who was a great scholar and an actual participant in the production of the seven fasciculi Chinese *Laṅkāvatāra* translation, has a better claim for authority, if choice is to be made between the literary remains of the time concerning the original texts, etc.

However this might have been, it is clear that the seven fasciculi translation is apparently the best of all the Chinese translations of this important Mahayana sutra, seeing that it was produced by the joint labour of competent scholars both Indian and Chinese. But, strangely, almost all the commentaries written seem to be based on the four fasciculi one by Guṇabhadra,[1] which is regarded as Bodhidharma's copy handed over to his disciple, Hui-k'ê.

To sum up: the first Chinese translation of the *Laṅkāvatāra Sūtra* was completed between A.D. 420 and 430, a second one appeared ten or twenty years later and each was made into four fasciculi. It took over a hundred years for the third in ten fasciculi to appear, while over two hundred years elapsed before the fourth in seven fasciculi was published, which means that the latest one came out over three hundred years after the first.

[1] One reason at least for the popularity of Guṇabhadra is that it is the shortest of all the translations.

There are two Tibetan translations[1] of the *Laṅkāvatāra-sūtra* preserved in the Kanjur:

1. འཕགས་པ་ལང་ཀར་གཤེགས་པ་ཐེག་པ་ཆེན་པོའི་མདོ།། (*ḥPhags-pa Laṅ-kar gÇegs-pa Theg-pa chen-poḥi mDo*). The Peking edition, LXVI, Sutra Division V, Case ངུ (*ṅu*), Folios 60b–208b; the Narthang, Sutra Division V, Case ཅ (*ca*), Folios 81–298; the Derge, Sutra Division, Case ཅ (*ca*), Folios 56a–191b.

2. འཕགས་པ་ལང་ཀར་གཤེགས་པ་རིན་པོ་ཆེའི་མདོ་ལས་སངས་རྒྱས་ཐམས་ཅད་ཀྱི་གསུང་གི་སྙིང་པོ་ཞེས་བྱ་བའི་ལེའུ།། (*ḥPhags-pa Laṅ-kar gÇegs-pa Rin-po-cheḥi mDo-las Saṅs-rgyas Thams-cad-kyi gSuṅ-gi Sñiṅpo Shes-bya-baḥi Leḥu*). The Peking edition, S.D., V, Case ངུ (*ṅu*), Folios 208–313; the Narthang, S.D., V, Case ཅ (*ca*), Folios 298–456; the Derge S.D., V, Case ཅ (*ca*), Folios 192a–284a.

The *Laṅkāvatāra* No. 1 consists of nine volumes (བམ་པོ) and is divided into seven chapters (ལེའུ) while the last one bears no special title. The Peking edition makes no mention of the translator, but the Narthang and the Derge are supplied with the following colophon: "This is the Blessed One's teaching, translated from the Chinese book (རྒྱའི་དཔེ) by ཆོས་གྲུབ (*Chos-grub*), a man from འགོས (*ḥGos*), and revised by himself" The question here is whether རྒྱ (*rGya*) is to be rendered as China or as India,

[1] The following section exclusively dealing with the Tibetan translations of the *Laṅkāvatāra* has been prepared by Mr. Bunkyō Sakurabe, of Otani Daigaku, Kyoto

for it means both, and when it stands by itself, generally China. The translator whose name is ཆོས་གྲུབ (*Chos-grub*), 法成 Fa-chang in Chinese, appears quite frequently in the Tibetan history of Buddhism as the one who translated the Tibetan into Chinese and the Chinese into Tibetan, and therefore there is no doubt that the colophon above referred to means that the *Laṅkāvatāra* is the translation by Chos-grub from the Chinese version. But the fact that this translation agrees so well with the Sanskrit original edited by Dr. Bunyū Nanjō and the fact that the Peking edition says nothing about Chos-grub or about the Chinese version, prove against the colophon found in the Narthang and the Derge. The latter, therefore, must have crept into the text for some unknown reason, probably by mistake on the part of the scribes. It is thus impossible to ascertain the translator and the date of the Tibetan *Laṅkāvatāra* No. 1.

As to the contents it agrees most with the Sanskrit text and in a lesser degrees with Bodhiruci (Wei) and Śikshānanda (T'ang).

The *Laṅkāvatāra* No. 2 is a translation of Guṇabhadra's Chinese version and the colophon reads: "By the order of དཔལ་ལྷ་བཙན་པ (*dPal-lha-btsan-po,* the auspicious heavenly king) this was translated and revised by the monk-translator, Chos-grub, a man from ḥGos, who collated [the text] with the commentary by Ācārya Wen-hui (文慧?) of China." "The auspicious heavenly king" here referred to is identified with king Ral-pa-can (རལ་པ་ཅན) who ruled Tibet in the middle of the ninth century, A.D. Chos-grub[1] figures as stated

[1] Concerning this translation from the Chinese and the translator, Chos-grub, see Pelliot's "Notes à propos d'un Catalogue du Kanjur" in the *Journal Asiatique,* July-August, 1914, pp. 128–129 and pp. 142–144; and also Mr. Juntaro Ishihama's article on 法成 (Fa-chang) and Prof. Toru Haneda's remarks on the article, both of which were published in 支那學 (*Chinese Studies*), Vol. III, No. 5; and also Prof. Haneda's Notes in *The Chinese MSS Excavated at Tun-huang,* Vol. I.

above as a great translator of the Buddhist texts in the Kanjur, and among the Chinese Buddhist sutras excavated at Tun-huang there are about ten works bearing his name as translator. He was a great Tibetan scholar flourishing in the first part of the ninth century and did most of his work at Hsiu-ta Ssŭ in Kan-chou (甘州·修多寺) and Yung-t'ang Ssŭ in Sha-chou (沙州·永唐寺).

The colophon regarding Wen-hui's commentary with which Chos-grub is said to have collated his translation is not quite clear. While there is no doubt that the present text is a translation of Guṇabhadra's (Sung) four fas. Chinese *Laṅkāvatāra* as we can testify by comparing the two, one variation at least we find in the Tibetan is the insertion of a passage after the gāthā on folio 213a, line 4. This passage does not appear in any of the texts Chinese, Tibetan, and Sanskrit, except Śikshānanda's, proving that the translator of the Tibetan *Laṅkāvatāra* No. 2 had this Chinese version with him.

The following is a tabular view of the corresponding pages between the Tibetan and the Guṇabhadra text:

Tibetan *Laṅkāvatāra* No. 2, Peking edition			Guṇabhadra's (Sung) Chinese *Laṅkāvatāra*, Taisho edition of Tripitaka			
Bampo	**Folio**	**Line**	**Fas.**	**Page**	**Column**	**Line**
I	208b	3	I	480	a	
II	221b	3		485	a	26
III	234b	6	II	489	a	
IV	247b	2		493	a	5
V	262b	6	III	497	c	
VI	274b	6		501	c	24
VII	285b	8	IV	505	b	
VIII	298b	8		509	c	25
	313a	8		514	b	

Generally speaking, there is just one Tibetan translation

for each one of the Buddhist texts making up the Tibetan Tripitaka, and in this respect the latter differentiates itself from the Chinese; for in the Chinese Tripitaka there are frequently more than one translation for the same text. That there are two translations of the *Laṅkāvatāra*, one from the Sanskrit and the other from the Chinese, is an exceptional case. This can also be said of the *Suvarṇaprabhāsa-sūtra,* which has also two translations, the one from the Sanskrit and the other from the Chinese of I-tsing. Incidentally, mention may be made of the statement in the *Chih-yüan Lu* (至元錄), the Buddhist Catalogue of the Chih-yüan Era (1264–1294), according to which the three Chinese translations of the *Laṅkāvatāra* are said from the same text (同本) and to correspond to the Tibetan text (與蕃本同); this is not exact, but there is no way here to find out whether this "Tibetan text" (蕃本) is in the singular or the plural.

II. Comparison of the Contents of the Three Chinese and One Tibetan Translations and One Sanskrit Text

A detailed comparison of the three extant Chinese and One Tibetan translations and the Sanskrit text of the *Laṅkāvatāra Sūtra* has not been attempted yet, except as to chapter-divisions and other general aspects. Before I present my own views concerning the result of such comparison, a tabular view of the contents as regards chapter-divisions of the five texts will be given on the following page.

This table shows at once (1) that the Guṇabhadra version[1] is very much simpler and shorter than all the others;

[1] Of the three existing Chinese translations, Guṇabhadra's is conveniently called the Sung version, Bodhiruci's the Wei, and Śikshānanda's the T'ang. Or, according to the number of fasciculi into which each version is divided, the Sung is often called simply the Four Fasciculi, the Wei the Ten Fasciculi, and the T'ang the Seven Fasciculi. In this chapter the translators' names will be used to designate the different versions.

(2) That Śikshānanda and the Tibetan[1] agree with the Sanskrit as regards chapter divisions; (3) That Bodhiruci has more chapter headings, i.e., is cut into shorter sections; (4) That in Guṇabhadra, the first and the last two chapters are missing altogether; (5) That Guṇabhadra has practically no chapter-divisions whatever, and that while "Sarvabuddhapravacanahṛidaya" has the character "*pin*" (品) suffixed which is the usual Chinese term for the Sanskrit "*parivarta*" (division), this title is almost like a sub-title to the *Laṅkāvatāra* itself, as if it were another name for the sutra.

What do these plain facts indicate? The first logical inference is that Guṇabhadra being the oldest translation represents a more primitive *Laṅkāvatāra* than the others. Possibly the later texts had these three extra chapters added during the one hundred years that elapsed between Guṇabhadra and Bodhiruci. That they were mechanically added is shown by their having no organic connection with the older parts. As they have nothing new to propose, we should not have missed them, if they were not found in the text. The first chapter where Rāvaṇa, the Lord of Laṅkā, asks the Buddha to deliver a discourse on his inner perception of truth, may superficially appear to be a sort of introduction needed for the development of the sutra; but there is no doubt that it was added later to supply this need, though really there was no such need from the beginning. The Rāvaṇa chapter was prefixed when there was a need on the part of the later Mahayanists to get the sutra connected with the story of Rāvaṇa and Rāmacandra as told in the *Rāmāyaṇa* when the latter came to assume a definite form as an epic, which, according to scholars, took place probably in the third or the fourth century of the Christian era. As the Guṇabhadra text stands, the interpolation of the Rāvaṇa

[1] That the Tibetan lacks a special title for the seventh parivarta as distinguished from the one on meat-eating into which apparently the former is merged is probably due to mere oversight on the part of the scribe.

incident has no special help to offer in the understanding of the sutra. The chapter of Dhāraṇī is a very short one, occupying about three pages of the Nanjō edition. This was also added when Dhāraṇi began to enter into the body of Mahayana literature, which took place much later in the history of Mahayana Buddhism in India. That the "Sagāthakam" was also a later attachment is easily shown from the examination of its contents, but for this I will devote a special paragraph later. The Sanskrit text and Śikshānanda are in full agreement as to chapter-divisions, which undoubtedly points to one original; but a more detailed examination will reveal that the Sanskrit is more frequently in accord with Bodhiruci. A safe conclusion may be that the texts were all different; while Bodhiruci belongs to a later redaction and is to a great extent mixed with notes and glosses, which fact makes it roughly 1.4 per cent. larger than Śikshānanda.

As I noted elsewhere[1] the whole *Laṅkāvatāra* is just a collection of notes unsystematically strung together, and, frankly speaking, it is a useless task to attempt to divide them into sections, or chapters (*parivarta*), under some specific titles. Some commentators have tried to create a system in the *Laṅkāvatāra* by making each paragraph somewhat connected in meaning with the preceding as well as the succeeding one, but one can at once detect that there is something quite constrained or far-fetched about the attempt. If this, however, is to be done successfully, the whole arrangement as it stands of the paragraphs must be radically altered; and this redaction is possible only by picking up and gathering together cognate passages which are found promiscuously scattered throughout the text, when for the first time a kind of system would be brought into the text. As the present form stands, passages of various connotations are juxtaposed, and a heading indicating one of the ideas contained in them is given to the whole section, thus arti-

[1] *Essays in Zen Buddhism,* Vol. I, p. 75.

ficially separating it from the rest. Guṇabhadra has done the wisest thing by simply designating the entire sutra as "The Gist of the Buddha's Teaching" (*buddhapravacanahṛidayam*).

The chapter-divisions in Bodhiruci are sometimes more or less rational, while we find four or five sub-divisions made into one chapter in Śikshānanda as well as in the Sanskrit. In this case, one Bodhiruci section expounds generally one main idea in prose which is abridged at the end in metric form. To be exact, for example, the chapter entitled "Anityatā" (Impermanency), which makes up the third chapter both in Śikshānanda and in the Sanskrit text, is sub-divided in Bodhiruci into five sections or chapters. The first sub-divided chapter on "Buddhacitta" (Buddha-mind) treats of fifteen different subjects, none of which make any direct reference to "Buddhacitta." This title, therefore, does not at all indicate the contents of the chapter except in a most comprehensive way. The fifteen subjects treated in this Bodhiruci chapter on "Buddhacitta" are as follows: (1) The Will-body (*manomayakāya*); (2) the five deadly sins; (3) Buddhatā; (4) the sameness of all the Buddhas; (5) that not a word was uttered for preaching by the Buddha during his long life; (6) being and non-being; (7) the experience-fact and preaching about it; (8) false discriminations; (9) language and meaning; (10) the three kinds of wisdom; (11) the nine changes taught by the philosophers; (12) the nine fetters and the true understanding; (13) the relation between false discriminations and existence; (14) that the world is a mere name; and (15) suchness and preaching about it.[1] Each subject treated here is expounded in prose as well as in verse. From this the reader can see how diversified are the topics treated and yet there is something more or less common running underneath them. Of the rest of the five sub-chapters in Bodhiruci the one on "Dharmakāya" can be further divided

[1] This is practically a repetition of (7).

into two sections, each of which is composed of prose and verse. Except these two sub-chapters on "Buddhacitta" and "Dharmakāya," all the chapters in Bodhiruci consist regularly of prose and verse parts.

The sixth chapter in Śikshānanda and the Sanskrit on "Momentariness" (*kshaṇika*), "Nirvana," etc., is divided in Bodhiruci into four sub-chapters: "Buddhatā," "Pañcadharma," "Gangānanda," and "Kshaṇika." Each of these consists normally of two sections, one in prose and the other in verse, showing that one topic of thought occupies one sub-chapter. In the Tibetan *Laṅkāvatāra* No. 1, which generally agrees with the Sanskrit, the chapter corresponding to "Nairmāṇika" has no title of its own. Taking all in all, the chapter-divisions of the *Laṅkāvatāra* in whatever version are, to say the least, arbitrary and of later elaboration.

A good practical way of reading the sutra without displacing the contents from their original setting will be to isolate in most cases one prose part with its metric repetition from another such part; and this will naturally cut up the text into many short independent sections.[1] There are some prose paragraphs without any corresponding gāthā-section, for instance, in the earlier part of Guṇabhadra and in the second chapter of the other versions. Guṇabhadra, when thus treated, will yield a little over fifty separate, individual chapters. The impression one gets after perusing the sutra carefully is that such independent statements dealing with the principal ideas of Mahayana Buddhism at the time when the sutra was compiled, were notes taken down by the author without any intention of arranging them in order. As was the case with the Pali Nikāyas, each of these independent paragraphs was perhaps a complete sutra in itself. Later, perhaps when there was a need for editing them under a

[1] Kumārajīva divides his Chinese translation of the *Diamond Sutra* into thirty-two sections, each of which consists of an irregular number of lines, sometimes of two or three lines only. This is quite a rational way of reading the sutra. Perhaps Kokwan Shiren followed Kumārajīva in his treatment of the *Laṅkāvatāra*.

title, they came to be known as the *Laṅkāvatāra*, or the *Buddhapravacanahṛidaya.* So long as we do not know how the Mahayana sutras were produced, all that we can say about their compilation has the nature of conjecture.

Were the sutras compiled one after another in time succession? Did one presuppose the existence of another, so that we can definitely trace the development of ideas backed by such documents? Or did they develop in different localities each one without knowing another? Is it possible as a matter of historical fact to arrange the Mahayana sutras in time sequence? Does logical development always coincide with historical events? That is to say, are fact and syllogism one? Does the one always and by nature precede, or follow the other? Until these questions are historically solved there will be many problems unsolved in connection with the make-up of the *Laṅkāvatāra Sūtra.*

That the first introductory chapter in which Rāvaṇa invites the Buddha to Laṅka to discourse on the truth inwardly realised by him, is a later addition, is also shown in the relation between the prose part and the verse. In this chapter, there is no such relation whatever between the two portions as is to be found in other parts of the sutra, that is, there is here no verse part that corresponds to or repeats the sense of the prose: the whole chapter is one complete piece, there is nothing fragmentary about it, it is altogether different in tone and style from the other parts of the sutra, the way the theme is developed and the style of the writing are quite distinct. In this respect, the chapter on meat-eating resembles this introductory one, although it has the verse part in correspondence with the prose. The meat-eating chapter may be a later addition, also, in spite of its being found in Guṇabhadra. It does not seem to fit in perfectly with the main part of the sutra. Did the author of the *Laṅkāvatāra* just put it in at the end as a kind of appendix, not standing in any organic relationship with the sutra proper, where highly metaphysical subjects are treated? And later did it accidentally get incorporated into the body of the sutra as forming a part of it?

Now we come to consider the last chapter entitled in the Sanskrit edition, "Sagāthakam," which occupies a special position in the structure of the *Laṅkāvatāra.* As the title indicates, it is composed entirely of gāthās. In the Sanskrit there are 884 couplets[1] taking up about one fourth of the whole text. Of these over 200 are found in the main text itself; therefore, about 680 gāthās are newly-added ones. In Śikshānanda these repetitions are systematically excluded from its gāthā chapter, while in Bodhiruci everything is thrown in and with something more. There are 890 quatrains in Bodhiruci and 656 in Śikshānanda, showing the relative amount of stanzas in each, as four Chinese lines are generally equivalent to one Sanskrit stanza.

As for the contents and their arrangement there is utter chaos in the "Sagāthakam." No doubt they chiefly concern the same themes as treated in the main text, but there are some original theses, and it is often hard to see why and how they came to be thrown in here. To read the "Sagāthakam" properly, therefore, it must be cut up into so many small portions, somtimes taking just one solitary śloka as expressing a complete idea, i.e., as a sort of aphorism. When this cutting-up process is brought to an end, we see that the "Sagāthakam," which appears on the surface as one solid chain of gāthās, is nothing but a heap of rubbish and gems.

How did this conglomeration come to be affixed to the *Laṅkāvatāra*? Why do we find so many gāthās taken from the sutra proper and mixed up with the rest? And the way they are mixed is most strange, seeing that while some are taken in bodily just as they are found in the sutra itself, others are broken up and interspersed fantastically among the rest. Was this done intentionally? Or did it happen just so? Does the "Sagāthakam" suggest an earlier origin than the sutra, in which the gāthā part was later elaborated

[1] The number includes occasional triplets.

in the prose in the way of commentary? But there is some reason to suppose that the "Sagāthakam" as a whole and in detail is later than the sutra proper, partly because it contains some historical matter which has no place in it, but chiefly because the thought expressed here seems to be more definite and developed than that in the body of the sutra. Taking all in all, the relation between the "Sagāthakam" and the rest of the sutra is a mystery because we have as yet reached no sure ground in the historical study of Mahayana literature in India. This much we may say that the "Sagāthakam" can easily be made into an independent text expounding the principal truths of the Mahayana philosophy. It reminds one of a notebook in which a student of the Mahayana took down some of the more important ideas as he learned them orally from his master, and in which at the same time he also put some other matter for his own benefit, though not necessarily in close relationship with the main contents of the notebook. In this respect the "Sagāthakam" shares the characteristics of the sutra as a whole. It may be noticed that Śikshānanda calls this part of the text the "Chapter of Gāthās" and Bodhiruci simply "General Chapter" (*Sāmānya*? 總品), while the Sanskrit edition is prefaced, "Listen to the jewel-made Gāthās preached in the Laṅkāvatāra-Sūtra, and free from the net of the [erroneous] views, [and containing] the wonderful Mahayana teaching," and concludes with this:

॥ इत्यार्यसद्धर्मलङ्कावतारो नाम महायानसूत्रं सगाथकं समाप्तमिति ॥

This may be rendered into English: "Thus is completed the Mahayana Sutra, the noble orthodox Dharma, called *Laṅkāvatāra*, together with the gāthās." According to the postscript thus translated, the gāthā section does not seem to have any special title for itself. For if *sagāthakam* means "that which is together with the gāthā," the designation must be regarded as applying to the whole sutra of *Laṅkāvatāra* and not to this last section exclusively made up with gāthās. What helps this interpretation is the Tibetan postscript which reads:

འཕགས་པ་ལང་ཀར་གཤེགས་པ་ཞེས་བྱ་བ་ཐེག་པ་ཆེན་
པོའི་མདོ་ཇི་སྙེད་པ་རྫོགས་སོ།།

This generally coincides with the Sanskrit except the one most important phrase, ཇི་སྙེད་པ , which may be Sanskritised *yathālabdham*. This means "as far as obtainable" or "as is available," which in the present case points to the possible existence of more gāthās or text belonging to the *Laṅkāvatāra* proper, showing at the same time the incompleteness of the sutra as we have it now. "*Yathālabdham*" is also found at the end of the *Āryamañjuśrīmūlakalpa* ("Trivandrum Sanskrit Series," LXXXIV, 1925, Trivandrum), which is one of the sutras having no usual sutra-ending, and also at the end of the *Gaṇḍavyūha,* which to all appearance is a complete sutra.

Incidentally, reference may be made to certain lines in the "Sagāthakam," which are often quoted by followers of Shin Buddhism as teaching Amitābha's Land of Bliss and also predicting the rise of Nāgārjuna. The lines are:

"The matured (*vaipākika*) Buddhas, and manifested (*nairmāṇika*) Buddhas, and beings, and Bodhisattvas, and [their] lands—they are in the ten quarters (140).

"The flowing (*nisyanda*) Buddhas, the reality (*dharma*) Buddhas, the transformed (*nirmāṇa*) Buddhas, and the manifested ones (*nairmāṇika*)—they all issue from Amitābha's Land of Happiness (141)."

Further: " 'My vehicle of self-realisation is beyond the attainment of the philosophers.' [Asked Mahāmati,] 'Pray tell me, after the Teacher passes, who would keep this up?'

" 'After the time when Sugata is passed away and no more, O Mahāmati, know that there will be one who can hold up the eye [of the Dharma].

" 'In the southern part of this country called Vedali there will be a Bhikshu of great and excellent reputation known as Nāgāhvaya, who will destroy the one-sided view of being and non-being.

" 'He will, while in the world, make manifest the unsurpassable Mahayana, and attaining the Stage of Joy, pass to the Land of Happiness' " (163–166).

In the Sanskrit text we have, instead of Nāgārjuna, Nāgāhvaya, and of course we do not know whether they are one person, or whether there is a mistake on the part of the scribe. From these passages alone it is difficult to infer anything historical concerning the age of the *Laṅkāvatāra* as a whole, and also its possible relation to the doctrine of Amitābha's Land of Bliss (*sukhāvatī*).

In short, the *Laṅkāvatāra-sūtra* may be divided as regards its textual construction into the following six specifically definable parts:

1. The Rāvaṇa chapter;
2. The section devoted to the enumeration of the so-called 108 questions and 108 terms;
3. The prose section in which no verses are found;
4. The prose-and-verse section, which may be subdivided:
   - *a.* The part devoted to a discourse carried on principally in verse, for instance, paragraphs on the system of Vijñānas;
   - *b.* The part containing ideas fully developed both in prose and verse, for example, meat-eating chapter;
   - *c.* The part containing ideas fully discussed in prose and supposedly recapitulated in verse, as in the greater parts of the text;
5. The Dhāraṇi section;
6. The "Sagāthakam."

III. Examples of the Textual Differences

This is not the place to dwell extensively on the textual differences between the various versions of the *Laṅkāvatāra*, for to do so would involve many questions which properly do not fall into an introductory part such as we intend this section to be. No doubt a detailed comparison of the different translations with the Sanskrit text, as well as with each other, will be instructive from the point of view of text-criticism and also from that of the history of Chinese Buddhist literature as translations. But as the writer wants to limit his attention chiefly to the inner significance of the sutra as an exposition of Zen Buddhism, and also as a most valuable text of the Mahayana, let us be content with the following extracts from the three Chinese translations and the Sanskrit text. A comparison of these extracts,[1] which may be considered as characteristic of each text, though they have been selected somewhat at random, will throw much light on the nature of the respective literatures. I have tried to give a literal English translation of the Chinese as far as it could be made readable.

[1] Sung—the Kōkyō Shoin Edition of 1885, 黃六, 二十六丁 a; Wei—六十三丁 a; T'ang—百八丁 b; Sanskrit Nanjo edition, pp. 228–229.

SUNG (GUṆABHADRA)	WEI (BODHIRUCI)
1. Further, O Mahāmati, the five categories (*dharma*) are: Appearance, Name, Discrimination,[1] Suchness, and Right Knowledge.	1. Further, O Mahāmati, the five categories are: Appearance, Name, Discrimination, Suchness, and Right Knowledge.
2. O Mahāmati, Appearance is such as is manifested in places, forms, colours, figures, etc.,—this is called Appearance.	2. O Mahāmati, what is Appearance? Appearance is what is seen in colours, forms, figures, which are distinctive and not alike,—this is called Appearance.
3. As when having such and such appearances, [things] are called a jar, etc., and by no other designation,—this is known as Name.	3. O Mahāmati, depending upon this appearing of things, there arises Discrimination, saying that "this is a jar", "this is a horse, a cow, a sheep, etc.," that "this is such and such", "this is no other thing"—this, O Mahāmati, is called Name.
4. Mind and what belongs to mind, whereby various names are set up and all kinds of appearances are brought out into view, such as a jar, etc., —this is called Discrimination.	4. O Mahāmati, depending upon these objects thus named, their characteristics are distinguished and made manifest, whereby such various names are set up as cow, sheep, horse, etc. This is called the Discriminating of mind and objects belonging to mind.
5. That Name, that Appearance —they are ultimately unattainable; [when] there is no intelligence from beginning to end, [when] there is no mutual conditioning in all things, and [when] Discrimination which is not real is put away,—this is known as Suchness.	5. O Mahāmati, when one surveys names and appearances even down to atoms, one never sees a single reality, all things are unreal; for they are due to the Discrimination stirred up in one's deceiving mind.

[1] For *Vikalpa*, Sung has 妄想, and not 分別 as in Wei and T'ang.

T'ANG (ŚIKSHĀNANDA)	SANSKRIT
1. Further, O Mahāmati, the five categories (*dharma*) are: Appearance, Name, Discrimination, Suchness, and Right Knowledge.	1. Further, O Mahāmati, the five categories (*dharma*) are: Appearance (*nimitta*), Name (*nāma*), Discrimination (*vikalpa*), Suchness (*tathatā*), and Right Knowledge (*samyagjñāna*).
2. Of these, by Appearance is meant that which we see,—each differs in colour, form, figure, etc. This is known as Appearance.	2. Then, O Mahāmati, by Appearance is meant that which is known as form, shape, distinctive figure, image, mark, etc. They are seen as Appearances.
3. Depending on these Appearances, names such as jars, etc., are set up, saying, "this is such and such," "this is no other,"—this is known as Name.	3. From these Appearances, ideas are formed such as a jar, etc., saying, 'This is it,' 'This is no other,'—this is Name.
4. By mind and what belongs to mind, various Names are set up, all kinds of Appearances are brought out into view,—this is known as Discrimination.	4. O Mahāmati, what is known as mind or as belonging to mind, whereby a Name is pronounced as indicating Appearance, or objects of like nature [are recognised]—that is Discrimination.
5. That Name, that Appearance [—they are all] ultimately non-existent: they are only due to the Discrimination by a perturbed mind of [things] mutually [related]. When one thus surveys the world until the disappearance of intelligence takes place, one has what is known as Suchness.	5. That Names and Appearances are ultimately unattainable [as realities] when intelligence[1] is put away, and that these things are not recognised and discriminated in their aspect of mutuality,—this is Suchness.

[1] *Buddhi* in this case is to be understood as "vikalpa-lakshaṇa-grāhābhiniveśa-pratishṭhāpikā" as is distinguished on p. 122.

SUNG (continued)	WEI (continued)
6. Reality, exactness, ultimate end, self-nature, the unattainable,—these are the characteristics of Suchness.	6. O Mahāmati, what is known as Suchness is non-emptiness, exactness, ultimate end, self-nature, self-substance, right seeing,—these are the characteristics of Suchness.
7. This is what I and other Buddhas have conformed to and entered into; we universally, for the sake of sentient beings, preach this according to the truth; [by us] this is set up and brought out into their view.	7. By myself and the Bodhisattvas and [other] Buddhas who are Tathagatas, Arhats, and All-knowing Ones, it is said that though names differ the sense is one.
8. When one conformably enters into right realisation which is neither discontinued nor permanent, no Discrimination arises, and one is in conformity with the noble path of self-realisation, which is not the state attained by all the philosophers, Śrāvakas, and Pratyekabuddhas, — this is known as Right Knowledge.	8. O Mahāmati, these are in conformity with Right Knowledge, neither discontinuing nor permanent and without Discrimination; and where Discrimination does not prevail one is conformed to the superior wisdom that is realised within one's inmost self. This is different from the false views entertained by all philosophers, Śrāvakas, Pratyekabuddhas, and from the incorrect views held by the partisans.
9. O Mahāmati, these are called the five Dharmas (categories); the threefold Svabhāva, eight Vijñānas, twofold Nairātmya, and all the Buddha-teachings are included therein.	9. O Mahāmati, in the five Dharmas (categories), the three Dharmalakshaṇas, the eight Vijñānas, the two Nairātmyas, all the Buddha-teachings are included in the five Dharmas.[1]
10. Therefore, O Mahāmati, you should discipline yourself in your own way and also teach others, but do not follow others.	10. Mahāmati, you and other Bodhisattva-mahāsattvas should discipline yourselves in order to seek this excellent knowledge. O Mahāmati, you know the five Dharmas when you

[1] Strangely, this is repeated.

T'ANG (continued)	SANSKRIT (continued)
6. O Mahāmati, reality, exactness, ultimate end, source, self-nature, the [un-]attainable,—these are the characteristics of Suchness.	6. Suchness may be characterised as truth, reality, exact knowledge, limit, source, self-substance, the unattainable.
7. This has been conformed to and realised by myself and all [other] Buddhas and is disclosed as it really is and preached by us.	7. This has been realised by myself and other Tathagatas, truthfully pointed out, recognised, made public and widely shown.
8. If one in conformity with this has an insight [into the nature of it] as neither discontinuous nor permanent, no Discrimination is stirred, and one enters upon a state of self-realisation which goes beyond the realm obtained by the philosophers and the two yānas. This is known as Right Knowledge.	8. When one, realising this, rightfully understands it, neither as discontinuous nor permanent, he becomes free from Discrimination, conforming himself to the superior wisdom in his inmost consciousness, which is a state other than that attained by the philosophers and is not the attainment of the Śrāvakas and Pratyekabuddhas. This is Right Knowledge.
9. O Mahāmati, in these five Dharmas (categories), the three Svabhāvas, the eight Vijñānas, and the two Nairātmyas, all the Buddha-teachings are wholly included.	9. O Mahāmati, these are the five Dharmas (categories), and in these are included the three Svabhāvas, the eight Vijñānas, the two Nairātymas, and all the Buddha-teachings.
10. O Mahāmati, with these categories you should by your own wisdom be skilfully conversant and also make others conversant therewith. Becoming conversant therewith, the mind is confirmed and is not led away by another.	10. Then, O Mahāmati, reflect well in this by yourself and let others do [the same], and do not allow yourself to be led by another.

SUNG (continued)

11. Then, wishing to reiterate this sense the World-honoured One preached the following gāthās:

The five Dharmas, the three
  Svabhāvas,
And the eight Vijñānas,
The twofold Nairātmya,—
They include all the Maha-
  yana.
Name, Appearance, Discrimi-
  nation,—
[These belong to] the twofold
  aspect of Svabhāva;
Right Knowledge and Such-
  ness,—
They constitute the Perfec-
  tion aspect.

SUNG TEXT IN THE ORIGINAL CHINESE

1. 復次大慧 五法者 相 名 妄想 如如 正智.

2. 大慧 相者 若處所 形相 色像等現 是名爲相.

3. 若彼有如是相 名爲瓶等 即此非餘 是說爲名.

4. 施設衆名 顯示諸相 瓶等心心法是名妄想.

5. 彼名彼相 畢竟不可得 始終無覺於諸法無展轉 離不實妄想 是名如如.

WEI (continued)

are not led by other teachings.

11. Then the Blessed One repeated this in the gāthās:

The five Dharmas, the Sva-
  bhāvas.
And the eight Vijñānas,
The twofold Nairātmya:—
They include all the Maha-
  yana.
Name, Appearance, and Dis-
  crimination—
These three Dharmas are
  aspects of the Svabhāva;
Right Knowledge and Such-
  ness—
These are aspects of the First
  Principle.

WEI TEXT IN THE ORIGINAL CHINESE

1. 復次大慧 五法 相 名 分別 眞如 正智.

2. 大慧 何者名爲相 相者 色 形相 狀貌 勝不如 是名爲相.

3. 大慧 依彼法相 起分別相 此是瓶 此是牛 馬 羊等 此法如是 如是不異 大慧是名爲名.

4. 大慧依於彼法立名了別示現彼相 是故立彼 種種名字 牛羊馬等 是名分別心心數法.

5. 大慧 觀察名相乃至微塵 常不見一法相 諸法不實 以虛妄心生分別故.

T'ANG (continued)

11. Then the Blessed One repeated this in the gāthās:

The five Dharmas, the three Svabhāvas,
And the eight Vijñānas,
The twofold Nairātmya,—
[They] wholly include the Mahayana.
Name, Appearance, and Discrimination,
Are included in the two Svabhāvas;
Right Knowledge and Suchness,—
They are Perfect Knowledge (*pariṇishpannalakshaṇa*).

T'ANG TEXT IN THE ORIGINAL CHINESE

1. 復次 大慧 五法者 所謂相 名 分別 如如 正智.

2. 此中相者　所謂見色等形狀各別是名爲相.

3. 依彼諸相立瓶等名 此如是 此不異 是名爲名.

4. 施設衆名 顯示諸相 心心所法 是名分別.

5. 彼名彼相畢竟無有 但是妄心展轉分別 如是觀察乃至覺滅 是名如如.

SANSKRIT (continued)

11. So this is said:

The five Dharmas and the Svabhāvas,
And the eight Vijñānas,
The two Nairātmyas,—
They comprise the whole Mahayana.
Name, Appearance, Discrimination:—
These are two aspects of Svabhāva;
Right Knowledge and Suchness:—
These are aspects of Perfect Knowledge (*parinishpanna*).

THE ORIGINAL TEXT IN SANSKRIT

1. punaraparaṁ mahāmate pañcadharmo nimittaṁ nāma vikalpas tathatā samyagjñānaṁ ca.

2. tatra mahāmate nimittaṁ yat saṁsthānākṛiti - viśeshākāra - rūpādi-lakshaṇaṁ dṛiśyate tan nimittam.

3. yat tasmin nimitte ghaṭādi saṁjñākṛitakam evam idaṁ nānyatheti tan nāma.

4. yena tan nāma samudīrayati nimittābhivyañjakaṁ samadharmeti vā sa mahāmate citta-caitta-saṁśabdito vikalpaḥ.

5. yan nāma-nimittayor-atyantānupalabdhitā buddhi-pralayād anyonyānanubhūtāparikalpitavād eshāṁ dharmāṇāṁ tathateti.

SUNG (continued)	WEI (continued)
6. 眞實 決定 究竟 自性 不可得 彼是如相.	6. 大慧 言眞如者 名爲不虛 決定畢竟盡 自性 自體 正見 眞如相.
7. 我及諸佛 隨順入處 普爲衆生 如實演說 施設顯示於彼.	7. 我 及諸菩薩 及諸佛如來 應正遍知 說名異義一.
8. 隨入正覺 不斷不常 妄想不起 隨順自覺聖趣 一切外道 聲聞 緣覺所不得相 是名正智.	8. 大慧 如是等隨順 正智 不斷不常無分別 分別不行處 隨順自身內證聖智 離諸一切外道 聲聞 辟支佛等惡見 明黨不正智中.
9. 大慧是名五法 三種自性 八識 二種無我 一切佛法悉入其中.	9. 大慧 於五法 三法相 八種識 二種無我 一切佛法皆入五法中.
10. 是故大慧 當自方便學 亦敎他人勿隨於他.	10. 大慧 汝及諸菩薩 摩訶薩 爲求勝智 應當修學 大慧 汝知五法 不隨他敎故.
11. 爾時世尊欲重宣此義 而說偈而言 五法三自性. 及與八種識. 二種無有我. 悉攝摩訶衍. 名相虛妄想. 自性二種相. 正智及如如. 是則爲成相.	11. 爾時世尊重說偈言 五法自體相. 及與八種識. 二種無我法. 攝取諸大乘. 名相及分別. 三法自體相. 正智及眞如. 是第一義相.

T'ANG (continued)	SANSKRIT (continued)
6. 大慧 眞實 決定 究竟 根本 自性 (不)可得 是如如相.	6. tattvaṁ bhūtaṁ niścayo nishṭhā prakṛitiḥ svabhāvo 'nupalabdhiḥ tat tathālakshaṇam.
7. 我及諸佛 隨順證入 如其實相開示演說.	7. mayānyaiśca tathāgatair anugamya yathāvad deśitaṁ prajñaptaṁ vivṛitam uttānīkṛitam.
8. 若能於此隨順悟解 離斷離常 不生分別 入自證處 出於外道二乘境界 是名正智.	8. yatrānugamya samyagavabodhānucchedāśāśvatato vikalpasyāpravṛittiḥ svapratyātmāryajñānānukūlaṁ tīrthakara-paksha-parapaksha-śrāvaka-pratyekabuddhāgatilakshaṇaṁ tat samyagjñānam.
19. 大慧 此五種法 三性 八識 及二無我 一切佛法普皆攝盡.	9. ete ca mahāmate pañcadharmāḥ, eteshveva trayaḥ svabhāvā ashṭau ca vijñānāni dve ca nairātmye sarvabuddhadharmāś cāntargatāḥ.
20. 大慧 於此法中 汝應以自智善巧通達 亦勸他人令其通達 通達此已 心則決定 不隨他轉.	10. atra te mahāmate svamatikauśalaṁ karaṇīyam anyaiś ca kārayitavyaṁ na parapraṇeyena bhavitavyam.
11. 爾時世尊重說頌言 五法三自法. 及與八種識. 二種無我法. 普攝於大乘. 名相及分別. 二種自性攝. 正智與如如. 名則圓成相.	11. tatredam ucyate: pañcadharmāḥ svabhāvaśca vijñānānyashṭa eva ca, dve nairātmye bhavet kṛitsno mahāyāna-parigrahaḥ. nāma-nimitta-saṁkalpāḥ svabhāva-dvaya-lakshaṇam, samyagjñānaṁ tathātvaṁ ca parīnishnanna-lakshaṇam.

A comparison of these four texts will give us some insight into the nature of each version; the variations are not necessarily due to the translators' individualism; they must have existed already in the original texts. Let me give another parallelism, this time one in verse. The extracts are from Chapter II, the opening gāthās of Mahāmati. The comparison will be only between the T'ang and the Sanskrit, as the Wei more or less agrees with the Sanskrit, while the Sung agrees with the T'ang, though the Sung as well as the Wei lack two verses corresponding to (4) and (5) of the Sanskrit. The most significant disagreement between T'ang and Sanskrit concerns "the awakening of a great compassionate heart." According to the Mahayanists, a heart is to be awakened in one that is above all forms of attachment and yet that feels suffering in the world as its own. In Sung and T'ang this idea is emphatically presented, whereas in Wei and Sanskrit it is missing. From this, can we not infer that there were at least two quite different texts of the *Laṅkāvatāra* from the early days of its existence as far as these gāthās are concerned? I do not know how the present Sanskrit text could be made to read like Sung and T'ang. The philosophy of the *Laṅkāvatāra* asserts the emptiness or the not-being-born of existence, and it is quite right to say that the world is like a dream or transcends birth-and-death, but we must remember that this position is not one of absolute nihilism, because the sutra teaches the reality of Prajñā itself or the truth of the "Mind-only" (*cittamātra*). So far the Sanskrit gāthās here reproduced accord well with the principal ideas of the *Laṅkāvatāra,* but there is another element in the Mahayana, which is love or compassion, and when the world is surveyed from this viewpoint, it is filled with sufferings, sorrows, and undesirable events. These are also in a way dreamy happenings, but compassion sees them in another light and strives to eradicate them by all sorts of "skilful means." For this reason, Sung and T'ang are preferable here to Wei and Sanskrit.

T'ANG[1]	SANSKRIT[2]
1. The world transcends birth and death, it is like the flower in the air; [transcendental] wisdom cannot be qualified as being or non-being, and yet a great compassionate heart is awakened.	1. When thou reviewest the world with thy wisdom and compassion, it is to thee like the ethereal flower, and of which we cannot say whether it is created or vanishing, as [the categories of] being and non-being are inapplicable to it.
2. All things are like the mirage, they are beyond the reach of mind and understanding; [transcendental] wisdom cannot be qualified as being or non-being, and yet a great compassionate heart is awakened.	2. When thou reviewest all things with thy wisdom and compassion, they are like visions, they are beyond the reach of mind and consciousness, as [the categories of] being and non-being are inapplicable to them.
3. The world is always like a dream. It is beyond nihilism and eternalism. [Transcendental] wisdom cannot be qualified as being or non-being, and yet a great compassionate heart is awakened.	3. When thou reviewest the world with thy wisdom and compassion, it is eternally like a dream, of which we cannot say whether it is permanent or it is subject to destruction, as [the categories of] being and non-being are inapplicable to it.
4. The wise know that there is no self-substance in a person, nor in an object, and that both passions and their objectives are always pure [in their nature] and have no individual marks; and yet a great compassionate heart is awakened in them.	4. The Dharmakāya whose self-nature is a vision and a dream, what is there to praise? Real existence is where rises no thought of existence and non-existence.
5. The Buddha does not abide in Nirvana, nor does Nirvana in the Buddha; it goes beyond	5. He whose appearance is beyond the senses and sense-objects and is not to be seen

[1] This partly appears in the section entitled "The *Laṅkāvatāra* and the Teaching of Zen Buddhism." See p. 214, et seq. The translation is from the Sung, but it mostly agrees with the T'ang as is observable here.

[2] The verses are quoted in my *Essays in Zen Buddhism*, pp. 76–77.

T'ANG (continued)

enlightenment and the enlightened, also being and non-being.

6. The Dharmakāya is like a vision, like a dream, and how could it be praised? When one realises that it has no substance, it is birth-less, this is called praising the Buddha.

7. The Buddha has no marks belonging to the senses and sense-objects. Not to see is to see the Buddha. How could there be praising and blaming in the Muni?

8. When one sees the Muni so tranquil and detached from birth [-and-death], this one not only in this life but after is free from attachments, has nothing to grasp.

SANSKRIT (continued)

by them or in them; how could praise or blame be predicated of him, O Muni?

6. With thy wisdom and compassion, thou comprehendest the egoless nature of things and persons and art eternally clean of the evil passions and of the hindrance of knowledge because they both are without signs [of individuality].

7. Thou dost not vanish in Nirvana, nor does Nirvana abide in thee; for it transcends the dualism of the enlightened and enlightenment as well as the alternatives of being and non-being.

8. Those who see the Muni so serene and beyond birth, are detached from cravings and remain stainless in this life and after.

1. 世間離生滅　譬如虛空華
智不得有無　而興大悲心

2. 一切法如幻　遠離於心識
智不得有無　而興大悲心

3. 世間恒如夢　遠離於斷常
智不得有無　而興大悲心

4. 知人法無我　煩惱及爾焰
常清淨無相　而興大悲心

5. 佛不住涅槃　涅槃不住佛
遠離覺所覺　若有若非有

1. utpāda-bhaṅga-rahito lokaḥ khapushpa-saṁnibhaḥ, sad-asan-nopalabdhas te prajñayā kṛipayā ca te.

2. māyopamāḥ sarvadharmāḥ cittavijñāna-varjitāḥ, sad-asan-nopalabdhas te prajñayā kṛipayā ca te.

3. śāśvatoccheda-varjataś ca lokaḥ svapnopamaḥ sadā, sad-asan-nopalabdhas te prajñayā kṛipayā ca te.

4. māyā - svapna - svabhāvasya dharmakāyasya kaḥ stavaḥ, bhāvānāṁ niḥsvabhāvānāṃ yo 'nutpādaḥ sa saṁbhavaḥ.

5. indriyārtha-visamyuktam adṛiśyaṁ yasya darśanam, praśaṁsā yadi vā nindā tasyo-

T'ANG (continued)	SANSKRIT (continued)
	cyeta kathaṁ mune.
6. 法身如幻夢 云何可稱讚 知無性無生 乃名稱讚佛	6. dharma-pudgala-nairātmyaṁ kleśa-jñeyaṁ ca te sadā, viśuddhamānimittena prajñayā kṛipayā ca te.
7. 佛無根境相 不見名見佛 云何於牟尼 而能有毀讚	7. na nirvāsi nirvāṇe na nirvāṇaṁ tvayi saṁsthitam, buddha-boddhavya-rahitaṁ sad-asat-paksha-varjitam.
8. 若見於牟尼 寂靜遠離生 是人今後世 離著無所取	8. ye paśyanti muniṁ śāntam evam utpatti-varjitam, te bhonti nirupādānā ihāmutra nirañjanāḥ.[1]

IV. A Further Examination of the Sutra as to its Inner Connections

Having finished what I wished to remark, though sketchily, about those chapters which are wanting in Guṇabhadra, and which, therefore, can logically be judged as later additions, I proceed to make some general statements about the sutra as to its form and contents and their inner connections.

The text takes throughout a form of dialogue between the Buddha and the Bodhisattva Mahāmati. No other Bodhisattvas or Arhats appear on the scene, though the dialogue is supposed to take place in an assembly of the Bhikshus and Bodhisattvas as in other sutras. Guṇabhadra fixes the scene of the sutra at the summit of Mt. Laṅkā in the Southern Sea, but in it there is no mention whatever of Rāvaṇa, who,

[1] This series of gāthās reappears in the "Sagāthakam," gg. 1–6, except the gāthās 4 and 5 which are missing in the "Sagāthakam"; and the order in the latter runs thus: 1, 3, 2, 6, 7, 8. The variations are: "viśuddham-animittena....." for "viśuddhamānimittena....." (6); "na nirvāsi nirvāṇe na nirvāṇaṁ...." for "na nirvāsi nirvāṇena nirvāṇaṁ....." (7); "te bhavantyanupādānā....." for "te bhonti nirupādānā....." (8).

in Bodhiruci and Śikshānanda, plays an important rôle, though in the first chapter only, as the initiator of the discourses that follow.

Mahāmati opens the dialogue by praising the virtues of the Buddha, whose wisdom sees that the world is a shadow but whose love embraces all suffering beings; Mahāmati then proceeds to ask the World-honoured One about one hundred and eight subjects (*ashṭottaraṁ praśnaśatam*). The Buddha answers: "Let sons[1] of the Victorious One ask me, and, O Mahāmati, you too ask, and I will talk to you about my inner realisation (*pratyātmagatigocara*)."

Now we ask, "What is the relation between the Buddha's inner realisation and Mahāmati's 108 questions, about which he wishes to be enlightened? Are all these subjects concerned with the realisation itself?" There must be some connection between the Buddha's replies and Mahāmati's questions. If not, they are certainly talking about things of no concern to each other.

Let us see, however, what questions issue from the lips of Mahāmati now and what are the subjects he is interested in. The questions are set forth in gāthās 12–59 inclusive, in Chapter II of the Sanskrit text. But what a conglomeration! Some of them are, indeed, quite to the point as they refer, for instance, to the origin of intellection (*tarka*) and mental confusion (*bhrānti*), and to their purification, emancipation, Dhyāna, Ālaya-vijñāna, Manovijñāna, Cittamātra, Non-ego, relative truth, phenomenality of existence, truth of suchness, the supreme wisdom (*āryajñāna*), Buddha of Transformation, Buddha of Recompense, absolute Buddhahood, enlightenment, etc. But at the same time there are questions concerning medicine, certain mythical gardens, mountains, woods, the capturing of elephants, horses, deer, the gathering of clouds in the sky, rules of prosody, the six seasons of the year, racial origins, etc. These do not seem to be properly asked of the Buddha, who is not a college

[1] *Jinaputra*, that is, Bodhisattva.

professor, or rather a primary school teacher, but the master of spiritual enlightenment. Why are the contents of the 108 questions of such a mixed character?

What is more astounding are the answers—that is, answers that are supposed to enlighten the questioner—given by the Buddha. The gāthās 61–96 (inclusive) are the words of the Buddha, who is the wisest man in the world and who is willing to disclose all the secrets of the Mahayana teaching that have been taught by all the Buddhas. He states in the beginning:

"Birth, no-birth, Nirvana, emptiness-aspect, transformation,—[all these are] without self-nature (*asvabhāvatva*); the Buddhas born of Pāramitā;

"Śrāvakas, sons of the Victorious One, philosophers, formless deeds (*arūpyacāriṇa*); Mt. Sumeru, the great ocean, mountains, isles, lands, earths;

"Stars, the sun, the moon; philosophers, deities, and also Asura; emancipation, Self-control, the Psychic Faculties, the Powers, Dhyānas, Samādhis,

"Nirodha and the miracles, the Bodhyaṅgas, and even the Paths; Dhyānas and Apramānas, Skandhas, and going and coming;

"Samāpatti and Nirodhas:—they are mental disturbances, only words. The mind, will, intelligence, non-ego, the five Dharmas—[so are they too]."[1]

So far, the answer, whatever be its exact purport, is more or less cogent to the main ideas of the *Lankāvatāra*; but what follows is strange not only from the doctrinal point of view but from literary construction. They are often not answers but questions, some of which are mere repetitions of the questions themselves. For instance, the Buddha is made to answer the 108 questions in this way:

[1] How far this is a correct rendering of the gāthās (62–66, pp. 29–30) is rather difficult to say; for the original merely enumerates all these items, sometimes repeating, and the grammatical relation between them is not to be definitely settled.

"How are the elephant, horse, and deer caught? You tell me. How is the conclusion (*siddhānta*) drawn from the combination of cause (*hetu*) and illustration (*dṛishṭanta*)? (69).

"What is meant by doing and being done? by various forms of mental confusion and the truth? They are both of "Mind-only" and are not visible, that is, not objective (*dṛiśya*). There is no gradation of the stages (70).

"What is the turning of the imageless?[1] Tell me, what about books, the medical sciences, artistic skill, the arts? (71)."

A glance is sufficient to see what kind of an answer this is. Questions and answers are curiously mixed up, and trifles and grave matters, too. The gāthās go on more or less like this until the Buddha concludes thus:

"O Son, thou askest me suchlike and many other questions. Each is in agreement with the [right] form, having nothing to do with erroneous views. I will tell thee now what the perfect doctrine is. Listen to me! According to the teaching of the Buddhas I will make a declaration in complete sentences of 108 clauses (*padam*). O Son, listen thou to me (97–98)."

With what [right] form are the questions proposed by Mahāmati supposed to be in conformation? From what erroneous views are they to be regarded as free? Whatever we may say about them, one thing is sure that all these questions and answers are incoherently strung together, and we fail to find any logical interpretation to the whole body of the gāthās making up the first part of the *Laṅkāvatāra Sūtra*.

Is some historical background needed to get a clue to the solution? Another source of confusion is discovered when we go on with Buddha's so-called 108 clauses, which

[1] Here is inserted the word "one hundred (*śatam*)" in all the texts except Sikshānanda. The insertion makes the confusion worse confounded.

are enumerated soon after. Evidently these clauses have nothing to do with the questions, although the number, which seems to be a favourite one, at least with the Buddhists, is substantially the same. The 108 clauses preached by the Buddhas of the past are a string of negations, negating any notion that happened to come into the mind at the moment, apparently with no system, with no special philosophy in them. These negations are another example of the irrationality of the *Laṅkāvatāra.*

"At that time Mahāmati, the Bodhisattva-Mahāsattva, said to Buddha, 'O thou Blessed One, what are these one hundred and eight clauses?'

"The Buddha said: 'What is termed as birth, is not birth; what is termed as eternal, is not eternal; what is termed as form, is not form; what is termed as abiding, is not abiding......'"

The negations go on like this concerning varieties of things not only religious and philosophical but of common experience. They comprise such terms as self-nature, mind, emptiness, cause and condition, passions, purity, master and disciple, racial distinctions, being and non-being, inner realisation, contentment with existence, water, number, clouds, wind, earth, Nirvana, dreams, mirage, heaven, food and drink, the Pāramitās, the heavenly bodies, medical science, industrial arts, Dhyānas, hermits, royalty, sex, taste, doing, measuring, seasons of the year, plants and vines, letters, etc. The number of terms, according to our calculation, seems to be a trifle less than 108, but this does not matter very much. What does matter is the subject-matter and the ultimate significance of the negations. Are all these negations from the point of view of absolute Śūnyatā philosophy? Why are the denials merely enumerated and no explanations given? Is it meant that these subjects are what engaged the attention of all the Buddhas of the past? But for what? Are they all important notions for the emancipation of sentient beings? Are they the subjects to be treated in the body of the *Laṅkāvatāra*? If so, how is it that the eight Vijñānas, which occupy a position of chief interest in the sutra, are not at all mentioned here? In short, the presence of these so-called 108 questions (*praśna*) forming the first section of the *Laṅkāvatāra* proper, can safely be cut off as not essentially belonging to the teachings.

A similar problem must have been in the mind of Fa-tsang (法藏), one of the helpers in the translation of Śikshānanda and a commentator of great importance, when he wrote the following in his 玄義 (*hsüan-i*):

"According to what I understand, the *Laṅkāvatāra* exists in three forms: the largest contains 100,00 ślokas, which, as is mentioned in the *Kaihuang Catalogue of the Tripitaka,* is preserved in the mountains of Nan-chê-chü-p'an (南遮俱槃國), of Yü-t'ien (于闐), not only of the *Laṅkāvatāra* but of ten other sutras, the largest of which consists of 100,000 ślokas each. The second large edition of the *Laṅkāvatāra* has 36,000 ślokas: of this mention is made in all the Sanskrit texts whose translations we have here. In this edition a chapter is devoted to answering in detail all the 108 questions: and Mi-t'o-shan (彌陀山), Master of the Tripitaka from T'u-huo-lo (吐火羅), is said to have personally studied the text while in India. It is also said that in the Western countries there is at present a commentary written by the Bodhisattva Nāgārjuna on this 36,000 śloka text of the *Laṅkāvatāra*. The smallest, the third text, contains only a little over 1,000 ślokas, and is known as the *Laṅkāhṛidya,* which translated means, 'the substance of the Laṅkā.' The present text is that. Formerly, it was designated as 乾栗太心 (*ch'ien-li-t'ai* or *hṛidayà-hsin*). The *Laṅkā* in four fasciculi is the one in which further abridgement was effected."

The existence of the three kinds of the *Laṅkāvatāra* text may be mythical as is the case with other sutras, of which a tradition of similar nature is stated; but it is probable that the *Laṅkāvatāra* which we have at present in the three Chinese translations and in the Nanjō Sanskrit edition is an abridgement of a larger and fuller text, that is, selections made from it by a Mahayana scholar who took them down in his notebook for his own use; and that in the larger text not only the 108 questions (*praśna*) but the 108 clauses (*pada*) are systematically answered and explained. In any event, something more than the present text of the *Laṅkāvatāra* is needed to understand it thoroughly and harmoniously.

The *Laṅkāvatāra* proper may be said to begin after the these "Questions" and "Clauses", each 108 in number; what follows here concerns the system of Vijñānas and their functions. But this paragraph does not last long, and after making some sketchy and not quite intelligible statements about the Vijñāna, it slides off into other subjects, such as seven kinds of self-nature or category (*bhāvasvabhāva*), seven kinds of truth (*paramārtha*), manifestations of self-mind, the problem of becoming, the world-conception and the religious life of certain Śramaṇas, who are evidently Buddhists, etc. When these subjects have received barely an outline treatment, the text returns to the Vijñāna, and after that a variety of subjects is discussed as is to be seen later when an index of the contents of the whole sutra will be given, but always in reference to the attainment of the inner realisation. Though the sutra makes frequent detours away from the main subject, which is inevitable from the nature of the textual construction, it revolves around the truth that the whole system of Mahayana philosophy is based on such notions as Śūnyatā (emptiness), Anutpāda (being unborn), Anābhoga (being effortless), Cittamātra (mind-only), etc., and that all these notions cannot be grasped and taken into one's life in their true perspective unless a spiritual insight is gained, when there issues transcendental knowledge and supreme enlightenment.

We can thus almost say that there are as many subjects treated in the *Laṅkāvatāra* as it can be cut up into so many separate paragraphs, each paragraph consisting sometimes of a prose part and its corresponding verse, but sometimes in long or short prose part only, not accompanied by verse. The same subjects are sometimes repeated more or less fully. The Japanese commentator Kokwan Shiren (虎關師錬),[1] who is also the author of a history of Japanese Buddhism known as the *Genko Shakusho* in thirty fasciculi (元亨釋書三十卷), divides the Guṇabhadra version of four fasciculi into eighty-six sections including the last chapter on "Meat Eating." This is the most rational way of reading the sutra, as in each of his sections only one subject is treated.

There is another thing which we must not let escape attention here. It is the refutation of the philosophies of other schools which were flourishing then in India. The Lokayata, Sāṅkhya, Vaiśeshika, and other schools are cursorily reviewed as not in agreement with the Buddhist teaching, or as not to be confused with it.

V. The Lankavatara and Bodhidharma, the Father of Zen Buddhism in China

That the *Laṅkāvatāra Sūtra* is closely connected with the history and teaching of Zen Buddhism in China has already been noted in the first volume of my *Essays in Zen Buddhism,* and I wish to present here a more detailed historical account of this relationship. According to Tao-hsüan's *Biographies of the High Priests* (道宣, 唐高僧傳), Bodhidharma (菩提達摩) handed his copy of the *Laṅkāvatāra* in four fasciculi to his first disciple, Hui-k'ê (慧可), saying, "As I observe, there are no other sutras in China but this, you take it for your guidance, and you will naturally save the world." By the non-existence of "other

[1] The commentary called the *Butsugoshin Ron* (佛語心論) in eighteen fasciculi was completed in 1325. He was a most learned Zen scholar and died in 1346 when he was sixty-nine years old.

sutras,'' Bodhidharma evidently meant that there were at that time no sutras other than the *Laṅkāvatāra* in China, which would serve as a guide-book for the followers of Zen Buddhism. This idea will grow clearer as we come to Tao-yüan's *Records of the Transmission of the Lamp* (道原, 傳燈錄) in which the author states:

''The Master further said, 'I have the *Laṅkāvatāra* in four fasciculi, which is handed over to you, and in this is disclosed the essential teachings of the Tathagata concerning his mental ground. It will lead all sentient beings to spiritual opening and enlightenment. Since I came to this country, I was poisoned about five times and each time I took out this sutra and tried its miraculous power by putting it on a stone, which was split into pieces. I have come from Southern India to this Eastern land and have observed that in this country of China the people are predisposed to Mahayana Buddhism. That I have travelled far over seas and deserts is due to my desire to find proper persons to whom my doctrine may be transmitted. While there was as yet no good opportunity for this, I remained silent as if I were one who could not speak. Now that I have you, [this sutra] is given to you, and my wish is at last fulfilled.' ''

According to this, it might seem that it was Bodhidharma himself who brought the *Laṅkāvatāra* to China; but Tao-hsüan and other records contradict it, and thus we have the following note under the above statement in the *Transmission of the Lamp,* though the writer of the note is not known. ''The following is taken from the report of the *Pao-lin Chuan* (寶林傳): Hsüan, the Vinaya Master, who is the author of the *Biographies of the High Priests,* says under the 'Life of K'ê, the Great Teacher', that in the beginning Bodhidharma took out the *Laṅkāvatāra* and handing it to K'ê said, 'As I observe that there are no other sutras in China but this, you take it for your guidance; and you will naturally save the world.' If this statement is correct, it means that it was before the second Patriarch attained to the realisation of the truth that Bodhidharma handed the *Laṅkāvatāra* to him, telling him to go over it. But, according to the *Transmission of the Lamp,* the sutra was evidently given to K'ê after the Law was entrusted to the hands of Hui-k'ê, together with the robe. Bodhidharma's further remark that he had the *Laṅkāvatāra* in four fasciculi which he would now give to Hui-k'ê, is probably quite correct. However, the remark that he had the sutra with him, sounds as if there never had been any *Laṅkāvatāra* before his coming to China. [This may not be quite exact.] The remark made later by Ma-tsu (馬祖) is to be regarded as more likely; for we read [in one of his sermons] to this effect, that [Bodhidharma] further quoted from the *Laṅkāvatāra* with which the mental ground of all sentient beings was given the [authoritative] seal: this does not conflict with the fact of the case.''

It is immaterial, as far as the historical relation between the *Laṅkāvatāra* and the father of Zen Buddhism in China is concerned, whether the sutra was handed by Bodhidharma to his disciple Hui-k'ê after the latter's realisation of the truth of Zen or before, and again, whether it was Bodhidharma himself or somebody else who first brought the sutra over to China; what we want to establish here is the mere fact of the relationship that historically exists between Bodhidharma and this sutra. Now as to this, we have ascertained it to be really so.

The reference to Ma-tsu (died 788) is important when the position of the *Laṅkāvatāra* in the history of Zen Buddhism after Hui-nêng is to be considered, though I do not wish to enter into its discussion here. I just quote the passage in question. Ma-tsu figures most prominently in Chinese Zen after Hui-nêng, for it was practically due to him and his contemporaries that Zen came to strike root most firmly in Chinese soil and grow up as a native product of Chinese genius. The passage reads thus: ''O monks, when you each believe that you yourself are the Buddha, your mind is no other than the Buddha-mind. The object of Bodhidharma who came from Southern India to this Middle Kingdom was to personally transmit and propagate the supreme law of One Mind by which we are all to be awakened to the truth.'' He further quotes from the *Laṅkāvatāra,* saying, ''The mental ground of all sentient beings was given the seal [of authority], because he was afraid of your being too confused in mind to believe that you yourself are the Buddha.''

In Ma-tsu's discourse, he does not expressly say that the *Laṅkāvatāra* was given to Hui-k'ê by his master, Bodhidharma, but simply that the existence of the Buddha-mind in each of us is certified by the teaching of the *Laṅkāvatāra.* The idea of the commentator who alluded to this passage in Ma-tsu was to strengthen the fact that the *Laṅkāvatāra* and Zen Buddhism were mutually related, not only historically but doctrinally. However this may be, Bodhidharma undoubtedly attempted to authorise the truth of his teaching by the *Laṅkāvatāra,* in which his unique method and the fact of spiritual enlightenment are expounded as from the Buddha's own ''golden mouth.'' But the narrative in the *Transmission of the Lamp* goes farther than that when it refers to the miraculous virtue of the *Laṅkāvatāra.* The belief in the magical power of an object considered to be holy is universal. It may be superstition, but if so it is of a wonderfully lasting character, as we find it throughout the world, civilised or uncivilised. May we not regard Bodhidharma's belief in the magical power of the *Laṅkāvatāra* to destroy the effect of poisons as an indication of the opposition of his enemies to his Zen teaching on the ground that it was not in agreement with their own experience of Buddhist life? If this were the case—and it is proved by other facts—the uniqueness of Zen Buddhism must have been quite a disturbing element in the Buddhist world of those days.

There was one noted Zen master of the Sung dynasty who denied the historical relation between the *Laṅkāvatāra* and Bodhidharma. His name is Ta-kuan T'an-ying (達觀曇穎, 985–1061). His standpoint is that of an absolute transcendentalist, ready to ignore anything relative and historical. According to 人天眼目 (*jên-t'ien yen-mu*, "The Eye for the Gods and Men"), a monk once asked, "Tradition says that Bodhidharma, the Great Master, brought along with him the four fasciculi of the *Laṅkāvatāra*: is this really so?" T'an-ying replied, "No, that is a mere invention of a busybody. Dharma simply transmitted the mind-seal which is above all letters; directly pointing to the mind itself he led people to see their real nature and attain Buddhahood. This being so, how could the *Laṅkāvatāra* have anything to do with Dharma?" The monk protested, "But this is the story told in the *Pao-lin-chuan.*" The master said, "The writer had not time enough to enquire with penetration. I will give my viewpoint. There are three translations of the *Laṅkāvatāra*: the first, in four fasciculi, was done by Guṇabhadra of Sung, who was a Tripitaka-master from India. The next one in ten fasciculi was by Bodhiruci in the Yüan-wei dynasty. The translator was a contemporary of Bodhidharma and it was he who poisoned Dharma. The last one was by Śikshānanda, who as a Tripitaka-master of Yü-t'ien came to China while the Heavenly Empress was ruling in T'ang. When these facts are put together, one can readity separate what is true from what is untrue. Yang-shan Chi (仰山寂), a great Zen master, too, had this once fully discussed and made the matter clear."

Ta-kuan's idea seems to be this: The *Laṅkāvatāra* was brought over to China and translated into Chinese by somebody else than Bodhidharma, who thus was not at all concerned with the sutra, and, therefore, it is evident that he never handed this to his disciple Hui-k'ê. Though there is no express reference to Hui-k'ê, we can infer the above from the way he writes about the translation of the sutra. From the very beginning he had no thought of connecting the father of Zen Buddhism with the *Laṅkāvatāra*. The writing of Yang-shan on the subject is now apparently lost.

In one respect Ta-kuan's view is even historically justified. During the Sung dynasty the relation between the Zen and the T'ien-tai school of Buddhism was quite tense, and each did its best to denounce the other as not being in harmony with the spirit of Buddhism. This was due, on the one hand, to T'ien-tai emphasising the intellectual study of the sutras as steps leading to spiritual development, whereas Zen, on the other hand, ignored all such literary and philosophical handbooks as altogether irrelevant to religious insight which is all in all in the realisation of the inner truth. The latter did not stop at this, its followers positively rejected all the literary authorities and treated the sutras and other sacred documents as if they were a mere heap of rubbish. This enraged the disciples of Chih-chê Tai-shih, one of whom writes disparagingly in his *History of Orthodox Buddhism,* fas III, (釋門正統, *Shih-mên Chêng-tung*): "The school calling itself Ch'an [that is, Zen] generally makes an all-sweeping negation its main business. All that is expounded in the sutras and śastras, all that is philosophically reasoned out, all that is regarded as morality—all such is put aside by followers of the Ch'an as having no value except on paper. When they are criticised for their extreme view, they declare, 'No disciplining, no realisation—this is the principle of our school.' Why don't they get cured of their diseases by studying our T'ien-tai philosophy of the six identities?" In another place (fas. VI), the author says, "The Zen followers declare their principle to be something directly transmitted from the Buddha outside his explicit teaching; but where can one find his teaching outside the sutras bequeathed to us and to them?" "It is really a pitiable sight to see a Zen master in the pulpit, who, not knowing what is what, scandalises the ancient worthies, abuses the sutras and their teachings, and confounds the minds of the ignorant and the learned." (Fas VII.) The quotations show well the valuation of the Zen school by its intellectualist opponents during the Sung dynasty.

The fact is, there are many things in common with Zen and T'ien-tai, and just because of this common ground, one side when it goes to an extreme is certain to be denounced by the other. The compiler of the *Jên-t'ien Yen-mu* prefaces Ta-kuan's apology in the following manner: "At the time followers of the philosophical school [of Buddhism, as distinguished from the intuitionalists] rose up strongly against the latter and concocting various arguments and reports scandalised the ancient worthies to the disparagement of the Zen school." Probably Ta-kuan was one of these extremely impassioned apologists who tried hard to silence his T'ien-tai opponents, but who at the same time only succeeded in stirring up their blood all the more. When Zen insisted on its being above all fetters of discursive reasoning, the T'ien-tai pointed out the fact that there is the historical fact of Bodhidharma handing the *Laṅkāvatāra* to his pupil Hui-k'ê, and further argued that if this be the case, how could the Zen followers justify their absolutism which cannot be separated from a sutra. In point of fact, the teaching of Zen is not derived from the *Laṅkāvatāra,* but is only confirmed by it. Zen stands on its own footing, on its own facts, but as all religious experience requires its intellectual interpretation, Zen, too, must have its philosophical background, which is found in the *Laṅkāvatāra.* For the sutra teaches, as will be shown in the subsequent chapters and elsewhere, that the final goal of the Buddhist life is to gain an inner insight into the truth underlying the relativity of all existence. The reason for this particular sutra's having been brought by Bodhidharma to bear upon his teachings can thus easily be understood. Ta-kuan went too far in his assertion, but his spirit is not altogether against Zen.

At the same time, the T'ien-tai philosophers were not quite right in thinking that Zen grew out of the letters of the *Laṅkāvatāra.* The transcendental intuitionalism of Zen and the teaching of Pratyātmagatigocara in the *Laṅkāvatāra* were what connected the two so closely.

VI. The Study of the Sutra after Bodhidharma in China and Japan

After Bodhidharma the study of the *Laṅkāvatāra* went on steadily as is shown in the history of Zen Buddhism. According to Tao-hsüan, the author of the *T'ang Kao Sêng Chuan* (唐高僧傳), we have under "The Life of Hui-k'ê" the following: "Therefore, Na (那), Man (滿), and other masters always took along with them the *Laṅkāvatāra* as the book in which spiritual essence is propounded. Their discourses and disciplines were everywhere based upon it in accordance with the instructions left [by the Master]." Na and Man were disciples of Hui-k'ê. Further down in Tao-hsüan's *Biographies* we come to the life of Fa-ch'ung (法冲), who was a contemporary of Tao-hsüan and flourished in the early middle of the T'ang, and who was an especial student of the *Laṅkāvatāra.* Here we have a concise history of the study of this sutra after Hui-k'ê.

"Fa-ch'ung, deploring very much that the deep signification of the *Laṅkāvatāra* had been neglected for so long, went around everywhere regardless of the difficulties of travelling in the far-away mountains and over the lonely wastes. He finally came upon the descendants of Hui-k'ê among whom this sutra was being studied a great deal. He put himself under the tutorship of a master and had frequent occasions of spiritual realisation. The master then let him leave the company of his fellow-students and follow his own way in lecturing on the *Laṅkāvatāra.* He lectured over thirty times in succession. Later he met a monk who had been instructed personally by Hui-k'ê in the teaching of the

Laṅkāvatāra according to the interpretations of the Ekayāna (one-vehicle) school of Southern India. Ch'ung again lectured on it over a hundred times.

"The sutra was originally translated by Guṇabhadra of Sung and written down by Hui-kuan; therefore, wording and sense are in good concord, practice and substance mutually correlated. The entire emphasis of its teaching is placed on Prajñā (highest intuitive knowledge) which transcends literary expression. Later, Bodhidharma, the Zen master, propagated this doctrine in the South as well as the North, the gist of which teaching consists in attaining the unattainable, which is to have a right insight into the truth itself by forgetting word and thought. Later, it grew and flourished in the middle part of the country. Hui-k'ê was the first who attained to the essential understanding of it. Those addicted to the literary teaching of Buddhism in Wei were averse to becoming associated with these spiritual seers. Among the latter there were some who had their minds truly enlightened by penetrating into the very heart of the teaching. As time passed on the younger generations failed to come to the real understanding of their predecessors."

Now we will trace the line of transmission from the beginning, from master to disciple, and show that the *Laṅkāvatāra* has its part in the history of Zen. Tao-hsüan continues: "After Bodhidharma there were his two disciples, Hui-k'ê and Hui-yü; the Master Yü, after attaining the truth, was absorbed in his inner life and did not take the trouble to talk about it. K'ê the Ch'an-shih (Zen Master) was followed by San (粲禪師), Hui (惠禪師), Shêng (盛禪師), Na-kuang (那光師), Tuan (端禪師), Chang (長藏師), Chên (眞法師), Yü (玉法師). They all orally discoursed on the deep meaning of the sutra, and did not leave any literature.

"After the Master K'ê, Shan (善師) produced a commentary in four fasciculi; Fêng (豐禪師), one in five fas.;

Ming (明禪師), one in five fas.; and Hu-ming (胡明師), one in five fas.

"Indirectly following the Master K'ê there were the Master Tai-t'sung (大聰師) who wrote commentary in five fas.; Tao-yin (道蔭師), who wrote one in four fas.; Ch'ung (冲法師), who wrote one in five fas.; An (岸法師), who wrote one in five fas.; Chung (寵法師), who wrote one in eight fas.; and Tai-ming (大明師) who wrote one in ten fas.

"There was another line, independent of the Master K'ê but depending upon [Asanga's] *Mahāyāna-saṁgraha;* Chien (遷禪師) wrote a commentary in four fas.; and Shan-tê the Vinaya Master (尙德律師), one in ten fas. After Na-kuang (那光師), there were Shih the Zen Master (實禪師), Hui (惠禪師), K'uang (曠禪師), and Hung-chih (弘智師) who is said to have been living at Hsi-ming (西明) in the capital; after his death the line was broken. Ming the Zen Master (明禪師) was succeeded by Chia (伽法師), Pao-yü (寶瑜師), Pao-ying (寶迎師), and Pao-ying (寶瑩師), whose line is still flourishing at present.

"Ch'ung, since he began to study the sutras, made the *Laṅkāvatāra* the chief object of his especial study and altogether gave over two hundred lectures on it. He has not, however, so far written anything about it. He went about with his lecturing as circumstances directed him, and he had no premeditated plans for his missionary activities. When one gets into the spirit of the teaching one realises the oneness of things; but when the letter is adhered to, the truth appears varied. The followers of Ch'ung, however, insisted upon his putting the essence into a kind of writing. Said the Master, 'The essence is the ultimate reality of existence; when it is expressed by means of language its finesse is lost; much more is this the case when it is committed to writing.' He however could not resist the persistent requests of his disciples. The result appeared as a commentary in five fasciculi, entitled *Szŭ Chi* 私記 [private notes], which is widely circulated at present."

This detailed story relative to the *Laṅkāvatāra* after Hui-k'ê is illuminating in many ways; it not only gives an insight into the historical relation between Zen and the sutra, but it gives the reason why the relationship exists between them. When the author refers to the specific features of the *Laṅkāvatāra* as consisting in attaining the unattainable, which is beyond the ken of reasoning, he at the same time describes the peculiarities of Zen teaching brought over to China by Bodhidharma. That the school of Dharma was not favourably received by students of Buddhist philosophy, that Hui-yü (慧育) who is better known as Tao-yü (道育), kept his mouth closed, knowing that the truth realised in his innermost mind was something beyond the phraseology of ordinary mentalities, that Fa-ch'ung (法冲) refused to commit his thoughts to writing because by doing so the exquisite colouring of his lively experience vanished; —all these statements made by Tao-hsüan (道宣) who was not yet acquainted with the later growth of Zen Buddhism, delineate with exactitude the characteristic point of Zen. The study of the *Laṅkāvatāra,* as especially related to Zen, was kept up to the time of Fa-ch'ung and Tao-hsüan, who were contemporaries, and this was about the time of Hung-jên (弘忍), the fifth patriarch of Chinese Zen Buddhism. Judging from these historical facts we know that the intellectual study and the practical discipline went on side by side, and that there were as yet none of the clear distinctions which later developed distinguishing Zen after Hui-nêng (慧能), the sixth patriarch, from what preceded him. So far none of all these numerous commentaries on the *Laṅkāvatāra* have been recovered.

There is one thing in the foregoing account given by Tao-hsüan of the history of the *Laṅkāvatāra* that requires notice: that there was another school in the study of the sutra than the one transmitted by Dharma and Hui-k'ê. This was the school of Yogācāra idealism. The line of Hui-k'ê belonged to the Ekayāna school (一乘教) of

Southern India which was also the one resorted to by Dharma himself when he wanted to discourse on the philosophy of Zen Buddhism. To this Ekayāna school belong the *Avataṁsaka* and the *Śraddhotpanna* as well as the *Laṅkāvatāra* properly interpreted. But as the latter makes mention of the system of the eight Vijnānas whose central principle is designated as Ālayavijñāna, it has been used by the Yogācāra followers as one of their important authorities. Ch'ien the Zen Master (遷禪師) and other teachers were those among whom the *Laṅkāvatāra* received an interpretation different from that given by Fa-ch'ung and his party. Though Fa-ch'ung is not recorded in any historical work on Zen in our possession at present, he was probably one of the earlier Zen followers. That he was not an ordinary scholar of the *Laṅkāvatāra* is proved by the following incident recorded by Tao-hsüan. When Hsüan-chuang (玄奘) came back from his long sojourn in India his influence in the Buddhist world of the day must have been immense. He was perhaps a little too self-confident and somewhat too presumptive when he declared that all the Chinese translations of the Buddhist sutras and śastras prior to him were not exact and reliable, and no discourses or lectures ought to be given on the older texts. When Fa-ch'ung heard of this, he retorted sharply, saying, "You are a Buddhist priest ordained according to the older texts; if you do not allow any further propagation of them, you should first take off the priestly robe and be reordained according to the newer texts. It is only when you listen to this advice of mine that you can go so far as to prohibit the spread of the older translations." This protest from one wandering monk-student of the *Laṅkāvatāra* in four fasciculi against the most powerful authority of the new translation school, whose reputation and influence must have been almost overwhelming, shows what kind of a man Fa-ch'ung really was. Everything recorded of him reminds one strongly of his Zen training and understanding.

The study of the *Laṅkāvatāra* after Fa-ch'ung seems to have declined, especially in connection with Zen Buddhism, and its place was taken by the *Vajracchedikā,* a sutra belonging to the *Prajñāpāramitā* group. It is quite interesting to enquire into the circumstances that brought about this change. For one thing the *Laṅkāvatāra* is a very difficult specimen of literature, and it requires a great deal of scholarship to read and understand it intelligently. Though Tao-hsüan remarks that its diction and sense are well in harmony (文理克諧), Su Tung-pei's (蘇東坡) criticism, which appears in his preface to the Chin-shan edition (金山板) of the Sung dynasty (1085), is more to the point: "The *Laṅkāvatāra* is deep and unfathomable in meaning, and in style so terse and antique, that the reader finds it quite difficult to punctuate the sentences properly, not to say anything about his adequately understanding their ultimate spirit and meaning which go beyond the letter. This was the reason why the sutra grew scarce and it became almost impossible to get hold of a copy." The real difficulty of properly punctuating the Chinese text of the *Laṅkāvatāra* in four fasciculi lies not necessarily, as Su Tung-pei judges, in the classical terseness of style, but rather in its adoption of the Sanskrit style of arranging words as is remarked by Fa-tsang. It was no easy task even for a most competent scholar to find exact Chinese expressions for the original phrases, and frequently he was obliged to follow the Sanskrit grammar. The Chinese translations, therefore, had occasionally to be read, not after their native laws of syntax, but after the Sanskrit. This is what Su Tung-pei really means by "terseness of style", and also the reason for Chiang Chih-chi's (蔣之奇) complaint that "I was much distressed with the difficulty of reading this sutra." When even scholars of the first grade found the *Laṅkāvatāra* so hard to read, the natural result was to leave it alone on the shelf for the worms to feed on it. Hence its decline as a help to the mastery of Zen. After Fa-ch'ung, who was contemporary with Hung-jên, the fifth patriarch of Zen Buddhism in China, the *Laṅkāvatāra* came gradually to be replaced by the *Vajracchedikā*. This does not mean that the former went altogether out of usage, but that the latter came to be thought more of in connection with Zen, especially as Zen grew to be more and more popular and appreciated by the general public outside the cloister. It must, therefore, be said that the fifth patriarch was far-sighted enough in this respect. The decline of the *Laṅkāvatāra* was, in fact, inevitable. The statement made by Chiang Chih-chi in his preface to the Chin-shan edition of the *Laṅkāvatāra* sheds light on the history of the sutra and also on the state of affairs in the Buddhist thought-world of his day (1085), and we give the following extract in which the two tendencies of Buddhism are referred to:

"The sutras preached by the Buddha are classified altogether into twelve divisions, which now make up as many as 5,000 fasciculi. While the Right Law (Dharma) still prevailed, the number of converts was beyond reckoning, who fathomed the depth of the Law by merely listening to a half stanza, or even to one phrase of the Buddha's teaching. But as we come to the age of similitude and to these latter days of Buddhism, we are indeed far away from the Sage; people at last find themselves being drowned in the letters; the difficulty is like counting the sands on the bottom of the ocean, and they do not know how to get at the one substance which alone is true. This was what caused the appearance of the Fathers, who, directly pointing at the human mind, told us to see here the ultimate ground of all things and thereby to attain Buddhahood. This is known as a special transmission outside the scriptural teaching. If one is endowed with superior talents and an unusual sharpness of mind, a gesture or an utterance will suffice to give one an immediate knowledge of the truth. Therefore, Ummon (雲門) treated the Buddha with the highest degree of irreverence, while Yakusan (藥山) forbade his followers to even study the sutras, since they were advocates of 'special transmission.'

"Zen is the name given to this branch of Buddhism, which keeps itself away from the Buddha. It is also called the mystical branch, because it does not adhere to the literal meaning of the sutras. It is for this reason that those who blindly follow the steps of Buddha are sure to deride Zen, while those who have no liking for letters are naturally inclined toward the mystical. The followers of the two schools know how to shake the head at each other, but fail to appreciate the fact that they are after all complementary. Is not Zen one of the six virtues of perfection? If so, how can it conflict with the teaching of the Buddha? In my view, Zen is the outcome of the Buddha's teaching and the mystical issues from the letters. There is no reason why a man should shun Zen because of the Buddha's teaching, nor need we disregard the letters on account of the mystical teaching. When we realise this, we come nearer to the truth. Jan-ch'iu (冉求) asked, 'Should I put everything I learn into practice?' Replied Confucius, 'Yes, do so conduct yourself.' When Tzŭ-lu (子路) asked the same question of the Master, the latter cautioned him, saying, 'As long as your parents are still alive, how can you put everything into practice as soon as you learn it?' Ch'iu was backward, so the Master urged him to go ahead, while Lu was too pushing, so he was told to be more circumspect. There is nothing cut and dried in Zen teaching, it is always directed at the onesidedness of human character. The fault of studying [scriptural] Buddhism lies in the danger of becoming sticklers for the scriptures, the meaning of which they fail to understand rightfully. Ultimate reality is never grasped by such, for them Zen would be salvation. Whereas those who study Zen are too apt to run into the habit of making empty talks and practising sophistry. They fail to understand the significance of letters. To save them the study of Buddhist literature [or philosophy] is to be recommended. It is only when these onesided views are mutually corrected that there is a perfect appreciation of Buddhist teaching.

"Of old when Bodhidharma was here from the West, he handed the mind-seal over to the second patriarch, Hui-k'ê, and afterwards said: 'I have here the *Laṅkāvatāra* in four fasciculi which I now pass to you. It contains the essential teaching concerning the mind-ground of the Tathagata, by means of which you lead all sentient beings to open their eyes to the truth of Buddhism.' According to this we know that Bodhidharma was not onesided, both the Buddhist sutra and Zen were handed over to his disciple, both the mystical and the letters were transmitted. At the time of the fifth patriarch, the *Laṅkāvatāra* was replaced by the *Vajracchedikā* which was given to the sixth patriarch. When the latter [while peddling kindling wood] heard his customer recite the *Vajracchedikā,* he asked him whence he got the text. He answered, 'I come from Mt. Wu-tsu (五祖山) east of Wang-mai (黃梅) in the province of Chin (蘄州) where Hung-jên the Great Master (弘忍大師), advises both monks and laymen to study the *Vajracchedikā,* which will by itself lead them to an insight into the nature of being and thus to the attainment of Buddhahood.' Thus the holding of the *Vajracchedikā* started with the fifth patriarch, and this is how the sutra came into vogue and cut short the transmission of the *Laṅkāvatāra.....*"

This long passage is quoted from Chiang Chih-chi's preface to the Chin-shan edition of the *Laṅkāvatāra,* as it is enlightening in more ways than one. First, we can infer from it that there was a strong antipathy between the philosophers of Buddhism and the Zen followers, each trying to get the upper hand; second, that the history of Zen Buddhism has been closely connected from the very beginning with the study of the *Laṅkāvatāra*; third, that the spread of the *Vajracchedikā* was coincident with the rise of Zen under the mastership of Hung-jên; and fourth, that the *Laṅkāvatāra* ceased to be studied as much as before, being replaced by the *Vajracchedikā,* but at the same time showing that the *Laṅkāvatāra* and Zen were most intimately related in spite of the Zen followers' general attitude of aloofness from all the sutras of Buddhist teaching.

There is, however, one point in Chiang Chih-chi's account which requires revision. He says that the *Laṅkāvatāra* lost its transmission after the adoption by Zen followers of the *Vajracchedikā,* but this is not entirely correct, for not only are allusions to the *Laṅkāvatāra Sūtra* found in Ma-tsu (馬祖) but the line of Shên-hsiu (神秀) seems to have been more partial to the *Laṅkāvatāra* than to the *Vajracchedikā,* as we see in Chang Shuo's stele-inscription (張說碑銘) for Shên-hsiu.[1]

As I remarked before, the chief defect in the *Laṅkāvatāra* which prevented its becoming popular, was its peculiar style and diction, which is not altogether native Chinese, and which made it difficult even for scholars to understand. On the other hand, the *Vajracchedikā,* like other sutras of the *Prajñāpāramitā* group, is easy to understand so far as its diction and phraseology go; and besides it is short in spite of its repetitious style. This advantage over the *Laṅkāvatāra* is sufficient to explain why the *Vajracchedikā* superseded it as a guide book to the mastery of Zen teaching. While the *Laṅkāvatāra,* according to my judgment, as regards pointing the way to the realisation of the inner truth, is nearer the mark, this advantage is easily upset by its unapproachability; and this advantage of the *Vajracchedikā* is in many ways decisive if Zen is to be studied and practised by a wider circle than scholars and specialists. That the *Laṅkāvatāra,* in spite of its literary shortcomings,

[1] Shên-shiu is not regarded as the sixth patriarch by the followers of Hui-nêng, who have been the transmitters of Zen teaching down to the present day. The line led by Shên-hsiu was broken off not long after his death, and records regarding him and his descendants are very scarce. But Chang-shuo's inscription states that Shên-hsiu was the sixth patriarch.

kept up its tradition throughout the development and wide propagation of Zen is proved by the existence still of a number of commentaries written in the T'ang, Sung, Ming, and Ch'ing, as well as in Japan. What, therefore, we can say of the *Laṅkāvatāra* after the fifth patriarch, is that it did not cease to be studied but was not so much in vogue as before, as for instance at the time of Fa-ch'ung and prior to him.

The supersession of the *Laṅkāvatāra* by the *Vajracchedikā* has another reason in the nature of Zen about which I wish to have a word here. Zen has no aversion to book-learning necessarily, but in point of fact Zen can be grasped more readily perhaps by the simple-minded and those who are not stuffed with intellectual accomplishments, as is proved, for instance, in the case of Hui-nêng, who to all appearance was not so erudite as his rival Shên-hsiu. This practical tendency has produced another tendency to discourage, sometimes to disregard, sometimes to positively slight the study of the sutras. Hence the above remarks of Chiang Chih-chi. But here is the lurking-place for the two divergent schools of Zen to emerge without being fully conscious of each other's characteristic standpoint. The one clings to the view that Zen is not controlled by the intellect, while the other upholds the fact that Zen is not by nature shy of erudition. The latter tends to be patronised by those whose natural bent is for learning and intellection; while the former is likely to be favoured by the more practical-minded. Hui-nêng belonged to the practical school both by disposition and by education, while Shên-hsiu was a scholar; for this reason Shên-hsiu held fast to the *Laṅkāvatāra,* and Hui-nêng to the *Vajracchedikā,* while both were being tutored by Hung-jên; for it is not true that Hung-jên was partial to the *Vajracchedikā;* indeed, for him the one was of as much importance as the other. Seeing that Hung-jên was about to paint the outside wall of his Meditation Hall with pictures illustrative of the *Laṅkāva-*

tāra, Hui-nêng inscribed his famous poem upon it.[1] What was a unity in the mind of the master, divided itself in the minds of his disciples, each of whom, according to his individuality, asserted one side more forcibly than the other, although not necessarily consciously. When a tendency is thus in the beginning given a strong impetus, it gains momentum, opening up its own course of movement. The *Vajracchedikā* school of Hui-nêng proved to be more in accord with the Chinese genius and consequently prospered more than the *Laṅkāvatāra* school of Shên-hsiu, though the latter was not entirely replaced by the former.

Hui-nêng was not such an illiterate peddler as is made out by his followers, though he was not so learned and scholarly as Shên-hsiu. But it was more politic for them to contrast their leader in this respect with his rival, who, was, indeed, the head of all the monks under Hung-jên not only in learning but in the disciplinary side of Zen as well. By emphasising this contrast Hui-nêng came out to be the greater Zen master, and the absolute aspect of Zen by which it transcends all the intricacies of learning and intellection received more emphasis than it actually needed. The *Laṅkāvatāra* thus finally ceased to be legitimately appreciated by Zen followers of the present day. Some scholars of Buddhism, chiefly modern Japanese, ignorant of the real nature of Zen, yet knowing enough of the historical relation between Hui-nêng and the *Vajracchedikā,* which was once edited by him with a preface, try to prove that Zen is the outcome of practical training of the mind to gain an insight into its real working. But its absurdity is patent to all serious students of Zen, for the *Prajñāpāramitā* is the result of the intellectual elaboration of the Zen experience which alone was the object of Hui-nêng's teaching in

[1] *Essays in Zen Buddhism,* Series I, p. 192:
"The Bodhi is not like the tree,
The mirror bright is nowhere shining;
As there is nothing from the first,
Where can the dust collect itself?"

connection with all the literary endeavours of scholars. He never took a dislike especially to the *Laṅkāvatāra,* his "ignorance" was altogether of a different order.

There are no records after Fa-ch'ung and after Hui-nêng as to the study by Zen followers of the *Laṅkāvatāra Sūtra,* except the commentaries which had been written on it by scholars and of which we are still in possession. The fact that during the Sung the sutra was much neglected has already been made clear by the preface of Chiang Chih-chi and Su Tung-pei to the Chin-shan edition of the sutra. But four commentaries of the Sung dynasty are still extant against two of the T'ang. One of the T'ang commentaries was written by Fa-tsang, as was stated previously, and this is a sort of general introduction to the study of the *Laṅkāvatāra* and is the most valuable literature ever written in connection with the sutra; for not only does it give the author's summarised interpretation of the *Laṅkāvatāra* as a whole and of its position in the system of Buddhism, but in it the reader can find Fa-tsang's view as a Buddhist philosopher. Quite a few commentaries have been written on this work of Fa-tsang's by Japanese scholars.

During the Ming dynasty the *Laṅkāvatāra* seems to have been studied much, for we have seven commentaries that are still in existence written on it during this period. written on it during this period that are still in existence. The Ch'ing dynasty has produced two, also extant. There are altogether fifteen expository writings on the *Laṅkāvatāra* from Chinese scholars, which are still in current circulation, as they are all included in the supplementary part of the Tripitaka compiled by Mr. Tatsuye Nakano, Kyoto, 1905–1912, and one is found in the main body of the Chinese Tripitaka itself.

In Japan during the Nara era in the eighth century it was a deed of merit to copy the *Laṅkāvatāra* with other sutras and śastras and to possess extra copies of them, but how earnestly and systematically it was studied is not known. We have many interesting and at the same time illuminating documents of this period, that is, of the first half of the eighth century, in which detailed entries are kept as to the various Buddhist writings that were copied by the official scribes as well as the business side of this pious undertaking which was constantly carried on during those days. Among these old valuable papers are references to the *Laṅkāvatāra* and its commentaries, and the most remarkable thing is that two of the commentaries mentioned are ascribed to Bodhidharma himself. How did such a tradition come over to Japan? As far as we know there are no records in China as to Bodhidharma's authorship of any such writings. If these were still in existence, they would shed much light on the history of Zen Buddhism in China.

The first serious study of the sutra was undertaken by a Zen monk called Kokwan Shiren (1278–1346) who was also a learned scholar being the author of a history of Buddhism known as *The Genko Shakusho* (元亨釋書三十卷) in thirty fasciculi, as was mentioned before. His commentary on the *Laṅkāvatāra* is called the *Butsugoshinron* (佛語心論十八卷), "Treatise on the Essence (or heart) of the Buddha-teaching," and consists of eighteen fasciculi. His dividing the sutra into eighty-six sections proves the keenness of his intellectual and analytical acumen. Tokugan Yōson (德巖養存) who published another commentary in 1687 followed Kokwan in the division of the sutra. His commentary is quite an improvement on his predecessor's. He mentions, among the *Laṅkāvatāra* commentaries he consulted with, two which are not included in the Supplementary Tripitaka of Kyoto. I wonder if they are accessible now?

A third Japanese work on the sutra is mentioned by Seigai Ōmura and Gisho Nakano who are the authors of the *Explanatory Notes* to the Nihon Daizokyo (日本大藏經解題) completed in 1921; the title of this Japanese book is *Ryōgakyō Kōyoku* (楞伽經講翼), by Kōken (光謙). Unfortunately, I have not yet been able to see it myself. In the same *Notes* seven works are mentioned written by Japanese scholars as commentaries on Fa-tsung's *Introduction to the Laṅkāvatāra* (楞伽心玄義).

Most recent Japanese works relative to the *Laṅkāvatāra* are Sōgen Yamakami's Japanese rendering of the *Laṅkāvatāra* by Śikshānanda; Shōshi Mitsui's concise exposition of the *Laṅkāvatāra* teaching; and Hōkei Idzumi's Japanese translation of the Nanjo edition of the Sanskrit original. Each in its way is helpful to the understanding of this neglected Mahayana literature.

VII. Introductory Chapter of the Lankavatara Sutra

In which Rāvaṇa, King of the Rakshasas, requests the Buddha to discourse on the realisation of the inmost truth

This introductory chapter which appears in all the *Laṅkāvatāra* texts except Guṇabhadra, the earliest Chinese version now extant, is, as I have remarked before, no doubt a later addition, and does not properly belong to the main text; but as it almost gives a summary, if any such thing is possible, of the *Laṇkāvatāra,* I have decided to incorporate its translation in this book. The translation is chiefly based upon the Nanjo edition of the Sanskrit text, and wherever it differs very much from the Chinese versions as regards the sense, the differences are quoted in footnotes.[1]

[1] The following translation is far from being satisfactory, and very likely it is laden with errors. Nobody can deny that the original text is corrupt to a great extent and requires for its complete revision greater learning and more critical intellect than the present translator can afford. But his over-zeal to have this important Mahayana sutra more widely known not only among those who are interested in Buddhism but among students of comparative religion will, he hopes, condone his audacity in sending out this partial and imperfect translation of the *Laṅkāvatāra* to the public at large. He will be more than pleased if critics will acquaint him with any criticisms and corrections which may occur to them.

(1)[1] Thus I have heard. The Blessed One once stayed in the Castle of Laṅkā which is situated at the peak of Mount Malaya in the great ocean, and which is adorned with flowers made of jewels of various kinds.[2] He was with a large assembly of Bhikshus and with a great multitude of Bodhisattvas, who had come together from various Buddha-lands. The Bodhisattvas-Mahāsattvas, headed by the Bodhisattva Mahāmati, were all perfect masters[3] of the various Samādhis, the [tenfold] Self-mastery, the [ten] Powers, and the [six] Psychic Faculties; they were anointed by all the Buddhas with their own hands; they all well understood the significance of the objective world as the manifestation of their own mind; (2) they knew how to maintain [various] forms, teachings, and disciplinary measures, according to the various mentalities and behaviours of beings;[4] they were thoroughly versed in the five Dharmas, the [three] Svabhāvas, the [eight] Vijñānas, and the twofold Non-ātman.

At that time, the Blessed One who [had been preaching] at the palace of the King of the Sea-serpents came out at the expiration of seven days and was greeted by an innumerable host of Śakra, Brahman, and Nāgakanyās, and looking at Laṅkā on Mount Malaya smiled and said, "By the Tathagatas of the past, who were Arhats and Fully-enlightened Ones, this truth (*dharma*) was made the subject of their discourse, at that castle of Laṅkā on the mountain-peak of

[1] These numerals in parentheses refer to the pages of the Sanskrit edition.

[2] Much more fully described in Bodhiruci (Wei).

[3] Literally, "sporting" (*vikrīḍita*).

[4] T'ang: According to the minds of beings, they manifest a variety of form and discipline them with [various] means.

Wei: [There are] various beings and various minds and forms; in accordance with these various minds and various changing thoughts, [the Bodhisattvas], by innumerable means of salvation, save [beings] everywhere, make themselves visible everywhere, so that their manifestations are universal.

Sung: [There are] various beings and various minds and forms; by innumerable means of salvation, [the Bodhisattvas] become variously visible to all classes [of beings].

Malaya,—the truth realisable by the supreme wisdom in one's inmost self, and not visible to the reasoning philosophers, nor conceivable by the consciousness of the Śrāvakas and Pratyekabuddhas.[1] I, too, would here for the sake of Rāvaṇa, Overlord of the Yakshas, discourse on this truth.''

[Inspired] by the spiritual power of the Tathagata, Rāvaṇa, Lord of the Rakshasas, heard [his voice and thought], ''Certainly, the Blessed One is coming out of the palace of the King of Sea-serpents, surrounded and accompanied by an innumerable host of Śakra, Brahman, Nāgakanyās; looking at the waves of the ocean and contemplating the mental agitations going on in those assembled, [he thinks of] the ocean of the Ālayavijñāna where the Vijñānas revolve [like the waves] stirred by the wind of objectivity.'' Then standing there, Rāvaṇa uttered an utterance: ''I will go and request of the Blessed One to enter into Laṅkā, which for this long night would probably profit, do good, and gladden (3) the gods as well as human beings.''

Thereupon, Rāvaṇa, Lord of the Rākshasas, with his attendants, riding in his floral celestial chariot, came up to where the Blessed One was, and having arrived there he and his attendants came out of the chariot. Walking around the Blessed One three times from left to right, they played on a musical instrument, beating it with a stick of blue Indra (sapphire), and hanging the lute at one side, which was inlaid with the choicest lapis lazuli and supported by [a band of] priceless cloth, yellowish-white like *priyaṅgu*, they sang with various notes such as Saharshya, Rishabha, Gāndhāra, Dhaivata, Nishāda, Madhyama, and Kaiśika,[2] which were melodiously modulated in Grāma, Mūrchana, etc.; the voice in accompaniment with the flute beautifully blended in the measure of the Gāthā.

[1] The Sanskrit text is here certainly at fault; there ought to be a negative particle somewhere in this passage, which is the case with the Chinese translations.

[2] Neither Bodhiruci nor Śikshānanda refers so specifically to these various notes.

1. "The truth-treasure whose principle is the self-nature of Mind, has no selfhood, stands away from reasoning, and is free from impurities; it points to the knowledge attained in one's inmost self; O Lord, show me here the way leading to the truth.

2. "The Sugata is the body in whom are stored immaculate virtues; in him are manifested [bodies] transforming and transformed; he enjoys the truth realised in his inmost self: may he enter into Laṅkā. Now is the time, O Muni!

3. (4) This Laṅkā was inhabited by the Buddhas of the past, and [they were] accompanied by their sons who were owners of many forms. O Lord, show me now the highest truth, and the Yakshas who are endowed with many forms will listen."

Thereupon, Rāvaṇa, the Lord of Laṅkā, further adapting the Toṭaka rhythm sang this in the measure of the Gāthā.

4. After seven nights, the Blessed One, leaving the ocean which is the abode of the Makara, the palace of the Sea-king, now stands on the shore.

5. Just as the Buddha rises, Rāvaṇa, accompanied by the Rakshasas and Yakshas numerous, by Śuka, Sāraṇa,[1] and learned men,

6. Miraculously goes over to the place where the Lord is standing. Alighting from the floral vehicle, he greets the Tathagata reverentially, makes him offerings, tells him who he is, and stands by the Lord.

7. "I who have come here, am called Rāvaṇa, the ten-headed king of the Rakshasas: mayest thou graciously receive me with Laṅkā and all its residents.

8. "In this city, the inmost state of consciousness realised, indeed, by the Enlightened Ones of the past (5) was disclosed on this peak studded with precious stones.

9. "Let the Blessed One, too, surrounded by sons of

[1] Said to be the ministers' names.

the Victorious One, now disclose the truth immaculate on this peak embellished with precious stones; we, together with the residents of Laṅkā, desire to listen.

10. "The *Laṅkāvatāra Sūtra* which is praised by the Buddhas of the past [discloses] the inmost state of consciousness realised by them, as it is not founded on any system of doctrine.

11. "I recollect that the Buddhas of the past surrounded by sons of the Victorious One recited this sutra; the Blessed One, too, will speak.

12. "In the time to come, there will be Buddhas and Buddha-Sons pitying the Yakshas; the Leaders will discourse on this magnificent doctrine at the peak adorned with precious stones.

13. "This magnificent city of Laṅkā is adorned with varieties of precious stones, [surrounded] by peaks, refreshing and beautiful and canopied by a net of jewels.

14. "O Blessed One, here are the Yakshas who are free from faults of greed, reflecting on [the truth] realised in one's inmost self and making offerings to the Buddhas of the past; they are believers in the teaching of the Mahayana and intent on disciplining one another.

15. "There are younger Yakshas, girls and boys, desiring to know the Mahayana. Come, O Blessed One, who art our Teacher, come to Laṅkā on Mount Malaya.

16. (6) "The Rakshasas, with Kumbhakarṇa at their head, who are residing in the city, wish, as they are devoted to the Mahayana, to hear about this inmost realisation.

17. "They have made offerings assiduously to the Buddhas [in the past] and are to-day going to do the same. Come, for compassion's sake, to Laṅkā, together with [thy] sons.

18. "O great Muni, accept my mansion, the company of the Apsaras, necklaces of various sorts, and the delightful Aśoka garden.

19. "I give myself up to serve the Buddhas and their

sons; there is nothing in me that I do not give up [for their sake]; O great Muni, have compassion on me!"

20. Hearing him speak thus, the Lord of the Triple World said, "O King of Yakshas, this mountain of precious stones was visited by the Leaders of the past.

21. "And, taking pity on you, they discoursed on the truth revealed in their inmost. [The Buddhas of] the future time will proclaim [the same] on this jewel-adorned mountain.

22. "This [inmost truth] is the abode of those practisers who stand in the presence of the truth. O King of the Yakshas, you have the compassion of the Sugatas and myself."

23. The Blessed One granting the request [of the King] remained silent and undisturbed; he now mounted the floral chariot offered by Rāvaṇa.

24. Thus Rāvaṇa and others, wise sons of the Victorious One, (7) honoured by the Apsaras singing and dancing, reached the city.

25. Arriving in the delightful city, [the Buddha was] again the recipient of honours; he was honoured by the group of Yakshas including Rāvaṇa and by the Yaksha women.

26. A net of jewels was offered to the Buddha by the younger Yakshas, girls and boys, and necklaces beautifully ornamented with jewels were placed by Rāvaṇa about the necks of the Buddha and of the sons of the Buddha.

27. The Buddha, together with the sons of the Buddha and the wise men, accepting the offerings, discoursed on the truth which is the state of consciousness realised in the inmost self.

28. Honouring Mahāmati as the best speaker, Rāvaṇa and the company of the Yakshas honoured and requested of him again and again,[1] [saying],

[1] Gāthās 20–28, inclusive, are in prose in T'ang.

29. "Thou art the asker of the Buddhas concerning the state of consciousness realised in one's inmost self, of which we here, Yakshas as well as sons of the Buddha, are desirous of hearing. I, together with the Yakshas, sons of the Buddha, and the wise men, request this of thee.

30. "Thou art the most eloquent of speakers, and the most strenuous of practisers (yogins); with faith I beg of thee. Ask [the Buddha] about the doctrine, O thou the proficient one!

31. "Free from the faults of the philosophers and Pratyekabuddhas and Śrāvakas is (8) the truth of the inmost consciousness, immaculate, and culminating in the stage of Buddhahood."

32.[1] Thereupon the Blessed One created jewel-adorned mountains and other objects magnificently embellished with jewels in an immense number.

33. On the summit of each mountain the Buddha himself was visible, and Rāvaṇa the Yaksha also was found standing there.

34. Thus the entire assembly was seen on each mountain-peak and all the countries were there, and in each there was a Leader.

35. Here also was the King of the Rakshasas and the residents of Laṅkā, and the Laṅkā created by the Buddha rivalling [the real one].

36. Other things were there, too,—the Aśoka with its shining woods, and on each mountain-peak Mahāmati was making a request of the Buddha

37. Who discoursed for the sake of the Yakshas on the truth leading to the inmost realisation; on the mountain-peak he was delivering a complete sutra with an exquisite voice varied in hundreds of thousands of ways.[2]

[1] From this point T'ang is in prose again.

[2] Thus according to Bodhiruci and Śiskhānanda. The Sanskrit text has: "hundreds of thousands of perfect sutras".

38. [After this] the teacher and the sons of the Buddhas vanished away in the air, leaving Rāvaṇa the Yaksha himself standing in his mansion.

39. Thought he, "How is this? What means this? and by whom was it heard? What was it that was seen? and by whom was it seen? Where is the city? and where is the Buddha?

40. "Where are those places, those jewel-shining Buddhas, those Sugatas? (9) Is it a dream then? or a vision? or is it a castle conjured up by the Gandharvas?

41. "Or is it dust in the eye, or a fata morgana, or the dream-child of a barren woman, or the smoke of a fire-wheel, that which I saw here?"

42. Then [Rāvaṇa reflected], "This is the nature as it is (*dharmatā*) of all things objectified in and by the mind, and it is not comprehended by the ignorant as they are confused by every form of discrimination.

43. "There is neither the seer nor the seen, neither the speaker nor the spoken; the form and usage of the Buddhist works—they are nothing but discrimination.

44. "Those who see things such as were seen before, do not see the Buddha; when discrimination is not aroused, then one indeed sees[1] the Buddha; the Buddha is a Fully-enlightened One; when one sees him, it is in a world unmanifested."[2]

The Lord of Laṅkā was then immediately awakened. Feeling a revulsion (*parāvṛitti*) in his mind and realising that the world was nothing but his own mind, he got settled in the realm of non-discrimination; was inspired by a stock of his past good deeds; acquired the cleverness of under-

[1] The Nanjo edition has here *na*, but I have followed the T'ang.

[2] T'ang has: "He who sees in the way as was seen before, cannot see the Buddha; when no discrimination is aroused, this, indeed, is the seeing." According to Wei: "If he sees things and takes them for realities, he does not see the Buddha. Even when he is not abiding in a discriminating mind, he cannot see the Buddha." Wei evidently reads somewhat like the Sanskrit.

standing all the texts; obtained the faculty of seeing [into things] as they were; was no more dependent upon others; observed things excellently with his own wisdom; gained the insight that was not of discursive reasoning; was no more dependent upon others;[1] became himself a great practiser of discipline; was able to manifest himself in all excellent forms; got thoroughly acquainted with all the skilful means; had the knowledge of the characteristic aspects of every stage whereby to surmount it skilfully; was delighted to look into[2] the self-nature of Citta, Manas, Manovijñāna; got a view whereby he could cut himself loose from the triple continuation; had the knowledge of disposing of every argument of (10) the philosophers; thoroughly understood the Tathāgata-garbha, the stage of Buddhahood, the inmost self; found himself abiding in the Buddha-knowledge; [when suddenly] a voice was heard from the sky, saying, "It is to be known by oneself."

"Well done, well done, O Lord of Laṅkā! Well done, indeed, O Lord of Laṅkā, for once more! The practiser is to discipline himself as thou doest. The Tathagatas and all things are to be viewed as they are viewed by thee; otherwise viewed, it is nihilism. All things are to be comprehended by transcending the Citta, Manas, and Vijñānas as is done by thee. Thou shouldst look inwardly and not get attached to the letters and a superficial view of things; thou shouldst not fall into the attainments, conceptions, experiences, views, and Samādhis of the Śrāvakas, Pratyekabuddhas, and philosophers; thou shouldst not have any liking for small talk and witticism; thou shouldst not cherish the notion of self-substance,[3] nor have any thought for the vainglory of rulership, nor dwell on such Dhyānas as belong to the six Dhyānas, etc.

"O Lord of Laṅkā, this is what is realised by the great

[1] This does not appear in T'ang, nor in Wei.
[2] T'ang: to go beyond.
[3] Wei and T'ang: Do not hold the views maintained in the Vedas.

practisers who can thus destroy the discourses advanced by others, crush mischievous views into pieces, properly keep themselves away from ego-centered notions, cause a revulsion in the depths of the mind fittingly by means of an exquisite knowledge; they are Buddha-sons who walk in the way of the Mahayana; and in order to enter upon the Tathagata-stage of self-realisation, the discipline is to be pursued by thee.

"O Lord of Laṅkā, conducting thyself in this way, be thou further purified in the way thou hast attained; (11) by disciplining thyself well in Samādhi and Samāpatti, follow not the state realised and enjoyed by the Śrāvakas, Pratyekabuddhas, and philosophers, as it is due to the imagination of those who discipline themselves according to the practices of the puerile philosophers. They cling to the visible forms created by their egotistical ideas; they maintain such notions as element, quality, and substance; they cling tenaciously to views originating from ignorance; they get confused by cherishing the idea of birth where prevails emptiness; they cling to discrimination [as real]; they fall into the way of thinking where obtains the dualism of qualifying and qualified.

"O Lord of Laṅkā, this is what leads to various excellent attainments, this is what makes one aware of the inmost attainment, this is the Mahayana realisation. He will accomplish and acquire a superior state of existence.

"O Lord of Laṅkā, by entering upon the Mahayana discipline the veils [of ignorance] are destroyed and one turns away from the manifold waves of mentation and falls not into the refuge and practice of the philosophers.

"O Lord of Laṅkā, the philosophers' practice starts from their own egotistic attachments. Their ugly practice arises from their adhering to the dualistic views concerning the self-nature of the Vijñāna.

"Well done, O Lord of Laṅkā! reflect on the signification of this as you did when seeing the Tathagata before; for this, indeed, is seeing the Tathagata."

At that time it occurred to Rāvaṇa: "I wish to see the Blessed One again, who has all the disciplinary practices at his command, who has turned away from the practices of the philosophers, who is born of the state of realisation in the inmost consciousness, and who is beyond [the dualism of] the transformed and the transforming. He is the knowledge (12) realised by the practisers, he is the realisation attained by those who are enjoying the perfect bliss of the Samādhi when there takes place an intuitive understanding which comes through meditation. Therefore, he is known as a great adept in the mental discipline.[1] May I see thus [again] the Compassionate One by means of his miraculous powers in whom the fuel of passion and discrimination are destroyed, who is surrounded by sons of the Buddha, who has penetrated into the minds and thoughts of all beings, who moves about everywhere, who knows everything, who keeps himself away from works (*kriyā*) and forms (*lakshaṇa*); seeing him may I attain what I have not yet attained, [retain] what I have already gained, may I conduct myself with non-discrimination, abide in the joy of Samādhi (meditation) and Samāpatti (concordance), and attain to the ground where the Tathagatas walk, and in these make progress."

At that moment, the Blessed One recognising that the Lord of Laṅkā is to attain the Anutpattikadharmakshānti[2] showed his glorious compassion for the ten-headed one by making himself visible once more on the mountain-peak studded with many jewels and enveloped in a net-work of jewels. The ten-headed King of Laṅkā saw the splendour again as seen before on the mountain peak, [he saw] the Tathagata, who was the Arhat and the Fully-enlightened One, with the thirty-two marks of excellence beautifully adorning his person, and also saw himself on each mountain-

[1] The original text here as it stands does not seem quite intelligible to me. Hence I have followed the T'ang which generally gives the best reading.

[2] This is explained later more or less fully as it is one of the most significant conceptions of Mahayana Buddhism.

peak, together with Mahāmati, in front of the Tathagata, the Fully-enlightened One, putting forward his discourse on the realisation experienced by the Tathagata in his inmost self, and, surrounded by the Yakshas, conversing on the literary teaching, recitation, and story [of Buddhism?]. Those (13) [Buddha]-lands were seen with the Leaders.[1]

Then the Blessed One beholding again this great assembly with his wisdom-eye, which is not the human eye, laughed loudly and most vigorously like the lion-king. Emitting rays of light from the tuft of hair between the eyebrows, from the ribs, from the loins, from the Śrivatsa[2] on the breast, and from every pore of the skin,—emitting rays of light which shone flaming like the fire taking place at the end of a kalpa, like a luminous rainbow, like the rising

[1] There is surely a discrepancy here in the text. T'ang reads: "In all the Buddha-lands in the ten quarters were also seen such events going on, and there was no difference whatever." Wei is quite different and has the following: "Besides, he saw all the Buddha-lands and all the kings thinking of the transitoriness of the body. As they are covetously attached to their thrones, wives, children, and relatives, they find themselves bound by the five passions and have no time for emancipation. Seeing this, they abandon their dominions, palaces, wives, concubines, elephants, horses, and precious treasures, giving them all up to the Buddha and his Brotherhood. They now retreat into the mountain-woods, leaving their homes and wishing to study the doctrine. He [Rāvaṇa] then sees the Bodhisattvas in the mountain woods strenuously applying themselves to the mastery of the truth, even to the extent of throwing themselves to the hungry tiger, lion, and Rakshasas. He thus sees the Bodhisattvas reading and reciting the sutras under a tree in the woods and discoursing on them for others, seeking thereby the truth of the Buddha. He then sees the Bodhisattvas seated under the Bodhi-tree in the Bodhi-maṇḍala thinking of suffering beings and meditating on the truth of the Buddha. He then sees the venerable Mahāmati the Bodhisattva before each Buddha preaching about the spiritual discipline of the inner life, and also sees [the Bodhisattva] surrounded by all the Yakshas and families and talking about names, words, phrases, and paragraphs." This last sentence is evidenty the translation of the Sanskrit *deśanāpāṭhakathām,* which is contrasted in the *Laṅkāvatāra* throughout with *pratyātmāryajñānagocara* (the spiritual realm realised by the supreme wisdom in one's inmost consciousness).

[2] Swastika.

sun, blazing brilliantly, gloriously—which were observed from the sky by Śakra, Brahman, and the guardians of the world, the one who sat on the peak [of Laṅkā] vying with Mount Sumeru laughed the loudest laugh. At that time the assembly of the Bodhisattvas together with Śakra and Brahman, each thought within himself:

"For what reason, I wonder, from what cause does the Blessed One who is the master of all the world (*sarva-dharma-vaśavartin*), after smiling first,[1] laugh the loudest laugh? Why does he emit rays of light from his own body? Why, emitting [rays of light], does he remain silent, with the realisation [of the truth] in his inmost self, and absorbed deeply and showing no surprise in the bliss of Samādhi, and reviewing the [ten] quarters, looking around like the lion-king, and thinking only of the discipline, attainment, and performance of Rāvaṇa?"

At that time, Mahāmati the Bodhisattva-Mahāsattva who was previously requested by Rāvaṇa [to ask the Buddha concerning his self-realisation], feeling pity on him, (14) and knowing the minds and thoughts of the assembly of the Bodhisattvas, and observing that beings to be born in the future would be confused in their minds because of their delight in the wordy teaching (*deśanāpāṭha*), because of their clinging to the letter as [fully in accordance with] the spirit (*artha*), because of their clinging to the disciplinary powers of the Śrāvakas, Pratyekabuddhas, and philosophers, —which might lead them to think how it were that the Tathagatas, the Blessed Ones, even in their transcendental state of consciousness should burst out into loudest laughter —Mahāmati, the Bodhisattva, asked the Buddha in order to put a stop to their inquisitiveness the following question: "For what reason, for what cause did this laughter take place?"

Said the Blessed One: "Well done, well done, O Mahāmati! Well done, indeed, for once more, O Mahāmati!

[1] This is wanting in the Chinese translations.

Viewing the world as it is in itself and wishing to enlighten the people in the world who have fallen into a wrong view of things in the three periods of time, thou undertakest to ask me the question. Thus should it be with the wise men who want to ask questions for both themselves and others. Rāvaṇa, Lord of Laṅkā, O Mahāmati, asked a twofold question of the Tathagatas of the past who are Arhats and perfect Buddhas; and he wishes now to ask me too a twofold question in order to have its distinction, attainment, and scope ascertained—this is what is never tasted by those who practise the meditations of the Śrāvakas, Pratyekabuddhas, and philosophers; and the same will be asked by the question-loving ten-headed one of the Buddhas to come."

Knowing that, the Blessed One said to the Lord of Laṅkā, thus: "Ask, O thou, Lord of Laṅkā; the Tathagata has given thee permission [to ask], delay not, whatever questions thou desirest to have answered, I will answer each of them (15) with judgment to the satisfaction of thy heart. Keeping thy seat of thought free from [false] discrimination, observe well what is to be subdued at each stage; ponder things with wisdom; [seeing into] the nature of the inner principle in thyself, abide in the bliss of Samādhi; embraced by the Buddhas in Samādhi, abide in the bliss of tranquillisation; going behind the Samādhi and understanding attained by the Śrāvakas and Pratyekabuddhas, abide in [the attainment of the Bodhisattvas] in the stages of Acalā, Sādhumatī, and Dharmameghā; grasp well the egolessness of all things in its true significance; be anointed by the Buddhas [with the water] of Samādhi at the great palace of lotus-jewels. [1]Surrounded by the Bodhi-

[1] The following sentence is done by the aid of T'ang, as the Sanskrit does not seem to give any sense. Literally translated it reads: "There by the becoming lotuses, by those lotuses that are blessed variously by the benediction of his own person...." Wei has: "O King of Laṅkā, thou wilt before long see thy person, too, thus sitting on the lotus-throne and continuing to abide there in a most natural manner. There are innumerable families of lotus-kings and

sattvas who are sitting on lotuses of various sorts each supported by the gracious power of the Buddhas, thou wilt find thyself sitting on a lotus and each one of the Bodhisattvas looking at thee face to face. This is a realm beyond the imagination. Thou shouldst plan out an adequate plan and establish thyself at a stage of discipline by planning out such a plan as would include [all kinds of] skilful means, so that thou comest to realise that realm which is beyond imagination; and then thou wilt attain the stage of Tathagatahood in which one is able to manifest oneself in various forms, and which is something never seen before by the Śrāvakas, Pratyekabuddhas, philosophers, Brahman, Indra, Upendra, and others.''

At that moment the Lord of Laṅkā being permitted by the Blessed One, rose from his seat on the peak of the jewel-mountain which shone like the jewel-lotus immaculate and glowing in splendour; he was surrounded by a company of celestial maidens of all kinds; garlands, flowers, perfumes, incense, unguents, umbrellas, banners, flags, necklaces, half-necklaces, diadems, tiaras,—all in every possible variety, (16) and other ornaments too whose splendour and excellence were never heard of or seen before, were created; music was played surpassing anything that could be had by the gods, Nāgas, Yakshas, Rākshasas, Gandharvas, Kinnaras, Mahoragas, and human beings; musical instruments were created equal to anything that could be had in all the World of Desire and also such superior musical instruments were created as were to be seen in the Buddha-lands; the Blessed One and the Bodhisattvas were enveloped in a net of jewels; a variety of dresses and high banners were raised high up in the air, as high as seven tālanga trees, to greet [the Buddha]; showering great clouds of offerings, playing music

innumerable families of Bodhisattvas there, each one of whom is sitting on a lotus-throne, and surrounded by those thou wilt find thyself and looking face to face at one another, and each one of them will before long come to abide in a realm beyond the understanding.''

which resounded [all around], and then descending from the air, [the Lord of Laṅkā] sat down on the peak of the jewel-mountain ornamented with magnificent jewel-lotus whose splendour was second only to the sun and lightning. Sitting he made courtesy, smiling first to the Blessed One for his permission, and proposed to him a twofold question: "It was asked of the Tathagatas of the past, who were Arhats, Fully-enlightened Ones, and it was solved by them. O Blessed One, now I ask of thee; [the request] will certainly be complied with by thee as it was by the Buddhas [of the past] in verbal teaching.[1] O Blessed One, duality was discoursed upon by the Transformed Tathagatas and Tathagatas of Transformation, but not by the Tathagatas of Silence.[2] The Tathagatas of Silence are absorbed in the blissful state of Samādhi, they do not discriminate concerning this state, nor do they discourse on it. O Blessed One, thou assuredly will discourse on this subject of duality. Thou art thyself a master of all things, an Arhat, a Tathagata. The sons of the Buddha and myself are anxious to listen to it."

The Blessed One said, "O Lord of Laṅkā, tell me what you mean by duality?"

The Lord of the Rākshasas, (17) who was renewed in his ornaments, full of splendour and beauty, with a diadem, bracelet, and necklace strung with vajra thread, said, "It is said that even dharmas are to be abandoned, and how much more adharmas (no-dharmas)! O Blessed One, why does this dualism exist that we are called to abandon? What are adharmas? and what are dharmas? How can there be a duality of things to abandon? Does not duality arise from falling into discrimination, from discriminating self-substance where there is none, from [the idea of] things

[1] That is, as far as the teaching could be conveyed in words. *Deśanāpātha* stands in contrast with *siddhānta* or *pratyātmagati* in the *Laṅkāvatāra*.

[2] In T'ang and Wei: "Original Tathagatas."

created and uncreated, because the non-differentiating nature of the Ālayavijñāna is not recognised? Like the seeing of a hair-circle as really existing in the air, [the notion of dualism] belongs to the realm of intellection not exhaustively purified. This being the case as it should be, how could there be any abandonment [of dharmas and adharmas]?"

Said the Blessed One, "O Lord of Lanka, seest thou not that the differentiation of things, such as is perceived in jars and other breakable objects whose nature it is to perish in time, takes place in a realm of discrimination [cherished by] the ignorant? This being so, is it not to be so understood? It is due to discrimination [cherished by] the ignorant that there exists the differentiation of dharma and adharma. Supreme wisdom *āryajñāna*), however, is not to be realised by seeing [things this way]. O Lord of Lankā, let it be so with the ignorant who follow the particularised aspect of existence that there are such objects as jars, etc., but it is not so with the wise. One flame of uniform nature rises up depending on houses, mansions, parks, and terraces, and burns them down; while a difference in the flames is seen according to the power of each burning material which varies in length, magnitude, etc. This being so, why (18) is it not to be so understood? The duality of dharma and adharma thus comes into existence. Not only is there seen a fire-flame spreading out in one continuity and yet showing a variety of flames, but from one seed, O Lord of Lankā, are produced, also in one continuity, stems, shoots, knots, leaves, petals, flowers, fruit, branches, all individualised. As it is with every external object from which grow [a variety of] objects, so also with internal objects. From Ignorance there develop the Skandhas, Dhātus, Āyatanas, with all kinds of objects accompanying, which grow out in the triple world where we have, as we see, happiness, form, speech, and behaviour, each differentiating [infinitely]. The oneness of the Vijñāna is grasped variously according to the evolution of an objective world; thus there are things seen inferior, superior, or middling, things defiled or free from defilement, things good or bad. Not only, O Lord of Laṅkā, is there such a difference of conditions in things generally, there is also seen a variety of realisations attained inwardly by each religious practiser as he treads the path of discipline which constitutes his practice. How much more difference in dharma and adharma do we not see in a world of particulars which is evolved by discrimination? Indeed, we do.

"O Lord of Laṅkā, the differentiation of dharma and adharma comes from discrimination. O Lord of Laṅkā, what are dharmas? That is, they are discriminated by the discriminations cherished by the philosophers, Śrāvakas, Pratyekabuddhas, and ignorant people. They think that the dharmas headed by Guṇa and Dravya are produced by causes—[these are the notions] to be abandoned. Such are not to be regarded [as real] because they are appearances. It comes from a man's clinging [to appearances] that the manifestations of his own mind are regarded as reality (*dharmatā*). (19) Such things as jars, etc., are products of discrimination conceived by the ignorant, they exist not; their substances are not attainable. The viewing of things from this viewpoint is known as their abandonment.

"What, then, are adharmas? O Lord of Laṅkā, what we call dharmas are not attainable, they are not appearances born of discrimination, they are above causality; there is in them no such [dualistic] happening as is seen as reality and non-reality. This is known as the abandoning of dharmas. What again is meant by the unattainability of dharmas? That is, it is like horns of a hare, or ass, or camel, or horse, or a child conceived by a barren woman. They are dharmas the nature of which is unattainable; they are not to be thought of [as real] because they are appearances. They are only talked about in popular parlance if they have any sense at all; they are not to be adhered to as in the case of jars, etc. As these [unrealities] are to be abandoned as not comprehensible by the mind (*vijñāna*), so are things (*bhāva*) of discrimination also to be abandoned. This is called the abandoning of dharmas and adharmas. O Lord of Laṅkā, your questioning as to the how of abandoning dharmas and adharmas is hereby answered.

"O Lord of Laṅkā, thou sayest again that thou hast asked [this question] of the Tathagatas of the past who were Arhats and Fully-enlightened Ones and that it was solved by them. O Lord of Laṅkā, that which is spoken of as the past belongs to discrimination; as the past is thus a discriminated [idea], even so are the [ideas] of the future and the present. Because of reality (*dharmatā*) the Tathagatas do not discriminate, they go beyond discrimination and futile reasoning, they do not follow (20) the individuation-aspect of forms, except when [reality] is disclosed for the edification of the unknowing and for the sake of their happiness.[1] It is by Prajñā that the Tathagata performs deeds transcending forms; therefore, what constitutes the Tathagatas in essence as well as in body is

[1] This is one of the most important sections in this first introductory chapter, but singularly all the three texts, perhaps excepting T'ang, present some difficulties for clear understanding. Wei: "O Lord of Laṅkā, what you speak of as past is a form of discrimination, and so are the future and the present also of discrimination. O Lord of Laṅkā, when I speak of the real nature of suchness as being real, it also belongs to discrimination; it is like discriminating forms as the ultimate limit. If one wishes to realise the bliss of real wisdom, let him discipline himself in the knowledge that transcends forms; therefore, do not discriminate the Tathagatas as having knowledge-body or wisdom-essence. Do not cherish any discrimination in [thy] mind. Do not cling in [thy] will to such notions as ego, personality, soul, etc. How not to discriminate? It is in the Manovijñāna that various conditions are cherished such as forms, figures, [etc.]; do not cherish such [discriminations]. Do not discriminate nor be discriminated. Further, O Lord of Laṅkā, it is like various forms painted on the wall, all sentient beings are such. O Lord of Laṅkā, all sentient beings are like grasses and trees, with them there are no acts, no deeds, O Lord of Laṅkā, all dharmas and adharmas, of them nothing is heard, nothing talked. O Lord of Laṅkā, all things in the world are like māyā. . . ."

wisdom (*jñāna*). They do not discriminate, nor are they discriminated. Wherefore do they not discriminate in the Manas? Because discrimination is of the self, of soul, of personality. How do they not discriminate in the Manovijñāna? [The Manovijñāna] is meant for the objective world where causality prevails as referred to forms, appearances, conditions, and figures. Therefore, discrimination and non-discrimination must be transcended.

"O Lord of Laṅkā, that which comes out in manifestation is [like] a figure inlaid in a wall, it has no sensibility [or consciousness]. O Lord of Laṅkā, all that is in the world is devoid of work and action because all things have no reality, and there is nothing heard, nothing hearing. O Lord of Laṅkā, all that is in the world is [like] an image magically transformed. This is not comprehended by the philosophers and the ignorant. O Lord of Laṅkā, he who thus sees things, is the one who sees truthfully. Those who see things otherwise walk in discrimination; as they depend on discrimination, they cling to dualism. It is like seeing one's own image reflected in a mirror, or one's own shadow in the water, or in the moon-

T'ang: "O Lord of Laṅkā, what you speak of as past is no more than discrimination, so is the future; I too am like him. [Is this to be read, "the present, too, is like it"?] O Lord of Laṅkā, the teaching of all the Buddhas is outside discrimination; as it goes beyond all discriminations and futile reasonings, it is not a form of particularisation, it is realised only by wisdom. That [this absolute] teaching is at all discoursed about is for the sake of giving bliss to all sentient beings. The discoursing is done by the wisdom transcending forms. It is called the Tathagata; therefore, the Tathagata has his essence, his body in this wisdom. He thus does not discriminate, nor is he to be discriminated. Do not discriminate him after the notions of ego, personality, or being. Why this impossibility of discrimination? Because the Manovijñāna is aroused on account of an objective world wherein it attaches itself to forms and figures. Therefore, [the Tathagata] is outside the discriminating [view] as well as the discriminated [idea]. O Lord of Laṅkā, it is like beings painted in colours on a wall, they have no sensibility [or intelligence]. Sentient beings in the world are also like them; no acts, no rewards [are with them]. So are all the teachings, no hearing, no preaching."

light, or seeing one's shadow in the house, or hearing an echo in the valley. People grasping their own shadows of discrimination (21) uphold the discrimination of dharma and adharma, and, failing to carry out the abandonment of the dualism, they go on discriminating and never attain tranquillity. By tranquillity is meant oneness, and oneness gives birth to the highest Samādhi, which is gained by entering into the womb of Tathagatahood, which is the realm of supreme wisdom realised in one's inmost self."

II

THE LANKAVATARA SUTRA AND THE TEACHING OF ZEN BUDDHISM

II

THE LANKAVATARA SUTRA AND THE TEACHING OF ZEN BUDDHISM

Preliminary Note

The study of the *Laṅkāvatāra* may best be approached in its especial relation to the teaching and history of Zen Buddhism. It was principally due to Bodhidharma, father of the Zen in China, that the sutra came to be prominently taken notice of by students of Buddhism, and it was mainly by his followers that its study was systematically carried on and its commentaries written. This has already been mentioned. It is true that the Yogācāra school, or the Dharmalakshaṇa sect（法相宗）of Chinese and Japanese Buddhism makes frequent references to it as supporting the psychological theories of their school, but this side of the sutra is incidental, its chief theme being the doctrine of self-realisation. Whatever psychology, or logic, or metaphysics it may contain, is to prove the main doctrine. The sutra is by no means systematically developed as has been repeatedly noticed, but the current running underneath the whole text is unmistakable. There is no doubt that this underneath current in spite of the memorandum-like nature of the sutra is in closest touch with the teaching of Bodhidharma and his school.

The study of the sutra, however, has not been so vigorously prosecuted as that of other Mahayana sutras, such as the *Saddharmapuṇḍarīka, Vimalakīrti, Avataṁsaka,* or *Sukhāvatīvyūha.* This neglect has especially been the case with the followers of Zen, who ought to have studied it most seriously, but whose indifference to philosophy and cognate subjects is notorious. Added to this, the fact that the sutra not only in the Chinese translations but in the original Sanskrit presents many difficulties in grammar and in meaning has increased the continued neglect of it. But the time is ripe for us to take it up and subject it to a serious study now that we have the Sanskrit edition completed by the unceasing efforts of the late Dr. Bunyū Nanjō. It is my intention here to treat it as the sutra *par excellence* in relation to the Zen teaching of Buddhism. While Zen as a rule abhors any connection with one special sutra or śastra, the undeniable fact remains that the *Laṅkāvatāra* was the book handed by Bodhidharma to his first disciple Hui-k'ê (慧可) as the sutra containing the essential teachings of his school. This being the case, it is natural for his followers of the present time to renew the investigation and study of it. Besides, no religious experience can stand outside a more or less intellectual interpretation of it. Zen may like to ignore its literary or philosophical side, and it is justified in doing so, no doubt, but to think that this implies the absolute ignoring of all attempts at any form of interpretation would be a grievous error.

PART I

A General Survey of the Principal Ideas Expounded in the Sutra

The Breadth of Mahayana Buddhism

Buddhism, especially Mahayana Buddhism so called, is like a vast ocean where all kinds of living beings are allowed to thrive in a most generous manner, almost verging on a chaos. Students who lightly step into it generally find it too complicated and overwhelming for their logical comprehension. But the fact is that Mahayana Buddhism is the outcome of long years of development of a religious system among a people furnished with a most fertile imagination. The student has to be patient. The best method of study may probably be found by taking up one principal Mahayana sutra at a time, and examining its contents historically, philosophically, and psychologically. The Chinese scholars encountered the same difficulties centuries ago, and as in those days there was no lower or higher criticism of the sacred texts, every tradition was respected on its face value. The scholars exhausted their ingenuity to make a logical, humanly plausible arrangement among the vast treasure of literature brought over from India and all claiming to have been delivered by the Buddha himself. This untenable position is now abandoned, and each sutra has come to be studied, historically, critically, and analytically. Each principal sutra may now be regarded as marking a certain stage or phase of development in the history of Mahayana Buddhism, which is indeed too huge and unwieldy to be handled as one solid piece of work completed within a few decades.

What, then, does the *Laṅkāvatāra* signify in the composite system of Mahayana Buddhism? What phase does it represent in the long history of Buddhism? What in short is the message of the *Laṅkāvatāra* as we have it now? What function does it or did it perform in the conservation of Buddhist thought and experience?

Each principal sutra has had its special work to accomplish in the unfoldment of the religious consciousness of the Buddhists. For instance, the *Saddharmapuṇḍarīka* marks the epoch in the history of Buddhism when Śākyamuni ceased to be conceived of as a historical personage subject to the fate of all transient beings; for he is no more a human Buddha but one who lives through eternity for the benefit of all creatures. All that he is recorded to have done in history is no more than one of his "skilful means" (*upāya*) to save mankind. So we read:

"I show the place of extinction, I reveal to all beings a device (*upāya*) to educate them, albeit I do not become extinct at the time, and in this very place [that is, Mount Gṛidhrakuta] I continue preaching the Dharma. Here I rule myself as well as all beings. But men of perverted minds in their delusion do not see me standing here. In the opinion that my body is completely extinct, they pay worship in many ways to the relics, but me they see not. They feel, however, a certain aspiration by which their minds become right. When such upright, mild, and gentle creatures leave off their bodies, then I assemble the crowd of disciples and show myself here on the Gṛidhrakuta. And I speak thus to them in this very place: I was not completely extinct at the time; it was but a device of mine, monks; repeatedly am I born in the world of the living......I see how the creatures are afflicted, but I do not show them my proper being. Let them first have an aspiration to see me; then I will reveal to them the true Dharma."[1]

The *Suvarṇaprabhāsa,* at least in part, belongs to the same period, when it says: "Every drop in the oceans may be counted up, but the age of Śākyamuni is altogether beyond calculation. Mount Sumeru may be pulverised and every particle is countable, but the age of Śākyamuni is altogether beyond calculation. However innumerable, every particle of dust composing the great earth may be counted up, but not the age of the Victorious One. However boundless space is, its ends may be reached, but the age of Śākyamuni is altogether beyond calculation. However long one may live through hundreds of kotis of eons, he cannot count up the age of the Buddha. There are two deeds whereby a man's life is prolonged: not to kill others and to give away much food. For this reason the age of the Great Man cannot be measured, it is like the measure of kalpas which are incalculable. Therefore, harbour not any shadow of doubt as to the age of the Victorious One which is indeed beyond the reach of measurement."[2]

The *Sukhāvatīvyūha* represents a stage in the history of

[1] S.B.E., Vol. XXI, pp. 307–308.

[2] Nanjo and Idzumi edition, pp. 9–10. This edition has so far only partly appeared in *The Eastern Buddhist,* Vol. V. No. 1.

Buddhist experience which ceased to be wholly satisfied with the intellectual presentation of the doctrine of enlightenment, when Buddhists began to be oppressed with the idea of sin and doubt hanging over them too heavily and acutely. Read the following in which the destiny of those Bodhisattvas is described who have not yet come to have an absolute faith in the wisdom of the Buddha but who try to save themselves by amassing their own stock of merit:

"And, O Ajita, there might be a dungeon belonging to an anointed Kshatriya king, inlaid entirely with gold and beryl, in which cushions, garlands, wreaths, and strings are fixed, having canopies of different colours and kinds, covered with silk cushions, scattered over with various flowers and blossoms, scented with excellent scents, adorned with arches, courts, windows, pinnacles, fire-places, and terraces, covered with nets of bells of the seven kinds of gems, having four angels, four pillars, four doors, four stairs; and the son of that king having been thrown into the dungeon for some misdeed is there, bound with a chain made of the Jambunada gold. And suppose there is a couch prepared for him, covered with many woollen cloths, spread over with cotton and feather cushions, having Kalinga coverings, and carpets, together with coverlids, red on both sides, beautiful and charming. There might be brought to him much food and drink, of various kinds, pure and well prepared. What do you think, O Ajita, would the enjoyment be great for that prince?

"Ajita said: Yes, it would be great, O Bhagavat.

"The Bhagavat said: What do you think, O Ajita, would he even taste it there and notice it, or would he feel any satisfaction from it?

"He said: No, indeed, O Bhagavat; but, on the contrary, when he had been led away by the king and thrown into the dungeon, he would only wish for deliverance from there. He would seek for the nobles, princes, ministers, women, elders, householders, and lords of castles, who might deliver him from that dungeon. Moreover, O Bhagavat, there is no pleasure for that prince in that dungeon, nor is he liberated, until the king shows him favour.

"The Bhagavat said: Thus, O Ajita, it is with those Bodhisattvas who, having fallen into doubt, amass a stock of merit, but doubt the knowledge of the Buddha......"[1]

It is very interesting to contrast these passages from the *Sukhāvatīvyūha* with the thought pervading the *Prajñāpāramitā-sūtra*. For the *Prajñāpāramitā* dwelling on the conception of unreality or emptiness (*śūnyatā*) seeks deliverance from the dungeon of existence, or rather interprets the Buddhist realisation purely from a metaphysical point of view. The doctrine of Śūnyatā[2] constituting the keynote of the *Prajñāpāramitā* is really the foundation of all the Mahayana schools of Buddhism including even the Yogācāra. What is known as primitive Buddhism denied the existence of an ego-substance (*ātman*), but its conception of the external world was that of the naïve realist. The *Prajñāpāramitā* philosopher insists on the non-existence of a particular body as such, that is, as an objective reality whose identity is absolute. Every being or every object, as he sees it, is relative, impermanent, and not worth attachment. This *Prajñāpāramitā* idea of unreality, or emptiness as the literal sense of the term *śūnyatā* is, is the foundation of the Buddhist theory of nature.

Thus, in the *Prajñāpāramitā*, supreme enlightenment is

[1] S.B.E. XLIX, *The Larger Sukhāvatīvyūha*, pp. 63–64.

[2] The theory of Śūnyatā (emptiness or void) is one of the best-known theories propounded by the Mahayana, but it is one of the least-understood especially by those whose thought has never run along the line of Mahayana ontology. But, even among Buddhist scholars, there are some who do not so fully comprehend the doctrine as one may expect of them, seeing that they must have been imbued with the idea since the beginning of their study. The reason is that the doctrine itself is quite liable to be wrongly or inadequately interpreted, owing to its subtlety or depth, or to its extreme simplicity, as it is variously approached and taken hold of. See also below where the doctrine of "Anutpāda" (no-birth) is treated.

identified with the attainment of Śūnyatā. In other words, the object of the Buddhist life is to find an unattached abode in this realisation. This abode is called *apratishṭhita,* not-abiding. Hence the noted phrase in the *Diamond Sūtra,* XIV: *na kvacit pratishṭhitaṁ cittam utpādayitavyam.*[1] The Tathagata has no dwelling place in the sense that all his thoughts and doings have no exterior or ulterior objects in view to which he desires to adapt himself, and therefore that he is like the sun that shines on everybody just and unjust, or like the lily in the field that blooms in its best even when there is nobody around to admire its supra-Solomonic array. So we have again in the *Ashṭasāhasrika,* Chapter II, p. 34: "A Bodhisattva-Mahāsattva should abide himself in the perfection of Prajñā by abiding in emptiness.... The Tathagata is so called because he is not abiding anywhere, his mind has no abode neither in things created nor in things uncreated, and yet it is not away from them." This is the message of all the sutras belonging to the *Prajñāpāramitā* class.

As to the *Avataṁsaka-sūtra,* it is really the consummation of Buddhist thought, Buddhist sentiment, and Buddhist experience. To my mind, no religious literature in the world can ever approach the grandeur of conception, the depths of feeling, and the gigantic scale of composition, as attained by this sutra. It is the eternal fountain of life from which no religious mind will turn back athirst or only partially satisfied. It is a great pity that this magnificent literature still remains concealed in a language not so universally accessible. Here not only deeply speculative minds find satisfaction, but humble spirits and heavily-oppressed hearts, too, will have their burdens lightened. Abstract truths are so concretely, so symbolically represented here that one will finally come to a realisation of the truth that even in a particle of dust the whole universe is seen reflected—not this

[1] "A Bodhisattva should have his thoughts awakened without abiding in anything whatever." In Chinese, 應無所住而生其心.

visible universe only, but a vast system of universes, conceivable by the highest minds only. Towards the end of this section I have translated the ten vows of the Bodhisattva Samantabhadra as given in the final chapter of the *Gaṇḍavyūha*, which forms a part of the Chinese *Avataṁsaka*.

The Teaching of the Laṅkāvatāra

Where does the *Laṅkāvatāra* stand then? It may be classed in a way with the *Avataṁsaka* inasmuch as it teaches the absolute idealism of the latter and is the disclosure of the inner mind of the Buddha, but it has a special message to give to the Buddhist world in a manner characteristic of the sutra. It is devoid of all symbolism, quite different in this respect from *Avataṁsaka*. It is, instead, straightforward in expression and notes down in a somewhat sketchy style almost all the ideas belonging to the different schools of Mahāyāna Buddhism. It is partly for this reason that the sutra requires a great deal of learning as well as an insight to understand all the details thoroughly. The principal thesis of the *Laṅkāvatāra*, however, may be regarded as summarised in the following passage:[1]

"Again, O Mahāmati, there may be other Śramanas and Brahmans who hold the following views: that all things have no self-substance (*niḥsvabhāva*),[2] they are like a cloud, like a circle traced out by a revolving fire-brand, or like the air-castle of the Gandharvas; that they are unborn (*anutpāda*),[2] that they are like māyā, or mirage, or the moon in water, or a dream; that external objects are manifestations of the mind erroneously perceived due to false discrimination (*vikalpa*)[2] since time immemorial, that by thus viewing the world one ceases to be conditioned by the false dis-

[1] This is done mainly from the T'ang version, the Kōkyōshoin edition of the Buddhist Tripitaka, 黄 (*huang*), VI, 87*b* f. Cf. the Sanskrit text (pp. 42 ff.). Throughout this book, wherever page-references are given, unless specified, they all refer to the Sanksrit text edited by B. Nanjō.

[2] As to the meaning of these terms, see below.

crimination worked out in one's own mind, one does away with the terminology belonging to such false discrimination and with the signification of words such as predicating and predicated; that when one understands that the body, property, and abiding-place[1] are the particularisations of the Ālaya-vijñāna (or *citta,* mind), one is freed from [ideas such as] perceived and perceiving, attains to a state of no-image, or shadowlessness (*nirābhāsa*).[2] O Mahāmati, such a Bodhisattva-Mahāsattva will before long realise the sameness of Saṁsāra and Nirvāṇa.

"O Mahāmati, by deeds of great love (*mahākaruṇā*), skilful means (*upāya*), and effortlessness (*anābhogacaryā*),[3] a Bodhisattva reviews all beings and knows that they are like māyā, they resemble shadows, they are not produced by causes; and, further, knowing that the world exists not outside the mind, he leads a life of formlessness (*animitta*). As he gradually goes up the higher stages (*bhūmi*), he will realise a state of Samādhi where he comes to the understanding that the triple world is Mind itself (*cittamātra*). The Samādhi he attains is called Māyā-like (*māyopama*). He will further free himself from all images, perfect his knowledge, and realise that things are unborn, and entering upon the Samādhi called Vajravimbopama, will obtain the Buddha-body. He will, always abiding in the suchness of things, manifest himself in transformed bodies, he will be endowed with the ten Powers, the six Psychic Faculties, and the ten-

[1] *Deha-bhoga-pratishṭha* is found generally in combination. It means this bodily existence with its material possessions and its physical surroundings; in short it stands for the world generally.

[2] This is a spiritual state of absolute purity in which one finds no traces of dualism. It is a complete identification of the self with the suchness or thusness (*tathatā*) of things, and there is no thought of birth, abiding, and disappearance, seeing that all things start from the evolution of one's own mind (*svacitta*).

[3] Or purposelessness, a state of perfect adjustment, when one is not at all conscious of doing anything special for any particular individual. The sun is said to be effortless or purposeless in its work when it shines on the just and on the unjust.

fold Self-mastery. O Mahāmati, adorned with Upāya (skilful means), he will visit all the Buddha-lands; and disengaged from the philosophical doctrines as well as from the Citta, Manas, and Vijñāna, he will experience a revulsion (*parāvṛitti*) within himself and by degrees will attain the Tathāgata-body.

"Therefore, O Mahāmati, if a Bodhisattva wishes to attain the Tathāgata-body, he should keep himself away from the Skandhas, Dhātus, Āyatanas, Cittam, causation, works, discipline, birth, staying and passing, and cease from discriminating, philosophising, and abide in the thought of the "Mind-only" (*cittamātra*).

"When the triple world is surveyed [by the Bodhisattva], he perceives that this existence is due to memory (*vāsanā*) that has been accumulated since the beginningless past but wrongly interpreted. He recognises that Buddhahood is a state imageless, unborn, and to be inwardly experienced by oneself, when the mind becomes fully controlled and purposeless deeds are accomplished. Like the Cintamaṇi (wish-gem), he will now manifest himself in a variety of forms according to the needs of sentient beings and lead them to the view that only Mind is, and then gradually compel them to ascend the stages. Therefore, O Mahāmati, let the Bodhisattva discipline himself well in the work of self-realisation (*svasiddhānta*)."

Being full of technical terms, the reader may find the import of the passage here quoted difficult to understand, but as we go on, it will, I hope, grow fully intelligible. In the meantime, the following paraphrase will help the reader to get a general idea of it.

The highest stage of Buddhist experience is reached when a man comes to realise that things are devoid of a self-substance, or that they are not after all final, irreducible realities, for they never have been created, they are what they are from beginningless past; if we say that they have come into existence, or that they exist as we perceive them through the senses, this will imply that individualisation is ultimate fact, which, however, is contrary to the truth inwardly perceived by an enlightened mind.

Individualisation is due to discrimination (*vikalpa*), which is falsely interpreted and adhered to by a heart blinded by desires and passions, and from this fact there issue all kinds of human tragedies and comedies. What really exists is mind, which is above all discrimination, that is, above logic and analysis. When this Mind which is designated in the sutra as the Ālaya or Ālayavijñāna is discriminated by an erroneously self-created and self-reflecting agent called Manas, this world of particulars develops in its misleading fulness and richness.

Discrimination is the result of memory (*vāsanā*) accumulated from the unknown past. *Vāsanā* literally means "perfuming," or "fumigation," that is, it is a kind of energy that is left behind when an act is accomplished and has the power to rekindle the old and seek out new impressions. Through this "perfuming," reflection takes place which is the same thing as discrimination, and we have a world of opposites and contraries with all its practical consequences. The triple world, so called, is therefore the shadow of a self-reflecting and self-creating mind. Hence the doctrine of "Mind-only" (*cittamātra*).

Reality as it is, or Mind in itself, is also called the suchness (*tathatā*) or sameness (*samatā*) of things, as herein are unified all forms of antithesis which constitute our actual world of sense and logic. The Bodhisattva abides in this suchness which transcends all our reasonings and discriminations. And because he abides in this transcendental realm, his all-loving heart works without the taint of selfishness and one-sided attachment, using all contrivances (*upāya*) whereby to save his fellow-beings from pain and suffering. These works of his are called purposeless for the reason that they are not actuated by any egotistic interests or desires or motives. They are called out from the abundance of his inner goodness which now shines forth free from all defilements of intellection as well as of conation.

The world is like māyā, or mirage, as his intellect is no longer snared in the meshes of dualistic logic, he intuitively perceives that the world of particularisation is no more than the reflection of his own mind. His life is thus designated as formless or imageless and his deeds effortless and purposeless. Yet he never relaxes his efforts to benefit all sentient beings. He knows from his transcendental position that Saṁsāra and Nirvāṇa are the same (*samatā*), and yet he knows not when to stop working for the realisation of the highest ideals and also for universal salvation. His inner mind is then said to be abiding in the Samādhi known as Māyopama (mirage-like).

This seems to be the highest state of spiritual attainment realisable by a mind encased in a human body; but there is still a higher state to be attained by the Buddhist. There is a higher body called Buddhakāya which is obtained when a man enters upon Vajravimbopama Samādhi. When this is obtained one is endowed with the ten Powers, the six Psychic Faculties, and the tenfold Self-mastery. He is then able to transform himself into various forms in order to benefit sentient beings in accordance with their desires and circumstances. He is also able to visit all the Buddha-lands and to perform all Buddha-deeds.

The main object of the Buddhist life is thus seen to consist in having a certain spiritual revulsion, whereby we are able to leap from the dualistic shore of this individualistic world to the other shore of Nirvana, where there are no egoistic impulses and desires in evidence any longer, though this means not at all the death of a loving heart itself. To effect this revulsion, spiritual discipline is needed which finally leads up to a certain exalted inner condition. Enlightenment, self-realisation, or the opening of an inner eye is the name given to it. The *Laṅkāvatāra* calls it Pratyātmāryajñānagocara, or Svasiddhānta, and the main object of its teaching is to acquaint us with the fact of an inner perception which causes a spiritual revolution in our whole life.

The reason why the *Laṅkāvatāra* is considered to be historically and doctrinally so closely related to Zen Buddhism is based on this fact that herein most emphatically asserted is the importance of an inner realisation as the source of all the religious virtues and blessings. Zen, of all the schools of Buddhism, is preëminently the religion of enlightenment. If the Buddhist life is to be regarded as consisting of Prajñā (higher knowledge) or Bodhi (wisdom), and Karuṇā (love), Zen indeed makes most of the Prajñā element at least during its first stages of training, and this Prajñā which it teaches is to be attained by transcending the relativity of worldly knowledge, which will free our desires and passions from the entanglements of the individualistic world-conception. It does not teach to destroy all the impulses, instincts, and affective factors that make up the human heart; it only teaches to clear up our intellectual insight from erroneous discriminations and unjustifiable assertions; for when this is done the heart knows by itself how to work out its native virtues. This is the position of Zen Buddhism, and in the following pages I wish to develop what the *Laṅkāvatāra* states on this subject, rather generally in the first part concerning the nature of the inner realisation, and in the second and the third part concerning its relations to logic, psychology, and the practical life.

The All-importance of an Inner Realisation

The ideas that things are devoid of self-substance (*svabhāva*), that is, they are by nature empty (*śūnya*), that the world is nothing but Mind, that in order to reach the ultimate end of Buddhahood one must transcend all the limitations of dualism and particularisation, and finally that the state of enlightenment must be realised within one's self, —these are the common property of Mahayana Buddhism; but in the *Laṅkāvatāra* these ideas are developed in a way peculiar to this sutra. By this I mean that it lays especial emphasis on the importance of self-realisation, without which the Buddhist life remains a mere philosophical exercise. The season why Bodhidharma (菩提達摩) handed this sutra over to Hui-k'ê (慧可) as containing the essence of Zen Buddhism must be sought in this that the constant refrain of the *Laṅkāvatāra* is the all-importance of an inner perception (*pratyātmagati*) or self-realisation (*svasiddhānta*). Therefore, the purpose of this sutra is highly practical in spite of its abstract speculations.

In the first chapter[1] which is added to the two later translations of the *Laṅkāvatāra,* we have this from the Buddha, who gently smiled looking at the palace of Laṅkā on Mount Malaya: "All the Buddhas of the past have discoursed on the truth of an inner realisation which can be attained only by the supreme wisdom (*āryajñāna*) of the Buddha and never by the speculation (*ṭarka*) of the philosophers[2] or by the discipline of the Śrāvaka and Pratyekabuddha. This truth I will now disclose for the benefit of Rāvaṇa, King of Laṅkā."[3]

And when the Bodhisattva Mahāmati finished praising the virtues of the Buddha in the beginning of Chapter II, (which is Chapter I of the Sung translation), the Buddha surveying the assembly made this remark: "O ye, sons of the Victorious One, and O thou, Mahāmati, ask and I will instruct you concerning the attainment of the inmost realisation (*pratyātmagati*)."

These statements are conclusive as showing that *Laṅkāvatāra's* special importance in the literature of Mahayana Buddhism lies in its perpetual upholding of this intuitive element in all religion. While the sutra has been made use

[1] For an English translation from the Sanskrit text, see supra.

[2] Whenever "the philosophers" are referred to in this book, they mean *tīrthya,* or *tīrthakara,* and 外道 (*wai-tao*) in Chinese, which literally means "other teachings."

[3] P. 2.

of to support the claims of a particular school such as the Yogācāra or the Avataṁsaka, in its connection with the doctrine of the Ālayavijñāna or Tathāgata-garbha, this connection is accidental. The thesis of the sutra must be regarded as centered upon the idea of an inner perception of the deepest truth, which goes beyond language and reasoning. The Buddhist discipline or exercise (*yoga*) as is told by the Buddha consists of two parts, philosophical and practical.[1] The philosophical discipline is to train the mind to absolute idealism and see that the world is Mind, and that there is in reality no becoming such as birth and death, and that no external things really exist; while the practical side is to attain an inner perception by means of supreme wisdom (*svapratyātmāryajñānādhigama*). Putting the practical side of Buddhist discipline first, we can say that when it is accomplished, the philosophical side follows by itself; that is to say, the world as seen in the light of self-realisation is to be interpreted in terms of absolute idealism. However this may be, the *Laṅkāvatāra* is decidedly rich in deep mystical speculations.

One thing I wish to notice in the *Laṅkāvatāra* before I proceed to describe the nature of the inner realisation, is that this sutra does not make one reference[2] to the awakening of the thought of enlightenment (*bodhicittotpāda*) made so much of, especially in the sutras of the *Prajñāpāramitā* group. The awakening of the thought of enlightenment

[1] P. 79 f. "To be great in the exercise that makes up Bodhisattvahood (*mahāyogayogin*), one has to be an expert in four things. [three of which are intellectual and the last one is practical]: (1) To perceive clearly that this visible world is no more than Mind itself; (2) to abandon the notion that birth, abiding, and passing-away really take place; (3) to look into the nature of things external and realise that they have no reality (*abhāva*); and finally (4) to train oneself towards the realisation of the truth in the inmost consciousness by means of supreme wisdom."

[2] This may not be quite an exact statement, as Mahāmati does refer once or twice to it, but the Buddha himself does not touch the subject. He always talks about the realisation of the inner truth.

means to take interest in the teaching of Mahayana Buddhism and to wish sincerely for the realisation of its truth. This is really the first step in the career of a Bodhisattva, for without this awakening no further progress in spiritual discipline will be possible. Therefore, in almost all the Mahayana sutras one is told to direct one's first thought toward enlightenment. When this is accomplished, one must come some day to the final attainment, however remote that day may be. In the *Laṅkāvatāra* no word is said about the awakening, but it goes directly to the heart of the matter, that is, it asks the Bodhisattva to come to the realisation at once, instead of making gradual advance toward the goal. In this respect, this sutra may be said to be an appeal to those Bodhisattvas who are already deeply steeped in the Mahayana teaching of Supreme Enlightenment.

Another thing that the student of the *Laṅkāvatāra* notices is that the Buddha here tells Mahāmati to attain to a state of inner realisation (*pratyātmagocara*) and not of enlightenment (*saṁbodhi*). These two are psychologically the same process; when one has Pratyātmajñāna, one is enlightened. But in the *Laṅkāvatāra* the ultimate goal of the Buddhist life is generally stated in terms of experience (*gocara*) and not intellectually as illumining.[1] I am inclined to think that the *Laṅkāvatāra* is unique in this respect explaining perhaps the reason why Bodhidharma, the father of Zen Buddhism in China, recommended it to his mystic followers.

When the *Laṅkāvatāra* refers to Gocara or Gatigocara, instead of to Bodhi or Saṁbodhi, we realise that the main

[1] This does not mean that the *Laṅkāvatāra* never refers to the attainment of the Bodhi, for the Bodhi is the cardinal idea in every school of Buddhism, and the sutra frequently speaks of it; for instance, see pp. 70, 73, 79, 85, 89, 112, 114, 148. We cannot help noticing however and emphasising the fact that the *Laṅkāvatāra* makes more frequent references to that higher state of consciousness in which is revealed the inmost truth of things, than to the attainment of supreme enlightenment.

object of the sutra centres on the acquirement and cultivation of a certain general subjective attitude towards the world and life, which is not merely philosophical or conceptual, but which comes from the experience of some definite turning in the activity of the mind. Saṁbodhi or enlightenment looks more toward the cognitive aspect of the revulsion (*parāvṛitti*) one experiences. This is all well as far as it goes, which is indeed the basis of all Buddhism, be it Hinayana or Mahayana. The *Laṅkāvatāra*, however, has come to see that the whole of the Buddhist life is not in merely seeing into the truth, but in living it, experiencing it, so that there will be no dualism in one's life of seeing and living: seeing must be living, and living seeing, with no hiatus between them, except in language. Hence the *Laṅkāvatāra's* reference so much to living or experience, Gocara or Gatigocara, that is, Pratyātmagocara.

The Inner Experience and Language

This inner perception or realisation is made possible by the presence of the Tathāgata--garbha within the heart of every sentient being.[1] The Garbha, which literally means "womb," or better, "something interiorly hidden," is the seed of Tathagatahood from which a fully-enlightened being grows up. This, however, is generally found covered up with defiled wrappings of false judgment (*parikalpa* or *vikalpa*) and irrational attachment (*abhiniveśa*). False judgment comes from not perceiving things as they are (*yathābhūtam*), that is, as not subject to the principle of individuation, which is imposed by the mind upon things considered external. As to the irrational attachment which causes in us all kinds of vexation, it is the inevitable result of false judgment. The Garbha, therefore, originally pure and immaculate, must be restored to its natural state free from attachments. It is thus generally likened to a priceless gem concealed under a soiled garment. Take the garment

[1] Pp. 77, 222.

off and the shining stone will begin to shed its natural light over things as they are. The illumination thus obtained is a state of self-realisation, and one can then see the Garbha as if held in one's own hand, even as plainly as the āmalaka fruit.[1] As the Garbha thus cleansed of its defilement is beyond the speculations of the philosophers and the attainment of the Hinayanists, the author of the *Daśabhūmika*[2] as well as the *Laṅkāvatāra* calls it Avikalpa, or Nirvikalpa-jñāna,[3] meaning knowledge of non-judgment or non-discrimination, a kind of direct perception, or again knowledge of thusness or suchness (*tathatājñāna*).[4]

In spite of the practical end it has in view, the *Laṅkāvatāra* is filled with abstract nomenclature, which sometimes turns away those unfamiliar with Buddhist literature from further pursuing their study of it. But this is unavoidable seeing that the experience on which the *Laṅkāvatāra* discourses is not within the reach of a consciousness ordinarily suffocated with contrary notions. The sutra is quite explicit in this respect as it declares that those who are tied (*saṁsakta*) to words do not understand the truth (*tattvam*),[5] or that "the superior state of self-realisation is beyond speech and analysis."[6] In fact, in this sutra the Buddha is never tired of repeatedly reminding us of the fact that language falls far too short of adequately representing the true state of self-realisation. This is in the nature of language. Language is always discriminative;

[1] P. 222. [2] Edited by J. Rahder, p. 64. [3] P. 158, etc.

[4] See also Sthiramati's commentary on the *Triṁśikā* by Vasubandhu, edited by Sylvain Lévi, pp. 40–41.

[5] Pp. 223, 224; "As the ignorant seize upon the finger-tip and not the moon, so, indeed, those who are fastened to letters comprehend not my truth."

[6] P. 148; "The truth of realisation is the superior condition of an inner attainment which goes beyond words, letters and discriminations and leads to the realm of non-outflowings; it is the ground of inner realisation itself, it has nothing to do with the reasonings of the philosophers and evil doers; destroying all these philosophers and evil doers, self-realisation shines out."

when we make reference to anything, it is to be distinguished from other things, thus limiting it to that extent and to that degree. But the supreme moment of self-realisation is not subject to any form of limitation and discrimination; perhaps the only way of describing it will be to say "that," or abstractly, "thusness" (*tathatā*), but even this is discriminating (*parikalpita*), and distorts the conception. As long as we are what we are, tied up to the exigencies of material existence and to the inherent needs of logical thinking, language is inevitable, and if we do not use words we have to resort to gestures and movements of some parts of the body in one way or another. As the *Laṅkāvatāra* remarks,[1] words are not necessarily used all over the world for the communication of ideas or feelings; for in some other Buddha-lands the Buddha-teaching is carried out by mere gazing, or by the contraction of the facial muscles, or by the raising of the eye-brows, by frowning or smiling, by clearing the throat, by the twinkling of an eye, by merely thinking, or by a motion of some kind. Articulate speech is not an absolute necessity for human intercourse. Mere gazing is said to be sufficient in the world of Samantabhadra to make one realise the highest state of enlightenment known as "Anutpattikadharmakshānti."[2] Even in this world, says the sutra, the ordinary business of life is carried on most successfully among the bees or ants that never use words. If so we never need wonder at those Zen masters who merely raise a finger or utter an unintelligible cry in order to demonstrate the profoundest experience ever attainable by human consciousness. When there is nothing in my mind which can readily respond to or which is already awakened to take in what is flashed out from another mind, the latter may use the finest expression possible in our language, and yet my mind may remain perfectly blind to its truth. If, on the other hand, there is a chord of harmony between

[1] P. 105.
[2] This is explained below. See pp. 125 ff. and pp. 226 f.

the two, a touch on either side will create a reverberation in the other. There is no power in a language as such, though we cannot dispense with it by any means.

The *Laṅkāvatāra* here makes a distinction between words (*ruta*) and meaning (*artha*),[1] and advises us not to understand meaning by merely depending upon words, to do which is quite ruinous to the comprehension of reality. A word (*ruta*) is the combination of sound and syllable, subject to our logical or intellectual understanding. (*Vāg-akshara-samyoga-vikalpa.*) It issues from the cavity of the mouth between the teeth, jaws, palate, tongue, and lips, when one is engaged in conversation; inflections, conjugations, and other grammatical and rhetorical modifications are effected according to the errors (*vikalpa*) and innate desires (*vāsanā*)[2] of the speaker. As to meaning (*artha*), it is an inner perception itself gained in self-realisation when one entering upon the path of Nirvana causes a revulsion (*parāvṛitti*)[3] in the deepest recesses of consciousness known as Ālayavijñāna. To gain this inner perception, a man retires into a solitary spot all by himself, and, by applying himself assiduously to abstract meditations and deep reflections, his inner sense (*prajñā*) or self-knowledge (*svabuddhi*) begins to shine out from underneath the residual accumulation (*vāsanā*) of the past thoughts, affections, and deeds since time immemorial. The meaning,

[1] Pp. 154, 193 ff.

[2] *Vikalpa*, literally means "to distinguish," "to determine," or "to discriminate," and is rendered in Chinese by 分別 (*fên-pich*), which is the characteristic function of thinking. *Vāsanā* is a more difficult term implying the whole philosophy or psychology of Mahayana idealism. No English equivalent is found. In this book, "memory," "habit energy," or "impression," is rather loosely used for it. For fuller explanation, however, see below, pp. 128, 178, etc.

[3] According to the T'ang translation, "They [the Hinayanists] do not understand that the great Nirvana is obtained when through an inner perception there takes place a revulsion in the Alaya upon which depends the existence of an external world." Vasubandhu's *Triṁśikāvijñaptikārikā* XXIX, also makes reference to this revulsion. The *Laṅkāvatāra,* pp. 62, 108, 238, etc. More about this revulsion later.

artha, thus realised in one's inmost consciousness is something no combination of the physical organs is capable of expressing in any way adequate to the experience. But as when searching for an object in the dark one has to rely on a lantern,[1] meaning is after all to be gathered by means of words, at least it is to be thus oriented. The understanding of the relation thus existing between *ruta* (words) and *artha* (meaning) will be necessary when we wish to know the nature of the inner perception (*svapratyātmajñāna*).

This relation between words and meaning, or between syllables (*akshara*) and reality (*tattvam* or *tathātvam*),[2] or between teaching (*deśanā*) and truth (*siddhānta*),[3] is like that between the finger and the moon.[4] The finger is needed to point out the moon but it ought not to be taken for the latter. The same disastrous result follows from regarding *akshara,* or *ruta,* or *deśanā* as the reality itself. Those who are not able to take their eyes away from the finger-tip will never realise the ultimate truth (*paramārtha*) of things.[5] It is again like feeding the baby with uncooked food,[6] it will be too late to resuscitate it when it has succumbed to the mother's unwise treatment. Those trained in the Buddhist doctrine ought to be quite discriminating in this respect. Naturally, we would not know what the teaching of the Buddha was if we had had no communication in words, words were very much needed, but when there is no correspondence between words and meaning the teaching itself will lose its sense. The *Laṅkāvatāra* thus reiterates throughout the text that the Tathagata never teaches the Dharma fallen into mere talk (*aksharapatita*), and it was

[1] "By means of the lamp of word and discrimination, the Bodhisattva-Mahāsattvas go beyond word and discrimination and enter upon the path of self-realisation." P. 155.

[2] Pp. 48, 196, etc.

[3] Pp. 148, 172.

[4] Pp. 196, 223.

[5] "The ignorant clinging desperately to the finger-tip of words are unable even unto their death to reach the ultimate truth." P. 196.

[6] P. 196.

for this reason that it was preached by the Buddha and other teachers of the Dharma that "the Tathagata had not uttered a word in answer or in discourse" during his lifetime between his Enlightenment and the Nirvana.[1] The idea is, "Do not cling to words!" (*Na deśanā-ruta-pāṭhā 'bhiniveśatam.*)[2] For "*dharmo naira ca deśito bhagavatā pratyātmavedyo yataḥ.*"[3]

Words are to be treated like the lunar reflection in water as far as they are related in meaning. The reflection is there, though the moon itself has not entered (*apravishṭam*) into the water; nor is it to be considered as standing in no relation (*nirgatam*) to the water, because the latter has something in it to reflect the moon.[4] Only let us not fall into the habit of superficially taking mere words for real meaning. This is the warning of the *Laṅkāvatāra*: *Yathārutārthābhiniveśasaṁdhau na prapatata.*[5]

Disastrous Complications Arising from Discrimination

The habit of regarding words as completely and adequately expressing all that can be found there comes from another habit of ours, which is, in the terminology of the *Laṅkāvatāra*, our wrong discrimination or interpretation (*vikalpa*) of the aspect of existence which may be designated as individuation (*prabhedanaya-lakshaṇa*,[6] or *vishaya-paric-*

[1] Pp. 144, 194, 240. The same idea is expressed in the *Tathāgata-guhya-sūtra*, which is quoted in Candrakīrti's Commentary on the *Madhyamika*, B.T. Society edition, p. 201.

[2] P. 193.

[3] *Sūtrālaṁkāra*, XII, 2, p. 77. "The truth has indeed never been preached by the Buddha, seeing that one has to realise it within oneself."

[4] *Jalacandra* or *udakacandra*; pp. 42, 72, 158, 193, 225, 227, etc. This is also used to show the Tathagata's ability to manifest himself as he is conceived variously by his devotees, and again to symbolise the nature of existence as mere appearance.

[5] P. 160, "Do not fall into the secret error of getting attached to the meaning as expressed in words."

[6] P. 127.

cheda-lakshaṇa[1]). When this aspect is well understood so that we shall no more be misled by wrong interpretation, we are able to get into a state of self-realisation. Individuation means to separate one object from another, and taking these separated, particular objects for final substances (*svabhāva,* or *dharmātmyalakshaṇa*), to cling to this notion and thereby to keep up the evil desires and passions burning all the time. According to the sutra, this wrong interpretation takes place in regard to several categories of thought and being such as (1) speech, (2) describable objects of thought, (3) appearances, (4) material wealth, (5) substance, (6) causal relations, (7) definite philosophical views, (8) reasonings as to the existence of an ego, (9) coming into existence, (10) not coming into existence, (11) dependence, and (12) bondage and release.[2] Logically considered, this kind of classification is baffling; but when we survey the Indian background which stimulated the Buddhist philosopher to speculate on such conglomerate subjects, we can readily enter into its spirit. For Buddhists, in fact for all Indian philosophers, there are no abstract problems of philosophy to be solved from a purely intellectual point of view. They are always tinged with religious sentiment, they have always some bearings on the most important practical question of life, which is how to get spiritual freedom. All the thinking carried on in this sutra, therefore, has always this question in view, and naturally those statements above referred to are to be explained according to the general trend of Buddhist thought.

The wrong consideration about speech (1) creates an attachment to musical or literary productions which are not always spiritually enhancing, and these are to be avoided. Objects of thought are describable and therefore are determinable (2), but the content of the inner perception forming the central theme of the *Laṅkāvatāra* is not subject to this

[1] P. 44.
[2] P. 128 et seq.

limitation, and if one gets a wrong idea here, there will be no salvation for him, as he takes a thing indescribable and inexpressible for a thing to be seen, to be touched, and to be possessed. Things describable have no permanency and consequently no spiritual value, but we are liable to judge them wrongly and get firmly attached to them. (3) We are in this respect like those who fancy watery appearances in the desert to be a real sheet of water. This faulty judgment may extend indefinitely over all appearances, and that the result will be ruinous goes without saying. Hence this warning. Attachment to material wealth or property (*artha*) is another case of false judgment as to appearance (4).

Substance (*svabhāva*) means in the *Laṅkāvatāra* a concrete individual object, a residue after the last analysis; and the adherents of the substance-theory maintain that there are really such things outside the mind (5). Owing to this misjudgment, the way to self-realisation is blocked. Errors of causal relation refer to the ideas of "to be" (*sat*) and "not to be" (*asat*), which are considered real inasmuch as they make it possible to establish causal relationship between things about us (6). But this idea of causality ought not to lead us to a first cause or a primary being from which all things derive their reality. As we know, Buddhist philosophy denies the existence of a first cause as such. The ideas of *sat* and *asat* are only relative and have no substantial existence besides being so named.

We next come to such philosophical views as were entertained by different schools of thought at the time of the *Laṅkāvatāra* (9); according to which such categories as "to be" (*asti*) and "not to be" (*nāsti*), as oneness (*ekatva*) and otherness (*anyatva*), or as bothness (*ubhaya*) and not-bothness (*anubhaya*), are actualities and for that reason to be adhered to. This is, however, wrong and is sure to lead one away from the inner realisation of the truth. (8) Reasoning (*yukti*) is concerned with the notion of the ego; when this is thought to be a reality our spiritual development stops short. The *Laṅkāvatāra,* loyal to the traditional view of Buddhist philosophy, refuses to countenance the theory of ego-substance, which may be regarded as a corollary to the general substance-theory. (9) The notion of "coming into existence" (*utpāda*) is related to that of causality. When certain causes and conditions are matured, people think something comes into actual existence and continues to exist until the causes and conditions cease to operate; for coming into existence and vanishing from it are both real facts as much as is the general law of causation. (10) The "no-birth" (*anutpāda*) view of things, on the contrary, argues that nothing has ever been brought into existence through causal relations, but that things are what they are prior to the operation of the law of causation. And this is one of the characteristic views of the *Laṅkāvatāra,* and a special treatment of the subject appears below.[1]

Dependence (*saṁbandha*) and bondage (*bandha*) are similar ideas. The relation between metal and wire is dependence, while a man tied with a cord is in bondage, from which he can later be released when the cord is broken. All such relations when conceived as real and permanent become dangerous to the spiritual growth of a true Buddhist, that is, of a Bodhisattva (11 & 12).

Words (*ruta*) and meaning (*artha*), therefore, are to be separated, as the former generally fail to give us an exact idea of the object described with them. They are of course indicative, suggesting where to look for the meaning. Numerous indeed are close attachments (*abhiniveśasaṁdhi*) a man makes to things and relations on account of a wrong understanding of their true nature and value, and, owing to these mistaken attachments, he wraps himself like a silk-worm in a cocoon, binding tight not only himself but others.[2]

[1] Pp. 183 ff, of these *Studies.*

[2] Pp. 161–163. "Since the ignorant, seizing upon words [as corresponding to] the knowledge of reality, do not comprehend its secret signification; they wrap themselves up like the silkworm with their own false discrimination (47)."

Imagining things where they are not, or not perceiving them where they are, men are addicted to evil desires and passions. Let them learn to look into reality, *yathābhūtam,* for to do this is to break through the net of wrong judgment and false imagination and to attain the inward perception which is emancipation.

The Meaning of Yathābhūtam and Māyā

To understand the world and selfhood as they really are —this is seeing *yathābhūtam,* one of the great trumpet-calls ringing through both Mahayana and Hinayana literature. But to know exactly what "*yathābhūtam*" means is the problem, for it does not allow of any definite description. The problem is to be settled only by appealing to experience, i.e., to direct perception when the truth has been grasped as such. In this respect Buddhist terminology is often graphic and full of power; think of such terms as *tathatā* (如如 or 眞如, i.e., suchness or thusness), *tattvam* (如實 or 眞實, thatness), or *satya* (眞諦, being-so), which are used to designate the content of the inner perception (*pratyātmajñāna*). This seeing *yathābhūtam* constitutes the mystical element of all religion; and if one is affectively inclined, "Tat" (that) will have to be taken in faith; but when the intellectual claim predominates, "Tat" will have to be perceived with "a noble eye of wisdom" (*āryaprajñacakshus*) and not by a divine (*divya*) or human (*māṁsa*) eye.[1]

The world seen through a divine or human eye is a world of māyā, but one disclosed to the Prajñā is the real one. Therefore, logically speaking, māyā is not a quality objectively attached to the world, it is not inherent in it, it rather belongs to the subject. As indeed the idealistic Mahayana does not admit the existence of an external world, whatever qualities we ordinarily think as belonging to the latter are creations or constructions of our own mind. But if we allow ourselves to be guided by the discriminating

[1] Pp. 40, 164. P. 13, *buddhyā na māṁsacakshushā.*

imagination (*parikalpa*), the world must be said to have in itself something of the nature of māyā; for its impermanence is patent to us all, it appears and disappears like lightning, having no self-substance in it. To say that this is an evanescent world is to say that it is always becoming, never in a state of being, that is, in constant flux as an ancient philosopher describes it. We must, however, be most careful not to be carried away by the ordinary method of interpreting the world and designate its transiency or constant becoming in Mahayanistic terminology. This is strongly coloured with an idealistic tinge, and to apply it in an objective realistic sense will be quite misleading. When the world is said to be like māyā, it is to be understood subjectively, and not objectively. Such objective terms as transiency or a flux of becoming presuppose realism, and are not, strictly speaking, in harmony with the absolutely idealistic standpoint adopted by Mahayanists.

So with the conception of Śūnyatā (emptiness), we must bear in mind the fact that the term is not to be found in a logician's dictionary, nor in one containing realistic terms only. For it is the word coined by the possessor of the Prajñācakshus (wisdom-eye) when he has reviewed the world as I look at a sheet of paper before me this very moment. By him the world is perceived *yathābhūtam* stripped of all its logical predicates and also its so-called objective trappings; the world thus appearing in its nakedness has been designated empty (*śūnya*), by the Mahayanists. It is in this sense, therefore, that it can be said there is nothing substantial in the world, nothing which has individuality (*ātman*), nothing which can be grasped; and that it slips through the hands, one predicate disappearing after another, so that it cannot be designated, as being (*sat*), nor by its opposite, not-being (*asat*). No term that admits of an antithesis can be applied to the world, as it is beyond the logic of opposites. To mention some such terms of antithesis used frequently in the *Laṅkāvatāra*, they are: (1) *asti* and *nāsti,* or *sat* and *asat,* (2) *śāśvata* and *uccheda,* (3) *svalakshaṇa* and *sāmānyalakshaṇa,* (4) *lakshya* and *lakshaṇa,* (5) *grāhya* and *grāhaka,* (6) *saṁsāra* and *nirvāṇa,* (7) *utpāda* and *nirodha,* (8) *kṛitaka* and *akṛitaka,* (9) *bāhyan* and *adhyātmaka,* (10) *anya* and *ananya,* (11) *anekatā* and *ekatā,* (12) *ubhaya* and *nobhaya,* (13) *nitya* and *anitya,* (14) *buddhi* and *boddhavya,* etc.[1] Before one term definitely fixes its quality, it runs over to the other alternative.

The *Laṅkāvatāra,* therefore, declares that the world as it is does not fall within the four propositions or points (*ćatushkoṭika*),[2] and in the first chapter even one hundred and eight negations are enumerated. The most truthful description of the state of things as we experience in this world of particulars, will be, from the Buddhist way of thinking, to compare it with māyā as created by the magician.[3] Making use of whatever objects a man chooses, he makes a variety of phantom creatures which appear to the spectators as real and substantial. But in this neither the magician nor the objects fancifully created are at fault; the fault lies with the spectators who make erroneous judgments permitting things where they are not. The sutra gives further analogical proofs[4] to impress upon us the truth of the māyā-conception or that of Śūnyatā. That a picture is seen as if it really had three dimensions, that

[1] (1) being and non-being, 有無, (2) eternal and discontinuous, 常斷; (3) individuality and generality, 自性共性; (4) predicable and predicate, 所相能相; (5) seizable and seizing, 所取能取; (6) birth-and-death and nirvana, 生死涅槃; (7) birth and extinction, 生滅; (8) made and not-made, 作非作; (9) external and internal, 內外; (10) other and not-other, 他非他; (11) not-oneness and oneness, 一不一, (12) both and not-both, 俱不俱; (13) eternal and not-eternal, 常無常; (14) knowledge and knowable, 覺所覺.

[2] They are: affirmation, "It is A"; negation, "It is not A"; double affirmation, "It is both A and not-A"; double negation, "It is neither A nor not-A."

[3] Pp. 56, 109, 129–130, 199, etc.

[4] Pp. 90 ff, etc.

a bedimmed eye imagines a hair-net (*keśoṇḍukam*), that a circle traced out by a fire-brand in quick motion is considered real, that a bubble is taken for a crystal ball, and, further, that the reflection of a tree in a lake, an image in the mirror, an echo reverberating through the valley, a mirage in the spring-field, and the wooden man operated by a goblin (*Piśāca*)—that each of these objects is regarded as an actuality, is due to the error of judgment on the part of an unenlightened mind, which, being placed under the permeating memory-influence (*vāsanā*) of past thoughts and desires, is self-incapacitated from looking into the truth of the matter. However, we must not take them for absolute illusions, for they are there and yet they are not there, so that the category of existence fails to be applied here. From the dualistic point of view, we feel inclined to interpret these terms objectively as denoting the idea of mere transiency or unreality, but when the whole trend of Buddhist thought is understood, we know that these similes are meant to describe a state of things, to which such logical conceptions as *sat* and *asat*, etc., are inapplicable, but which must be directly experienced in the inmost consciousness with the understanding of reality as it is.

The *Laṅkāvatāra* says:[1]

"The sky [or space], the hare's horns, and a barren woman's child—
They are not, only talked of; so are things discriminated.
In the totality of causes and conditions, the ignorant imagine birth;
Not knowing this reason, they go astray in the triple world."

This may seem to mean: All things are mere names, their existence is not more than a matter of subjective discrimination; to think that things are really born, stay, and disappear in the system of causes and effects, is an illusion.

[1] P. 105.

All these realities, so called, have no objective validity; and, therefore, the world is altogether empty, void, unreal, and a mass of nothingness. To think this way, however, is not the position of the Mahayanist. What he wants us to do is that we should have a revulsion of the whole system of mentality and get a new point of view where we may survey the world *yathābhūtam*. The sutra, therefore, states a little further down[1] that the difference between the wise and the ignorant is that the former are free from the Viparyāsa (顛倒, *tien-tao*), while the latter are not. *Viparyāsa* literally means, "inversion" or "error"; it means imagining things as they are not, taking error for truth. The wise not hampered by this imagination see that the world is like māyā and has no reality, but at the same time they know that it is there, that it is not pure nothingness. Why? Because they have gone beyond the relativism of being and non-being. The waters of the Ganges are not visible to the Preta, but since other people see them they cannot be said to be non-existent. In a similar way, the wise have a correct view of things for they are free from errors in their perception of an objective world, which exists only in relation to their own mind. An objective world is really an error (*bhrānti*, 妄法, *wang-fa*) in so far as it is discriminated as existing externally and individually. Or we may say that an external, particularised world is an illusion as long as the ignorant are unable to break through the fetters of Vikalpa, wrong discrimination; whereas to the wise the phenomenal world is true in its suchness (*tathatā*). What, therefore, is an error to one is truth to the other, because the latter is entirely free from all forms of discrimination (*sarvakalpanāvirahitam*).[2]

To repeat: the objective world is an error, there is nothing real about it, it is māyā, it is empty (*śūnya*); but this does not mean that it is altogether non-entity and merely

[1] Pp. 106 ff.
[2] P. 108.

a vast expanse of vacuity; the world, even if it is error, is there to the wise as well as to the ignorant, but the wise know that it is of an illusive nature and in this cognition they are neither perverted nor unperverted, they just see it in reality (*yathābhūtam*), they perceive the world as it truly is. And while they do this, the world or what is regarded as such by the ignorant, is eternal (*śāśvata* or *nitya*), and beyond the reach of every possible dualistic category. It is in this sense that the *Laṅkāvatāra* declares: *bhrāntiḥ śāśvatā, bhrāntis tattvam,*[1] "this world of error is eternity itself, truth itself." If the wise, as the sutra states, cherish even an incipient stirring of thoughts rooted in discrimination or particularisation of forms and signs (*nimitta-lakshaṇa-bhedatva*), they are far from the reality and thought of supreme wisdom (*āryajñāna*) and the wise fall into the rank of the ignorant.

It, however, is to be remembered that the existence of this erroneous and confusing world makes it possible for the wise to cause a revulsion (*parāvṛitti*) in their minds and awaken their supreme wisdom from the narcotic effect of evil memory (*vāsanā*) accumulated since time immemorial. This narcotic effect manifested in so many aspects of consciousness as Citta, Manas, Manovijñāna, etc., causes it to differentiate reality as in a dream into subjects and successive appearances and thus accepting them as real and final to cling to them as to the truth. But, realising the illusive nature of these intellectual discriminations, the wise rise above them and seeing them as errors transmute falsehood into truth, phantasm into reality. And on account of this realisation they know that what confront them is neither reality (*vastu*) as imagined by the ignorant nor unreality (*avastu*) as inferred by the unreflecting. The world is such as it is, it is neither existence nor non-existence, no such predicates are applicable to it, and for this reason what is to be termed an error

[1] Pp. 106, 107.

(*bhrānti*) for the ignorant is Tathatā (suchness) for the wise. Though this statement sounds paradoxial or even irrational, the position of the *Laṅkāvatāra* will readily be comprehended when we abandon our dualistic standpoint and see the world *yathābhūtam,* from its aspect of eternity (*nityatā*). So we have:

"The wise do not see the erroneous world (*bhrānti*), nor is there any reality (*tattvam*) in the midst of it. [But] since the erroneous world is reality, there is reality in the midst of it.

"If, by abandoning all that is of the erroneous world, something (*nimittam*) is to rise, this something is an error, like the cataract which has not yet been cleared off the eye."[1]

In short, all such apparent paradoxes are designed to adjust our thoughts *yathābhūtam* to the actuality of existence, with which no ordinary rules of logic are compatible. To say, "It is," is eternalism (*śāśvatavāda*), to say that "It is not" is nihilism (*ucchedavāda*); and the object of Buddhist reasoning is to avoid both of these two antithetic views, though not necessarily attempting to establish idealistic monism, but to lead us to the way of experiencing it in its inwardness as well as in its totality.

"O Lord of Laṅkā," reads the sutra, "he who sees thus sees rightly;[2] if seen otherwise, it is 'carrying on discrimination' (*vikalpa*), because here is discrimination which leads to dualism. It is like seeing one's own face in water, or like seeing one's own shadow in the moonlight or by the lantern, or listening to an echo of one's own voice in the valley, wherein discrimination takes place leading to attachment. In like manner, to separate "Dharma" from "Adharma" (or *a* from not-*a*) is only due to discrimination, and on account of this one finds it impossible to do away with the distinction, thereby creating all forms of falsehood. One is thus unable

[1] P. 109. The lines are repeated in the "Sagāthakam", gg. 127 and 128.

[2] *Sa samyak-paśyati,* p. 20.

to realise tranquillity (*śānti*). By tranquillity is meant oneness of objects, and oneness of objects is the highest Samādhi, from which grows an inner perception by supreme wisdom. The Tathāgata-garbha is its objective."[1]

As we see here, any thought that permits of opposition or antithesis such as *sat* and *asat*, *dharma* and *adharma*, is considered to be the outcome of discrimination (*vikalpa*) ; and as long as this is cherished, one can never realise the standpoint of pure idealism (*cittamātra*) and the *yathābhūtam* understanding of absolute oneness will never take place.

"If this world is an error as is taught by thee, is it to be regarded as existent or as non-existent?" Mahāmati is made to ask the Buddha in the *Laṅkāvatāra*.[2] The natural conclusion as we ordinarily see it will be: "This erroneous world does not exist." But the Buddha says: "It exists as māyā, and no aspects of it are worth while clinging to. If there are any aspects of it worth clinging to, there can be no rejecting the notion of substance (*svabhāva*), and the theory of causation (*pratītyasamutpāda*) will be upheld as is done by the philosophers who assume the existence of a final cause." If this erroneous world is like māyā, does this not lead to the creation of another error? "No, it does not, because māyā is not the cause of the error, because it does not produce faults and fallacies. Māyā, indeed, does not produce faults and fallacies. O Mahāmati, māyā is not the product of discrimination, but evolves from the magic formulas pronounced by another person; it owes not its existence to the power of self-discrimination and fallacious habit-energy; it does not produce faults. Whatever faults there are in connection with this erroneous world come from the clinging of the ignorant to that which is nothing but the delusion of their own minds. The wise, however, are free from all this."

[1] The concluding passage of the first chapter, the *Laṅkāvatāra*, after the T'ang version.

[2] Pp. 108–109.

What is Meant by Being Unborn?

When māyā is understood in the sense as elucidated above, we shall find light shed over the statement that all things are uncreated, or, literally, unborn (*anutpannaḥ sarvabhāvaḥ*). This is one of the phrases quite frequently met with in all Mahayana literature, and those who are not familiar with it will certainly find the phrase devoid of sense, as they may regard it as having no connection with self-realisation. But this again is a part of viewing things *yathābhūtam*. For if existence is not to be annotated by any one of the four propositions (*catushkoṭika*) and is above the alternation of *sat* and *asat*, and not controlled by the law of causation (*hetupratyaya*), it cannot be described in any other way than by calling it unborn (*anutpanna*),—unborn not in the sense of eternity, nor in that of uncreatedness. Things are unborn simply because no categories admitting contradiction or alternation or antithesis are applicable here. Eternity contrasts with non-eternity or impermanence; uncreatedness if it has any relative meaning stands in opposition to creation; and if being unborn is taken in a similar way it limits itself and our perception of things will be no more *yathābhūtam* but affected by Parikalpa. For this reason, the Buddha in the *Laṅkāvatāra* repeatedly warns us not to get confused here, but to understand *anutpādaṁ sarvadharmāṇāṁ* in its absolute, unconditioned sense.

"Why is existence regarded as unborn or unoriginated? Because there is neither creating nor created, and, therefore, there is no causer [i.e., creator]."[1] Again,[2] things are unborn because they are to be regarded as māyā, and because the Buddha desires that the philosophers should look beyond logic and its necessary limitations. As long as the antithesis of *sat* and *asat* is considered objectively real, as held by some philosophers, there will be the real coming into existence and the real passing away from it. Those

[1] P. 115. [2] P. 111.

who are taken to the passing-away aspect of existence are nihilists, while those who look for the eternal aspect are eternalists; and neither of them has the right view of it. They are attached to one thing or another, they are far from attaining the point where all things are perceived in their true bearings, that is, as manifestations of Mind itself (*cittamātradṛiśya*). The *Laṅkāvatāra* calls this viewpoint "seeing into the abode where things are in their suchness" (*yathābhūtāvasthāna-darśana*, 如實處見)."[1] The gāthā reads:

"Because there is no causing, there is no birth;
Where existence is admitted, there is the holding of birth and death.
When it is seen as being like māyā, etc.,
No discrimination takes place as regards appearances."[2]

This Buddhist idea of being unborn is liable to be confused with eternalism as is suggested by Mahāmati.[3] But when we know that Anutpāda, "to be unborn" is not an idea contrasted to Utpāda, "to be born," or an idea subject to the principle of causation, but an idea absolutely going

[1] Pp. 112, 184, and 200 (line 6): *yathābhūtārthasthāna-darśana*, seeing into the abode of reality in its truthful signification. Again p. 124, line 1, *yathābhūta-svalakshaṇāvasthānāvasthitam* (住如實處, or 如實自相處). It is the point where things are perceived in their proper bearing.

[2] P. 112.

[3] Pp. 111, 116, etc. Eternalism may not be an appropriate term for that school of philosophy which holds that all things have been what they are and remain for ever as such. This is the Śāśvata (eternal or persistent) view of existence and stands opposed to the other view known as the Uccheda (destruction or extirpation). According to the latter, there is nothing in the world that is real, eternally abiding, and that will retain its identity for ever. The doctrine of Śūnyatā is sometimes taken for this. Buddhism goes the middle way between the two extremes; for, according to it, existence is neither temporal and forever vanishing, nor eternal and forever abiding. Objectively stated, it is in a state of constant becoming, which in terms of Mahayana philosophy is called like māyā, or it is *śūnya* (empty, another difficult word to translate properly), it is unborn, it is not dualistic, it has no self-substance. This is the Buddhist teaching known as "*Śūnyatā, anutpāda, advaya, niḥsvabhāva-lakshaṇaṁ sarvadharmāṇām.*" P. 73.

beyond opposites, we come nearer to the truth. We need an inner perception to see into the true nature of existence; otherwise, like the ignorant and confused, we see things where there is really nothing, and imagine them to be actualities though they are like the hare's horns[1] or the tortoise's hair. Vikalpa takes place here, and all looks distorted. So we read in the sutra:

"According to my doctrine, there is neither being nor non-being, for existence (*sarvabhāva*) is not to be characterised as being born, nor as disappearing. Why is there no non-being? For it is like seeing various objects created by the magician or in a dream. [As long as there are things actually seen, they cannot be said to be non-existent.] Why is there no being? For the self-nature of all things that appear to be here, is really non-existent, they are seen and yet not seen, they are taken hold of and yet not taken hold of. Therefore, I say that things are neither existent nor non-existent. If a man, realising that there is nothing but what is seen of mind, abides in the suchness of things where no individuation (or discrimination, *vikalpa*) takes place, he will see that all doings in the world cease. To discriminate is the business of the ignorant and not of the wise. O Mahāmati, it is due to the mind that discriminates that there appears a world destitute of reality, such as the palace of the Gandharvas or the phantom creations of the magician. To distinguish between the born and the not-born, between the created and the un-created, is like talking about the works of the magician, that have never been in existence and therefore that will never disappear. The ignorant fail to see the self-nature of existence (*bhāvasvabhāva*) because their views are perverted. When they are thus perverted, they are unable to realise a state of aloofness, and as they are unable to do so, they cannot disengage themselves from false discrimination. As long as one sees things particularised in forms, there is a perception of the born and the

[1] P. 62.

unborn, and as a result discrimination goes on. Nirvana is where there is no birth, no extinction; it is seeing into a state of suchness (or thatness) absolutely transcending all categories constructed by mind; for it is the Tathagata's own inner consciousness.''[1]

In connection with the Anutpāda (not-being-born) idea, it may not be out of place to say a few words about the Mahayana conception of what is known as "Anutpattika-dharmakshānti." One meets with this phrase quite frequently in Mahayana sutras, though not so much in the *Laṅkāvatāra*. Literally rendered, it means "not-born-object-patience" and 無生法忍 (*wu-shêng-fa-jên*) in Chinese. This evidently baffled some of the European translators of Mahayana texts.[2] But we shall be able to understand it much better now than they as we have already explained what the Mahayanists mean by all things not being born (*sarvadharmāṇām anutpādaḥ*). The idea is simply that reality or Dharma or existence in general is beyond all predicable attributes, and therefore in the failure of language and intellect, definition is impossible, and being outside the ken of all but direct perception, all we can state of it is emptiness or unborn-ness in the absolute sense. *Anutpattikadharma* is a statement concerning existence from the Mahayana point of view. In this connection *dharma* does not mean "la loi," nor a "consequence," nor an "idea."

But the last term of the compound, *kshānti*, may be

[1] Abridged, pp. 198–200. For a fuller translation see pp. 265 ff.

[2] M. E. Burnouf has in his French translation of the *Saddharma-puṇḍarīka* (p. 85), "Une patience miraculeuse dans la loi"; Max Müller in his *Sukhāvatīvyūha* (S.B.E. XLIX, pp. 39–40, and p. 51), "Resignation to consequences which have not yet arisen"; Cecil Bendall and W. H. D. Rouse in their English translation of Śāntideva's *Śikshasamuccaya* (p. 297), "Resignation to the idea of not being re-born"; and H. Kern in his English *Saddharma-puṇḍarīka* (S.B.E. XXI, p. 134), "Acquiescence in the eternal law." These show how these great Sanskrit scholars struggled to get at the exact meaning of *anutpattikadharmakshānti*. Also see Sylvain Lévi's *Sūtrālaṃkāra*, French translation, p. 123.

somewhat puzzling. What has patience to do with this existence that is to be designated as unborn? *Kshānti*, of course, means "patience" here as when it is one of the six Pāramitās, or resignation, or acquiescence, but not in its ordinary sense. For *kshānti* here does not mean "to endure," or "to suffer patiently"; endurance or suffering implies unwillingness and resistance to a certain extent. The sense of Buddhist *kshānti*, however, is a willing compliance or acceptance. When the *anutpanna* view of existence is truthfully recognised and accepted, it becomes the principle of one's conduct, determining the whole attitude of mind. The Chinese scholars generally take 忍 (patience) for 認 (recognition) as they are both pronounced *jên*; but, strictly speaking, the term is not an intellectual one, it belongs to the will, it is a whole-hearted acceptance of the ultimate fact (*tattvam*) as perceived by a mind free from errors or wrong judgments (*vikalpa*).

In the *Avataṁsaka-sūtra*, a chapter[1] is devoted to an explanation of ten kinds of Kshānti.[2] (1) Kshānti in sounds means to listen to the oral teaching of the Buddha, to accept it without fear or hesitation and to abide in it whole-heartedly. (2) Kshānti of obedience is to reflect upon the nature of things, and, truthfully penetrating into it, to keep the mind pure and serene. (3) Kshānti in the unborn

[1] Śikshānanda, Chapter XXIX "On Kshānti."

[2] Cf. *Sukhāvatīvyūha*, S.B.E. XLIX, p. 51 § 32, where three kinds of Kshānti are mentioned: (1) Ghoshānugā-kshānti, (2) anulomikī-kshānti, (3) Anutpattika-dharma-kshānti. They evidently correspond to the first three of the ten Kshāntis here explained from the *Avataṁsaka-sūtra*. In a Śāstra called *On the Awakening of Bodhicitta* (發菩提心論, 縮刷大藏經, 來一), ascribed to Vasubandhu, there is a chapter devoted to the explanation of "Śūnyatā (emptiness) as having no distinguishing marks," in which the author also gives three kinds of Kshānti: (1) Kshānti of faith, (2) Kshānti of obedience and (3) Dharma-kshānti. The first is to believe (信, *hsin*) in the various teachings of the Buddha, such as the Fourfold Noble Truth, the Twelvefold Chain of Origination, the Four Virtues of Infinite Greatness, (goodwill, compassion, joy, and equanimity), and the Six Virtues of Perfection which lead one finally to liberation in one form

nature of existence has already been explained. The rest of the ten are realised when one attains to the knowledge of things as like māyā (4), mirage (5), dream (6), echo (7), shadow (8), phenomenal (9), and empty (10)). That this way of looking at existence is generally Mahayanistic and that it is not the same as regarding existence as altogether unsubstantial from the relative point of view, has been already made clear, as I hope, in the preceding section.[1]

How is Nirvana Explained?

Nirvana has been the central object of the Buddhist life ever since the Buddha's own time, though in the Mahayana we do not come across the term so much as in the Hinayana. The idea has been replaced to a certain extent by such conceptions as Prajñā, Saṁbodhi, Dharmakāya, Tathatā, Pratyātmajñāna, etc., as Buddhist thought drifted towards intellectual intuitionalism. The *Laṅkāvatāra*, however, has not forgotten to make reference to Nirvana and to interpret it in its own characteristic manner. According to its author, whoever he may be, Nirvana is realised when one can see into the abode of suchness (*yathābhūtārthasthānadarśanam*).[2] Here is the point the intellect as such (*vikalpa*) cannot enter; for it dissects and establishes somewhat to take hold of (*grahaṇa*), and it will then see that something coming into existence (*utpāda*) and disappearing (*nirodha* or *apravṛitti*). But Nirvana has no tangible form (*nimitta*)

or another. The (2) Kshānti of obedience (順, *shun*), is to see into the truth that there is no self-substance in any individualised object, animate or otherwise, and, therefore, that there is neither actor nor sufferer, and things are eternally such as they are. When a man comes to accept this truth though he may not yet have fully realised its meaning, he has the obedience. (3) The Dharmakshānti (法忍, *fa-jên*) which is apparently an abbreviation for Anutpattikadharmakshānti is attained when he fully realises the truth and knows that all is empty including emptiness itself.

[1] For further definition of "Anutpattikadharmakshānti" see below, pp. 226–227.

[2] P. 200; see also supra.

and it neither comes into existence nor ceases from working. To attain Nirvana, therefore, is to see into the truth of things *yathābhūtam,* that is, as unborn, as not affected by categories of intellectual construction.

To attain Nirvana which is a state of emptiness (*śūnyatā*) inherent in the nature of things and which again is a state of self-realisation obtained by means of supreme wisdom (*āryajñāna*), there must be a revulsion (*parāvṛitti*) at the deepest seat of consciousness known as the Ālayavijñāna.[1] The latter is a kind of mental receptacle where all the memory of one's past deeds and psychic activities is deposited and preserved in a form of energy called Vāsanā (習氣 *hsi-chi,* in Chinese, habit-energy). But as this energy is so contaminated with ignorance and wrong judgments and all sorts of attachment (*abhiniveśa*), it reacts upon an external world in a way detrimental to the realisation of Nirvana, and, therefore, to the perception of the truth *yathābhūtam.* The old conditions must now be overhauled in order to create a new situation in our consciousness. To do this, we must free ourselves from views nihilistic (*uccheda*) and eternalistic (*śāśvata*) and also from the notions of being (*bhava*) and non-being (*abhava*).

When this revulsion is effected, Nirvana is found to be devoid of all predicates. In it nothing is gained, nothing is cast aside, no extermination, no eternity, no unity, no diversity, one finds here. Nirvana is the mind of all holy ones and the goal of Buddhist discipline.[2]

The Hinayanists do not know this; when they realise that Nirvana is something above particular conditions and tranquil in nature, they feel that they have it in its completeness in their Nirvana, so called. But in fact they distinguish it from birth-and-death (*saṁsāra*), and seek it for fear of being caught up in the net of transmigration. They cherish dualism, and so long as they do so, there is no true

[1] Pp. 62, 98, etc.

[2] P. 99.

Nirvana for them. Nirvana, according to the *Laṅkāvatāra*, is not to be found in contradistinction to birth-and-death or Saṁsāra; for thus to distinguish one from the other is the result of a wrong judgment (*vikalpa*), which imagines a future when the world of the senses is altogether annihilated, which is their Nirvana. The Mahayanistic Nirvana goes, however, beyond the dualism of Nirvana and Saṁsāra. It is to be found where there is the identity of Nirvana and Saṁsāra.

So long as dualism is adhered to, there is no Nirvana, no self-realisation. Light and shadow, long and short, black and white—they are mutually related; when they stand alone each by itself, they have no meaning. So with Nirvana. When it is sought after in relation to Saṁsāra, we have a sort of Nirvana. But this kind vanishes when separated from the condition of mutuality in which it exists. True Nirvana is that which is realised in the oneness of Nirvana and Saṁsāra, absolute or *śūnya* in its nature, and above the relativity of eternalism and nihilism. Mahayana followers strive to realise this kind of Nirvana.[1]

The following passages[2] from the *Laṅkāvatāra* will give us some ideas of Nirvana prevalent at the time when this sutra was compiled:

"The Buddha said, O Mahāmati, what is regarded as Nirvana by the philosophers is not in accordance with the true features of Nirvana. Listen, O Mahāmati, I will tell you what it is.

"Some philosophers, seeing how impermanent things are, do not cling to the individual conditions; to them no external world exists, nor does the subjective mind exist; they do not think of the past, present, and future. Like the light that shines no more, like the seed that has no life, like the fire that no more burns, all attachments are gone with them, no individualising reflections take place, and this they

[1] Pp. 76, 126.
[2] Pp. 182 ff. The translator has here mainly followed T'ang.

consider to be Nirvana. But inasmuch as they see something destroyed, their Nirvana is not a true one, O Mahāmati.

"Again, there are some who think that departing to another realm is Nirvana; there is no external world of particulars for them; it is like wind ceasing to blow.[1]

"Again, some think that not to see the distinction between the knowing subject and the known object is Nirvana.

"Again there are some who, holding to the view that all individual appearances are real, cherish the feeling of pain; for they are ignorant of the truth that all is the manifestation of mind-only. And just because of this ignorance they are frightened with appearances and seek for a state where there are no-appearances. An intense longing for this is regarded by them to be Nirvana.

"Again, there are some who, reviewing things inner as well as external in their individual and universal aspects and as existing in time, think that here is self-substance, not subject to destruction; and in this they find Nirvana.

"Again, there are some who believe in the indestructibility of all things such as ego, being, life, growth, and personality, and think this to be Nirvana.

"Again, some philosophers, not being intelligent enough, imagine the reality of Prakṛiti and Purusha and think that the Guṇas in various transformations constitute all objects; and in this they see Nirvana.

"Again, some philosophers see Nirvana in the extinction of both merit and demerit, others in the extinction of evil passions by means of knowledge, and still others hold that Iśvara is in truth the creator.

"Again, there are some who think beings come into existence mutually conditioning and not through any other cause. As they are without wisdom, they are unable to understand rightly, and because of their not understanding rightly, they imagine Nirvana in their own way.

[1] This last sentence does not properly belong here. There must have been some transposition in the text.

"Again, there are some who, wrongly imagining what they have seen to be the true path, find Nirvana here.

"Again, some philosophers, holding to the view that quality and substance are one and yet two, and mutually related and yet not-related, think Nirvana to be in this relationship.

"Again, there are some naturalists who believe in spontaneous creation, saying of the peacock's variegated beauty, the thorn's pointedness, and the production of the various kinds of precious stones from the mine,—who is the maker of all these things? Nobody but Nature. And this is their Nirvana.

"Again, some find Nirvana in the understanding of the twenty-five principles (*tattva*).

"Again, some cherish the opinion that the looking after the welfare of the subjects by the observance of the six virtues (*guṇa*) is Nirvana.

"Again, some think time is Nirvana, from which issues the world.

"Again, there are some who see Nirvana in that the world (*bhava*) exists, or that the world (*bhava*) exists not, or that the world exists and exists not, or that the world and Nirvana are not two different things.

"Again, there are some[1] who, differing from all these philosophers, and in possession of all-knowledge (*sarvajñā*), proclaim like a roaring lion that to understand thoroughly what is meant by the manifestation of Mind itself (*citta-*

[1] This is evidently the Mahayanist view of Nirvana, though it is treated as if it were one held by the philosophers also not belonging to Buddhism. In fact, the Sung version has this entire paragraph moved towards the end of the whole section on Nirvana, and begins with, "According to my view, Nirvana is ....," showing that this is the Buddhist conception of Nirvana. The conclusion of the paragraph is: "O Mahāmati, you and other Bodhisattva-Mahāsattvas should discipline themselves in this so that they could quickly get away from all these other views of Nirvana as upheld by the philosophers." This transposition clears off the difficulty at once. The Wei version is like the T'ang and the Sanskrit.

mātra), not to get attached to the external world (*bāhya-bhāva*), to be disengaged from the four propositions, to abide in the *yathābhūtam* view of things,[1] not to fall into the errors of dualism, to be free from the ideas of subject and object, to stand above all forms of knowledge, not to get attached to any one form of truth, to abide in the realisation of the truth revealed to one's inmost consciousness (*svapratyātmāryadharmādhigama*), to perceive the twofold truth of egolessness, to be devoid of the two kinds of evil passions (*kleśadvaya*), to be cleansed of the two kinds of hindrance (*āvaraṇadvaya*), to discipline oneself in all the stages [of Bodhisattvahood] one after another, whereby, entering upon the state of Buddhahood, to realise all the great Samādhis such as Māyā, and forever to go beyond the Citta, Manas, and Manovijñāna:—this is indeed to attain Nirvana.

"O Mahāmati, all these philosophers' views [except the last mentioned] are based on the imagination (*tarka*) and are not in accordance with the truth (*yukti*); they are forsaken by the wise, for they are dualistic and Nirvana is imagined where it is not. There is really no Nirvana where one may enter or come out. The philosophers each adhering to his own thesis, fall into erroneous views contrary to reason, thereby achieving nothing but the wanderings and tribulations of the mind and will. O Mahāmati, therefore, you and other Bodhisattvas should avoid them."

To quote the gāthās attached here:

"Nirvana is variously viewed and discriminated by the philosophers, but they are no more than imaginations, there is no way in them that leads up to emancipation (*moksha*) (69).

"The philosophers who are not released from [the dualism of] fettered and fettering and who are far apart from the right way of thinking (*upāya*), imagine emancipation where there is no [real] emancipation (70).

[1] See also above, p. 123.

"All sorts of doctrines are maintained by various philosophers, but as they issue from the wrong discriminations of confused minds their emancipation is not a true one (71).

"As all the philosophers are fascinated with the ideas of something done and something doing, they are upholders of doctrines of being and non-being, and their emancipation is no true one (72).

"Those ignorant ones who delight in debating and idle talk cannot have a wider view of truth; mere talking is the source of sorrow in the triple world. It is the truth only that destroys sorrow (73).

"It is like an image reflected in a mirror, it is seen there but it is not real; the one Mind is seen as a duality by the ignorant when it is reflected in the mirror constructed by their habit-energy (*vāsanā*) (74).

"From not knowing that all that is seen is of mind-only, there takes place discrimination and hence duality; but when it is known that it is nothing but Mind, no discrimination evolves (75).

"It is true that mind reveals itself as multitudinousness, but in itself it is devoid of predicates (*lakshyalakshaṇa*); appearances are there but not to be seen in the way discriminated by the ignorant (76).

"The triple world is no more than [the product of] discrimination, there is no external world of objects; it is owing to discrimination that the multidinousness of things appears, which, however, is not understood by the ignorant (77).

"In various sutras discrimination is the subject of discourse, it is on account of ideas and names, for apart from naming (*abhidhāna*) no meaning (*abhidheya*) is attainable (78)."[1]

The Essence of Buddhahood.

The self-realisation that is to be attained by the Bodhisattva is none other than the Buddha's own inner con-

[1] Pp. 185–187.

sciousness, self-illuminating as well as world-illuminating. Therefore, when we know what is the nature of this enlightenment attained by the Buddha (*svabuddhabuddhatā*), we shall also have some glimpse of the content of the Pratyātmāryajñānagocara, the subject-matter of the *Laṅkāvatāra*. According to the sutra,[1] what constitutes the essence of the Buddhahood (*buddhatā*) is neither a thing made nor a thing not-made, it is neither cause nor effect, it is neither predicable nor unpredicable, it is neither describable nor indescribable, neither subject to perception nor beyond perception. Why? Because by applying any one of these terminological explanations (*nirukti*) to this case, we commit a logical offence. If Buddhatā, the essence of Tathagatahood, is something made, it is impermanent; and if it is impermanent, all things made will be Tathagatas—which is impossible. If, on the other hand, it is a thing not made, it will be without a substance (*ātmakatva*), and all efforts to realise it will be to no purpose, as it is like the hare's horns or a barren woman's child. For are they not all not-made, unreal, merely imagined?

"Again, if the essence of Tathagatahood is neither cause nor effect, it is then neither being (*sat*) nor not-being (*asat*). And this being the case it lies outside the four propositions (*catushkoṭika*). The latter belong to the worldly way of talk and what lies outside them is no more than talk, it is like speaking of a barren woman's child. This exists only in talk and does not come under the four propositions. As it does not come under them, the wise know it is beyond their logical survey (*pramāṇa*). The meaning of all the Tathagatas' words is to be thus understood by the wise."[2]

This passage is taken from the Sanskrit text, which coincides with one of the Chinese versions, the T'ang; but when we weigh the meaning of the passage, we grow somewhat confused about it because it is apparent contradiction

[1] Pp. 187 ff.
[2] P. 188.

to the general drift of thought that has been explained above as characteristic of the *Laṅkāvatāra* teaching. For if the essence of Buddhahood is something like the barren woman's child existing only in name and placed beyond the survey of the wise in the sense that it has no truth in it, the object of all Buddhist discipline will be set at naught. If, however, it could be understood in the sense that the truth is beyond the logical survey of even the wise, and, therefore, it is an object of direct intuition, altogether beyond the reach of popular parlance which is made up of the four propositions, the quoted passage would be consistent with the rest of the text. The sentence referring to the barren woman's child as mere talk and beyond the four propositions will have to be altered. In fact, the Wei translation reads quite differently: "The four propositions belong to the worldly way of talk. O Mahāmati, if the truth does not go beyond the four propositions, it is no more than a word like when speaking of a barren woman's child. O Mahāmati, this belongs to mere speech, coming under the four propositions, and if the truth should come under them, the wise would not take it up." Evidently there is some discrepancy in the text. The earliest Chinese version in fact, that is, the Sung reads simply and is quite intelligible, showing perhaps that this is a more original text, not mixed with gloss and other addenda. "O Mahāmati, if it is neither an object (*vastu*?) nor a cause, then it is neither being nor non-being, it lies outside the four propositions. The latter belong to worldly talk. When it [or the essence of Buddhahood] lies outside the four propositions it is beyond them, and being beyond them as such the wise accept it. The meaning of all the Tathagata's propositions is to be understood by the wise thus [that is, as beyond the four propositions]."

When Buddhism speaks of the egolessness (*nirātmana*) of all things (*sarvadharma*), this must be understood in the way suggested above, that is, in the sense that while all things have their characteristic marks (*svalakshana*), they are without self-substance (*ātman*). Inasmuch as the cow is not the horse and the horse is not a cow, they are quite distinct one from the other. Their individuality is to be reckoned with, but as to each possessing any substance in itself or anything that remains eternally so except its appearance (*lakshaṇa*), that cannot be. Therefore, things in one sense are as they are, but in another sense they are not. This is what is meant by Buddhist phenomenalism, but we are not to be carried away by its doctrine of emptiness as was explained before, as Buddhism has after all something to affirm. Its superficially paradoxical way of presenting the truth is often baffling to logicians. The *Laṅkāvatāra* proceeds to say that the ignorant and confused use their own way of discrimination (*vikalpa*) to grasp the theory of non-ego, but as existence is really beyond any system of categories, the Tathagata's wisdom alone is capable of penetrating into reality. It is, therefore, declared by him that he is not distinct from the Skandhas, nor is he identical with them.[1]

The two horns of a cow are distinguished one from the other, for the one is longer or shorter than the other, and in colour they may differ, but they are of one nature as they are both horns. In a similar way, the Tathagata is different from what constitutes matter, and yet he is not different. Again, he is designated as one who is emancipated (*moksha*), but he is not one with emancipation, nor is he different from it. Therefore, the essence of Buddhahood is neither eternal nor transient, neither made nor not-made, neither composite nor un-composite, neither knowledge nor the known, neither predicable nor unpredicable, neither of the Skandhas nor not of them, neither describable nor indescribable. It is beyond all measurement, it is not to be brought under any forms of category. We may talk of it as talk we must, but we can never reach it through words. For it is unborn, and consequently not subject to destruc-

[1] P. 188.

tion. It is like unto the sky beyond logical construction, and no amount of intellectual tricks (*prapañca*) will bring it within one's grasp. The essence (*buddhatā*) transcends measurement (*pramāṇa*) and the senses (*indriya*).[1]

"[The nature of enlightenment] is not limited by measurement and senses, it is neither an effect nor a cause, it is neither enlightening nor enlightened. It is neither predicated nor predicating (79).

"The Skandhas, causation, enlightenment are not visible anywhere to anybody;[2] how can any statement be made concerning that which is not visible anywhere to anybody (80)?

"It is neither something made nor something not made, neither an effect nor a cause, neither Skandhas nor no-Skandhas, nor indeed is it of any other composition (81).

"It is not something that is subject to discrimination and hence perceptible, nor is it for that reason to be understood as non-existent; it is the very nature of things as they are (82).

"Non-being goes along with being, and being goes along with non-being; when non-being is not knowable, being too is not to be discriminated (83).

"Those who cling to words only, not comprehending the egolessness of an ego [so called], are drowned in dualism; they destroy themselves, they destroy the ignorant (84).

"When they see any teaching shorn of all faults, they then see things rightly; they do not vilify the leaders (85)."

The *Laṅkāvatāra* is quite anxious to have us realise that the theory of non-ego does not conflict with that of the Tathagata's Womb (*tathāgata-garbha*), of which mention is made in various connections.[3] When the Tathāgata-garbha is spoken of as a kind of storage where all the seeds (*bīja*) of

[1] P. 189 ff.

[2] Here Sung and T'ang have: The Skandhas and causation in their relation to enlightenment—whether they are one or different, nobody can see. Wei: The causal relations and the five Skandhas, the Buddha sees nothing [here].

[3] See pp. 105–106, 177, etc., and also under "Ālayavijñāna."

the past deeds and psychical activities are preserved, philosophers are apt to take it for an ego-soul. But, says the *Laṅkāvatāra,* the Tathāgata-garbha is empty in its nature yet real, it is Nirvana itself, unborn, without predicates, without affections (*apraṇihita*), and, further, it is attained where no false discrimination (*nirvikalpa*) takes place, where no shadow (*nirābhāsa*) of particularisation falls. There is nothing here for the Buddhas or Bodhisattvas to take hold of as an ego-soul. They have gone beyond the sphere of discriminations and judgments, and it is due to their wisdom and skilful device (*upāda*) that they set up all kinds of names and phrases in order to save their followers from mistaken views of reality. Hence the following:[1]

"O Mahāmati, it is like the potter who, out of a mass of atoms of clay of one kind, produces various kinds of vessels by applying on it his artistic skill and manual labour, knowing how to make use of the stick, water, and string; just so, O Mahāmati, is the Tathagata who points out the egolessness of things (*dharmanairātmya*)—the truth transcending everything characteristic of discrimination—by a variety of skilful means, which is joined with Prajñā, that is, sometimes by the doctrine of Tathāgata-garbha, and sometimes by the doctrine of non-ego, or sometimes like the potter by the aid of words, suggestions, and synonyms. For this reason, O Mahāmati, the doctrine of Tathāgata-garbha is not the same as the doctrine of ego as advocated by the philosophers. Thus indeed the doctrine of Tathāgata-garbha is taught by the Tathagatas in order to induce the philosophers advocating the ego-theory [which latter in a superficial way may be regarded as resembling the Buddhist conception of Tathāgata-garbha] and further indeed in order that those who have fallen into the view of discriminating an unreal ego [as real] may become possessed of the realm of the triple emancipation and speedily realise the highest supreme enlightenment. For this reason the Tathagatas who are Arhats

1. Pp. 78, 79.

and Fully-enlightened Ones talk of the doctrine of Tathāgata-garbha which is thus to be differentiated from the ego-theory of the philosophers. Therefore, O Mahāmati, in order to keep thyself away from the ego-theory of the philosophers thou shouldst seek the doctrine of the Tathāgata-garbha that is based on non-ego.

"Pudgala (soul, 人 or 士夫), Saṁtati (continuity, 相續), Skandha (aggregate 陰 or 蘊), Pratyaya (causation, 緣), Aṇu (atom, 微塵), Pradhāna (supreme soul, 勝), Iśvara (god, 自主), Kartṛi (creator, 作者):—some such ideas are entertained by the philosophers, but they are mere constructions of mind."[1]

The World-Transcending Knowledge

The inner consciousness of the Buddha, which constitutes the essence of Buddhahood (*svabuddhabuddhatā*), is the highest form of knowledge (*jñāna*). Of knowledge the *Laṅkāvatāra* distinguishes three forms: (1) worldly knowledge (*jñānaṁ laukikam*), (2) supra-worldly knowledge (*lokottaram*), and (3) supreme supra-worldly knowledge (*lokottaratamam*). The first is relative as cherished by ordinary minds whose thinking is determined by ideas of being and non-being; the second is one possessed by Hinayanists who cannot go beyond the categories of particularity (*svalakshaṇa*) and generality (*sāmānyalakshaṇa*); while the the third and highest is the knowledge attained by the Buddhas and Bodhisattvas who view the world from an absolute standpoint, for they know that the world is beyond all characteristics, that is, has never been brought into existence and will never be annihilated, that it is designable neither as being nor as non-being. It is by means of this highest knowledge that the Bodhisattva finally comes to the realisation of the egolessness (*nairātmya*) of all things, thus entering upon the path of Tathagatahood.[2] This

[1] Pp. 78, 79.

[2] P. 156 ff.

supreme supra-worldly knowledge is none other than the supreme wisdom (*āryajñāna*) of the Bodhidsattva, which enables him to enter into the inmost nature (*svapratyātma*) of all the Buddhas, and which constitutes the central theme of the *Laṅkāvatāra-sūtra*. Its three aspects are now distinguished.[1] The first is its not being mere appearance (*nirābhāsa*), that it is reality, as distinguished from the way it is regarded generally by the Hinayanists and philosophers. The second is that it is awakened by the will (*praṇidhāna*) and power (*adhishṭhāna*) of all the Buddhas. That is to say, supreme wisdom is aroused in the mind of the Bodhisattva by virtue of the Buddhas' earnest desire for universal enlightenment and salvation; their earnest desire or will sends out strong waves of vibration throughout the universe, and all sentient beings there feel its effect according to their capacities. Thirdly, sustained by this and going beyond the relative knowledge of the Hinayanists, the Bodhisattva's mind is freed from all predicable forms and is ready for realising in himself a psychic state termed Māyopamasamādhikāya (如幻三昧身). This means the body attained by a Bodhisattva when he enters into the Samādhi known as Māyā-like, that is, the Samādhi that enables one to look intuitively into the nature of existence and realise that it has no self-substance and is like māyā. The following passage[2] will shed light on the Māyā-like Samādhi: "The Tathagata, for the sake of the Bodhisattvas whose minds are still distracted by individuality and generality, preaches the path of particularisation based on their relative knowledge of existence. When the nature of relative knowledge and particularisation is fully comprehended, they are able to realise the egolessness of an individual person and an external object, and gain an insight into the stages of Bodhisattvahood; they will pass beyond the Dhyānas, Samādhis, and Samāpattis belonging to

[1] P. 49.
[2] Pp. 50–51.

the Śrāvaka, Pratyekabuddha, and philosopher, and walk on the path and enter into the realm of Tathagatahood, which is outside the ken of the ordinary understanding; they will abandon the path belonging to the five Dharmas (五法) and embellish themselves with the highest wisdom (*prajñā*) which comes from the Dharmakāya of all the Tathagatas, and entering into the realm of māyā will visit all the Buddha-lands, abide in the palace of Tushita and reach the highest place where they will obtain the Tathagata-body." Māyā, Śūnyatā, Anutpatti, Apraṇihita, Nirābhāsa,— they are all synonymously used in the *Laṅkāvatāra*. The Bodhisattva is now fairly on the way to the final stage of Buddhist discipline.

In Buddhism no distinction is made between knowledge and knower. Supreme wisdom (*āryajñāna*) is at once the inner perception and the mental power that brings about this perception. This is quite in accordance with the general mode of thinking in Buddhism; for if there is something at the back of the knowledge, or if this is the function of a certain higher faculty of the mind, there will be a dualism which is so strongly combatted by the Mahayanists. Knowledge after all must be absolute; so Prajñā, which is the same thing as Āryajñāna is described as one of the six Pāramitās (virtues of perfection) in the following manner:[1] As the Hinayanists cling to the idea of Nirvana for their own spiritual enjoyment (*ātmasukha*), they are unable to think of the welfare of their fellow-beings. With the Mahayanists it is different, they are ever bent on practising the six Pāramitās in their highest possible form; and, therefore, in Prajñā their minds are free from false discrimination (*vikalpa*); because they are awake to the suchness of reality they do not fall into any of the opposing predicates; they are thus able to cause a revulsion (*parāvṛitti*) in the whole field of their consciousness, though this does not mean that they destroy the work of their own past karma. Prajñā

[1] P. 238.

thus leads them finally to the realisation of the inmost truth deeply concealed under the wrappings of attachment and intellectualism.

Doctrine of the Triple Body[1]

When the *Laṅkāvatāra* was compiled, the doctrine of the Triple Body (*trikāya*) was apparently not yet formulated in the shape we have it today. We thus have terms corresponding to the three Bodies and the indications of the underlying idea, but no specified relationship is established between them. Only the absolute state of self-realisation is considered as belonging to the Dharmatā-Buddha, who is evidently the Dharmakāya of the later periods.

There are other forms of Buddhahood known as Nishyanda-Buddha and Nirmāṇa-Buddha. *Nishyanda* literally means "flowing down" or "flowing into," and the Nishyanda-Buddha is a Buddha into whom Dharmatā flows and who shines in splendour. The two later Chinese translators have rendered it as 報佛, *pao-fo,* 報 meaning "to requite," "to compensate"; while the Sung by Guṇabhadra has 依佛 *i-fo,* 依 meaning "to depend," "to rely upon." The latter is nearer to the sense of the Sanskrit *nishyanda,* and it is hard to know how the later translators came to have 報 *pao* for it instead of 依 *i.* Did they try to read their own thought into it? For they were doubtless acquainted in their own day with the doctrine of Trikāya, one of which, generally known as Sambhogakāya, corresponds to Vipākaja (報生),[2] or Vipākasthā (報住?)[3] in the *Laṅkāvatāra.*

The other form of the Buddhahood mentioned in the *Laṅkāvatāra* is Nirmāṇika, or Nairmāṇika, or Nirmāna.[4] This is generally done into Chinese by 化佛 or 變化佛, i.e., Transformation-Buddha, corresponding to the Nirmāṇakāya

[1] This subject is more fully treated in Section III under the same heading; see p. 308 et seq.

[2] P. 28.

[3] P. 34.

[4] Pp. 28, 34, 56, 93, etc.

of the Triple Body. As to what this Transformation-Buddha is, the sutra does not offer any explanation. But when the distinction is made between the Nirmāṇa-Buddha and the Dharmatā-Buddha as to their method and material of preaching, we can have a glimpse into the specific features of the Nirmāṇa-Buddha. The *Laṅkāvatāra*[1] makes the latter the teacher of the ordinary people known as "*bāla* and *prithagjana*"[2] (愚夫 or 愚痴凡夫) in Buddhist literature, while the Dharmatā-Buddha discusses an inner perception penetrating into the suchness of truth, or the self-absorbing contemplation by supreme wisdom (*āryajñāna*) of the ultimate condition of things which cannot be reached by logical categories. The class of beings designated as "Bāla and Pṛithagjana," which includes almost all of us who drift over the ocean of contrary ideas, is not able to see behind the veil of ignorance and wrong judgment (*vikalpa*), and to lead this unfortunate group of sentient beings to salvation and enlightenment, the Nirmāṇa-Buddha would discuss the aspects of particularity (*svalakshaṇa*) and generality (*sāmānya-lakshaṇa*) as objects of the intellect. His preaching is thus concerned with the individualising side of existence (*prabhedapracāra*), which is dealt with in Buddhist philosophy under such categories as the six Pāramitās, five Skandhas, twelve Āyatanas, eighteen Dhātus, methods of emancipation (*vimoksha*), modes of consciousness, and other subjects.[3] The object of these discourses is naturally to go beyond the teachings of the various philosophical schools of the day. The Dharmatā-Buddha, on the other hand, is meant for the Bodhisattvas whose aim is to

[1] P. 93.

[2] *Bāla* means "not fully developed" and *prithagjana* means "different people or race." Thus Bāla stands against the enlightened, and Pṛithagjana against the noble (*ārya*). In Buddhist literature they represent people whose minds have not yet been opened to the teaching of the Buddha. I have translated them in this book as "the ignorant," or the "simple-minded," or "stupid and vulgar people."

[3] P. 57.

come to the highest realisation of truth, which is known as Pratyātmāryajñānagatigocara in the *Laṅkāvatāra*.

The distinction between the Nirmāṇa-Buddha and the Nishyanda-Buddha is not quite clear as far as the *Laṅkāvatāra* is concerned. For it describes the latter as performing almost the same function as the Nirmāṇa-Buddha.[1] His teaching is said to consist of such topics as particularity, generality, habit-energy (*vāsanā*) conserved in the deep recesses of consciousness, wrong judgments about it, and their interrelations causing multitudinousness of objects to apppear, and then our inordinate attachment to them, but in reality the non-existence of all these phenomena. Of these topics, the Dharmatānishyanda Buddha will speak thus: the conception of an individual ego-substance arises from our wrong judgment concerning the nature of existence and the law of causation, both of which fail to apply beyond the world of relativity which is empty(*śūnya*) ; it is like the creation of the magician, he knows how to produce a variety of unrealities depending upon some objects of the senses, such as plants, brick, etc.; the spectators are induced to take them for real objects, though in fact there are none such. To the ordinary mind, the law of causation is made to extend beyond the world of relativity, which is also the world of wrong judgments and attachments; whereas the world which supplies a subject-matter for the Dharmatā-Buddha is altogether unsupported (*nirālamba*) and disengaged from dependence (*ālambavigata*), that is to say, it is not to be subsumed under such notions as creation, sense-perception, inference, and others, as it is not to be found among the contents of thought cherished by ordinary ego-bound minds, in which the Hinayanists and philosophers are included. The Dharmatā-Buddha points directly to the truth of immediate perception in which the Bodhisattva stands alone detached from the hypothetical creations of the mind.

This gives us an insight into what the Dharmatā-Buddha

[1] P. 56 ff.

teaches in contradistinction to the two other Buddhas, the Nirmāṇa and the Nishyanda; but as to the distinguishing marks between the latter two we fail to get any definite and specific ideas. When the universe is divided into two aspects, absolute and relative, the absolute belongs to the Dharmatā, while the relative one is the common province of the Nirmāṇa and the Nishyanda. One may ask, Why the distinction, then? As far as the *Laṅkāvatāra* goes, this question is not explicitly answered. We can say only this, that the doctrine of Trikāya must have already been in progress at the time of the *Laṅkāvatāra* and the compiler of the sutra took it for granted that his readers were acquainted with the idea. It was evidently some time later that the doctrine came to be dogmatised. The term "Dharmakāya" occurs at several places[1] in this sutra but no "Sambhogakāya," (except once in the "Sagāthakam," p. 314, g. 384), nor "Nirmāṇakāya," perhaps except once on p. 241.[2] However, that the Buddha is able if he wills to manifest himself as a Nirmāṇakāya in response to the earnest desire of his followers or in order to execute his own purposes, is foreshadowed in the conception of Manomayakāya, "mind-made-body," or "will-body."[3] This is a kind of Nirmāṇakāya.

[1] Pp. 51, 70, 192, 212, etc.; as Tathāgatakāya, pp. 42, 43, 51.

[2] One difference between the Transformation-Buddha and the Dharmatā-Buddha is described to be as follows:

"The Tathagata of Transformation (*nirmita-nairmāṇika*) is attended by Vajrapāṇi, but not the original Tathagata (*maula-tathāgata*). The original Tathagata is beyond all senses and reasonings, cannot be known by the simple-minded, Śrāvakas, Pratyekabuddhas, and philosophers. He abides in a state of bliss which follows from the perception of the truth as he has perfected himself in the doctrine of wisdom and patience. He requires no attendance of Vajrapāṇi. No Buddha of Transformation (*nirmita-buddha*) are born of karma (*na karma-prabhava*), yet they are neither the same nor different with the Tathagata. Like the potter who produces articles by bringing various conditions together, the Transformation-Buddhas preach the Dharma when circumstances are provided for them, but they are incapable of discoursing on the state of consciousness realised by supreme wisdom which leads to an inner perception of truth." (P. 242.)

[3] Pp. 81, 136, 192.

One thing I wish to emphasise in this statement concerning the three forms of Buddhahood is that the story of the inmost perception to be gained by the Bodhisattvas, forming the central theme of the *Laṅkāvatāra,* is told only by the Mūla-tathāgata, or true Tathagata (眞實如來) as in the T'ang version, because he is above all senses, all logical measurements (*sarvapramāṇa*), and cannot be perceived by the Śrāvakas and Pratyekabuddhas, nor by the philosophers; because he abides absorbed in the bliss of realisation and in the perfection of the highest knowledge.[1] The doctrine of the *Laṅkāvatāra* is thus seen to be the direct revelation of the absolute Buddha as he is.

This sketchy and incidental reference to the doctrine of the Triple Body is far from being satisfactory. In a chapter exclusively devoted to the treatment of the subject a fuller exposition is presented.

The Highest Knowledge and a First Cause

We know now that supreme wisdom realised in the inmost depths of consciousness (*pratyātmāryajñāna*) is something absolutely defying all description and altogether unpredicable, and that it is therefore the topic to be properly dealt with by Dharmatā-Buddha himself and not by any beings subject to the principle of relativity. This knowledge is thus eternal, unconditioned, and beyond the reach of all analysis and discursive understanding, as it belongs to the highest principle of cognition from which all relative knowledge is derivable. Now the question is, "In what respect does this differ from the first cause (*kāraṇa*) considered by the philosophers to be also eternal (*nitya*) and beyond thought (*acintya*)?" This is answered by the author of the *Laṅkāvatāra* in the following manner:[2]

What is claimed to be first cause by the philosophers cannot really be so, because a cause always presupposes some-

[1] P. 242.

[2] Pp. 59 ff.

thing beyond and cannot be its own cause. The idea of causation belongs to a world of relativity, and what is relative cannot be eternal and is always within the sphere of thought. If we take a thing belonging to the relative world and therefore to a realm of action, as a first cause from which everything else has its beginning, this will be a wrong form of inference; for we jump from relativity to transcendentality, from impermanence to eternity, from a thing that is to a thing that is on the other side of being and non-being. Therefore, what is regarded by the philosophers as the first cause eternal and beyond thinkability is not to be identified with supreme wisdom attainable by the Buddhas and Bodhisattvas.

That the supreme wisdom is eternal and cannot be made a subject of thought, comes from its intrinsic nature. For it is a state of mind realised personally by the Buddhas when they deeply delve into the ultimate principle itself which is not conditioned by any category of thought. It is not to be designated as a cause which is bound up with its antecedents and consequents, it stands alone "quietly" as absolute knowledge flashed through one's consciousness, it is a fact of experience which does not allow of any arguments. It is Tathatā (suchness), Tattva (thatness), perceived in the inmost consciousness of the Tathagata. As it is not an object external to him, it is a self-sufficient cause not depending on anything. We may say that this is a state of pure perception (*pratyātmagati*).

And it is for this reason that the *Laṅkāvatāra* is ever persistent in making this pure perception not an object of discursive understanding for the ordinary minds, for the philosophers, for the Hinayanists. It is not only too exalted a subject for them to comprehend, but quite beyond logic and liable to be wrongly and disastrously interpreted by them. It is meant for those only who are not at all surprised, or alarmed, or frightened at hearing that there is a thing beyond one's power of thinking, for such belong to the family of Tathāgatayāna.[1] The Mahayanist does not deny the reality of the objective world as regards its relativity, where all conditions obtain; he only refuses to extend these to a realm where they do not apply; and of the existence and reality of such a realm he is firmly convinced because his inner perception testifies to it. What stronger and more intimate and more convincing proof could one ever expect to offer for a truth? Therefore, the *Laṅkāvatāra* boldly declares:[2]

"Srotāpatti-phala (預流果), Sakṛidāgāmi-phala (一來果), Anāgāmi-phala (不還果), and Arhattva (羅漢果)[3]—they are all perturbed states of mind. Sometimes I speak of the Triple Vehicle, sometimes of the One Vehicle, and sometimes of No-vehicle; all these distinctions are meant for the ignorant, for men of inferior wisdom, or even for the noble-minded. As to the entering into the ultimate truth (*paramārtha*), it goes beyond dualism. When one is abiding where there are no images (*nirābhāsa*), how could the Triple Vehicle be established? All kinds of Dhyāna, Apramāṇa, Ārūpya, Samādhi, and the Extinction of Thoughts[4]—they do not exist where there is Mind-itself (*cittamātra*)."

The Parable of the Sands of the Gangā

From the absolute point of view, no use is apparently to be found for anything in the world; no talk is needed, no sermoning avails, and therefore, let the world go as it pleases and work out its own salvation if it ever wants; for what are the Buddhas and Bodhisattvas after all? This is then the question awaiting the absolutist's solution. The following passages concerning the parable of the sands of the Ganges will be edifying in this respect:[5]

[1] P. 64. [2] P. 65.

[3] These are the spiritual attainments of the Hinayanists, Arhatship being the highest of the four.

[4] Summarily stated, these are all different forms of meditation.

[5] P. 229 ff.

"At that time Mahāmati asked the Blessed One, Thou teachest in the scriptural text (*deśanāpāṭha*)[1] that the Tathagatas of the past, present, and future, are like the sands of the Gangā; is this to be understood literally? Or is there another meaning to it? Explain it to me, O Blessed one!

"To this the Blessed One answered: O Mahāmati, do not understand it literally. The Buddhas of the past, present, and future are not to be measured, according to the measure of the sands of the Gangā. Why? Because the comparison goes beyond this world, it is no fair comparison, there is something resembling in it but not quite exact. And, O Mahāmati, the Tathagatas do not hold up a comparison going beyond this world and not of complete resemblance. What has been told by myself and the Tathagatas is no more than a small portion of real resemblance. When I say that there are Tathagatas equal to the sands of the Gangā, it is meant to make those stupid and vulgar people tremble, who, following the modes of feeling and the erroneous views which are cherished by some philosophers, get attached to them, thinking that there is an eternal being or that there is not, go on revolving around the wheel of existence, of birth-and-death. How are they to be kept away from the strait pass of the wheel of existence so that they come to long for a superior object and lay hold of a superior object? Thus it is shown that Buddhahood is easy to attain. If it is told that the appearance of a Tathagata is like the blooming of the udumbara, they may not exert themselves. [Therefore, I preach that the Tathagatas are like the sands of the Gangā. But again,] considering what people are to be led, I hold out in the scriptural text that the appearance of the Tathagata is a matter of as great rarity as the blooming of the udumbara plant. O Mahāmati, the udumbara flower has never been seen by anybody, while the Tathagatas have already appeared in the world and are here even now. To

[1] For this term T'ang has simply 標, while Sung translates it as 所說句 and Wei as 名字說.

say that the appearance of the Tathagata is as rare an event as the blooming of udumbara plant is not a statement put forward in accordance with my inner knowledge. When a statement is shown in accordance with my inner knowledge, it goes beyond, it oversteps any comparison that may be made in the world, because of its unbelievableness, and it will not be believed by stupid and vulgar people. No comparisons hold good in the realm of the supreme wisdom which is attained by an inner realisation, because the truth (*tattvam*) goes beyond those marks visible to the Cittam, Manas, and Manovijñāna. The truth is the Tathagata, therefore no comparisons are adequate here.

"Nevertheless, O Mahāmati, just a little of comparison is given, that is, Tathagatas are said to be equal to the sands of the Gangā, they are equal, they are not different, yet the comparison is not proper, nor erroneous. O Mahāmati, for instance, the sands of the river Gangā are violently trampled on by fishes, tortoises, porpoises, crocodiles, buffaloes, lions, elephants, etc., but the sands are not troubled, have no ill feelings, nor are they unconscious of being trampled on; they are without imagination, beautifully clear and devoid of impurities. Even so with the Tathagatas, O Mahāmati, their supreme wisdom attained by an inner perception is the great river of Gangā, and their Powers, Psychic Faculties, Self-mastery are the sands; and they are trampled by the philosophers, stupid people, and antagonists, who are the fishes, but they are not troubled, they have no ill feelings. The Tathagatas, because of their original vows, fulfilling all the bliss that accrues from perfect mental concordance (*samāpatti*) for the sake of all beings, are not troubled, have no ill feelings. Therefore, the Tathagatas, like the sands of the river of Gangā, do not particularise, as they are above likes and dislikes.

"O Mahāmati, the sands of the river of Gangā do not lose their earthly quality even when fire breaks out on earth at the end of the kalpa, because the sands are of the nature of the earth itself. And, O Mahāmati, as the earth is one with fire, it will never consume away though it is imagined by stupid and vulgar people who are fallen into the way of untruthfulness that the earth will burn up because of continuity. But it will never consume away because it is the element on which fire subsists. Even so, O Mahāmati, the Tathagata's Dharma-body, like the sands of the Gangā, is not destructible.

"O Mahāmati, as the sands of the river Gangā are immeasurable, even so, O Mahāmati, the Tathagata's rays of light are immeasurable, which are shed by the Tathagatas over the assemblies and circles of all the Buddhas in order to effect the ripening and inspiring of all beings.

"O Mahāmati, as the sands of the river Gangā, retaining their quality of being themselves, do not change into anything else, even so, O Mahāmati, the Tathagatas, because of their severance from the cause of conditional existence, have gone beyond the realm of birth-and-death.[1]

"O Mahāmati, as the sands of the river Gangā are unconcerned whether some of them are taken away or whether more are thrown in, even so, O Mahāmati, the Tathagatas' wisdom (*jñāna*) which is engaged in the ripening of all beings knows neither decrease nor increase, for the Dharma is without corporeality. Beings endowed with the body, O Mahāmati, are destructible, not so with beings without the body; and the Dharma is without the body.

"O Mahāmati, as a man cannot obtain ghee or oil or such things from the sands of the river Gangā, however hard he may squeeze them to get it, even so,[2] O Mahāmati, the Tathagatas however painfully hard they may be oppressed for the sake of all beings, never neglect the fulfilling

[1] Literally, "are neither produced nor vanishing in Saṁsāra."

[2] This analogy does not hold good as far as the getting of ghee from the sands is concerned; but we may take the hard squeezing part as compared with the ever-unrequited labour of the Tathagata who works hard for all sentient beings though the latter fail to appreciate the love so ungrudgingly bestowed upon them.

of their original vows which they cherish in the depths of their hearts in the Dharmadhātu [i.e., realm of the Dharma], so long as all beings are not led into Nirvana by the Tathagatas, and this is due to the latter's being endowed with great compassion.

"O Mahāmati, as the sands of the river Gangā flow along the banks of its water and not where there is no water, even so, O Mahāmati, all the discourses by the Tathagatas on the Buddha-dharma take place in accordance with the stream of Nirvana. For this reason the Tathagatas are said to be like sands of the river Gangā. O Mahāmati, the sense of transmigration here does not apply to the Tathagatas, O Mahāmati, decay is the sense of transmigration. And, O Mahāmati, the ultimate end of birth-and-death is not to be known. Not being known, how am I to disclose the Dharma in the sense of transmigration? Annihilation is the sense of transmigration. O Mahāmati, this is not known to stupid and vulgar people.

"Mahāmati asked: If, O Blessed One, the ultimate end is not knowable, how is it possible for all sentient beings to obtain deliverance as they are living in the midst of birth-and-death?

"Said the Blessed One: O Mahāmati, when the cause is removed which is the memory [i.e., habit-energy or *vāsanā*] or erroneous reasoning and faulty discrimination during beginningless time, and when there takes place a revulsion at the seat of discrimination by realising that external objects are appearances or manifestations of one's own mind, then there is deliverance, which is not annihilation. Therefore, O Mahāmati, there is no occasion for speaking of endlessness. An endless end is a synonym of discrimination, O Mahāmati; and apart from discrimination, there is no being whatever present. When the inner world or the outer one is surveyed with wisdom (*buddhi*), we find indeed, O Mahāmati, all objects transcending the dualism of knowing and being known. Only because of ignorance of the discriminating mind, discrimination takes place; when this is realised, it disappears.

"On this occasion this was uttered:

"Those who perceive the Buddhas like the sands of Gangā as unrelated to destruction, or to transmigration, they truly see the Tathagatas.

"As the sands of Gangā are free from all defects, always flowing along the current, so is the substance of Buddhahood."

PART II

(A) The Intellectual Content of the Buddhist Experience

Having elucidated to a certain extent though not so exhaustively as a thorough survey of the *Laṅkāvatāra* may require, as regards its general contents and especially the nature of the inmost consciousness of the Tathagata known as Pratyātmāryajñāgocara, let us now proceed to see what intellectual equipment is needed for a Bodhisattva before he can attain to this inner realisation so emphatically acclaimed in the sutra. This intellectual equipment consisting of two parts, logical and psychological, is in a way the philosophical content of the intuitive experience attained by the Bodhisattva. It may be regarded either as the intellectual attitude to be acquired by him before he enters upon the path of Buddhist discipline, or as the philosophy of what he has realised, which as a rational being he is to elaborate later on. In either case, the *Laṅkāvatāra* offers us a thoroughgoing idealism along with the message of self-realisation, and this has been the point of discussion as referred to before among the Buddhist exegetists who wished to decide which was the more important topic of the sutra. Whatever this may be, we are now prepared to see what is the philosophical background of the Buddhist experience.

Historically, the *Laṅkāvatāra* has been considered as an

exposition of the following subjects: the five Dharmas, three Svabhāvas, eight Vijñānas, and two Nairātmyas. Buddhist scholars, Indian, Chinese, and Japanese were always quite inclined to what may be termed a numerical method of analysis. The whole text was first analysed into so many parts, and each part again into so many sections, and so on; and the important ideas developed in them were picked up and gathered up numerically in order, one, two, three, and so on. They often thus failed to see one central thought running through the text, like the mountaineer whose attention is constantly arrested by the details in his way and fails to take in the mountain as a whole. Now, the *Laṅkāvatāra's* philosophy is absolute idealism and all these numerical headings are details used to establish the main theme. But I will here first discuss each subject separately and then arrange it so as to bring out the whole system in a more centralised shape.

The Five Dharmas

To begin with, "dharma" is a very troublesome word to handle properly and yet at the same time it is one of the most essential technical terms in Buddhism. As it is used in many different senses, the serious business of a translator or a commentator is to know exactly what the term means in a given context. Etymologically, it comes from the root *dhṛi* "to hold," "to bear," "to exist"; there seems always to be something of the idea "to endure" also going along with it. The commonest and most important sense given to it in Buddhism is "truth," "law," "religion," as exemplified in *saddharma, dharmakāya, dharmacakra, dharmaparyāya*, etc. Secondly, it is used in the sense of "existence," "being," "object," or "thing," as, for instance, in *sarvadharmaśūnyatā, dharmanairātmya*, etc. Thirdly, it is synonymous with "virtue," "righteousness," "norm," not only in the ethical sense, but in the intellectual one also. In the latter case, it is "truth," "standard," "category," or a general name for a class of things or ideas. Fourthly, it is occasionally used in a most comprehensive way, including all the senses mentioned above, and it is in this case that we feel inclined so often to leave the original untranslated rather than to seek for an equivalent in a foreign language. For example, when *dharma* and *adharma* are contrasted, *dharma* is here used most evidently in its widest connotation; it is not especially the Buddha's teaching, nor is it a moral standard set up against unrighteousness, nor does it refer to existence generally. In fact it includes all these. The term may be understood to mean anything of which something can be asserted; and its opposite *adharma* means everything that negates the affirmation, logical or ontological, or merely physical or ethical. *Dharma* and *adharma* are used in this sense toward the end of the first chapter of the *Laṅkāvatāra*. *Sarvadharma* may be regarded as being just as comprehensive in its significance; indeed, it may even include *adharma* as well as *dharma,* for *adharma,* too, is a *dharma* so far as it is another form of assertion. *Sarvadharma* is interchangeable with *sarvabhava.* Still another comprehensive use of *dharma* may be found in *Buddhadharma,* for this includes not only all the teachings that go in the name of the Buddha but all the activities, institutions, physical objects, mental operations, and indeed everything that is connected with Buddhism in any possible manner. Thus "Buddhadharma" may come to include the entire universe and all that is found there. The "Dharma" in the five Dharmas may approximately be rendered as "category."

The five Categories (*dharma*) are Name (*nāma*), Appearance (*nimitta*), Discrimination (*vikalpa*), Right Knowledge (*samyagjñāna*), and Suchness (*tathatā*).[1] Those who are desirous of attaining to the spirituality of the Tathagata are urged to know what these five categories are; they are unknown to ordinary minds and, as they are unknown,

[1] Pp. 224 ff, 228.

the latter judge wrongly and become attached to appearances. Now Names are not real things, they are merely symbolical (*saṁketa*, 假立, *chia-li*), they are not worth getting attached to as realities. Ignorant minds move along the stream of unreal constructions, thinking all the time that there are really such things as "me" and "mine." They keep tenacious hold of these imaginary objects, over which they learn to cherish greed, anger, and infatuation, altogether veiling the light of wisdom. These passions lead to actions, which, being repeated, go on to weave a cocoon for the agent himself. He is now securely imprisoned in it and is unable to free himself from the encumbering thread of wrong judgments. He drifts along on the ocean of transmigration, and, like the derelict, he must follow its currents. He is again compared to the water-drawing wheel (*ghaṭīyantra*) turning around the same axle all the time. He never grows or develops, he is the same old blindly-groping sin-committing blunderer. Owing to this infatuation, he is unable to see that all things are like māyā, mirage, or like a lunar reflection in water; he is unable to free himself from the false idea of self-substance (*svabhāva*), of "me and mine," of subject and object, of birth, staying and death; he does not realise that all these are creations of mind and wrongly interpreted. For this reason he finally comes to cherish such notions as Iśvara, Time, Atom, and Pradhāna,[1] and becomes so inextricably involved in appearances that he can never be freed from the wheel of ignorance.

By Appearances (*nimitta*) are meant qualities belonging to sense-objects such as visual, olfactory, etc.; and by Discrimination (*vikalpa*) is meant the naming of all these objects and qualities, distinguishing one from another. The text reads: "Then again, O Mahāmati, Discrimination is that by which names are set up. Expressions are given to appearances, saying, 'This is such and not otherwise'; and

[1] Pradhāna is a kind of the Primary Germ, which, according to the Sāṅkhya philosophy, becomes the cause of all material appearances.

we have names such as elephant, horse, wheel, footman, woman, or man, wherein Discrimination takes place."[1]

Right Knowledge (*samyagjñāna*) consists in rightly comprehending the nature of Names and Appearances as predicating or determining each other. It consists in seeing mind as not agitated by external objects, in not being carried away by dualism such as nihilism and eternalism, and in not falling into the state of Śrāvakahood and Pratyekabuddhahood as well as into the position of the philosopher.

When a world of Names and Appearances is surveyed by the eye of Right Knowledge the realisation is achieved that they are to be known as neither non-existent nor existent, that they are in themselves above the dualism of assertion (*samāropa*) and refutation (*apavāda*), and that the mind abides in a state of absolute tranquillity undisturbed by Names and Appearances. With this is attained with the state of Suchness (*tathatā*), and because in this condition no images are reflected the Bodhisattva experiences joy.[2]

The Three Forms of Knowledge.

The three forms of knowledge known as Svabhāvalakshaṇatraya[3] are more or less a recapitulation or reclassification of the five Dharmas. *Svabhāva*, or *sva-bhāva*, literally means "self-nature," "self-substance," or "existence as it is in itself," and *lakshaṇa* is the "characteristic mark" or marks that distinguish one thing from another. The combination thus literally understood looks as if it had nothing to do with knowledge. The meaning however is this, that as existence (*bhava*) is conceived or cognised by mind, it allows itself to be understood in three different and characteristic ways, and that each of these three ways of understanding or three views of existence is taken as final

[1] P. 226.

[2] An English translation of a part of this section is given elsewhere in this book (pp. 25–33), where a comparison is made between the three Chinese versions and one Sanskrit text. Pp. 225–229.

[3] Pp. 67, 227.

and true to the self-nature of existence by those who may hold that particular view. Thus, the phrase *sva-bhāva-lakshaṇa* may apply to the nature of knowledge itself and also to its object, that is, to existence in general. The motive underlying the classification is to see what knowledge or view of existence is required for the attainment of the truth that brings release from the pain and bondage of existence, and the three characteristic marks so called will more properly describe the nature of knowledge than that of its object. *Svabhāva* in this case is to be understood as an epistemological term.

The first of the three Svabhāvas is known as the Parikalpita (*pari+kalpita,* contrived or imagined), wrong discrimination of judgment, and proceeds from rightly comprehending the nature of objects, internal as well as external, and also the relationship existing between objects as independent individuals or as belonging to a genus. The second is the Paratantra, literally, "depending on another," is a knowledge based on some fact, which is not, however, in correspondence with the real nature of existence. The characteristic feature of this knowledge is that it is not altogether a subjective creation produced out of pure nothingness, but it is a construction of some objective reality on which it depends for material. Therefore, its definition is "that which arises depending upon a support or basis (*āśraya*)." And it is due to this knowledge that all kinds of objects, external and internal, are recognised, and in these individuality and generality are distinguished.[1] The Paratantra is thus equivalent to what we nowadays call relative knowledge or relativity; while the Parikalpita is the fabrication of one's own imagination or mind. In the dark a man steps on something, and imagining it to be a snake is frightened. This is Parikalpita, a wrong judgment or an imaginative construction, attended with an unwarranted excitement. He now bends down and examines it closely and finds it to be

[1] P. 67.

a piece of rope. This is Paratantra, relative knowledge. He does not know what the rope really is and thinks it to be a reality, individual and ultimate.

While it may be difficult to distinguish sharply the Parikalpita from the Paratantra from these brief statements or definitions, the latter seems to have at least a certain degree of truth as regards objects themselves, but the former implies not only an intellectual mistake but some affective functions set in motion along with the wrong judgment. When an object is perceived as an object existing externally or internally and determinable under the categories of particularity and generality, the Paratantra form of cognition takes place. Accepting this as real, the mind elaborates on it further both intellectually and affectively, and this is the Parikalpita form of knowledge. It may be after all more confusing to apply our modern ways of thinking to the older ones especially when these were actuated purely by religious requirements and not at all by any disinterested philosophical ones.

The third form of knowledge is the Parinishpanna, perfected knowledge, and corresponds to the Right Knowledge (*samyagjñāna*) and Suchness (*tathatā*) of the five Dharmas. It is the knowledge that is available when we reach the state of self-realisation by going beyond Names and Appearances and all forms of Discrimination or judgment (*vikalpa*). It is Suchness itself, it is the Tathāgata-garbha-hṛidaya, it is something indestructible (*avināśa*).[1] The rope is now perceived in its true perspective. It is not an object constructed out of causes and conditions and now lying before us as something external. From the absolutist's point of view which is assumed by the *Laṅkāvatāra*, the rope is a reflection of our own mind, it has no objectivity apart from the latter, it is in this respect non-existent. But the mind out of which the whole world evolves is the object of the Parinishpanna, perfectly-attained-knowledge.

[1] Pp. 67, 227.

The following gāthās are translated from the Sanskrit text,[1] where the relation of the three Svabhāvas is treated somewhat in detail. This is one of the difficult series of the gāthās to be found in the *Laṅkāvatāra,* for the meaning is obscure. I have given here my interpretation of it rather than a translation, which latter when reproduced as it stands in the original would be quite unintelligible to the average reader. This series of gāthās is broken up into five sections and is reproduced with more or less variations in the "Sagāthakam" part of the sutra. The gāthās run thus:

"When the mind (*citta*) is bound by an objective world, the intelligence (*jñāna*) is awakened and reasoning takes place; but the highest wisdom (*prajñā*) obtains where there are no images,—a higher level of consciousness (182).

"Owing to the Parikalpita conception of existence it appears real; from the Paratantra point of view there is no such reality; the Parikalpita discrimination holds good as long as there is a state of confusion; in the Paratantra view of existence there is no [subjective] discrimination (183).

"Though a variety of things may be produced by māyā, there is no validity (*siddhi*) in them; so also in the Parikalpita discrimination which causes the multiplicity of appearances there is no validity (184).

"Appearance is due to the evil way of the past, the effect of a fettered mind; it becomes for the ignorant the object of their Parikalpita conception which is formed on the Paratantra [relative] nature of things (185).

"Existence of which the Parikalpita conception is formed [by the ignorant] has the nature of relativity; and it is as regards this relative nature of existence that the discrimination creates multitudinous appearances (186).

"There is worldly [knowledge, *saṃvṛiti*], and ultimate truth (*paramārtha*), and a third is the doctrine of causelessness (*nāstihetukam*); the Parikalpita belongs to worldly

[1] Pp. 130–133.

knowledge; when it is cut asunder, there is revealed the realm of the wise (187).

"As in the case of the magician who reveals multiplicity out of oneness, though there is really no multiplicity, so is the nature of the Parikalpita view of existence (188).

"As with cataract of the eye which makes one imagine various forms though the cataract itself has nothing to do with forms or no-forms, so is the relative nature of existence to the unenlightened (189).

"Like unto pure gold, water free from dirt, and the sky clear of clouds, pure is the nature of the discriminated (190).

"There is no reality as discriminated in the Parikalpita view of the world, but Relativity (*paratantra*) itself exists; assertion and refutation are done away with, which are the products of discrimination (191).

"If the Parikalpita is non-existent because of the nature of Relativity (*paratantra*), what is existent has no existence, and what is existent is produced from non-existence (192).

"Depending upon the Parikalpita, discrimination there obtains Relativity (*paratantra*); from the relationship of Names and Appearances there rises the Parikalpita-discrimination (193).

"But the Parikalpita is not ultimately complete, it has no other way of birth [than depending upon Relativity]; thus it is known that Ultimate Truth is pure in its self-nature (194).

"There are ten[1] kinds of Parikalpita and six kinds of Relativity; as to that which is recognised as Suchness in one's inmost consciousness there is no differentiation in it (195).

"The five Dharmas are truth, and so are the three Svabhāvas; when the Yogin has an insight into this he does not go outside Suchness (*tathatā*) (196).

"What is known as Appearance [and] Relativity, that

[1] In all the Chinese translations we have twelve instead of ten.

is due to Discrimination; but the phenomena of Parikalpita take place depending upon Relativity (197).

"When, however, [existence] is truthfully discerned (*vivecya*) by the intelligence (*buddhi*), there is neither Paratantra nor Parikalpita discrimination. Nor is there anything to be called Perfect Knowledge (*parinishpanna*), and how can there be anything to be discerned by the intelligence (198)?

"That which is Perfect is beyond the dualism of being and non-being; how can there be these two views of existence [known as Parikalpita and Paratantra] (199)?

"In the Parikalpita view of existence dualism is established, and with these dualistic establishments, multiplicity is seen discriminated, but pure is the realm of the wise (200).

"Multiplicity is discriminated indeed, it is discriminated depending upon Relativity (*paratantra*); if a man's discrimination takes place in any other way, he follows the doctrines of the philosophers (201).

"The discriminating is said to be the discriminated; the idea of causation grows from trying to formulate philosophical views; when the dualism of discrimination is gotten rid of, there is indeed that perfect view of existence (*parinishpanna*) (202)."

The relation[1] between the five Dharmas and the three Svabhāvas may be tabulated as follows:

The Five Dharmas			The Three Svabhāvas
	Nāma Nimitta	. . . . Parikalpita	
	Vikalpa	. . . . . . Paratantra	
	Samyagjñāna Tathatā	Parinishpanna	

In going over this tabulation as in the study of other parts of Buddhist philosophy we must keep one thing always

[1] P. 68, g. 134; see also p. 229, g. 6; and p. 285, g. 156.
Nimittaṁ nāma saṁkalpaḥ svabhāvadvayalakshaṇam,
Samyagjñānaṁ hi tathatā paranishpannalakshaṇam.

before our minds, as I stated elsewhere, which is, that Buddhist thought is always the outcome of Buddhist life; that its logic, or psychology, or metaphysics cannot be understood adequately unless we realise that facts of Buddhist experience are at its basis, and, therefore, that pure logic is not the key to the understanding of Buddhist philosophy.

The Two Kinds of Knowledge

The division of knowledge of truth (*satya*) into two forms, Saṁvṛiti and Paramārtha,[1] is also known to the author of the *Laṅkāvatāra*, but it was due to the Madhyamika school of Nāgārjuna that the distinction was thoroughly formulated into a system, and they made most of it to account for the dual aspect of experience in their treatises on the doctrine of the Middle Path. In the *Laṅkāvatāra* we may say that the idea is foreshadowed when it makes reference to "Vyavahāra" (practical experience) according to which the Buddha concedes the possibility of such concepts as being and non-being, birth and death, caused and causing, grasped and grasping, etc. "Vyavahāra"[2] belongs to ordinary life where rules the principle of individuation, and as long as the relative and provisional existence of māyā is admitted, common parlance too has to be permitted for practical purposes. When the sutra, however, goes on further down to explain the characteristic features of the Paratantra form of knowledge, the terms Saṁvṛiti and Paramārtha occur, as we have just noted in the gāthās quoted—the former as leading to particularity and the latter as a mental state when this is transcended. The gāthās throw some light on what is meant by the Parikalpita and the Paratantra view of ex-

[1] The term "Paramārtha" is sometimes (p. 87) used in opposition to the "realm of words, discrimination, and intelligence" (*vāg-vikalpa-buddhi-gocara*) or to the "discrimination of individuality and generality" (p. 89). In this case Paramārtha is synonymous with the supreme wisdom realised in one's inmost consciousness, which is the main thesis of the *Laṅkāvatāra*.

[2] *Vyavahāra* means "usage" or "worldly way." P.85.

istence and at the same time on their relationship to the Madhyamika conception of Saṁvṛitisatya. They are very complicated in meaning and difficult to expound exactly and in full. But the main idea seems to be this: Mind is set in motion when it allows itself to be conditioned by the principle of individuation. The Parikalpita and the Paratantra follow from this stirring up of mentation. The Paratantra is intellectual, for it operates depending on something outside itself. It is a kind of representation. It may not always be correct, but it does not create anything out of itself. The Parikapita, on the other hand, weaves its own imaginative world regardless of its objective value. It is always in the wrong not only in a logical sense but psychologically. The main point about it is that it discriminates "me and mine" from what is not "me and mine," and holding this distinction to be real and final, becomes attached to it, which culminates in moral egoism. When this is once asserted, all the evils follow that are to be found in connection with life. The Paratantra which may be innocent in itself becomes the most efficient hand-maid to the Parikalpita, and what is created by it is also intellectually confirmed with all its practical consequences. The Paratantra and the Parikalpita are mutually dependent. The Parinishpanna is to go beyond both these forms of knowledge. This is Paramārtha, the highest transcendental wisdom, while the Saṁvṛiti form of truth prevails in the world of Parikalpita and Paratantra.

The two kinds of Buddhi (knowledge)[1] which are elsewhere distinguished in the sutra may be considered to correspond to Saṁvṛiti and Paramārtha. In the following lines[2] which are repeated in the "Sagāthakam" (gg. 54–55), truth or reality (*bhūtakoṭi*) is contrasted with its reflected image or semblance (*pratibimba*): "As the king or householder gives his children all kinds of playthings looking like

[1] P. 122.
[2] P. 88.

deer and other animals and alluring and pleasing them by these, finally gives them real things; so I do, for I tell my children, by the aid of various forms reflecting realities, the ultimate truth which is to be realised in their inmost consciousness.'' Buddhi is a higher power of reasoning, but it also denotes any form of intelligence. The first is called Pravicayabuddhi,[1] which is a kind of absolute knowledge corresponding to the Parinishpanna. *Pravicaya* means, "to search through," "to examine thoroughly," and the Buddhi so qualified penetrates into the fundamental nature of all things, which is above logical analysis and cannot be described with any of the four propositions (*catushkoṭika*). The second Buddhi is called Pratishṭhāpika,[2] that is, the intelligence that sets up all kinds of distinction over a world of appearances, attaching the mind to them as real. Thus it may establish rules of reasoning whereby to give judgments to a world of particulars. It is logical knowledge, it is what regulates our ordinary life. But as soon as something is established (*pratishṭhāpita*) in order to prove it, that is, as soon as a proposition is made, it sets up something else at the same time and goes on to prove itself against that something else. There is nothing absolute here.

This setting up or establishing is elsewhere designated as Samāropa.[3] The four establishments are given: (1) characteristic marks (*lakshaṇa*), (2) definite views (*dṛishṭa*), (3) a cause (*hetu*), and (4) a substance (*bhāva*)—all where there are none such in reality. Owing to these proposotions definitely held up as true, opposite ones will surely rise and there will take place a wrangling or controversy (*apavāda*)[4] between the opposing parties. The sutra thus advises the Bodhisattva to avoid these one-sided views in order to attain a state of enlightenment which is beyond the positive as well as beyond the negative way of viewing the world.

[1] 觀察智, *kuan-ch' a-chih.* [2] 建立智, *chien-li-chih.* (T'ang).
[3] 建立, pp. 70, 96, 156. [4] 誹謗, pp. 70, 96.

The Twofold Non-Atman Theory.

We now come to a third distinctive feature of the philosophy of the *Laṅkāvatāra,* which is known as the twofold non-Atman theory, i.e., Nairātmyadvaya.[1] The non-Atman or non-ego theory is known among all Buddhist students as the most differentiating mark of Buddhism, but the denial of an Atman or self-substance (*svabhāva*) in external objects is the specific property of the Mahayana and may require some explanation. To translate *ātman* always by "ego" or "self" or "soul" may not be right; and especially when its denial is applied to an objective world, egolessness has no meaning, it is merely the source of misapprehension. An Ātman means something substantial in possession of a number of qualities, and a free agent not bound by the principle of relativity. When its existence, therefore, is denied in us, it means that we have no such free agent within ourselves, enjoying a substantial existence even above the concatenation of cause and effect. When we deny its reality in the world external to us, it means that there is no self-substance (*svabhāva*) in individual objects which come into existence, abide for a while, and finally disappear according to certain laws. In this case, *nairātmya* is *niḥsvabhāva,* and when it is understood in this way, the idea falls in harmoniously with the other views maintained by Mahayanists. Though not yet formulated numerically by Buddhist scholars, there are four distinguishing marks in Mahayana ontology which constitute its very kernel. They are, (1) that all things are empty (*śūnya*), (2) unborn (*anutpanna*), (3) not dual (*advaita*), and (4) without self-substance (*niḥsvabhāva*).[2] This sums up the metaphysical aspect of Mahayanism, and the dual non-Atman theory is merely a partial recapitulation of it.

[1] P. 68, etc.

[2] Pp. 73, 188, etc. These somewhat correspond to what is generally known as the three Samādhi or Vimokshamukha; śūnya, animitta, and apraṇihita. Cf. pp. 78, 166, 163, etc.; and also pp. 138, 141 etc., of these *Studies.*

The *Laṅkāvatāra* explains the theory in the following manner:[1] The Skandhas, Dhātus, and Āyatanas have nothing personal in them, there is no "me and mine" in them, they are created by the ignorant affirmation of the desire to have,[2] and attachment takes place when they are comprehended by the senses. The material world as well as the physical body are manifestations of the mind known as Ālayavijñāna, and when they are discriminated as particular existences, we are discriminating our own mind-made. When thus created they are seen in constant transmigration, they never remain even for a moment as they are, they flow like a stream, they change like a seed, they flicker like a candle light, they move like the wind or like a cloud. And when affections are stirred up, they are pursued by us, we behave like the monkey who is ever restless, or like the fly that runs after filthy food, and not knowing when we are satiated, and evidently to no good purpose, we burn like fire. Owing to the habit-energy (*vāsanā*) accumulated since time immemorial through wrong reasoning and attachment, we now transmigrate from one state to another revolving like a wheel, like a machine, like a phantom creation, or like a walking ghost. When we realise this, we are said to have the knowledge of the non-existence of an individual ego-soul (*pudgalanairātmya-jñānam*).

Dharma-nairātmya-jñānam (法無我智),[3] as I said before, is gained by extending the knowledge of the non-existence of an individual ego-soul to the external world. The two ideas are interrelated, and when the one is asserted the other follows inevitably. To say that all objects are devoid of self-substance is to recognise a most complicated system of

[1] P. 68 ff. [2] *ajñāna-karma-trishna.*

[3] It is sometimes argued that the Hinayana too denies the existence of Dharmātman and that Dharmanairātmya-jñānam is not the exclusive property of the Mahayana. The argument may be true as far as it goes, but what most distinguishes the Mahayana is the doctrine of Śūnyatā which necessarily follows from the egolessness of all things, and its application to the Bodhisattva's practical life.

relationship running through all existence. This was noticed by the Buddha himself when he discovered what is known as the chain of origination, but as his immediate interest was to free his disciples from ignorance and attachment, his statement stopped short at the theory of non-ego. With the development of Buddhist experience and thought, the psychology grew up into metaphysics, and the doctrine of Śūnyatā (emptiness) came to occupy the minds of Mahayanists. And this doctrine is another way of saying that all objects are without self-substance. When the theory of non-ego is once established, all these stock ideas of Mahayana Buddhism are the necessary inferences: Śūnyatā (空), Dharmanairātmya (法無我), Niḥsvabhāva (無自性), Anutpāda (不生), Anābhāsa (無影像), Nirvāṇa (涅槃), Mayopama (如幻), etc.

The denial of self-substance means that just as the Skandhas, Dhātus, Āyatanas, are devoid of an ego-soul and have no other creator than the desire to possess (*tṛishṇa*) which expresses itself in deeds, thereby subjecting itself to an endless concatenation of cause and effect, so all things are by nature above such categories of particularity and generality, are distinguished as concrete individuals only through wrong discrimination which is so intensely cherished by the ordinary mind. The wise are not thus confused, however, they are free from unwarranted inferences and attachments, as they know, by rightly reviewing the world of particulars (*sarvadharma*), that the latter is devoid of mind (*citta*), will (*manas*), intelligence (*manovijñāna*), the five Dharmas, and the three Svabhāvas (self-nature).[1] When this is attained, the knowledge concerning the absence of Ātman in all things is attained.

"To be devoid of mind, etc.," means that the real nature of existence cannot be designated by any category of thought, for to be predicated means to be determined, to be limited. The truth, if it is really something that gives complete satisfaction to the yearnings of our religious consciousness, must

[1] P. 69.

be absolute, and to be absolute and thoroughly convincing such truth must be inwardly experienced. When an appeal is made to logic a statement or proposition is to be proved according to rules of thought, and these rules are sure to be conditional, and, therefore, more or less one-sided and prejudicial. When the Mahayanists have to assert (*asti*) or deny (*nāsti*), they run the risk of being judged by the rules of thought, and perhaps all they can establish in the circumstances is to say that all things are devoid of "mind, will, etc." as above referred to. This is where Mahayana philosophers are always in a quandary, and this is the reason why the Mahayana teaching looks on the surface at least as self-contradictory or full of paradoxes.

To apply the term, "ātman," ego, soul, not only to a person (*pudgala*) but to all inanimate objects may sound strange at first sight as was stated above, but when it is realised that Buddhist philosophy has no special intellectual interest in the discussion itself except from the most pragmatical point of view, i.e., as concerned with life, with this person, with its salvation and enlightenment, the extension of the term "self" or "soul" over to all existence seems justified and appropriate. At any rate the dual non-ego theory is one of the features of the Mahayana as differentiated from the Hinayana.

(B) The Psychology of Buddhist Experience

The Doctrine of Mind-only

Having finished that phase of equipment which may be called logical, for the upward career of the Bodhisattva, let us now pass on to the psychological phase, that is, the doctrine of consciousness, technically known as the theory of the eight Vijñānas. As I wish to repeat, Buddhism being a religion has no abstract interest in logic, or psychology, or metaphysics *per se,* and especially in the case of the *Laṅkāvatāra* the chief problem is to reach a state of self-realisation which is the *sine qua non* of Buddhahood, and of Bodhisattvahood as well. All efforts are to be directed towards this goal, and it would be entirely against the spirit of the sutra to discuss the psychology of the *Laṅkāvatāra*. I am doing this simply for the benefit of the modern reader who wants to get a better perspective of the text than in its original confusion.

Psychology is, however, the most difficult part of the *Laṅkāvatara*, and it is not an easy matter to get a clear insight into the meaning of it. What I have done here may not be quite correct as far as the reading of the text is concerned, and I am open to conviction from the hand of a more competent interpreter.

Most Buddhist scholars are often too ready to make a too sharp distinction between the Madhyamika and the Yogācāra school, taking the one as exclusively advocating the theory of emptiness (*śūnyatā*) while the other is bent single-mindedly on an idealistic interpretation of the universe. They thus further assume that the idea of emptiness is not at all traceable in the Yogācāra and that idealism is absent in the Madhyamika. This is not exact as a matter of historical fact. Though it is impossible just at present to fix the date of the *Laṅkāvatāra* definitely, we find in it the tendencies that might have developed into the Yogācāra as well as into the Madhyamika; and these tendencies must be regarded as prior to the development of these two schools each distinctly claiming its special province of interest. The differentiation must have taken place after the sutra and not before; for it is natural to infer that composite tendencies appear first and then their decomposition into separate ideas and further development each along its specified line.

However this may be, the main point we must never forget in the study of the *Laṅkāvatāra* is that it is not written as a philosophical treatise to establish a definite system of thought, but is to discourse on a certain religious experience. What philosophy or speculation it offers is only incidental as an introduction or as an intellectual interpretation necessitated by the rational nature of humanity. This latter phase of religious experience may be more predominant in Buddhism than in some other religions, but it is not for us to overlook the essence of the matter for the sake of its more or less unimportant accessories, however inevitable they may be in the understanding of it.

As was definitely stated, the principal theme of the *Laṅkāvatāra* is Pratyātmāryajñānagocara, the state of consciousness in which the inmost truth is directly presented in one's mind. This being an immediate perception of the truth it cannot be imparted to others by means of logic, but without it the perception itself ceases to be operative, which is the same thing as not existing at all or being unreal. The experience itself is without content, and must be given to it by the intellect to make it workable in our social living. The psychology of the *Laṅkāvatāra* is also to be treated thus, that is to say, its doctrine of "Mind-only" (*cittamātra*) with all its accompaniments is meant to explain the mental experience of the Bodhisattva. We have always to bear in mind this subordinate position of psychology or logic or metaphysics in the teaching of the *Laṅkāvatāra*.

The doctrine of the Vijñānas is described in this wise:[1]

"As the waves of the ocean depending on the wind are stirred up and roll on dancing without interruption (99);

"So the Ālaya-flood constantly stirred up by the wind of individuation (*vishaya*) rolls on dancing with the waves of the various Vijñānas (100);

"As dark blue, red, and other colours with salt, conch-shell, milk, and honey; fragrance with fruits and flowers; rays of light with the sun:—they are neither different nor not-different one from another (101);

"So the seven Vijñānas which are the waves of the ocean rise in conjunction with mind (*citta*) (102);

[1] Pp. 46 ff. These gāthās are in some places not quite clear as to their meaning. Perhaps the text ought to be more thoroughly re-arranged, which to a certain extent the author hopes to do later.

"Manifold are the waves evolved in the ocean; likewise indeed the Ālaya sets in motion a variety of Vijñānas (103);

"Citta, Manas, and [Mano-]vijñāna are spoken of [as different] because of appearances; in fact the eight [Vijñānas] have no specific qualifying marks: there is neither that which qualifies nor that which is qualified (104).

"As there is no differentiation in the ocean's waves, so no modification obtains in Citta as regards the Vijñānas (105).

"Citta gathers up karma, Manas inspects, the Vijñāna distinguishes, and the five Vijñānas discriminate the visible [world] (106).

"[Mahāmati asked]:

"Dark blue and red and suchlike are known to be the Vijñāna of mankind; tell me, O Mahāmuni, how a likeness is obtained between waves and mind (*citta*) (107).

"[The Buddha answered]:

"Dark blue and red and suchlike are indeed not in the waves, it is for the sake of the ignorant that mind is described as evolving due to appearances (108).

"There is no evolving in mind, mind in itself is free from that which is perceived; where there is that which is perceived there is that which perceives; the case is the same with the waves (109).

"Body, property, and abode[1] are known to be the Vijñāna of mankind, in which an evolution is thus observed; the analogy holds good with the waves (110).

"[Mahāmati said]:

"The ocean with its dancing waves is discernable, and why is not the evolution of the Ālaya likewise perceived by intelligence (111)?

"[The Buddha replied]:

"In accordance with the intelligence and discrimination

[1] *Deha*, *bhoga*, and *pratishṭha* are usually enumerated together in the *Laṅkāvatāra*, symbolising the entire material world. *Deha* is the physical body, *bhoga* stands for everything that belongs to an individual and is enjoyed by him, while *pratishṭha* is his entire physical environment where he finds his place of living. 身, 資財, 所住, (T'ang).

of the ignorant, the Ālaya is compared to the ocean, and the likeness of waves and the evolution [of mind] is pointed out by a simile (112).

"[Mahāmati requested]:

"Like unto the sun that illumines equally above and below, thou art indeed the light of the world; announce the truth for the sake of the ignorant (113). Thou hast already begun the exposition of the Law, why dost thou not announce the truth [*tattvam*]?

"[The Buddha then replied]:

"Even when there is a man who discourses on the truth, there is in his mind no [special object to be called] truth (114).[1]

"As the waves are stirred on the ocean, as images are seen in a mirror, in a dream, simultaneously, so is the mind in its own field (115).

"To discriminate objects, an evolution [of Vijñānas] takes place in succession: the Vijñāna distinguishes, and Manas again reflects (116).

"The visible world manifests itself to the five Vijñānas; there is no successive evolution when mind is in a state of

[1] In Bodhiruci's translation this verse is put into the mouth of Mahāmati with all that follows; in the Sanskrit text it forms the second half of the verse (114) where *bhāshāmi* in the footnote may be a more logical reading. My reading is here after the Sung and the T'ang version. The sense of the verse, however, as it is phrased here may not be quite clear to the reader, for it may be taken as meaning that the Buddha speaks of a thing which is not really in his mind, that is, that he is a liar and that he is confessing the fact himself. The intended idea is that the truth (*tattvam*) is something elusive and beyond specification, or that defies logical definition; when it is said that here is the truth, it is no more there, for in this case "here" fails to include what is "not-here," and to be the truth it must transcend all possible limitations ascribed by human thought. The *Laṅkāvatāra*, in fact the whole system of Mahayana speculation, is built upon this idea of truth. Tattvam is *tathatā* (如如 or 如實) which literally means "suchness" or "thatness" or "thusness," and is therefore said to be unattainable (*alabdha*, 不可得). The reader must get used to this Mahayana way of describing the absolute character of ultimate reality when he tries to understand the psychology of the Mahayana Buddhist.

collectedness. As a painter or his disciple (117) arrays his colours in order to produce a painting, so do I preach; the picture is not in the colour, nor in the canvas, nor in the plate (118).

''In order to attract all beings, the picture is produced in colours; preaching may err, but the truth is beyond words (119).

''Being the master of all the doctrines, I preach the truth to the devotees, and the truth is to be attained by an inner perception, as it goes beyond both the distinguished [objects] and the distinguishing [subject] (120).

''I preach for the sake of sons of the Buddha, this preaching is not for the ignorant; the manifoldness of things is seen as like māyā, and exists not (121).

''Preaching is thus done in various ways, subject to errors; when the preaching is not in good accord [with the mentality of the hearer], it is then for him no preaching (122).

''A good physician administers medicine according to his patients; so indeed do the Buddhas discourse in accordance with the mental capacity of beings (123).

''The masters thus preach the state of consciousness attained by their inner perception, which does not belong to the realm of the philosophers and Śrāvakas (124).''[1]

According to the *Laṅkāvatāra,* the mind, inclusive of Citta, Manas, and the other six Vijñānas, is in its original nature (*svabhāva*) quiet, pure, and above the dualism of subject and object. But here appears the principle of particularisation known as ''Vishaya'' (境界), which comes from the root *vish* meaning ''to act,'' ''to work''; and with the rise of this wind of action, the waves are agitated over the tranquil surface of the mind. It is now differentiated or evolves (*vṛitti*) into eight Vijñānas: Ālaya, Manas, Manovijñāna,

[1] In the ''Sagāthakam'' section all these gāthās, 99–124, are reproduced, but are broken up into four parts, while gāthās 101–123 are kept solid. See pp. 271, 272, 314–315, and 320.

and the five senses;[1] and simultaneously with this evolution the whole universe comes into existence with its multitudinous forms and with its endless entanglements. The following is indeed the constant echo reverberating through the sutra:

"The visible [world] which is mind does not exist [as seen by the senses]; but mind is set in motion by being seen [i.e., objectified]; the body, property, and the abode are the manifestations of the Ālaya [inherent in all] mankind (125).

"Citta, Manas, and Manovijñāna, Svabhāva, the five Dharmas, the two forms of Nairātmya (egolessness), purity —these are elucidated by the Buddhas (126).

"Long and short and suchlike come to exist mutually conditioned; not-to-be grows effective by to-be and to-be by not-to-be (127).

"When things are analysed into atoms, there remains nothing to be discriminated as objects. Those who hold wrong views do not believe in the ever-abiding ground where the mind-only [doctrine is established] (128).

"The masters point out the state of consciousness attained by their inner perception, which goes indeed beyond the mental calibre of the philosophers and Śrāvakas (129)."[2]

The Important Terms Explained

Before going further, it may be desirable to explain the more important technical terms constantly used in Buddhist psychology.

As is seen here, the conception of the Ālayavijñāna plays a chief, though silent, rôle in the evolution of the

[1] That is, Vijñānas. When *vijñāna* is used in its most comprehensive sense, it is equivalent to mind as distinguished from unthinking matter, *rūpa*. In its specific, technical sense, it is the perceiving and discriminating activity of mind. (See also infra.)

[2] Pp. 54–55. This last gāthā (129) is also found as the concluding line on the previous page. In fact, it is the favorite theme of the *Laṅkāvatāra*. This string of gāthās is repeated in the "Sagāthakam," page 320.

idealistic philosophy of the *Laṅkāvatāra*. It is often called simply "Citta," or "Tathāgata-garbha." *Ālaya* means a storage-house (*tsang*, 藏 in Chinese) where all kinds of goods are kept in storage, and it is the Ālayavijñāna's function to store up all the memory (*vāsanā*) of one's thoughts, affections, desires, and deeds. The seeds (*bīja*) thus stored remain in the Ālaya perfectly quiescent and neutral.

Citta which is used as a synonym of the Ālaya may be translated "mind" as distinguished from Manas, that is, in its more specific sense. *Citta*, according to the sutra, apparently comes from the root *ci*, which has two senses, (1) "to gather," "to pile," "to acquire," and (2) "to perceive," "to look for." *Citta*, therefore, may mean either "collection" or "perception," and in the present case, that is, when it is identified with the Ālaya, Buddhist scholars take it in the sense of accumulation. So we read in the *Laṅkāvatāra*, "Citta gathers up karma," or "karma is gathered up by Citta."[1] Ordinarily, it may correctly be rendered "thought," or "mind." The great source of confusion, however, comes from Citta being used frequently for the whole system of Vijñānas as well as for the Ālaya alone.

Vijñāna is one of the significant terms in Buddhism, it is difficult to find one English word for it. *Jñā* means "to know," "to perceive," but Vijñāna in Buddhism has a technical sense; it is not mere cognition or understanding, it is a sort of principle of conscious life as distinguished from the body, and it is also the power or faculty of discrimination. It has, however, essentially an intellectual connotation, faithfully retaining its original sense. In the case of Ālayavijñāna, there is no discrimination in it, no intellection; for it simply accumulates all the impressions, all the memory-seeds (*bīja*) that are produced and left behind by the activities of the other Vijñānas.

[1] Pp. 46, 158: *cittena cīyate karmam.* Also cf. the "Sagāthakam," g. 754, *tair ācitāni karmāṇi*; and g. 829, *cittam anādi-mati-saṁcitam.*

Tathāgata-garbha, which is another name for the Ālaya, is also a sort of store-room or receptacle where the seeds of Tathagatahood are retained and matured. It has a religious shade of meaning in contradistinction to the Ālayavijñāna which is a more philosophical term. *Garbha* is generally done into Chinese as 藏 (*tsang*), same as *Ālaya,* but literally it means "womb" (胎, *tai*). It is strange that the Chinese translators never, as far as I know, rendered *tathāgata-garbha* by 如來胎, but always, 如來藏, except when in the Shingon sect the Garbha-kośa-dhātu (胎藏界) is spoken of as contrasting with the Vajradhātu (金剛界). But the meaning is clear because the Tathāgata-garbha is the womb where the Tathagatas are conceived and matured, and as we are all possible Tathagatas except that we sit generally bound like mummies by the heavy intellectual and affective coverings known as *jñeyāvaraṇa* and *kleśāvaraṇa.* These two obstructions lie in our way of attaining supreme enlightenment. The intellectual one may not be so difficult to overcome as far as the intellect alone is concerned as it is detached altogether from the influence of the passions; but these passions constituting the very root of personality from the hardest knot to be untied by all earnest followers of Buddhism. The Buddhists, however, have no desire to extinguish all the affective factors that make up the human heart. What they mean when they say that one should extirpate all the passions (*kleśa*) in order to attain perfect freedom is that our passions, as they are generally harboured, are deeply rooted in the idea of self and inseparably joined with all the egotistic impulses, and that therefore they should be disjoined and set free for the working of Mahākaruṇā (great compassionate heart), which, in conjunction with Prajñā, supreme wisdom, makes up the life of the Mahayana Buddhist.

Manas (from *man*), meaning "to think," "to imagine," "to intend." is that seat of intellection and connation, corresponding to the Western conception of mind. It is the one term in Buddhist psychology that has no *vijñāna* attached at its end. It is often confused, and justifiably, with Manovijñāna which is one of the six Vijñānas recognised by all the schools of Buddhism. In the *Laṅkāvatāra* Manas occupies a definite position and performs a specific function in the hierarchy of psychical activities, which will be described later. *Manovijñāna,* like the other five Vijñānas, has a field of its own as the perceiving of the rationality of things internal as well as external. The *Cakshur-vijñāna* is meant for the visibility of things, the *Śrotra-vijñāna* for their audibility, ad so on. The Manovijñāna functions sometimes independently of the five Vijñānas and sometimes simultaneously and conjointly with them. To a certain extent, it may be considered equivalent to the intellect, while Manas is conative and affective besides being intellectual. Therefore, it is sometimes called Klishṭamanas, meaning "Manas in defilement." The spiritual defilement starts nowhere else but in the Manas, the root of intellection and conation.

Vāsanā is quite a new conception in the development of Mahayana Buddhism, and the knowledge of it is indispensable to the understanding of the Ālayavijñāna. *Vāsanā* comes from the root *vas* meaning "to dwell," "to stay," or "to perfume," and in the Mahayana sutras it is used in the two senses combined, that is, in the sense of a perfuming energy that leaves its essence permanently behind in the things it has perfumed. The Chinese translators generally have 習氣 *hsi-ch'i,* or 薫習 *hsün-hsi,* for this term; *hsi* meaning "habit," "long usage," or "repeated experience." Vāsanā, therefore, is a kind of super-sensuous energy (*acintya-vāsanā-pariṇāma,* 不思議薫變) mysteriously emanating from every thought, every feeling, or every deed one has done or does, which lives latently in the store-house called Ālayavijñāna. It is often qualified as *daushṭhulya* whose Chinese equivalent is 惡 *wu,* or 過惡 *kuo-wu,* meaning "erroneous" or "evil." Vāsanā is morally evil and logically erroneous inasmuch as it creates an external world and causes us to cling to it as real and final. In modern psychology, we can say that Vāsanā corresponds to memory in its widest sense. This perfuming or leaving impressions is sometimes known as sowing seeds (*bija*). It is a technical term with the Yogācāra philosophers, though the *Laṅkāvatāra* does not make many references[1] to it.

The Theory of Mind-Only

When the sutra says that all things are nothing but Mind (*citta*), what is meant by it? Does Citta refer to the Ālaya, or to the whole system of the Vijñānas, or to the interaction of the Ālaya and the Manas? When it is said that Citta is under the bondage of Vishaya, *cittaṁ vishaya-saṁbandham,* as on page 130, or that bondage is mind-made, *bandhanaṁ citta-saṁbhavam,* on the same page, what is meant by this Citta? What does the phrase, *svacittadṛiśya-mātra* (the seen-only-by-one's-own-mind), or *citta-vikal-palakshaṇa* (appearances-discriminated-by-mind), which occurs so frequently throughout the *Laṅkāvatāra,* really refer to? When mention is made of "purifying the outflows of the visible world from one's own mind" (*svacittadṛiś-yadhārāviśuddhi*),[2] what is this mind?

In my view, Citta or mind refers in some cases to the Ālaya alone, in other cases to Manas, or even to the whole system of Vijñānas. When the sutra says that if there is no revulsion (*parāvṛitti*) in the Ālayavijñāna called by the name of Tathāgata-garbha, there will be no extinction of the seven functioning Vijñānas,[3] or that when the Tathāgata-garbha is united with the seven Vijñānas, from attachment arises dualism, and that when this is thoroughly perceived the error is removed,[4] we realise that the Ālaya is the most important conception on which the whole mechanism of the psychic life hangs. "Mind-only"(*cittamātram*) must then mean that there is nothing but the Ālayavijñāna (*ālayavijñānamātram*). In fact the Ālaya is a depository of all kinds of karma-seeds,

[1] Pp. 45, 95, 294, etc.
[2] P. 55. [3] P. 221. [4] P. 223.

good as well as bad,[1] and so long as it is not stirred up by Vishaya, the principle of individuation, it will remain tranquil, retaining its original purity[2] or neutrality, inefficiency, aloofness, and the primary quality of not being contaminated by defilements. However, the Ālaya is always found in company with the seventh Vijñāna or Manas,[3] and when it is found working, all the other Vijñānas are in action.[4] This being the case, the "Mind-only" may also involve the whole mental apparatus, especially with the Ālaya strongly in alliance with Manas.

It may be more appropriate to consider Citta designating the whole system of Vijñānas as a unit, instead of looking at each Vijñāna as an independent yet interrelating element. The whole mind is then conceived as operating or functioning in eight different modes, while each mode also shares in the general activity of the mind either as Citta or Vijñāna. Unless Citta is especially referred to as distinguished from Manas and the Vijñānas, we can safely state that Citta, when mentioned independently in such phrases as *cittamātram*, *svacittadṛiśyam*, or *cittamātravinirmuktaṁ nopalabhyate*, means the whole system of conscious life which is generally designated as mind by Western philosophers. For instance, we have in the T'ang version the following verse corresponding to the gāthā in the Sanskrit text, p. 70:

"The body, property, and abode—
These are no other than the shadow of the mind;
The ignorant, unable to understand it,
Are engaged in theory-making and in controversy.
But what they establish is merely mind-made,
And outside mind nothing is obtainable."

In this quotation Citta (mind) no doubt stands for the

[1] *Tathāgatagarbho mahāmate kuśala-akuśala-hetukaḥ*. P. 220; see also p. 242.

[2] *Atyanta-prakṛiti-pariśuddhi*. Pp. 221, 222; see also pp. 298, 357, 358, etc.

[3] P. 220. [4] P. 221.

totality of the Vijñāna system. Indeed, when the Ālaya is separated from its company, it ceases to work, that is, to exist, and we have here nothing left but the name.

The doctrine expounded in the *Laṅkāvatāra* and also in the *Avataṁsaka-sūtra* is known as the Cittamātra and never as the Vijñānamātra or Vijñaptimātra as in the Yogācāra school of Asanga and Vasubandhu. Throughout the *Laṅkāvatāra* no mention is made of "*vijñānamātra,*" but either "*vijñaptimātra,*" or "*prajñaptimātra,*" and they are used synonymously. The instances are:

(1) *prajñāptimātraṁ tribhavam* (p. 168, line 7; p. 274, line 10; p. 275, line 13);
(2) *vijñāptimātravyavasthānam* (p. 169, line 5; p. 170, lines 9–10);
(3) *lokaṁ vijñāptimātram* (p. 270, line 1);
(4) *vijñaptināmamātreyam* (p. 96, line 4);
(5) *prajñaptimātrakam* (p. 33, line 11);
(6) *prajñaptimātraṁ ca katham* (p. 26, line 17);
(7) *prajñaptināmamātreyam* (p. 267, line 1).

Of these phrases quoted from the sutra, (1) and (2) are the more important; (3) appears in the "Sagāthakam" which evidently being a later addition I have not made much use of in the preparation of this book. *Prajñapti,* or *Vijñapti* is not here understood in the sense of 了別 (discernment) nor of 識 (knowledge or cognition) as is rendered by the later translators, but it means "construction," or "elaboration" (施設 or 假設), or "provisionary name" (假名). Where the triple world (*tribhavam*) is said to be nothing but *vijñapti* or *prajñapti,* it means that the world is mere subjective construction, having no reality or self-substance (*svabhāva*). The doctrine of Cittamātra, (mind-only, or pure-mind-only), as advocated in the *Laṅkāvatāra,* however, differs from this in that it does not deny the existence of mind itself, from which the objective world appears with all its forms of particularisation. The fault lies in our not recognising this truth and consequently in adhering to a world of particulars as final reality, instead of turning back into our own inner world where we can perceive the Tathāgata-garbha in its unity and immaculacy. The Tathāgata-garbha itself is free from the wrong judgments and discrimination which end in stirring up all kinds of defilements, passions, and outflowings. More will be said about the difference between the *Laṅkāvatāra's* position and that of the Yogācāra as regards the doctrine of Cittamātra when the subject is treated later on more specifically. As far as the idealistic way of looking at the world is concerned, both systems have something in common; especially the *Laṅkāvatā* may be interpreted more or less consistently by means of the Yogācāra psychology, and indeed this has been frequently attempted by scholars. But as is the case with Aśvaghosha's *Awakening of Faith,* the *Laṅkāvatāra* differs from the Yogācāra in one important point, i.e., that while the latter maintains that the Ālaya is absolutely pure and has nothing to do with defilements and evil passions, the *Laṅkāvatāra* and Aśvaghosha maintain the view that the Tathāgata-garbha or the Ālaya is the storage of the impure as well as the pure, that it is both immanent and transcendental, both relative and absolute.

The Evolution of the Vijñāna System

The whole Vijñāna system is explained in the *Laṅkāvatāra* from various points of view which are very difficult to present adequately in another language in which there is no tradition of thought corresponding to the Indian or Buddhist way of thinking. I hope the following interpretation of mine has not altogether misrepresented the original conceptions of the *Laṅkāvatāra.*

The Vijñāna system is describable from three points of reference: its evolution (*pravṛitti*), its modes of being (*lakshaṇa*), and its function (*karma*). By evolution is meant the rise (*utpāda*), abiding (*sthiti*), and disappearance[1] (*nirodha*) of the Vijñāna. Of this there are two forms, Prabandha (相續), and Lakshaṇa (相). Prabandha, meaning incessant continuation, is concerned with an uninterrupted activity of the Vijñāna, while Lakshaṇa, meaning external mark, refers to its manifested aspect. When the habit-energy (*vāsanā*) stored up in the Ālaya by the imprints left behind by thinking, feeling, willing, and acting, either good or bad, is destroyed, there will be no visible signs of them left. This is called the destruction or disappearance of the Vijñāna as to their Lakshaṇa. When not only the cause of the subject (*āśraya*) in dependence upon which the Vijñānas can function, but that which supports them (*ālambana*), or that which provides them with material, is removed, there will be no more continuation of activity in the Vijñānas. This is the case of disappearance both with the Prabandha and with the Lakshaṇa of the Vijñānas, and the same conditions will also hold good with their rise and continuance.

As the sutra, however, does not give any further explanation concerning the difference between, for instance, the disappearance of the Prabandha and that of the Lakshaṇa, the above statement is not enough to show why this distinction between the two is necessary, not only logically but psychologically; for the difference specified above does not seem to be sufficiently warranted. All that we can gather from this is that there is Vāsanā amassed in the Ālaya, which acts as cause to the other Vijñānas, and that there is another thing which serves as object to the latter, and, finally, that by the interaction that goes on between subject and object all the Vijñānas grow either active or dormant according to the case.

[1] P. 37 ff. But this does not mean that the Ālaya itself disappears as is maintained by some philosophers. If this should take place, the doctrine of Cittamātra would not hold good, and there would be no such spiritual event as is known as "turning" (*parāvṛitti*).

The one most important conception in the system of Vijñānas is Vāsanā. What is this? Psychologically, as was stated before, Vāsanā is memory, for it is something left after a deed is done, mental or physical, and it is retained and stored up in the Ālaya as a sort of latent energy ready to be set in motion. This memory or habit-energy,[1] or habitual perfuming[2] is not necessarily individual; the Ālaya being super-individual holds in it not only individual memory but all that has been experienced by sentient beings. When the sutra says that in the Ālaya is found all that has been going on since beginningless time systematically stored up as a kind of seed, this does not refer to individual experiences, but to something general, beyond the individual, making up in a way the background on which all individual psychic activities are reflected. Therefore, the Ālaya is originally pure, it is the abode of Tathagatahood, where no defilements of the particularising intellect and affection can reach; purity in terms of logic means universality, and defilement or sin means individuation, from which attachments of various forms are derived. In short, the world starts from memory, memory in itself as retained in the Ālaya universal is no evil, and when we are removed from the influence of false discrimination the whole Vijñāna system woven around the Ālaya as centre experiences a revulsion toward true perception (*parāvṛitti*). This is the gist of the teaching of the *Laṅkāvatāra*.

This revulsion marks the culmination of the practical psychology of the *Laṅkāvatāra*, for it is through this fact that the realisation of Pratyātmāryajñānagocara is possible, and this realisation is the central theme of the discourse. As this event takes place in the Ālaya, or what is the same thing, in the Tathāgata-garbha, which is the basis of all things, it is known as *āśraya-parāvṛitti*, a revulsion at the basis.[3] *Āśraya*

[1] 習氣 (*hsi-ch'i*).
[2] 熏習 (*hsün-hsi*).
[3] 轉依 (*chuan-i*).

means that on which anything is dependent, and in this case the Ālaya is the Āśraya on which hangs the working of the Vijñānas and consequently the birth of the whole universe. The new orientation takes place when the ego-centric and evil-creating discrimination based upon the dualism of subject and object ceases by the realisation that there is no external world besides what is perceived within the self; and this realisation is effected by the cultivation of the intellect known as non-discriminative and transcendental (*nirvikalpa-lokottara-jñānam*). As long as our ordinary understanding which is dualistically conditioned prevails, we cannot go beyond the realm controlled by the seven Vijñānas, and if we cannot go beyond this, we have no chance of penetrating into the reality of things (*dharmatā*), which means an ever-lasting transmigration in the world of birth-and-death. We must look now in the opposite direction, towards the quarter where no Vikalpa takes place, and where no evolution (*pravṛitti*) of the Vijñānas has set in. An opening must be made to the non-discriminative and transcendental intellect. The opening is called revulsion. The eye that used to open to the external world thinking it was reality and got egotistically attached to it, now turns within to see what lies here. It is in this inner world that so many things we have been looking after are accessible now: the Inner Perception,[1] Nirvana,[2] Tathatā,[3] Emancipation,[4] Prajñāpāramitā,[5] the cessation of the seven Vijñānas,[6], etc.

This sudden turning is in a sense re-turning, the Ālaya or Tathāgata-garbha returns by this to its original purity (*śuddha*), happiness (*sukha*), and eternal nature which is above *pravṛitti* and *nirvṛitti* (rise and disappearance).[7] The

[1] *Svacittadṛiśyagocara*, p. 62, etc.
[2] Pp. 62, 98, 238, etc.
[3] P. 108.
[4] *Moksha*, p. 233.
[5] P. 238.
[6] P. 221.
[7] P. 222.

Ālaya has been contaminated by external impurities (*āgantu-kleśa*) amassed by all kinds of philosophising (*vitarkadar-śana*) bassed on the discrimination of subject and object. When the discrimination is in the right direction, it is right, for it points towards the returning; but when it goes astray as in the case with every one of the ignorant and un-enlightened, it stirs up all sorts of trouble, not only intel-lectually but affectively, the latter being the worst of all trouble-makers. As Buddhism like other Indian systems of thought puts the first emphasis on intellectual integrity, the right seeing into the situation performs the most important office in the whole programme of Buddhist experience. When the intellectual outlook is distorted, the affective and conative disturbances follow, which in turn react upon the essential purity of the Ālaya and contaminate it thoroughly. Incorrectness in every form is described by Buddhists in terms of chromatics. Hence the Ālaya is dyed (*upaklishṭa*) by external impurities. *Kleśa* is generally translated in Bud-dhism as 煩惱, "tormenting and afflicting," "causing vexa-tions of spirit," but here in the *Laṅkāvatāra* it is stated as 塵, "dust" or "impurity" as it spoils the immaculate Ālaya. And since this dust is not native to the Ālaya, it is called *āgantu,* the "guest" who is uninvited.[1]

The Three Modes of the Vijñāna

The Vijñānas may be described from their modes of being, that is, from the lakshaṇa point of view: there are three signs from which their being may be approached. The first is the Vijñāna as evolving (*pravṛitti*), the second the Vijñāna as producing definite effects (*karma*), and the third the Vijñāna as remaining in its original nature (*jāti*).[2] The Pravṛittivijñāna is a collective name for all the parti-cular Vijñānas that evolve out of the Ālaya, when they are considered from the point of view of evolution, while the

[1] P. 222; also cf. p. 77, and *The Sūtrālaṁkāra,* p. 88, vv. 18–19.
[2] P. 37 ff.

Ālaya is the Vijñāna or Citta that remains undisturbed in its native abode. The Karmavijñāna describes the Vijñāna in its functioning capacity. The Vijñāna in itself does not show any signs of becoming; but these three aspects belong to one Citta; thus they are, as the sutra says, "neither different nor not-different." The following extract will show us the relation of the Pravṛitti-vijñāna to the other aspects of the Vijñāna:

"As atoms of clay and a lump of clay are neither different nor not-different from each other, so are gold and articles of ornament made of it. If, O Mahāmati, a lump of clay is different from its atoms, nothing will be produced out of them, but as something is produced out of them, they are not different. But if they are identical, not different, no distinction is possible between atoms of clay and the lump. Likewise, O Mahāmati, if the evolved Vijñānas are different from the Ālaya each in its original nature, the Ālaya will not be their primary cause. If they are identical, the disappearance of the Vijñānas will be the disappearance of the Ālaya, but there is no disappearance of their original nature. Thus, O Mahāmati, there is no disappearance of the original nature of the Vijñānas, but only the disappearance of the karma-aspect of the Vijñānas. If, however, their own original nature should disappear, the Ālaya itself would disappear. With the disappearance of the Ālaya, the distinction will cease to exist between the Buddhist doctrine and nihilism of some philosophers. According to the latter, when the comprehension of an external world ceases, the Vijñānas cease to continue, their uninterrupted activity since beginningless time will be broken. O Mahāmati, the philosophers may explain an uninterrupted evolution [of the Vijñānas] by a cause, and deny that the evolution (*pravṛitti*) is produced by the united action of the eye-sense with form and light. They assume another cause; the cause is Pradhāna (unevolved nature), Purusha (supreme spirit), Īśvara (supreme lord), Time, or Atom." (Pp. 38–39.)

Having thus roughly illustrated the relation of the Ālayavijñāna to its evolute-vijñānas, the sutra after a while returns to the question of the actual stirring up of the sense-vijñānas which are uninterruptedly set in motion like waves in the ocean of Ālaya, this being what constitutes the contents of the Dharmakāya.[1] The following quotation gives a glimpse into the working of the Vijñānas and the rise of the Manovijñāna though it is difficult to understand it clearly in details.

"O Mahāmati, the eye-sense (*vijñāna*) is awakened by four causes (*kāraṇa*). What are the four? Being attached to the visible world, not knowing that it is mind-made (1); the tenaciously clinging to forms due to the habit-energy of unwarranted speculations and erroneous views from beginningless time (2); the self-nature of the Vijñāna itself (3); and an eager desire for the multitudinousness of forms and appearances (4). O Mahāmati, owing to these four causes, the waves of the evolving Vijñānas are set in motion in the Ālaya which flows like the waters in the midst of the ocean. O Mahāmati, as with the eye-sense, so [with the other senses, the perception of] the objective world takes place simultaneously and regularly [i.e., constantly] in all the sense-organs, atoms, and pores; it is like the mirror reflecting images (*vimba*), and, O Mahāmati, like the wind-tossed ocean, the ocean of mind is disturbed by the wind of objectivity (*vishaya*) and the [Vijñāna-]waves rage without ceasing (*avyucchinna*). The cause and the manifestation of its action are not separated the one from the other; and on account of the karma-aspect of the Vijñāna being closely united with the original-aspect, the self-nature of form [or an objective world, *rūpasvabhāva*] is not accurately ascertained, and, O Mahāmati, thus evolves the system of the five Vijñānas. When together, O Mahāmati, with these five Vijñānas, the objective world is regarded as the reason of the differentia-

[1] Pp. 43–44: *udadhi-taraṅgālayavijñanagocaraṁ tathāgatānugītaṁ dharmakāyaṁ prabhāshasva.*

tion (*pariccheda*) and appearances are definitely prescribed, we have the Manovijñāna. Caused by this is the birth of the body [or system of the Vijñānas, *pañcavijñānakāya*]. They do not, however, reflect thus: 'we, mutually dependent, come to get attached to the visible world which grows out of one's own mind (*svacittadṛiśya*) and is discriminated by it.' They [i.e., the Vijñānas and Manovijñāna] rise simultaneously, mutually conditioning, and not broken up, but each taking in its own field of representations (*vijñapti-vishaya*).

"[The way the Ālayavijñāna works in our system of Vijñānas is extremely subtle, and it is the privilege of the highly-trained mind of the Bodhisattva only that can fully grasp the inner significance of the Ālaya.] Those who train themselves in tranquillisation are not always conscious of the subtlety of the working of their habit-energy, and they imagine that they enter into a perfect state of tranquillisation by annihilating all the Vijñānas. But the fact is, they have not annihilated the Vijñānas though they may be in a state of tranquillisation, for their seeds of habit-energy are not fully destroyed; what they have destroyed is simply the [habit of] grasping and discriminating the objective world of particulars. So subtle indeed, O Mahāmati, is the working of the Ālayavijñāna that only the Tathagatas and those Bodhisattvas who are already advancing through the stages of Bodhisattvahood can penetrate into it; it is beyond the powers of the Samādhi and Prajñā acquired by Śrāvakas, Pratyekabuddhas, and philosophers."[1]

The Functions of the Eight Vijñānas

From the functional point of view, there are eight Vijñānas: Ālaya, Manas, Manovijñāna, and the five sense-vijñānas; but they may be grouped under two headings: Khyāti-vijñānas and Vastu-prativikalpa-vijñāna.[2] *Khyāti*,

[1] Pp. 44–45.

[2] 現識 (*hsien-shih*) and 分別事識 (*fen-pieh-shih-shih*).

from *khya*, means "to perceive," "to manifest," and this function of the Vijñāna is to perceive or to reflect things that appear before it just as the mirror reflects all forms before it.[1] This is the function of the Ālaya. It looks into itself where all the memory (*vāsanā*) of the beginningless past is preserved in a way beyond consciousness (*acintya*) and ready for further evolution (*pariṇāma*); but it has no active energy in itself; it never acts, it simply perceives, it is in this sense exactly like a mirror; it is again like the ocean, perfectly smooth with no waves disturbing its tranquillity; and it is pure and undefiled, which means that it is free from the dualism of subject and object. For it is the pure act of perceiving, with no differentiation yet of the knowing one and the known. The waves, however, will be seen ruffling the surface of the ocean of Ālayavijñāna when the principle of individuation known as Vishaya (境界) blows over it like the wind. The waves thus started are this world of particulars where the intellect discriminates, the affection clings, and passions and desires struggle for existence and supremacy.

This particularising agency sits within the system of Vijñānas and is known as Manas; in fact it is when Manas begins to operate that a system of the Vijñānas manifests itself. They are thus called "object-discriminating-vijñāna" (*vastu-prativikalpa-vijñāna*). The function of Manas is essentially to reflect upon the Ālaya and to create and to discriminate subject and object from the pure oneness of the Ālaya. The memory accumulated (*cīyate*) in the latter is now divided (*vicīyate*) into dualities of all forms and all kinds. This is compared to the manifoldness of waves that stir up the ocean of the Ālaya. Manas is an evil spirit in one sense and a good one in another, for discrimination in itself is not evil, is not necessarily always false judgment (*abhūta-parikalpa*) or wrong reasoning (*prapañca-daushṭhulya*). But it grows to be the source of great calamity

[1] P. 37.

when it creates desires based upon its wrong judgments, such as when it believes in the reality of an ego-substance and becomes attached to it as the ultimate truth. For Manas is not only a discriminating intelligence, but a willing agency, and consequently an actor.

In these activities Manas is always found in company with Manovijñāna. In fact, it may be more proper to say that Manas and Manovijñāna conjointly working produce the world of particulars, and when reference is made to Vastu-prativikalpa-vijñāna it includes both Manas and Manovijñāna. The function of Manovijñāna is by hypothesis to reflect on Manas, as the eye-vijñāna reflects on the world of forms and the ear-vijñāna on that of sounds; but in fact as soon as Manas evolves the dualism of subject and object out of the absolute unity of the Ālaya, Manovijñāna and indeed all the other Vijñānas begin to operate.[1] It is like a complicated machine now, the whole system of the Vijñānas, each singly and also conjointly with others, is set in motion. When the system is thus in full swing, we cannot distinguish one Vijñāna from another, they so intimately interact, and the mirroring Ālaya is not distinguishable from the discriminating Manas and from the other Vijñānas, reflecting, reasoning, desiring, and acting. The Khyāti and the Vastu-prativikalpa have now no differentiating marks (*abhinnalakshaṇa*),[2] they re-act upon each other, the one acting in turn as the cause to the other (*anyonyahetuka*).

In the beginning there was the memory amassed in the Ālaya since the beginningless past as a latent cause, in which the whole universe of individual objects lies with its eyes closed; here enters Manas with its discriminating intelligence, and subject is distinguished from object; Manovijñāna reflects on the duality, and from it issues a whole train of judgments with their consequent prejudices and attachments, while the five other Vijñānas force them to

[1] P. 44.
[2] P. 37, l. 18; p. 44, l. 18.

become more and more complicated not only intellectually but affectively and conatively.[1] All the results of these activities in turn perfume the Ālaya, stimulating the old memory to wake while the new one finds its affinities among the old. In the meantime, however, the Ālaya itself remains unmoved retaining its identity.

The following extracts from the *Laṅkāvatāra* elucidate for us the relation between the Ālaya and the other Vijñānas and also that between Manovijñāna, including Manas, and the remaining part of the Vijñāna system.

When the Buddha said that Buddhist Nirvana consisted in turning away from the wrongfully discriminating Manovijñāna, Mahāmati asked, "O Blessed One, dost thou not establish eight Vijñānas?" Being assured of this, Mahāmati proceeded, "If this be the case, why dost thou not speak of one's turning away from the seven Vijñānas instead of Manovijñāna?" The Buddha answered to the following effect: "With Manovijñāna as cause (*hetu*) and support (*ālambana*), there takes place the evolution of the seven Vijñānas. Further, O Mahāmati, when Manovijñāna discerns and clings to an external world of particulars, all kinds of habit-energy (*vāsanā*) are generated therefrom, and by them the Ālaya is nurtured. Together with the thought of 'me and mine,' taking hold of it and clinging to it, and reflecting upon it, Manas thereby takes shape and is evolved. In substance (*śarīra*) [however, Manas and Manovijñāna] are not different the one from the other, they depend upon the Ālaya as cause and support. And when an external world is tenaciously held as real which is no other than the presentation of one's own mind, the mentation-system (*citta-kalāpa*), mutually related, is evolved in its totality. Like the ocean waves, O Mahāmati, [the Vijñānas] set in motion by the wind of an external world which is the manifestation of one's own mind, rise and cease. Therefore, O Mahāmati, the seven Vijñānas cease with the cessation of Manovijñāna. Thus it is said:

[1] P. 235.

"My Nirvana has nothing to do with Substance (*bhāva*), nor with Action (*kṛiyā*), nor with Appearance (*lakshaṇa*).[1] With the cessation of the Vijñāna which is caused by discrimination, there is my cessation [i.e., Nirvana].

"Depending upon it as cause and support, the whole system of mentation finds its refuge here; the Vijñāna supplies cause to the mind (*citta*) and is its dependant.

"As when the great flood runs its course there are no more waves, so with the extinction [of Manovijñāna] all the Vijñānas cease to rise."[2]

The above shows the importance of the Manovijñāna in the body of Vijñānas including the Ālaya; let us now proceed to see what rôle the Ālaya, besides supplying material to the activity of the Manovijñāna, plays, or rather how it stands by itself especially in connection with the idea of the Tathāgata-garbha. The following will be of great help to our understanding the significance of the Ālaya, which is needed in the bringing about of an inner experience known as Pratyātmajñānādhigama:

"O Mahāmati, the Tathāgata-garbha contains in itself causes alike good and not-good, and from which are generated all paths of existence. It is like an actor playing different characters without harbouring any thought of 'me and mine.' From not comprehending this, there arises the union and interaction of three causes producing results. The philosophers not understanding this become attached to the fixed idea of a creator. Infused with the habit-energy of various kinds of speculations and errors which have been carried on since beginningless time, the name of Ālayavijñāna obtains, [as *ālaya* means all-conserving]. It is in company with the seven Vijñānas which are generated in the dwelling-house of ignorance. The body [of the Vijñānas] is stirred uninterruptedly and all the time like the waves of the great ocean,

[1] These are the views held by the non-Buddhist philosophers of the time.

[2] Pp. 126–127.

but [the Ālaya itself] is free from the fault of impermanence and devoid of the thought of ego and is in its ultimate substance perfectly immaculate. As to the other seven Vijñānas beginning with Manas and Manovijñāna, they originate and come to an end and are characterised by momentariness; This is due to our erroneously discriminating things that are not; they are intimately related to and dependent upon an external world of forms and images; tenaciously attached to names and appearances, they fail to comprehend that forms and appearances are manifestations of the mind; they do not realise what is pain and what pleasure, they are no producers of emancipation; firmly standing on names and appearances [as realities], they are begotten of the desire to have (*rāga*) and further beget the same desire; [the desire and the Vijñānas are] thus mutually conditioning. When what are known as the perceiving senses are destroyed and disappear, others [Vijñānas], immediately following this, cease to function. There is [still] a self-discriminating knowledge; and seeing that no pain, no pleasure is felt, that there follows the extinction of thought and sensation, and the attainment of mental tranquillity and the four Dhyānas, together with skilfulness in [the understanding of] truth and emancipation, the devotees (*yogin*) think that they have [really] attained emancipation. But as long as the Ālaya-vijñāna known by the name of Tathāgata-garbha is not set in motion and differently oriented, the cessation of the seven evolving Vijñānas will never take place. Why? Because, depending on the Ālaya as cause, the Vijñānas are evolved; because this is not within the reach of all Śrāvakas, Pratyekabuddhas, philosophers, and yoga-devotees; because [while] they understand that there is no ego-substance in a person, they are [still] attached to the ideas of individuality and generality as really existing in the Skandhas, Dhātus, and Āyatanas. The Tathāgata-garbha is awakened and grows quiescent as one perceives what is meant by the five Dharmas, [three] Svabhāvas, and the non-existence of ego-substance in particular objects; and when there takes place the revulsion [in the Ālaya] by gradually ascending the steps [of perfection, i.e., Daśabhūmikā], a man will never be led astray by the methods and views held by the philosophers......

"The Tathāgata-garbha is found united with the seven Vijñānas: from attachment duality sets in, from knowledge (*parijñāna*) it disappears.

"The mind is to be regarded as mirror-like, perfumed by speculation [-habit] since the beginningless [past]: when things are truly (*yathābhūtam*) observed, they are not as they appear.

"As the ignorant see the finger-tip and not the moon, so those who are addicted to letters understand not the thatness (*tattvam*) of the things I teach.

"The mind (*citta*) dances like the dancer, Manas resembles the jester [or companion actor], the Vijñāna, in company with the five, imagines the visible [world] as a stage."[1]

The Function of Manas

The question may rise now, What is the significance of Manas? Cannot the other Vijñānas do without this one acting, as it were, between the Ālaya and the other particularising six Vijñānas? This seems to be quite a natural question to ask, seeing that the Manovijñāna can directly deal with the Ālaya without the interference of Manas. According to my way of interpreting the *Laṅkāvatāra,* which may not be correct, the Ālaya is a sort of universal consciousness, and Manas individual empirical consciousness. In the Ālaya everything is stored, good and bad, in a state of quiescence and potentiality, but no discrimination, which latter, however, appears with the initiation of Manas. Manas is the active source of all the mental activities we ordinarily experience in this world of particulars. The possibility of consciousness lies in its dualistic nature, for without that which grasps (*grāhaka*) and that which is grasped (*grāhya*),

[1] Pp. 220–224.

there will be no conscious life. The duality of subject and object is fundamental, but this dualism is impossible without assuming behind it something which is not dual. Therefore, at the back of the six Vijñānas there must be Manas, the principle of individuation, and also the Ālaya, which goes even beyond the foundation of consciousness. When we admit that the six Vijñānas are fundamentally conditional by the principal of individuation, we admit the existence of Manas. And when Manas is admitted, we inevitably go on to the Ālaya which allows itself to be reflected by Manas as its condition and yet at the same time transcends it because the Ālaya is not an individual object of experience but universal in its nature. And it is owing to this universal nature of the Ālaya that all the individual Manas are capable of reflecting one and the same universe and of engaging in discussion. The Ālaya is thus most appropriately compared to the ocean.

This ocean of the Ālaya is disturbed by the wind of the particularising principle, psychologically known as Manas and epistemologically as Vishaya. While Manas is conceptually separable from the other six Vijñānas, it is practically involved in them. In our psychological life itself the whole Vijñāna system is engaged and we cannot very well talk individually of its components. So the *Laṅkāvatāra* is always careful to guard us from getting confused about this point: the Ālaya and the Vijñānas are different and yet not-different, i.e., one. Without the Ālaya, the cause disappears and the whole mental apparatus collapses; and when that which makes the cause operative ceases to react, the cause itself ceases to act though this does not mean its disappearance or destruction.

The Manas is the discriminating agency, but as this is possible only in the Ālaya, on which Manas with all its retinue of Vijñānas is dependent, the Manas and the Ālaya are in the closest possible relationship. For this reason, the Ālaya is dependent upon Manas for consciousness of itself and its unity. On the other hand, the six Vijñānas cannot function in harmony with one another unless Manas comes between them and the Ālaya. Manas is the connecting link. The position occupied by Manas in the system of Vijñānas is thus peculiarly complicated and is apt to get confused sometimes with the Ālaya and sometimes with Manovijñāna. In the *Laṅkāvatāra,* the Ālaya is the reservoir of things good and bad, but it is perfectly neutral and not conscious of itself as there is as yet no differentiation in it. The differentiation is caused by Manas, the defiling Vijñāna as it is sometimes called. The differentiation or defilement itself is neither good nor bad, but when it is adhered to as final, irreducible reality, there ensues the idea of an ego-substance internally and externally, and from this all evils are generated. As a result the mind loses its native tranquillity. What is now most needed is to cause a revolution (*parāvṛitti*) in the whole system of Vijñānas, especially in the Ālaya itself, which, contaminated by Manas and Manovijñāna, has had its neutrality, purity, and innocence all exiled. To look into the matter squarely and clearly is called to see *yathābhūtam* by direct perception, which leads to emancipation and serenity.

To summarise: the Ālaya is mind in its deepest and most comprehensive sense; while it manifests itself as individualised in our empirical consciousness and as subject to the momentary changes that are taking place in them, it never loses its identity and eternality. In this respect, it is different from the Ātman or ego which is regarded by the ignorant as something like the Ālaya. Though it is pure and immaculate in its original nature, it allows itself to be affected by Manas, the principle of individuation. And thus affected the dualism of subject and object is created in it, which issues in the appearance of a world of particular objects. The latter comes in contact with the five sense-vijñānas, and all the impressions gained from this contact are presented to Manovijñāna which is a sort of door-keeper between Manas and the five Vijñānas. All the impressions and reports gathered at Manovijñāna are here classified according to the categories of "me and not-me"—this being the function of Manovijñāna given by Manas. The authority of Manas thus increased by its faithful servant and backed inwardly by the presence of the Ālaya, gains strength in the conviction that there is an ego on the one hand and an objective world in all its reality on the other hand. From the disciplinary point of view the most refractory agent is Manas supported by Manovijñāna. When this pair, especially Manovijñāna, is put back to its proper function and made to see things in their true bearings inwardly as well as outwardly, the Vijñāna-system ceases to be an evil-creating machine and becomes the storage of things good and pure (*kuśalānāsravāḥ*).

Let us conclude this paragraph with a quotation on the Buddhist doctrine of momentariness (*kshaṇikam*):[1]

"There are eight Vijñānas: (1) The Tathāgata-garbha, known under the name of Ālayavijñāna, (2) Manas, (3) Manovijñāna, and the five sense-vijñānas grouped together as is pointed out by the philosophers. This system of the five sense-vijñānas is in union with Manovijñāna and this mutuality makes the system distinguish between what is good and what is not good, etc., and further being bound up together so closely and continuously, the Vijñāna-system evolves as one solid undivided body. The evolution thus goes on, but when the nature of a visible world is not understood as Mind, there is a constant rise and disappearance of the Vijñānas; Manovijñāna in union with the five sense-vijñānas grasps forms and appearances in their multitudinous aspect; and there is not a moment's cessation of activity. This I call the momentary character [of the Vijñānas]. There is this momentariness again, O Mahāmati, when the Tathāgata-garbha known under the name of the Ālaya-vijñāna, in union with Manas, is together with the memories of the evolute-vijñānas. If, on the other hand, it is together

[1] Pp. 235–236.

with those free from [evil] outflowings, there is no momentariness. This is found hard to understand for the ignorant who are addicted to the doctrine of momentariness. As they do not understand what is meant by the momentariness and the not-momentariness of all things, they cherish a nihilistic view of existence, and are apt to regard things (*dharma*) belonging to the category of uncreates (*asaṁskṛita*) as subject to destruction.

"O Mahāmati, the body of the five sense-vijñānas is exempt from transmigration, is not susceptible to pleasure and pain, and has nothing to do with the attainment of Nirvana. It is the Tathāgata-garbha, O Mahāmati, that is affected by pleasure and pain, becomes the cause [of Nirvana], is subject to evolution and disappearance, and becomes stupefied by the four kinds of habit-energy (*vāsanā*). The ignorant do not understand this because they are infected by discrimination which is based on the view of momentariness.

"Again, O Mahāmati, gold, diamond, and the Buddha's śarīra [bony relics] equally pass through ages of existence and show the unique character of indestructibility. If the wise who have attained enlightenment have the nature of momentariness they must be said to be lacking in wisdom. Gold and diamond, however long they may be in existence, remain the same; they show no sign of increase or decrease. How can the ignorant be expected to understand my esoteric doctrine, who, discriminating in all things inner and outer, cherish the thought of momentariness?"

These long passages, occasionally deeply involved in obscurity, have been quoted partly to describe the relation between the various Vijñānas as a system, and partly, also, to present the Mahayana Buddhist view of momentarism as regards the Tathāgata-garbha or Ālaya-vijñāna. The gāthās at the end of this chapter on "Kshaṇikam" are to be replaced immediately after the above quotation and not after the account of the six virtues of perfection (*pāramitā*) as they stand now in the original texts, Sanskrit and Chinese.

The Awakening of Prajñā

How do we now get Prajñā awakened in order to see into the true state of things, *yathābhūtam*? Where does this Prajñā come, and how do we attain self-realisation by directly experiencing the truth? And what is the truth? The sutra refers constantly to Prapañca,[1] Parikalpa,[2] Vikalpa,[3] Abhiniveśa,[4] Bhrānti,[5] Daushṭhulya,[6] Vāsanā,[7] etc., which are tossing up the roaring waves over the Ālaya-ocean; but when does Pratyātmāryajñāna get its start so that the stormy sea will grow calm and the world be perceived without discrimination or disturbance of any kind? Says the sutra: "The Bodhisattva who aims to be great in his spiritual discipline is required to be perfect in the following four things: (1) He must have a penetrating comprehention (*vibhāvana*) as regards the nature of the manifestation of Mind; (2) He must be free (*vivarjana*) from such notions as birth, abiding, and destruction; (3) He must observe (*upalakshaṇa*) that external objects do not exist; and (4) He must earnestly desire (*abhilashaṇa*) a state of realisation by directly seeing into the inmost self."[8] How can this be achieved?

If it were due to the appearance of the principle of particularisation or discrimination (*vikalpa*) that the Ālaya ceases to be the seat of Tathagatahood, and if without this principle no sentient beings could ever come to the perception of the Ālaya even in its disturbed, distorted, and altogether false reflections, it must be again this principle that will set us aright in the position that we may have a correct view of Ālaya. In other words, if it were the work of Manas and Manovijñāna that an external world came to be recognised as external, it must be their work again, properly executed this time, that we come to look at the world as having evolved out of our own being. Formerly, the Vijñāna was wrongly

[1] 戯論. [2] 妄計. [3] 分別. [4] 執着. [5] 迷惑. [6] 過惡. [7] 熏習.
[8] Pp. 79–80.

attached to the principle of particularisation and thus to the undesirable part of the Vāsanā, memory, in the Ālaya. There must be a turning of the waves, the course of Manas and Manovijñāna must be altered towards another direction than that which has been pursued hitherto. If we all thought of the Ālaya as external and subject to changes, we must now retrace our steps and look within ourselves and see if there is anything that transcends the principle of particularisation. To transcend this principle, that is, for Manas and Manovijñāna to transcend themselves, means the obliteration of themselves, their disappearance from the field of operation, the transcending of the dualism of *grāhya* and *grāhaka*, of *sat* and *asat*, one and many, particularity and generality. When this is accomplished, where do we find ourselves? Where is the ultimate abiding place for us? This is the abode of Tathagatahood, and belongs to the realm of Ālayavijñāna to be known as Tathāgata-garbha, and realisable only through immediate perception (*pratyaksha*).[1] For this no more belongs to the sphere of logic and analysis, but is an experience attained immediately within oneself (*pratyātmagatigocara*). A knowledge that is not of particularisation and discrimination, must be one of direct experience in which the Ālaya reveals itself in its original purity and not in its distorted and defiled forms as it ordinarily does to the Vijñānas.

When we thus come to have an immediate knowledge of transcendental nature, the Vijñāna system will cease to be treated psychologically. We have now to return to the chapter preceding this, where the so-called logical aspect of the inner experience is treated. The awakening of Prajñā which is dynamic rather than non-discriminative knowledge (*nirvikalpajñāna*) beyond the realm of mentation (*acintya* or *acitta*), is a practical question in the *Laṅkāvatāra*, and this will be treated in what is to follow.

[1] P. 222; *pratyaksha* stands against *vitarka, vikalpa, prapañca,* etc.; see also p. 41.

PART III

Life and Works of a Bodhisattva

Self-discipline and Adhishṭhāna

The logical and psychological equipment must be followed up by practical discipline without which the Bodhisattva could not be more than an idealistic philosopher. "As all the sacred doctrines leave no room for option [and doubt as to the import of self-discipline] let the Bodhisattva retire into a quiet and solitary place and reflect within himself by means of the intelligence (*buddhi*) which lies in his inmost mind, not to be led by anybody else. Then he will be able to free himself from views based upon discrimination and by degrees advance towards the state of Tathagatahood."[1] This not depending upon another (*aparapraṇeya*) is emphasised not only in Mahayana literature but in the Āgamas or Nikāyas; for Buddhism is emphatically the doctrine of enlightenment which is to be realised within oneself. So, it is urged for the Bodhisattva who wishes to penetrate behind the screen of contrasts and dialectics that he should rid himself of all the hindrances (*nivaraṇa*) that may arise from noisy confusion, from heaviness of mind, and from sleepiness, and also that he should assiduously engage in disciplining himself throughout the night, not at all mindful of the philosophies of other schools, including the Hinayanist.[2]

Can the Bodhisattva, however, reach his goal by his own effort and without any outside assistance? Is there really no "other power" that will come to his help? Here we have

[1] P. 133; see also p. 155, where the distinction between words and meaning is discussed.

[2] Pp. 49, 97–98. When the Bodhisattva-Mahāsattva is urged to exercise his own intelligence and not to be dependent upon another, this means that the truth of enlightenment must develop from within oneself and intuitively grasped, which being the ultimate object of the Dhyāna discipline recommended in the *Laṅkāvatāra*.

one of the special features of Mahayana Buddhism distinguishing itself from the Hinayana. The *Laṅkāvatāra* calls it the "Adhishṭhāna of all the Buddhas which issues from their Praṇidhāna."[1] Without this Adhishṭhāna on the part of the Buddha, the Bodhisattva with all his assiduity and penetrating insight may be incapable of realising the highest truth in himself and may not finally be taken up among the community of the Buddhas of the past, present, and future. *Adhishṭhāna* (*adhi* + *sthā*) means "basis," "position," "power," etc., translated into Chinese by 加持力 (*chia-chih-li*), "the power that is added to and sustaining." It is the power emanating from the will of the Buddha whose loving heart embraces the whole universe, and is added to that of a Bodhisattva to sustain him, to encourage him, and finally to carry him over to a state of self-realisation. Not only in the present sutra but in other Mahayana sutras we frequently come across the sentence, "Through the Anubhāva or Prabhāva [that is, power] of the Buddha, a Bodhisattva rose from his seat and asked thus of the Buddha, or preached thus." This is a form of authorisation, but in the case of Adhishṭhāna, it is more than that, for here the Buddha's power sustains the Bodhisattva throughout his long laborious career of discipleship. Read the following:[2]

"And again, O Mahāmati, sustained in two ways by the power (*adhishṭhāna*) of the Buddhas, the Bodhisattva falls down at their feet and asks them to settle controversial points for him. What are the two ways? The one is the power by which the Bodhisattva is made to attain states of mental tranquillisation, and the other is that by which the Buddha personally appears before the Bodhisattva and anoints him with his own hands.

"It is thus due to the power of the Buddha that the Bodhisattva at the first stage attains the Samādhi known as the Light of the Mahāyāna, and that having attained this Samādhi the Bodhisattva finds himself now blessed by the

[1] Pp. 49 f. [2] Pp. 100 ff.

personal presence of all the Buddhas from the ten quarters who will with their own body and speech accumulate their power upon him. It is like the case of the Bodhisattva Vajragarbha and others who are furnished with all these meritorious attributes.

"O Mahāmati, in this wise the Bodhisattva at the first stage is sustained by the power of the Buddhas in his attainment of the states of tranquillisation. In virtue of a stock of merit accumulated for hundreds of thousands of kalpas, he will in succession ascend the stages, and qualifying himself with the virtues of perfect control, reach the stage of Bodhisattvahood called Dharmamegha (Cloud of the Law). Seating himself on a throne in the Palace of the Great Lotus, he is surrounded by Bodhisattvas like himself and wears a tiara adorned and embellished with all kinds of jewels. The Buddhas will now come from all the ten quarters of the universe, shining like the brilliant full-moon with yellowish, golden, champaka-like rays, and with their lotus-like hands anoint the forehead of the Bodhisattva seated on the throne in the lotus palace. He is like the crown-prince of a great sovereign, who, being thus anointed by the Buddhas personally with their own hands, assumes full power. This Bodhisattva and such others are said to be sustained, thus hand-anointed by the power of the Buddhas. These are the two ways in which the Bodhisattva is sustained by the power of the Buddha; and when he is thus sustained he will see all the Buddhas face to face. In no other way are the Tathagatas, Arhats, the Fully-enlightened Ones to be seen.

"And again, O Mahāmati, whatever the Bodhisattva accomplishes in the way of Samādhi, psychic attainments, or preaching, is thus done by being sustained in two ways by the power of the Buddhas. If the Bodhisattva could at all preach intelligently without being sustained by the power of the Buddhas, the ignorant would also preach intelligently. Why? It all depends upon whether or not one is sustained by the Buddhas' power. If it is sustained by the entrance of the Tathagata into it, [the whole universe with its] grasses, shrubs, trees, and even mountains, and also [with its] musical instruments of all kinds, utensils, towns, dwellings, palaces, and seats,—all will make music. How much more conscious beings! The deaf, blind, and mute will be emancipated from their defects. Such is the power of the Tathagata, so distinctive, and so full of great virtues.

"Mahāmati asked, Why do the Tathagatas sustain the Bodhisattva by their power when he abides in the state of tranquillisation as well as when he is at the superior stage? Said the Blessed One: It is to keep him away from the evil one and from evil passions, it is to let him not fall into the Dhyāna and stage of the Śrāvakas, but to make him attain to the self-realisation of the Tathagata-stage and grow in the virtues already acquired by him. For this reason, the Bodhisattva is sustained by the power of all the Tathagatas. O Mahāmati, if he is not thus sustained he may fall into the way of thinking as cherished by bad philosophers, Śrāvakas, and the Evil One, and will not be enlightened in the Supreme Enlightenment. For this reason, the Bodhisattva is favoured by the Tathagatas who are Arhats and Fully-enlightened Ones."[1]

The Purification (viśuddhi) of the heart

The conception of Praṇidhāna which is usually translated in Chinese as 誓願 (*shih-yüan*) or simply 願 (*yüan*), meaning "vow" or "prayer" is peculiar to the Mahayana. A Bodhisattva as a rule makes a number of vows before he begins his career, for his desire to attain the final stage of Bodhisattvahood is not only for his own benefit but for all the worlds visible and invisible. The forty-eight vows of Dharmākara are one of such examples, who became Amitābha Buddha the world-saviour when his vows were all fulfilled. The Bodhisattva's universal vow or prayer or earnest desire

[1] Pp. 100–103, abstract; see also p. 212 f.

is, therefore, that all his fellow-beings, inclusive of non-sentient beings, sooner or later, attain to the supreme enlightenment of the Buddha. To accomplish this end, he begins with the preparation of the ground which consists in "maturing" the minds and hearts of all sentient beings, supported by the adhishṭhāna of all the Buddhas. He who is literally the embodiment of the vow to benefit others is thus ever bent on awakening them in enlightenment. Hence in the *Prajñāpāramitā* and other sutras the awakening of the thought of enlightenment (*bodhicittotpāda*) is constantly spoken of as the first step towards gaining access to the truth of Tathagatahood. But the *Laṅkāvatāra* does not tell us so much about this awakening, in fact I think there is no reference to this idea in the sutra. When the Anuttara-samyak-sambodhi is mentioned, it refers to its attainment and not to the awakening of thought towards it. Whatever this may be, there is a paragraph in the *Laṅkāvatāra* which is concerned with the purification by the Buddha of the hearts or minds of sentient begins from the effects of defilement that has been going on in them since the beginningless past due to their wrong discrimination regarding the signification of the objective world. This process of purification to be carried on by the Buddha may be considered to correspond to the awakening of the thought of enlightenment in the *Prajñāpāramitā* sutras.

Mahāmati now raises a question as to the time needed for the purification by saying: "Is the cleansing which is effected by the Buddha instantaneous or by degrees—the cleansing of all beings from the outflowings of the mind whereby they cling to the reality of an objective world?" To this the Buddha gives an answer as is quoted below, according to which his cleansing or purification takes effect sometimes instantaneously, sometimes by degrees. This variation evidently comes from the workings of the individual habit-energy (*vāsanā*). The Buddha's statement here, however, seems to lack the word "sometimes" and I think we have to supply it in order to make the sense of the whole context not too glaringly contradictory. Indeed, the reading of the *Laṅkāvatāra* is not altogether an easy task as was already remarked elsewhere, and in many cases varied interpretations are possible.

"Mahāmati asked,[1] when the mind is cleansed by the Buddha of its own outflowings, it is done all at once or by degrees? Answered the Buddha: "The cleansing is done by degrees, not all at once. It is like the ripening of the āmra fruit which takes place gradually and not at once. It is again like the potter's making pots, the work is done gradually and not at once. The Tathagata's cleansing of all beings of their minds from which external manifestations flow, is carried out by degrees and not all at once. It is again like the shooting of grass, shrub, herb, or a thicket on

[1] Mainly done after the T'ang version. Cf. pp. 55–56, of Nanjō edition. *Svacittadṛiśyadhārā*, for which the T'ang has 自心現流, means "that which perpetually flows out of one's own mind and is perceived as something external to oneself." This combination occurs in these passages only. Is "*dhārā*" in any way related to the idea of Āsrāva (oozing or flowing-out)? "That which flows" in the mind owing to our attachment to an external world must be thoroughly purified as it stains the entire fabric of our spiritual life. The process needed by the Buddha for the cleansing is sometimes gradual and sometimes abrupt. But the notion of revulsion or up-turning (*parāvṛitti*) leads us to imagine the process to be abrupt rather than gradual, while in our actual experience of life what the psychologist calls conversion takes place in either way, gradual or abrupt. The fact may be ascribed to the innate construction of the mind, or, to use Buddhist terminology, to the working of individual karma. Still, one may say, when the process of purification is so gradual and quiet that the man in question never becomes conscious of the changes taking place in his spiritual life, would he ever experience what is termed in the *Laṅkāvatāra* as revulsion? Psychologically this is a phenomenon suddenly happening in the consciousness. When a man was walking in a certain direction all the time, his steps are all of a sudden made to turn back; he faces now the North instead of the South. This abrupt shift of the vista is a revolution, a revulsion; he is sure to be strongly conscious of the transformation. The unconscious process that preceded it may have been gradual, but as far as his conscious mind is concerned, the revulsion has taken place instantaneously. This is however a mooted question in the psychology of religion.

earth, it is gradual and not at once; so does the Tathagata cleanse all beings of their mental outflows. It is again like one's learning the arts of dancing, singing, writing, playing the lute, etc.; it is mastered by degrees and not all at once; so does the Tathagata his purifying work.

"[But sometimes the cleansing is done at once and not by degrees] as in the case of the mirror's reflecting all forms simultaneously and without discrimination. In a similar way, the Tathagata cleanses the minds of all beings from their outflowing manifestations, making them at once pure and free from discrimination and leading them to a state of no-images. Again, as the sun or the moon illumines all forms and appearances at once with its beams of light, so does the Tathagata reveal at once the spiritual state of Buddhahood which is the object of intuitive knowledge (*acintyajñāna*) by freeing all beings of their self-imagined manifestations, errors, and habit-energy (*vāsaṇā*). Again, as the Ālaya-vijñāna reveals simultaneously an external world of individual objects as manifestations of the individual mind, so that Nishyanda-Buddha,[1] at once maturing all beings, enables them to discipline themselves as religious devotees at their abodes in the celestial palace of Akanishṭha.[2] Again, as the Dharmatā-Buddha shines instantly with the light of the Nishyanda-Buddha and the Nirmāṇa-Buddha, so does the inner realisation of the ultimate truth shine forth all at once superseding the wrong views based upon ideas of being and not-being."

The Will-body (*manomayakāya*)

No definite statement of the Triple Body dogma is found in the *Laṅkāvatāra*, but all the component ideas seem to be present as is recognisable here: Dharmatā-Buddha, Nishyanda-Buddha, and Nirmāṇa-Buddha, which apparently cor-

[1] For the explanation of this, see supra (pp. 142 ff).

[2] See also gāthās 38, 774, in the "Sagāthakam"; and pp. 28, 33, 51, 215, etc.

respond to the later trinity of Dharma-kāya, Sambhoga-kāya, and Nirmāṇa-kāya. It would be interesting to discuss here the development of the dogma[1] if the author were not going to restrict himself in this chapter to such topics in the *Laṅkāvatāra* as are more or less directly connected with the absolute idealism developed in the sutra and with the intuitive knowledge of the truth which is its principal theme—these being the foundation of Zen Buddhism. He wishes, however, to touch upon the idea of Nirmāṇa-Buddha as it is closely related to that of Praṇidhāna, the Bodhisattva's vow. Being thoroughly idealistic, whatever is most vehemently desired by the Buddha or Bodhisattva whose interest extends over the whole field of beings, must take effect in one way or another in this world even of our ordinary life. To have, however, a wish realised successfully, one may have frequently to exceed the limitations of this physical body, which is tied to space-time relations. A body not so limited will be needed in this case,—a body that can be manifested anywhere and at any time as is wished. The Buddha of Bodhisattva has this body known as Manomaya-kāya, which means "mind-made body," or simply "will-body."

The definition of Manomayakāya (意生身 or 意成身), according to the *Laṅkāvatāra,* is this: "By *manomaya* ['as willed'] is meant the power to move about as speedily and unobstructedly as is willed. Like the mind that moves unobstructedly over mountains, walls, rivers, trees, and other objects, even beyond many hundreds of thousands of yojanas, by merely thinking of objects seen and perceived previously, with its own thought continuously and uninterruptedly working regardless of the limitations of the body; so when the Manomayakāya is obtained in the realisation of the Samādhi known as Māyopama [Māyā-like], one acquires the ten Powers (*bala*), the tenfold Self-mastery (*vaśita*), and the

[1] The author discusses the dogma of the Triple Body later in this book as far as the *Laṅkāvatāra* can shed light on the subject.

six Psychic Faculties (*abhijñā*), is adorned with the distinguishing marks, and born in the family of Holy Path, and, thinking of the objects of his original vow which is to bring all beings to full maturity, moves about among them as unobstructedly as the mind moves on."[1]

The three kinds of Manomayakāya ("will-body") are distinguished in the *Laṅkāvatāra* somewhat foreshadowing the later systematisation of the Triple Body dogma: the three are (1) the will-body attainable in the bliss of Samādhi;[2] (2) the will-body born of the knowledge of the self-nature of the Dharma,[2] and (3) the will-body whose deeds are not calculative, being born among the order of the holy ones.[2] The first kind is the product of a perfect mental control which takes place as the Bodhisattva ascends through the third, the fourth, and the fifth stage of spiritual discipline, and realises that the mind in its true nature is above its evolved Vijñānas, and, seeing into the phenomenality of objects, is tranquil like the ocean undisturbed by waves. The second form comes from a deep penetration into the truth of all things, which is enjoyed by the Bodhisattva above the eighth stage; for as he perceives that all things are mere appearances like māyā and non-entities, there takes place a revulsion in the recesses of his consciousness, and he enters into the Samādhi called Māyopama and then into other Samādhis. He is now adorned with flowers, with various attributes such as the tenfold Self-mastery and the six Psychic Faculties, etc., moves as quickly as thought itself; and the body attained now is like the lunar reflection in water or an image in a mirror, or a vision in a dream; it is not made of the four elements and yet resembles one so made, it is furnished with all the parts of the material body; he will now enter into all the Buddha-lands, their circles and as-

[1] Cf. p. 81.

[2] (1) *samādhi-sukha-samāpatti-manomayakāya* (三昧樂正受意生身), (2) *dharma-svabhāvā-'vabhoda-m.* (覺法身性意生身), (3) *nikāya-sahajā-'saṁskāra-kriyā-m.* (種類俱生無所作意生身). T'ang.

semblies. As he has thus perfectly penetrated into the nature of the Dharma, he has the second form of the will-body. The third will-body comes from deeply experiencing the bliss of the inner realisation enjoyed by all the Buddhas.''[1]

Of the three kinds of Manomayakāya, the second is the most important, and when the Body is mentioned without qualifications, it generally means this, as we have for instance on pp. 125–126 and pp. 80–81. We quote the statement on pages 80–81: ''How does a Bodhisattva-Mahāsattva keep himself above the view [that upholds the reality of] birth, abiding, and disappearance? Let him regard all things as dreams or māyā-created forms; they never have been born because self, others, and all of them are non-existent. When things are viewed in conformity with the doctrine of ''Mind-only,'' when external objects are seen as having no real existence, the Vijñānas do not revolve; when the idea of causal accumulation is done away with, the triple world is seen originating from wrong discrimination; when thus all things, external and internal, are viewed as having no self-substance and unattainable [i.e., unreal], a Bodhisattva can keep himself away from the idea of birth; he will acquire what is known as resignation to the idea that all things are unborn, as they have the self-nature of māyā, etc. Such Bodhisattvas have now reached the eighth stage; they know the significance of Citta, Manas, and Manovijñāna, the five Dharmas, the three Svabhāvas, the twofold Nairātmya (egolessness), and have realised a revulsion in their inner being, and because of this they now have the will-body. Thus, O Mahāmati, it is that the Bodhisattva-Mahāsattva keeps himself above the view that upholds the reality of birth, abiding, and disappearance.''

In this connection let me notice that the *Laṅkāvatāra* makes reference[2] to two kinds of death (*cyuti*) which takes

[1] Pp. 136–137, abstract.
[2] Pp. 140, 134, 307, etc.

place in the life of a Bodhisattva. The first is the natural death happening to his physical body which is acquired as the result of his past karma committed through his evil passions and outflowings. In Chinese this death is called 分段 (*fên-tuan*), meaning "graded," because the end of life variously comes to individuals. The other is "inconceivable-transformation-death" (*acintya-pariṇāma-cyuti*, 不思議變易死). This happens to the subtile body of a Bodhisattva which he assumes as the consequence of his karma and intellectual hindrance which has not yet been thoroughly destroyed. The life-limit of this super-material body is indefinite as it depends upon the original vows of the Bodhisattva. If his compassionate heart makes him wish to live eternally among mortal beings in order to save the last one, he may live in this body until then. And again he may have it in any size he desires, and be able to perform wonderful deeds of all kinds, and also go through as many transformations as required. He achieves this spiritual existence when he enters upon the path of Bodhisattvahood.

It will be quite an interesting study to inquire into the historical facts which prompted Buddhist scholars to conceive the idea of a spiritual body which could be acquired as the outcome of one's moral training. There is no doubt that the Manomayakāya is the forerunner of the Nirmāṇakāya as one of the Triple Body, and that all these conceptions were needed by early Mahayanists to interpret the religious significance of the historical Śākyamuni side by side with the conception of Dharmakāya.

The inner realisation (*pratyātmādhigama*) referred to in the third Manomayakāya is the common property of all the Buddhas, and when a Bodhisattva attains this insight into his inmost being, he has thereby attained the passport into the spiritual community of all the Buddhas, past, present and future. If a critic insists that this subjectivity ought to be verified objectively, i.e., must have some objective ground on which the experience is to be set up, the *Laṅkāva-*

tāra says that there is what is to be called Paurāṇasthitidharmatā,[1] something that has been in existence from the timeless past, or thingness that abides eternally in things, or an absolute reality that exists regardless of the appearance or non-appearance of the Buddhas. This reality exists in the world as gold exists concealed in the ore, for it is this that makes things abide, makes them arrange themselves in order and establish a realm among themselves, and constitutes their essence. It is eternally there. It is the suchness of things.[2]

Therefore, when the Bodhisattvas or Buddhas attain to realisation, the experience is not something altogether new to them. It is an old story, as it were. It is like walking in an old city which one happens to discover in the midst of the desert. The streets are smoothly paved as ever. One enters into it, and quietly enjoys a peaceful life. The Buddha did not create these things, they have been there from the beginning. The Dharma he has an insight into is something enduring (*dharmasthititā*), a regulative principle (*dharmaniyāmatā*), and suchness of things (*tathatā*), it is reality (*bhūtatā*), truth (*satyatā*).[3] And it was for this reason that the Buddha declared that ever since his enlightenment night he had not uttered a word.[4] This is indeed, according to the *Laṅkāvatāra,* the esoteric teaching (*saṁdha*) of Buddhism.[5]

The conception of Paurāṇasthitidharmatā, or Pūrvadharmasthititā[6] is the doctrine of universal Ālayavijñāna ontologically stated. The Pratyātmagati consists in realising this originally-abiding Dharma, which is variously described as Tathāgatagarbha, the Ālaya, suchness of things. It is beyond the signs of speech, analysis, and description, and in it all the Buddhas, Bodhisattvas, and sentient

1 本住法性.
2 P. 143. 3 本住, 法位, 眞如, 實性, 諦性.
4 Pp. 143, 144, 194, 240; see also above.
5 P. 144. 6 P. 241.

beings are united, and have an ever-enduring community —Nirvana. But the function of the Bodhisattva is not to stay forever in this happy society but to come into a world of particulars. His vows are to be fulfilled, and in this he is said truly to be a Bodhisattva.

The Bodhisattva and Social Life

The central theme of the *Laṅkāvatāra* has been explained as being the attainment of an insight into the inmost consciousness, and to attain this we have seen that the sutra approaches the subject in two ways, logical and psychological. But as Buddhism is a religion and as every religion has its practical and social side, without which it will lose its reason of existence, the *Laṅkāvatāra* also prepares the Bodhisattva for his mission as one of the members of a cooperative life. In fact, this is what distinguishes the Mahayana from the Hinayana, for the latter's object of spiritual discipline does not extend beyond his own interest, however exalted it may be in itself,—the object being the attainment of Arhatship, a solitary saintly life. This is all well as far as it goes, but as we are all living within a most complicately organised communal body, not excepting even a Buddha or a Bodhisattva, we have to think of this side of life. The conception of a Bodhisattva was thus inevitable. If he attained to a state of self-realisation which he finds so full of peace, bliss, and strength, his natural desire is to impart it to his fellow-beings. Technically, when he has finished benefiting himself (*ātmahitam*),[1] his next step is to go out into the world and benefit others (*parahitam*).[2] In reality, he cannot do good for himself without letting others share in it. The sutra, therefore, now proceeds to tell the reader what is the practical, i.e., social life of the Bodhisattva. It may be said that the object of gaining an insight into the inner truth of things is really to qualify oneself for social work.

[1] 自利. [2] 利他.

Before proceeding, a question may be raised as to the value of doing anything for others inasmuch as, according to the doctrine of *Svacittamātram* or self-mind-only, or to that of *Sarvadharmānāṁ śūnyatā-anutpāda-advaya-niḥsvabhāva-lakshaṇam,*[1] there is nothing or nobody in the world that can be the object of salvation, or upon whom any kind of benefit may be bestowed. From the absolutely idealistic point of view, we may even ask if life is at all worth living. Is it not really much ado about nothing that the Bodhisattva should try to save the world when the latter is no more than the illusion of his own mind? Is it not really like a monkey trying to take hold of the moon in water?

This is what is called by the Mahayanists as Uccheda-darśanam or nihilism which does not understand *yathā-bhūtam* the truth of things. That the world is like a mirage, that it is thus empty, does not mean that it is unreal in the sense that it has no reality in any sense. But it means that its real nature cannot be understood by a mind that cannot rise above the dualism of "to be" (*sat*) and "not to be" (*asat*). Therefore, the Sung translation of the *Laṅkāvatāra* opens with this stanza recited by Mahāmati: (1) "The world transcends [the dualism of] birth and death, it is like the flower in air; the wise are free from [the ideas of] being and non-being, yet a great compassionate heart is awakened [in them]."

The last sentence: "Yet a great compassionate heart is awakened in them" is repeated in the first four verses. This is the most important passage not only in the philosophy of the *Laṅkāvatāra* but in the whole teaching of Mahayana Buddhism. Therefore says the *Ashṭasāhaśrikā-prajñā-pāramitā Sūtra*:[2] "Sāriputra asked Subhūti, If as you say the Bodhisattva is unborn, how is it that he works hard and suffers much for the sake of all sentient beings? To this answers Subhūti: I do not wish the Bodhisattva to think that

[1] P. 73, 一切法空, 無生, 無二, 無自性相.

[2] Mitra edition, pp. 25–26.

he is working hard and suffering much. If he does, he is no Bodhisattva. Why? If he does cherish such thoughts, he cannot except to benefit sentient beings whose number exceeds calculation. Rather let him rejoice over his doings, and, towards all sentient beings, feel like mother or father, son or daughter, and let him, feeling like this among men and women, walk in the path of Bodhisattvahood. Further than that, let him feel towards all beings as if they were himself, and think, 'If I am to be completely free from all woes, let them also be so in the same measure. I cannot leave them to their fate. I must save them from the innumerable pains they suffer, and even if I were cut up to pieces many times over?' This I would not cherish any uncharitable feeling toward them is the way a Bodhisattva-Mahāsattva should feel toward all beings and there will be no thought of hardship with him. . . .''

The doctrine of effortless or purposeless deeds (*anābhogacaryā*) is rooted in the possibility of awakening as is here stated a loving heart for all beings even though they have from the metaphysical point of view no self-substance (*niḥsvabhāva*) and are therefore only relative in existential value. That is to say, the world is only a temporal phenomenon, and whatever evils and sufferings we encounter they have no finality as far as they go; but the pitying heart that transcends the cold and severe contemplation of the reasoning philosopher has no inclination to ignore the reality of particularisation; it is determined to eradicate all the evils that are in the world and to save all the suffering ones in the sea of transmigration. This compassionate heart has no ulterior motive except that it moves spontaneously and universally like the sun that shines on the righteous and on the unrighteous. This heart is called pure and undefiled because it is above the relativity of being and non-being, and yet it never ceases to function out of its over-flowing goodness.

The Sanskrit text of the *Laṅkāvatāra* that we have now,

reads somewhat differently from what we have here. We have taken it from the Sung translation which agrees with the T'ang. The Wei reading is in accord with the Sanskrit. This fact has already been noticed before. It shows that there must have been at least two original texts of the *Laṅkāvatāra* already at the time of the Wei translation. And, moreover, there were some reasons for the T'ang translation to adopt the first reading instead of the second (or Wei). What I would now like to know is the reason for this deviation from the Wei. What was really the reason that made the T'ang adopt the Sung rather than the Wei? To say that the texts varied is not enough. According to Fa-tsang's commentary notes on the *Laṅkāvatāra,* the T'ang is the outcome of five Sanskrit texts and the two Chinese translations being carefully collated by the best scholars of the time under the Imperial auspices. The T'ang is, therefore, the result of mature scholarship and authoritative revision. The result thus attained in the T'ang reading is naturally in full accordance with the spirit of Mahayana Buddhism, whereas the Wei and the present Sanskrit text do not bring out the inner sense of the *Laṅkāvatāra* so clearly and adequately. That the world appears like the ethereal flower, etc., is only when seen by the transcendental eye of wisdom (*prajñā*) and not when felt by the compassionate heart of the all-loving Buddha. The heart particularises and feels pity for the sufferings of the world. This is the common teaching of the Mahayana. If the world is like a vision even when perceived in the love of the Enlightened One, where is the framework in which to build up the temple of universal salvation? The opening verses of the *Laṅkāvatāra* must be read as in the Sung and in the T'ang, and not according to the Wei and the present Sanskrit edition.

The Bodhisattva Never Enters into Nirvana

According to the *Laṅkāvatāra* there are five orders of beings from the religious point of view. (1) Those who belong to the Śrāvaka order, (2) Those of the Pratyekabuddha order, (3) Those of the Tathāgata order, (4) Those who belong to no definite order, and (5) Those who are altogether outside these orders.[1] Those belong to the Śrāvaka order who are delighted at listening to such doctrines as concern the Skandhas, Dhātus, or Āyatanas, but take no special interest in the theory of causation, who have cut themselves loose from the bondage of evil passions but have not yet destroyed their habit-energy. They have attained the realisation of Nirvana, abiding in which state they would declare that they have put an end to existence, their life of morality is now attained, all that is to be done is done, they would not be reborn. These have gained an insight into the non-existence of an ego-substance in a person but not yet into that in objects. Those philosophical leaders who believe in a creator or in the ego-soul may also be classed under this order.

The Pratyekabuddha order comprises those who are intensely interested in anything that leads them to the realisation of Pratyekabuddhahood. They would retire into solitude and have no attachment to things worldly. When they hear that the Buddha manifests himself in a variety of forms, sometimes in group, sometimes singly, exhibiting miraculous powers, they think these are meant for their own order, and immensely delighted in them they would follow and accept them.

The Tathagata order may be again divided into three: those who gain an insight into the truth that there is no individual reality behind what one perceives, those who know that there is an immediate perception of the truth in one's inmost consciousness, and those who perceive that besides this world there are a great number of Buddha-lands wide and far-extending. They may listen to discourse on such subjects as manifestations of mind, or transcendental realm of the Ālaya, from which starts this world of particulars,

[1] P. 63 et seq.

and yet they may not at all feel astonished or frightened. These belong to the order of Tathagatas.

The fourth one is of indeterminate nature, for those who belong to it may take to either one of the above three orders according to their opportunities.

There is still another class of beings which cannot be comprised under any of the four already mentioned; for they have no desire whatever for emancipation, and without this desire no religious teaching can enter into any heart. Two sub-classes, however, may be distinguished here, those who have forsaken all roots of merit, and those who have vowed at the beginning to save all beings. They both belong to the Icchantika[1] order so called. Into the former fall all those who vilify the doctrines meant for the Bodhisattvas, saying that they are not in accordance with the sacred texts, rules of morality, and the doctrine of emancipation. Because of this vilification they forsake all the roots of merit and do not enter into Nirvana. The second group is that of the Bodhisattva, who wishing to lead all beings to Nirvana

[1] This is generally understood to have been derived from *icchā* "desire." According to Dr. Unrai Wogiwara, however, it comes originally from *itthamtvika* or *aitthamtvika*, meaning "being worldly" or "belonging to this world." (The *Mahāvyutpatti*, ed. by himself, notes, p. 23.) Linguistically, he may be right, but psychologically there is no harm in deriving *icchāntika* from *icchā*, wish or desire; for the Icchantika are those devoted followers of hedonism either in its bad or good sense. The Bodhisattva is a hedonist in the good sense, his not entering into Nirvana is his own desire or pleasure, he simply desires to remain in this world in order to save his fellow-beings from misery, and he does this not from any sense of duty or moral desirability; he does this merely from his altruistic impulse as it were, that is, he is following the bent of his own mind, which is pleasure to him. But in the case of a sensuous hedonist "he does not believe in the law of causality, he has no feeling of shame, he has no faith in the working of karma, he is unconcerned with the present, with the future, he never befriends good people, he does not follow the teaching of the Buddha." (Quoted by Dr. Wogiwara as the definition of the Ichchantika given in the *Nirvāṇa-sūtra*, the Kōkyōshoin edition of the Chinese Tripitaka, 昃 VII, 96a, 1.9.) As far as the pursuit of pleasure is concerned, the hedonist-Bodhisattva and the worldly sensuous hedonist belong to the same order as are classified in the *Laṅkāvatāra*.

denies himself this bliss. He vowed in the beginning of his religious career that until every one of his fellow-beings is led to enjoy the eternal happiness of Nirvana he himself would not leave this world of pain and suffering, but must strenuously and with every possible means (*upāya*) work towards the completion of his mission. But as there will be no termination of life as long as the universe continues to exist, the Bodhisattva may have no chance for ever to rest himself quietly with his work finished in the serenity of Nirvana. The time will come even to those who speak evil of the Bodhisattvayāna when through the power (*adhishṭhāna*) of the Buddhas they finally embrace the Mahayana and by amassing stock of merit enter into Nirvana, for the Buddhas are always working for the benefit of all beings no matter what they are. But as for the Bodhisattva he never enters into Nirvana as he has a deep insight into the nature of things which are already in Nirvana even as they are. (*Bodhisattvecchantiko 'tra mahāmate ādiparinirvṛitān sarvadharmān viditvā 'tyantato na parinirvāti.*)[1]

Thus, we know where the Bodhisattva stands in his never-ending task of leading all beings into the final abode of rest. So, says the sutra: "He will through his ten never-ending vows bring all beings to maturity, and, manifesting himself in various forms in response to the needs of all beings, will never know where to rest from his task; and yet his mind is always abiding in the state of self-realisation and in the enjoyment of perfect meditation."[2]

Elsewhere[3] we read again:

"Again, O Mahāmati, when Śrāvakas and Pratyekabuddhas enter upon the eighth stage of Bodhisattvahood, they become so intoxicated in the enjoyment of the Samādhi of Cessation, that they are unable to comprehend the doctrine that all things visible are due to "Mind-only"; their habit-

[1] P. 66; 大慧, 彼菩薩一闡提, 知一切法本來涅槃, 畢竟不入 (T'ang).

[2] P. 123.

[3] P. 214.

energy prevents their seeing beyond individuality and generality, they come to uphold the one-sided view of the egolessness of persons and things; their knowledge and understanding of Nirvana is based upon discrimination, and fails to penetrate into the truth of solitude.[1] The Bodhisattvas, on the contrary, O Mahāmati, who rejoice in the bliss of the Samādhi of Cessation are well furnished with the original vows and a pitying and compassionate heart, and, realising the import of the ten inextinguishable vows, do not enter into Nirvana. They are already in Nirvana because their views are not at all beclouded by discrimination. To them no discrimination takes place as to things seized and seizing. As they understand what is meant by the doctrine of "Mind-only," they cherish no discrimination regarding existence; they are kept awav from discriminating and attaching themselves to such ideas as Citta, Manas, Manovijñāna, the self-substance of things external, and their forms. They keep, however, the source of all things in action that belong to the Buddha; they put supreme wisdom (*jñāna*) forward as they thus attain the Tathagata stage of self-realisation."

The Bodhisattva's Vows and His Effortless Works

According to his transcendental insight into the truth of things, the Bodhisattva knows that it is beyond all predicates and not at all subject to any form of description, but his heart full of Karuṇā (love) for all beings who are unable to step out of the dualistic whirlpools of *sat* and *asat*, he directs his intense vows towards their salvation and emancipation. His own heart is free from such attachments as are ordinarily cherished by the unemancipated, but that which feels persists, for his insight has not destroyed this, and hence his Pūrvapraṇidhāna, his Upāyakauśalya, his Nirmāṇakāya. Yet all that he does for the maturity (*paripācana*) of all beings in response to their needs, is like the

[1] *Viviktadharmamatibuddhi*, 寂滅慧(T'ang), p. 214, line 2; or simply *viviktadharma* (寂滅之法, p. 215, or 寂靜法, p. 125).

lunar reflection in water (*jalacandravat*),[1] showing himself in all forms and appearances he preaches to them on the Dharma. His activity is what is in Mahayana phraseology called Anābhogacaryā,[2] deeds that are effortless, effectless, and purposeless, which may be considered to correspond to the Christian love of God.

When the Bodhisattva enters upon the first stage called Joy, Pramuditā, in the career of his spiritual discipline, he makes the following solemn vows, Praṇidhāna, ten in number, which, flowing out of his most earnest determined will, are as all-inclusive as the whole universe, extending to the extremity of space itself, reaching the end of time, exhausting all the number of kalpas (ages), and functioning uninterruptedly as long as there is the appearance of a Buddha. The first is to honour and serve all the Buddhas, one and all, without a single exception; the second is to work for the preservation and perpetuation of the teaching of all the Buddhas; the third is to be present at the appearance of each Buddha, wherever and whenever it may be; the fourth is to practise the proper conduct of Bodhisattvahood which is wide and measureless, imperishable and free from impurities, and to extend the Virtues of Perfection (*pāramitā*) towards all beings; the fifth is to induce all beings in the most comprehensive sense of the term to turn to the teaching of the Buddhas so that they may find their final abode of peace in the wisdom of the all-wise ones; the sixth is to have an inner perception of the universe, wide and inexhaustible, in all its possible multitudinousness; the seventh is to realise the most closely interpenetrating relationship of each and all, of all and each, and to make every land of beings immaculate as a Buddha-land; the eighth is to be united with all the Bodhisattvas in oneness of intention, to become intimately acquainted with the dignity, understanding, and psychic condition of the Tathagatas, so that the Bodhisattva can enter

[1] Pp. 227, 193, 158, etc.
[2] Pp. 42, 43, 89, 161, 266, etc.

any society of beings and accomplish the Mahāyāna which is beyond thought; the ninth is to evolve the never-receding wheel whereby to carry out his work of universal salvation, by making himself like unto the great lord of medicine or the wish-fulfilling gem; and lastly, the tenth is to realise the great supreme enlightenment in all the worlds, by going through the stages of Buddhahood, and fulfilling the wishes of all beings with one voice, and while showing himself to be in Nirvana, not to cease from practising the objects of Bodhisattvahood.[1]

These ten vows or prayers made by the Bodhisattva at the beginning of his spiritual career, that is, when he has entered upon the first stage of Bodhisattvahood or rather Buddhist life, called Pramuditā, do not quite describe the inner consciousness of the Bodhisattva in its deepest signification; for he has not yet entered the stage of Anābhoga-caryā where all his conscious efforts are dropped and he moves about as the sun shines on the unjust as well as on the just, or as the moon in water. While a great compassionate heart (*mahākaruṇā*) is always the most powerful driving force throughout his spiritual progress, he may not attain to a higher stage unless his heart transcends dualism and his behaviour leaves no taint of discrimination (*vikalpa*). Up to the seventh stage (called Dūraṁgamā) of Buddhist life, the Bodhisattva has not been free from the sense of making effort for the attainment of a certain definite object, he has so far always been conscious of strain and strenuosity, he has been making a definite attempt at accomplishing something, at bringing forth some tangible result as the outcome of his labour. But he has now completed this part of his work, he has now graduated, so to speak, from an effortful

[1] This is a mere abstract. For details see the *Daśabhūmika-sūtra*, edited by J. Rahder, pp. 14–16. Also cf the *Sikshāsammuccaya*, translated into English by E. Bendall and H. W. D. Rouse, pp. 265–268. Quite interesting it is to compare the English version with the various Chinese translations of the *Daśabhūmika-sūtra* as an independent text and also as one of the chapters in the *Avataṁsaka-sūtra*.

life (*prāyogikacaryā*, 加行), he is now on the way to a life of Anābhogacaryā, where no efforts are made, no consciousness of strain is left though he is far from being a sleepy lithargic good-for-nothing fellow now.[1]

So we read in the *Avataṁsaka-sūtra*, or in the *Daśabhūmika-sūtra*,[2] that up to the seventh stage the Bodhisattva has endeavoured not to be affected or contaminated by a life of evil passions (*kleśa*), but has not yet been able to go beyond it (*samatikram*). He is like a great king who goes about riding on a fine elephant. He knows thus that there are many poverty-stricken people in his country, but he himself has no fear of becoming one of these unhappy creatures. He is quite free indeed from such contamination, but he cannot be said to be a super-man who has passed beyond the frailty of a mortal being. He can attain to this transcendental state only by abandoning his kingly position and being born in the Brahman world, where, enveloped in the celestial light, he looks down at thousands of worlds and freely walks among them. The Bodhisattva, up to the seventh stage, has gone through the world riding in the carriage of the Pāramitās (virtues of perfection), and due to these virtues he has been secluded from the contamination of this world though he knows well that there are defiled lives enough here. But he cannot be called yet to be one who has gone altogether beyond evil passions and deeds following them. If, however, he abandons all his conscious strivings or purposeful efforts, that is, if he finally passes from the seventh to the eighth stage, and, riding in the Bodhisattva's carriage of immaculacy, walks through the world, free from contaminations, he is really one who has altogether gone beyond.

When thus the Bodhisattva, discarding all effortful works (*sarvābhogavigata*), attains to the effortless state of consciousness, he enters upon the eighth stage known as

[1] Cf. Rahder, p. 57.
[2] Cf. Rahder, p. 58.

Acalā, the Immovable. But we must remember that effortlessness is the outcome of intense effort, and that when the former is not preceded by the latter, it can never be realised. Says the *Daśabhūmika*: It is like a man who in a dream finds himself drowning in a river; he musters all his courage and is determined at all costs to get out of it. And because of these very efforts and desperate contrivances he is awakened from the dream and when thus awakened he at once perceives that no further doings are needed now. So with the Bodhisattva: because of the great determination and the constant strivings that he has put forward in order to save all beings from drowing in the river of ignorance and confusion, he has at last reached the eighth stage, and once here all his conscious efforts are set aside, his perception is not obstructed by dualistic considerations, nor by appearances.

The *Laṅkāvatāra* also has this dream illustration, but its application somewhat differs from that in the *Daśabhūmika*.[1] "It is like a man's attempting to cross a great river in a dream. While exerting himself eagerly to cross to the other side of the water, he is awakened even before getting there. Being awakened, he thinks, 'Is this real? or is it not real?' Then he recalls, this is neither real nor unreal. [That which took place in the dream] is due to the discrimination that has been going on since the beginningless past as regards forms and figures in their multitudinousness, —the discrimination that is the outcome of the memory experienced in seeing, hearing, thinking, and cognition; it is not to be viewed by the categories of being and non-being; it is to be regarded as something that has been experienced during a dream by the Manovijñāna. It is likewise with the Bodhisattva-Mahāsattva, who, passing from the first stage on to the seventh, realises at the eighth that no discrimination has ever been proceeding in him, that all things as they are seen in full realisation are like māyā, etc., that

[1] Rahder, p. 64.

all things are free from the imagination that longs for seizing and being seized, and that mind and what belongs to it appear as the result of discrimination. Seeing all this, the Bodhisattva strives to realise everything that belongs to the Buddha; he enlightens all who have not yet attained enlightenment. This is the Bodhisattva's Nirvana. It is not annihilation. As he is removed from Citta, Manas, Manovijñāna, and thoughts of discrimination there is in him an acceptance of all things as unborn. O Mahāmati, in ultimate truth (*paramārtha*) there is no gradation, no continuity, no imagery, no discrimination, and this is known as the truth of solitude (*viviktadharma*).''[1]

This effortlessness is again compared in the *Daśabhūmika*[2] to a great seafaring boat. When the boat is not yet at sea, much labour is needed to make it move forward, but as soon as it reaches the ocean, no human power is required; let it alone and the wind will take care of it. One day's navigation thus left to itself in the high seas will surely be more than equal to one hundred years of human labouring while still in the shallows. When the Bodhisattva accumulating the great stock of good deeds sails out onto the great ocean of Bodhisattvahood, one moment of effortless activity will infinitely surpass deeds of conscious striving.

By these analogies, the reader will be able to form some idea as to the significance in Buddhism of a life of effortlessness. When the Bodhisattva reaches this stage of Buddhist life he is said to be standing on the stage of immovability (*acalā*), for he has now realised Anutpattika-dharmakshānti. This is defined in the following terms in the *Daśabhūmika*[3] showing where is the spiritual background of the Anābhogacaryā, which is really the quintessence of Bodhisattvahood.

''The Bodhisattva Vajragarbha said, O venerable sons

[1] Pp. 214–215. [2] Rahder, p. 67.
[3] Rahder, p. 63 f.

of the Buddha, when the Bodhisattva, while at the seventh stage, has thoroughly finished examining what is meant by cleansing the paths with transcendental wisdom and skilful means (*prajñopāya*), has accumulated all the preparatory material (*sambhāra*), has well equipped himself with the vows, and is sustained by the power of the Tathagatas, procuring in himself the power produced from the stock of merit, attentively thinking of and in conformity with the powers, convictions, and unique characteristics of the Tathagata, thoroughly purified, sincere in heart, and thoughtful, elevated in virtue, knowledge, and power, great in pity and compassion which leaves no sentient beings unnoticed, and in pursuit of the path of wisdom that is beyond measurement; and, further, when he enters, truly, as it is, upon the knowledge that all things are, in their nature, from the first, unborn (*anutpanna*), unproduced (*ajāta*), devoid of individualising marks (*alakshaṇa*), have never been combined (*asaṁbhūta*), are never dissolved (*avināśita*), nor extinguished (*anishṭhita*), nor changing (*apravṛitti*), nor ceasing (*anabhinivṛitti*), and are lacking in self-substance (*abhāva-svabhāva*); when he enters upon the knowledge that all things remain the same in the beginning, in the middle, and in the end, are of suchness, non-discriminative, and entering into the knowledge of the all-knowing one; [and finally] when he thus enters upon the knowledge of all things as they really are; he is then completely emancipated from such individualising ideas as are created by the mind (*citta*) and its agent (*manovijñāna*); he is then as detached as the sky, and descends upon all objects as if upon an empty space; he is then said to have attained to the acceptance of all things as unborn (*anutpattika-dharma-kshānti*)."[1]

"Those that have no self-substance are unborn and in their nature are like the sky; dharmas sought outside the concatenation are the products of discrimination by the ignorant. There is, however, an unborn reality other [than

[1] See also supra, pp. 125–126.

those just mentioned] which is the one attained by the wise; its birth consists in not being born, and in this not being born, there is their Kshānti."[1]

"The triple world thus has nothing to depend upon, either inside or outside; seeing this existence unborn there is the Kshānti of no-birth."[2]

All these quotations point to the correctness of my interpretation of the phrase, "Anutpattikadharmakshānti."[3]

This may seem from the point of view of ordinary terminology almost too abstract, too metaphysical, but to those who are well acquainted with the Mahayanistic way of thinking and feeling, the definition of Anutpattika-dharmakshānti here quoted from the *Daśabhūmika* is exact and adequately describes the highest object of the Buddhist life as far as this kind of phraseology allows. In the *Laṅkāvatāra,* the same ideas are more concretely expressed from another angle by means of an analogy, though the sutra says that such analogies do not do justice to the true state of affairs. The truth as intuitively seen by the Buddhas and Bodhisattvas surpasses all symbolism and is beyond the understanding of ordinary minds, but when some indications are not given, the truth may forever be kept away from us, perhaps worse than that, vilified and denounced to our own spiritual ruination. The analogy has already[4] been quoted when Tathagatahood was compared to the sands of the Ganges.

There are some other important points in the *Laṅkāvatāra* concerning which I intend to write in the following chapters; my object here has been to treat the sutra as most intimately connected with Zen Buddhism, and, therefore,

[1] P. 203, gg. 108–109.

[2] P. 273, g. 67.

[3] Cf. Sylvain Lévi's French translation of the *Sūtrālaṁkāra,* p. 123 footnote, and Asanga's remarks on the "eight unborn dharmas" (*Sūtrālaṁkāra,* XI, 52.)

[4] See supra, page 148 et seq.

as containing some of the most salient ideas of Zen. Therefore, I opened this study with an account of Pratyātmagatigocara which forms the central thesis of the *Laṅkāvatāra* and also is the object of the Zen discipline. No doubt all the schools of Mahayana Buddhism, (and for that matter the Hinayana, too), aim at gaining an immediate personal insight into the essence of Buddhahood, but this aspect of Buddhist life I find more clearly and emphatically and straightforwardly brought out in the *Laṅkāvatāra* than in any other sutra. But as all religion requires a philosophical background without which it limps, I have tried to show how the *Laṅkāvatāra* gives a logical and psychological account of the inmost experience called Pratyātmagatigocara, or Pratyātmāryajñāna. With this the theoretical side of Zen Buddhism finishes, while its active side is to be developed if it has to bear fruit in this practical life. Hence towards the end of this study I have tried to describe the disciplinary life of the Buddhist as far as it is presented in this sutra.

Buddhist nomenclature is frequently too intellectual and the Indians have their own peculiar way of presenting their ideas; for this reason one is apt to regard the Mahayana as a philosophy too abstract and too high-flying and not at all religious; but the fact is that the Mahayana stands firmly on two legs, Prajñā and Karuṇā, transcendental idealism and all-embracing affection for all kinds of beings, animate as well as inanimate. The former sees into the unity of things, and the latter appreciates their diversity. The Bodhisattva weeps with suffering beings and at the same time realises that there is one that never weeps, being above sufferings, tribulations, and contaminations. Buddhist life finds its perfect realisation in a harmonious blending of the two conceptions: philosophically, the one and the many, *sat* and *asat*; religiously the pure and the defiled. And this balancing is seen in the Bodhisattva's Praṇidhāna or vow. "There are two worlds, the defiled and the immaculate, and between the two there is no way to cross from the one to the other, except by the power of the Bodhisattva's great vow, transcendental wisdom, skilful means, and psychic penetration (*abhijñā*)."[1]

The Ten Vows of Bodhisattva Samantabhadra

It may be appropriate to conclude this part of the study of the *Laṅkāvatāra* by quoting the ten vows of the Bodhisattva Samantabhadra which forms the concluding chapter of the *Gaṇḍavyūha-sūtra*. The following abstract[2] is taken from the Chinese translation by Prajñā, master of the Tripitaka, which is popularly known as the *Kegon-Kyo* (*Avataṁsaka-sūtra*) in forty fasciculi.[3]

After praising the excellent virtues of the Tathagata, the Bodhisattva Samantabhadra said to all the Bodhisattvas assembled including Sudhana: The virtues of the Tathagata are so great that nobody, however long and however incessantly he may talk about them, cannot even begin to describe them adequately, and if you wish to perfect these virtues yourselves you must practise the following ten great vows (*mahāpraṇidhāna*). What are they? They are: 1. To honour all the Buddhas; 2. To praise all the Buddhas; 3. To make extensively all kinds of offerings to the Buddhas, especially what may be termed "moral offerings". (*dharmapūja*); 4. To repent all sins ever committed by yourselves; 5. To be sympathetically joyful over whatever merits are acquired by others; 6. To ask the Buddha to revolve the Wheel of the Dharma; 7. To ask the Buddha to stay on living in this world; 8. To be always learning from the life of the Buddha; 9. To look after the spiritual welfare of all beings; 10. To turn all your merits towards the promotion of goodness and

[1] The *Daśabhūmika Sūtra*. Cf. Rahder, p. 58.

[2] This prose part is lacking in the Sanskrit *Gaṇḍavyūha*, where we find the verse only. Prof. Hokei Idzumi, of Otani College, has lately collated various MSS containing this verse section and published it in the *Journal of Otani College* for the spring term this year. An English translation together with the original text will appear in *The Eastern Buddhist* Vol. V, No. 2, 1929.

[3] Translated into Chinese in A.D. 796–798.

the suppression of evils. These are the ten,[1] and in the execution of them, a Bodhisattva will not know when to get rested from his work, for it will have to continue as long as there is space extending in the ten quarters, as long as there is one being left in the universe to be saved, as long as there is one evil desire to be destroyed, a Bodhisattva will thus work incessantly, continuously, without interruption, with his body, speech, and mind, to the very end of the world.[2]

(1) By the vow to pay reverence to all the Buddhas is meant this: There is an inconceivable number of Buddha-lands filling up the ten quarters of the universe, their number is indeed inconceivable as the number of atoms composing the earth; and there is an inconceivable number of Buddhas residing in these innumerable Buddha-lands through the three divisions of time. And because of the virtue of Samantabhadra's life of vows a deep faith is awakened in a Bodhisattva's heart, and he will feel as if he were in the presence of all these Buddhas, whom he will salute with his body, speech, and mind that are pure; and dividing his one body into as many bodies as there are Buddhas in these innumerable Buddha-lands—innumerable as atoms composing the worlds, he will salute every one of them; he will not feel fatigued in doing so till the end of the universe.

(2) By the vow to praise the Tathagatas is meant this: The number of the Buddha-lands filling up the entire extent of the universe and the three divisions of time is as numberless as that of atoms composing the earth, and in each one of these numberless Buddha-lands there is again as innumerable a number of Buddhas as that of atoms composing

[1] A comparative study of these ten vows of Samantabhadra and those to be made by a Bodhisattva in the beginning of his spiritual career will be very interesting. We can say that these two sets of vows sum up the contents of the Buddhist experience. The vows of Samantabhadra are known in the *Laṅkāvatāra* as Daśānishṭhāpada (the ten inexhaustible clauses, 十無盡句). Pp. 123, 160, 214, 227, etc.

[2] Something like this is repeated at the end of each of the ten vows.

the earth. The Buddha is found surrounded by an ocean of Bodhisattvas in every one of these Buddha-lands, and a Bodhisattva will present himself before each one of these Buddhas with a deep understanding and a clear perception. The ocean of the merits of the Tathagata will then be praised with a tongue far more exquisite and eloquent than that of Sarasvatī, each tongue expressing a sea of inexhaustible voices, and each voice articulating a sea of words in every form possible. And this praising will go on without cessation till the end of the world and as long as there is a being in existence, and yet a Bodhisattva will never feel tired of his work.

(3) The vow to make all kinds of offerings to the Buddhas consists in offering to every one of these innumerable Buddhas as above mentioned such things as flowers, wreaths, music, umbrellas, garments, and all kinds of incense and ointment, and many other things—and all these offerings in such a large quantity as is equal to clouds or to a mountain; and a Bodhisattva will also burn before every one of the innumerable Buddhas all sorts of oil in such a measure as compares to an ocean. But of all the offerings one could thus make to a Buddha the best is that of the Dharma, which is to say, disciplining oneself according to the teaching, benefitting all beings, accepting all beings, suffering pains for all beings, nurturing every root of goodness, carrying out all the works of a Bodhisattva, and at the same time not keeping himself away from the thought of enlightenment. None of those material offerings above mentioned begin to compare with this form of moral offerings (*dharmapūja*). The former are not equal even to an infinitesimal fraction of the latter. Why? Because all Buddhas are born of moral offerings of this kind, because these are the true offerings, because the practising of the Dharma means the perfection of an offering one could make to a Buddha. A Bodhisattva will make these offerings without cessation to every one of those innumerable Buddhas till the end of the world and as

long as there is one being in existence, and in doing so he will never feel tired.

(4) The vow to repent all the sins committed by oneself and thereby to get rid of one's karma-hindrance is usually expressed in this formula:

> Whatever sins committd by me,
> They are due to my greed, anger, and folly,
> And done with my body, speech, and mind:
> All these I now make full confession and repent.

According to the sutra, all these sins, if they were really substantial, are thought to have filled the universe to its utmost ends and even over-flowing, of which a Bodhisattva now vows to repent without reserve from the depths of his heart, vowing that such will never be committed again by him, for he will henceforward always abiding in the pure precepts amass every sort of merit. And of this he will never get tired even to the end of the world.

(5) To be in sympathy with all beings for whatever good things they think, or feel, or do, constitutes the fifth vow of the Bodhisattva. All the Buddhas had gone through untold hardships before they attained full enlightenment. Since their first awakening of the thought of enlightenment, they never hesitated to accumulate all the merit that tended towards the attainment of the goal of their life, they never raised a thought of egotism even when they had to sacrifice their life and all that belonged to them. The Bodhisattva now vows to feel a sympathetic joy for all these doings of the Buddhas. Not only with the Buddhas does he this, but for every possible deed of merit, however insignificant, executed by any being in any path of existence, of any class of truth-seekers. The Bodhisattva with this vow will never be tired of putting it into practice till the end of the world and as long as there is one being in existence in this world.

(6) A Bodhisattva vows to ask every one of the Buddhas to revolve the Wheel of the Dharma, who are residing in these innumerable Buddha-lands filling up all

the worlds which are indeed as inconceivably numerous as atoms of the earth.

(7) And further the Bodhisattva will ask every one of the Buddhas not to enter into Nirvana if any is so disposed, he will ask this even of any Bodhisattvas, Arhats, Śrāvakas, or Pratyekabuddhas; for he wishes these superior beings to continue to live in the world and keep on benefitting all beings. He will never stop in this request as long as there is one being left in this world.

(8) The Bodhisattva vows to learn from the life of a Buddha who in this saha-world ever since his awakening of the thought of enlightenment have never ceased from exercising himself ungrudgingly, not even sparing his own life, for the sake of universal salvation. His reverential attitude towards the Dharma had been such as to make paper of his skin, a brush of his bones, and ink of his blood wherewith he copied the Buddhist sutras to the amount of Mount Sumeru. He cared not even for his life, how much less for the throne, for the palaces, gardens, villages, and other external things! By practising every form of mortification he finally attained supreme enlightenment under the Bodhi-tree. After this, he manifested all kinds of psychical powers, all kinds of transformations, all aspects of the Buddha-body, and placed himself sometimes among Bodhisattvas, sometimes among Śrāvakas, and Pratyekabuddhas, sometimes among Kshatriyas, among Brahmans, householders, lay-disciples, and sometimes even among Devas, Nāgas, human beings, and non-human beings. Wherever he was found, he preached with perfect eloquence, with a voice like thunder, in ordr to bring all beings into maturity according to their aspirations. Finally, he showed himself as entering into Nirvana. All these phases of the life of a Buddha, the Bodhisattva is determined to learn as models for his own life.

(9) In this universe life manifests itself in innumerable forms, each one differing from another in the way of its birth, in form, in the duration of life, in name, in mental

disposition, in intelligence, in aspiration, in inclination, in demeanour, in garment, in food, in social life, in the mode of dwelling, etc. However different thus they are, the Bodhisattva vows to live in accordance with the laws that govern every one of these beings in order to serve them, to minister to their needs, to revere them as his parents, as his teachers, or Arhats, or as Tathagatas, making no distinction among them in this respect. If they are sick, he will be to them a good physician; if they go astray he will show them the right path; if they are sunk in poverty he will supply them with a treasure; thus uniformly giving benefits to all beings according to their needs. Why does he do this? Because the Bodhisattva is convinced that by serving all beings he is serving all the Buddhas, that by revering all beings, by making them glad, he is revering and gladdening all the Buddhas. Why? Because a great compassionate heart is the substance of Tathagatahood. It is because of all beings that this compassionate heart is awakened, and because of this compassionate heart the thought of enlightenment is awakened, and because of this awakening supreme enlightenment is attained. It is like a great majestic tree growing in the desert: that it spreads out so luxuriously its stems, branches, leaves, flowers in all direction, is due to the supply of water under the ground. So with the majestic tree of enlightenment growing in the wilderness of birth-and-death, the roots are deeply planted among all beings, while it blooms out and bears fruit as Buddhas and Bodhisattvas. That these roots are well nourished is due to the pouring of the water of great compassion, without which there will indeed be no flowers and fruits of enlightenment as attained by Buddhas and Bodhisattvas. Why? Because of the water of great compassion all beings are benefitted and perfected as to attain the highest supreme enlightenment. Therefore, enlightenment is dependent upon beings. If there were no beings, there would be no Bodhisattvas attaining supreme enlightenment. Thus the Bodhisattva must have a good understanding in this. As he regards with impartiality the minds of all beings, he is able to perfect his great compassionate heart, and as he moves among all beings with this great compassionate heart in accordance with their modes of living and feeling and thinking, he is able to complete his offerings to the Tathagatas. In doing this the Bodhisattva will know no fatigue even to the end of the world.

(10) Whatever merits the Bodhisattva acquires by paying sincere respect to all the Buddhas and also by practising all kinds of meritorious deeds as already described, they will all be turned over to the benefits of all beings filling up this entire universe. He will thus turn all his merits towards making beings feel at ease, free from diseases, turn away from evil doings, practise all deeds of goodness, so that every possible evil may be suppressed and the right road to Nirvana be opened for the gods and men. If there be any beings who are suffering the results of their evil karma committed in the past, the Bodhisattva will be ready to sacrifice himself and bear all the pains for the miserable creatures in order to release them from karma and finally make them realise supreme enlightenment. In this transference of merit onto another, the Bodhisattva knows indeed no fatigue to the end of the world, etc.

Then concludes the Bodhisattva Samantabhadra, "These are, O sons of good families, the Bodhisattva-Mahasattva's ten great vows."

III

SOME OF THE IMPORTANT THEORIES EXPOUNDED IN THE LANKAVATARA

III

SOME OF THE IMPORTANT THEORIES EXPOUNDED IN THE LANKAVATARA

When the *Laṅkāvatāra* is studied apart from its connection with the philosophy of Zen Buddhism, it is usually as one of the text-books of the Yogācāra school. As was already stated in the first part of the present work (p. 53), this was done very early in the history of the sutra when the Chinese Buddhist scholars belonging to the school of the *Mahāyāna-parisaṁgraha-śāstra* attempted to interpret the sutra according to Asanga's teaching. Whether this view is correct or not is another question, but the fact is that the sutra contains the theories relating to the so-called psychological explanation of existence such as the doctrine of Cittamātra (mind-only)[1] and the system of eight Vijñānas, which also make up the contents of the Yogācāra philosophy. To complete, therefore, the study of the *Laṅkāvatāra,* these theories are also to be examined even though cursorily.

Next, the doctrine of Emptiness (*śūnyatā*) or No-birth (*anutpāda*) is the foundation of Mahayana Buddhism; it is not necessarily confined to the Madhyamika school of Nāgārjuna, though this has been exaggerated too far so that some scholars are led to regard Emptiness as the exclusive property of this school. The fact as it stands is that it is a common possession of all the Buddhist schools psychological as well as logical. The *Laṅkāvatāra* is thus insistent too on the doctrine of Emptiness, indeed as much as the *Prajñā-pāramitā-sūtras,* only it uses the term "no-birth" or "unborn" (*anutpāda* or *anutpattika*) more frequently than "emptiness" or "vacuity." Both connote the same thing

[1] The distinction between the Cittamātra and the Vijñaptimātra or Vijñānamātra has been noticed elsewhere in this book (pp. 181, 182), but for its specific treatment see p. 278 et seq.

and are quite interchangeable. A chapter has thus been reserved in this book for the treatment of this idea as expounded in the *Laṅkāvatāra.*

The question of Buddhahood is another important idea in a work claiming to elucidate the *Laṅkāvatāra* in its various aspects. Not only is its conception of the Tathagata to be examined but also that of the Triple Body (*trikāya*). Though these two are closely related—indeed they are two sides of the same shield—I think it best to treat them separately. The doctrine of the Triple Body is not yet formally systematised in the sutra, as is for example in the *Suvarṇa-prabhāsa* which has a special chapter devoted to the treatment of the subject.[1] The adumbration of the theory is, however, clearly traceable in the *Laṅkāvatāra.* I have tried to make the point clear in the following pages apart from the notion of Tathagatahood.

The four topics have thus been chosen as requiring special consideration in the *Laṅkāvatāra* when it is dissociated from the teaching of Zen Buddhism, which are: (1) The Doctrine of "Mind-only" (*cittamātra*), (2) The Idea of No-birth (*anutpāda*), (3) The Dogma of the Triple Body (*trikāya*), and (4) The Tathagata. These, however, do not exhaust the whole range of thoughts finding expression in the *Laṅkāvatāra,* there is more material which may claim room in these *Studies.* No doubt, what is left after the four topics just mentioned and outside its connection with Zen, is not so weighty as to require any extensive treatment, as far as the sutra itself is concerned. The last chapter is then devoted to these minor subjects: (1) The One Vehicle and the Three Vehicles, (2) The Five Fatal Sins, (3) The Six Pāramitās, (4) The Four Dhyānas, and (5) Meat-eating.

[1] Though this is missing in the Sanskrit MSS in our possession, it appears in the Tibetan as well as in the Chinese translation.

1. THE DOCTRINE OF "MIND-ONLY" (*cittamātra*)

One of the Principal Theories in the Sutra

Something about the doctrine of "Mind-only" has already been stated (pp. 169 ff), but more will have to be written about it if the *Laṅkāvatāra* is to be treated as an independent Mahayana sutra, not necessarily in connection with the teaching of Zen Buddhism. There is no doubt that the purpose of compiling the sutra was, on the part of the author or editor, to emphasise the all-importance of the self-realisation of the truth (*pratyātmadharma*) in its practical bearing on the life of the Bodhisattva. But when self-realisation is to be given its content so that the experience becomes communicable, that is, when it is made the subject of a philosophical discourse, something more has to be said. The mere statement of the fact that the truth realised in the inmost consciousness constitutes the reason of the Buddhist life, is altogether too inadequate to convince other people: the *Laṅkāvatāra* has to be more than an utterance of the inner experience. To be consistent with the general philosophical tradition of Mahayana Buddhism, it has to advocate the doctrine of "Mind-only." We may, therefore, say that the teaching of Zen Buddhism, philosophically stated, is a pure idealism. This chapter will now be devoted to an elucidation of the *Laṅkāvatāra* doctrine of "Mind-only" (*cittamātra*).

What is then meant by the "Mind-only"? Let me quote some gāthās[1] relative to the subject.

"When things existent are regarded as being free from [the bondage of] mutual dependence, there is decidedly nothing but Mind, I say, nothing but Mind (25).

"[Mind] is the measure [of all things], it is the abode of their self-nature, and has nothing to do with causation and the world; it is perfect in its nature, absolutely pure. This is the measure indeed, I say (26).

[1] Pp. 153–154, gg. 25–33.

"The worldly way of thinking (*prajñaptisatyatā*) views [the Mind] as the individual self (*ātman*), but there is no such substantial reality. So with the substance (*skandhatā*) of the Skandhas, the worldly way of thinking views it as real; in reality it has no existence (27).

"There are four sorts of sameness for those who discipline themselves in religious life: appearance, causation, coming into existence, and the fourth is egolessness (28).[1]

"[Mind] is beyond all philosophical views, is apart from discrimination, it is not attainable, nor is it ever born: I say, there is nothing but Mind (29).

"It is not an existence, nor is it a non-existence; it is indeed beyond both existence and non-existence; it is Suchness,[2] it is even released from mind: I say, there is nothing but Mind (30).

"Suchness, emptiness, the limit, Nirvana, Dharmadhātu, variety of will-bodies—they are nothing but Mind, I say (31).

"Out of Mind spring innumerable things, conditioned by discrimination and habit-energy; these things people accept as an external world. I say, there is nothing but Mind (32).

"What appears to be external does not exist in reality, it is indeed Mind that is seen as multiplicity; the body, property, and abode—all these, I say, are nothing but Mind (33)."[3]

In the "Sagāthakam" we have the following stanzas (358–359, 366–370):

"When the "Mind-only" is understood, external objects are set aside. discrimination ceases; and we have the Middle Way (358).

"There is the 'Mind-only,' there are no objects to be

[1] It is difficult to know what these four sorts of sameness mean and in what connection they stand to the verses above and below.

[2] For *tathatā* T'ang has *tathā*, reading "so it is with mind which is detached."

[3] Gg. 32–33 are placed between gg. 28 and 29 in the Sung translation.

seen; when there are no objects to see, Mind is not born; and this is called by myself and others the Middle Way (359).

"Without being born they are seen as born; they are not dead but are seen as dead; they are simultaneously visible in myriads of countries even as the moon is reflected in many waters (366).

"One is seen as many, they make it rain, they ignite fires, as is willed by their minds; so they declare that there is the 'Mind-only' (367).

"To say the 'Mind-only' is by mind, is also born of mind; particular forms and figures in all possible varieties, when thoroughly understood, are no more than Mind itself (368).

"Of Buddhas, Śrāvaka-forms, Pratyekabuddha-forms, and other various forms, it is declared by them that they are nothing but Mind (369).

"Their forms, although really of no-form, are seen as having forms by all beings from the world of no-form down to the hells; they are nothing but the workings of Mind itself (370)."

From these quotations some of which are more shrouded in obscurity than others, the reader may gain a general idea as to what the doctrine of "Mind-only" means. The sutra sometimes makes summary statements like these:

1. *Cittamātraṁ lokam.* (The world is nothing Mind.) P. 73, g. 136.
2. *Cittabāhyādarśanam.* (Nothing is to be seen outside the Mind.) P. 42, lines 10–11.
3. *Svacittamātraṁ traidhātukam.* (The triple world is Mind itself.) P. 80, line 7; p. 42, line 12; p. 123, line 17; p. 213, lines 11–12; etc.
4. *Cittaṁhi traidhātuka-yoniḥ.* (Mind produces the triple world.) P. 268, g. 36.
5. *Tribhavacittamātram.* (The triple existence is nothing but Mind.) P. 208, line 13.
6. *Cittaṁ hi sarvam.* (All is Mind.) "Sagāthakam," g. 134.

7. *Sarvarūpāvabhāsaṁ hi yadā cittaṁ pravartate.* (When Mind evolves, all forms are manifested.) "Sagāthakam," g. 93.

Speaking in the modern way, the theory of "Mind-only" is a form of pure idealism. All that we habitually consider having an objective value, such as our own body (*deha*), property (*bhoga*), and the land (*pratishṭhāna*) where we have our abodes, are no more than our own mind projected and recognised as externally extending and real. Even Nirvana, the truth of suchness, emptiness, reality—all these are but our mental creations, having no objective validity as far as they are forms of discrimination. We, ordinary mortals, see the Buddha in his multifarious manifestations, which, however, are the reflections of our ideas formulated in the mind by virtue of inherited memory (*vāsanā*) mysteriously working from time immemorial.

Passages Quoted Relative to the Doctrine

The doctrine of "Mind-only" runs through the *Laṅkāvatāra* as if it were warp and weft of the sutra. To understand it is to realise the ultimate truth, and not to understand it is to transmigrate through many a birth-and-death. The sutra lays much emphasis on the importance of the doctrine, so much, indeed, that it makes everything hinge on this one point, the salvation of the world, not to say anything of the individual. Read the following passages culled at random from the sutra:

1. The "Mind-only" leads to the realisation of the ultimate truth (*paramārtha*). "Language, O Mahāmati, is not the ultimate truth; what is attainable by language is not the ultimate truth. Why? Because the ultimate truth is what is enjoyed by the wise; by means of speech one can enter into the truth, but words themselves are not the truth. It is the self-realisation inwardly experienced by the wise through their supreme wisdom, and does not belong to the domain of words, discrimination, or intelligence; and, therefore, dis-

crimination does not reveal the ultimate truth itself. Moreover, O Mahāmati, language is subject to birth and destruction, is unsteady, mutually conditioning, and produced according to the law of causation; and what is mutually conditioning and produced according to the law of causation is not the ultimate truth, nor does it come out of such conditions, for it is above aspects of relativity, and words are incapable of producing it, and again as the ultimate truth is in conformity with the view that the visible world is no more than our own mind, and as there are no such external objects appearing in their multifarious aspects of individuation, the ultimate truth is not subject to discrimination."[1]

"O Mahāmati, when a man sees into the abode of reality where all things are, he enters upon the truth that what appears to him is not other than mind itself."[2]

2. The "Mind-only" is grasped by pure thought. "Absolute intelligence (*prajñā*) does not belong to the two Vehicles; it has, indeed, nothing to do with particular objects; the Śrāvakas are attached to the notion of being; absolute intelligence, pure in essence, belongs to the Tathagata who has entered upon the 'Mind-only.' "[3]

3. Bodhisattvas do not enter into Nirvāna because of their understanding of the truth of the "Mind-only." "All the various doings in the triple world (*traidhātuka*) such as the grading of stages in the discipline of the Bodhisattva and his steady promotion are nothing but the manifestations of Mind. This is not understood by the ignorant, therefore all these things are taught by the Buddhas. And again, the Śrāvakas and the Pratyekabuddhas, when they reach the eighth stage, become so intoxicated with the bliss of mental tranquillity (*nirodha-samāpatti*) that they fail to realise that the visible is nothing but the Mind. They are still in the realm of individuation, their insight into reality is not yet pure (*vivikta*). The Bodhisattvas, on the other hand, are alive to their original vows flowing out of their all-embracing

[1] Pp. 87–88. [2] P. 112. [3] P. 158.

loving hearts; they do not enter into Nirvana; they know that the visible world is nothing but the manifestation of Mind itself; they are free from such ideas as mind (*citta*), will (*manas*), consciousness (*manovijñāna*), external world, self-substance, and distinguishing marks."[1]

4. The "Mind-only" and the dualistic conception of being and non-being, which is the outcome of wrong discrimination (*vikalpa*), stand opposite to each other, and are irreconcilable until the latter is absorbed into the former. Its teaching, intellectually speaking, is to show the fallacy of a world-conception based on discrimination, or rather upon wrong discrimination, in order to get us back into the right way of comprehending reality as it is. "As the ignorant and unenlightened do not comprehend the teaching of the 'Mind-only,' they are attached to a variety of external objects; they go from one form of discrimination to another, such as the duality of being and non-being, oneness and otherness, bothness and not-bothness, permanence and impermanence, self-substance, habit-energy, causation, etc. After discriminating these notions, they go on clinging to them as objectively real and unchangeable, like those animals who, driven by thirst in the summer-time, run wildly after imaginary springs."[2]

"To think that primary elements really exist is due to wrong discrimination and nothing else. When the truth of the 'Mind-only' is understood, there are no external objects to be seen; they are all due to the discrimination of what one sees in one's own mind."[3]

5. Not to understand the "Mind-only" leads one to eternal transmigrations. "As the philosophers fail to go beyond dualism, they hurt not only themselves but the ignorant. Going around continually from one path of existence to another, not understanding that what is seen is no more than

[1] An abstract of pp. 213–214.
[2] Cf. pp. 90, 104, 149, 208, 234, etc.
[3] P. 123.

their own mind, and adhering to the notion that things external are endoved with self-substance, they are unable to free themselves from wrong discrimination."[1]

6. As to the relation between the "Mind-only" theory and the conception of the Ālayavijñāna, mention will be made later; here let it only be remarked that the rising of the Ālaya is due to our taking the manifestations of the mind for a world of objective realities. "The Ālayavijñāna is its own subject (=cause) and object (=support); and it clings to a world of its own mental presentations, a system of mentality that evolves mutually conditioning. It is like the waves of the ocean, stirred by the wind; that is, a world made visible by Mind itself where the mental waves come and go."[2] This ocean-and-waves simile is a favourite one with Mahayana Buddhists.

7. Thus we see that there is nothing in the world that is not of the mind, hence the "Mind-only" doctrine. And this applies with especial emphasis to all logical controversies, which, according to the *Laṅkāvatāra,* are mere subjective fabrications. "The body, property, and abode—these are no more than the shadows of Mind (*citta*), the ignorant do not understand it. They make assertions (*samāropa,* 建立) or refutations (*apavāda,* 誹謗), and this elaboration is due to Mind only, apart from which nothing is obtainable."[3] The author of the *Laṅkāvatāra* does not stop here, he goes further on and declares that even the spiritual stages of Bodhisattvahood are merely the reflections of mind. "The [Buddha-] abodes and the Buddha-stages are of Mind only in which there are no shadows; that is what is taught by the Buddhas past, present, and future."[4]

8. Lastly, when all forms of individuation are negated, there takes place a revulsion (*parāvṛitti*) in our minds, and

[1] P. 62.

[2] P. 127.

[3] Cf. p. 70. The reading of this gāthā varies in all four of the texts, one Sanskrit and three Chinese. I have followed the T'ang.

[4] P. 215.

we see that the truth that there is nothing but Mind from the very beginning and thereby we are emancipated from the fetters of wrong discrimination.[1]

The Citta and its Evolution

Now the question naturally suggesting itself is: what is really meant by *cittamātram,* or "mind-only"? It is often phrased, *svacittadṛiśyamātram,* meaning "own-mind-seen-only." What is the Citta that is here rendered as "Mind"?

Let us see first what the *Laṅkāvatāra* means by Citta. Citta as noticed elsewhere is used in two ways, general and specific Where it is used in a general way, it is the name given to the sum of all mental activities, including both the mind proper and its various functions. But where the mind is divided into Citta, Manas, Manovijñāna, and the five Sense-vijñānas, (eye, ear, nose, tongue, and body), the Citta gains a specific signification. It is the principle of unification by which all the activities are understood as issuing from one centre. The Manas is a discriminating agency by which the homogeneous, undifferentiated Citta is divided into two parts: the one as the seer and the other as the seen; the one as the grasping ego and the other as an object grasped. The Manas is not only an intellective but also a conative principle. The Vijñāna, that is, the Manovijñāna is separated from the Manas, only retaining the latter's intellective function, and may be translated as the intellect; in which case the Manas may be regarded as corresponding to the will and the affection. The five Vijñānas are thus the five senses which discriminate a world of individual forms, each within its own sense-field.

When the Citta is thus considered in its specific sense, it may seem to be an abstract principle devoid of content. But, according to the *Laṅkāvatāra,* this is not the case: for the Citta is rich in content, and just because of this inner richness, it is able to evolve out of itself a world of infinite multitudinousness. It is, indeed, an inexhaustible reservoir

[1] The "Sagāthakam," gg. 275–282.

of seeds (*bīja*) which have been accumulated therein since the beginningless past. So the definition of Citta is as follows: *Cittena cīyate karma.*[1] That karma is accumulated by Citta means that the latter takes in all that goes on in the mind and also all that is done by the body. Technically stated, every deed (*karma*), mental and physical, leaves its seeds behind which are deposited in the Citta, and the Citta has been hoarding them since time immemorial. It is the rich repository of all the thoughts, feelings, desires, instincts, etc., no matter how they have come to act, that is, whether merely stirred up in the inmost recesses of one's consciousness, or carried out by the body into deed, or checked in the incipient stages of their activity. Psychologically, the Citta may thus be regarded as corresponding to the Subcouscious.

This repository-Citta, so long as it remains contented in and with itself, is absolutely quiet and no waves are seen stirring on its *cittam avyākṛitaṁ nityam.*[2] It is in its nature non-discriminative, it does not pretend to divide and analyse itself. It may dance like the dancer (*naṭavannṛityate cittam*),[3] but if there is nobody to keep company with her and no audience to applaud her, what is the use of her dancing? A solitary dance is the same as no dance whatever, the dancing is the same as no dancing; but it gains significance as soon as there appears some one beside the dancer.

This somebody is at hand who keeps company with the Citta; not only that, it calls up an audience and creates the stage on a grand scale. The panoramic world of particular objects now comes up into view, the manager's name is Manas.

> "Citta dances like the dancer,
> Manas resembles the jester,
> The Vijñāna, in company with the five, imagines
> What is presented [i.e. an external world] to be
> the stage."[4]

[1] Pp. 158, 38. [2] "Mind eternally quiescent," p. 278, l. 3.
[3] "The mind dances like a dancer," p. 224, l. 2.
[4] P. 244. See also p. 195 of the present work.

The Manas is not, however, an independent agent acting on the Citta from the outside, it is indeed the creation of the Citta itself. "Depending upon the Ālaya [=Citta[1]], the Manas arises; allied with the Citta and Manas, the Vijñāna arises."[2] Again, "[with the Citta] as its cause and supporting it, the Manas walks along depending on the Citta; the Citta is caused to move by the Vijñāna, and there is an interdependence among them."[3] From this it is evident that the Manas depends on the Citta for its existence, and at the same time Citta takes Manas for the object of its activity. Without Manas there will be no mentation, and without mentation Citta's own existence will not be known. The one, thus, gives support to the other, and at the same time is supported by the other.

The business of Manas is thus twofold: (1) to reflect on the Citta, and (2) to make Citta visualise itself as object. This is called "arranging " (*vidhīyate*),[4] or "putting in order" (*vicīyate*),[5] or "reflecting" (*manyati*),[6] which is the function of the Manas. It is again described as "walking in two ways" (*mano hyubhayasaṁcaram*),[7] which means the dualistic character of the Manas, as against the absolute unity of the Citta. One Citta has now been differentiated into Citta and Manas, and this latter particularised Citta is no more neutral, non-discriminative, and non-functioning; for all the karma-seeds hitherto lying dormant in the absolute Citta have now begun to sprout out in full vigour. These germinating seeds are now distinguished or discriminated (*chindati*),[8] by the Vijñāna known as Manovijñāna, by the aid of the five senses, wherewith creating a world of indivi-

[1] *Cittam-ālayavijñānam*, p. 278, g. 102.

[2] P. 300, g. 269.

[3] "*Tad hetukam tad ālambya manogatisamāśrayam, hetuṁ dadāti cittasya vijñānaṁ ca samāśritam*" (p. 127, g. 180).

[4] P. 158, l. 3.

[5] P. 46, l. 17. One MS reads, *vidhīyate*.

[6] P. 323, g. 461; p. 278, l. 1; p. 48, g. 116.

[7] P. 278, g. 103.

[8] P. 323, g. 461.

duals. The latter is called "the seen," or "what is presented" (*dṛiśya*), which is now imagined (*kalpeti*) as real and substantial, and from this arise all kinds of spiritual tribulations.

The distinction between Manas and Manovijñāna is that Manas is conative and Manovijñāna is intellective (*vijānāti*, or *manyate*).[1] While intellection is not lacking in Manas, what predominates is the will, especially since the intellective function has more or less effectively been surrendered to the Vijñāna, i.e., Manovijñāna. In fact, however, all these function together and simultaneously, as we have seen in the simile of the theatre.[2] Further quotations from the "Sagāthakam" will be helpful.

"Depending upon the Ālaya there evolves the Manas; and depending upon Citta and Manas there evolves the Vijñāna (869).

"There are the maturing and development of Manas and Vijñānas, that is, Manas is born of the Ālaya and the Vijñānas of the Manas (870).

"From the Ālaya are stirred up all the mental activities like waves; with habit-energy as cause they are born in accordance with [the law of] origination (871).

"Grasping mind as their objects and bound by a chain of successive moments, the Mano[-vijñāna], eye[-vijñāna], etc. are evolved to create forms, signs, and figures (872).

"Bound by bad habit-energy of the beginningless past, something resembling an external world is produced, and the mind is seen in the aspect of multiplicity—this is what blocks the understanding of the philosophers (873).

"With that [i.e., *vāsanā*] as cause and depending on it, other things [i.e. vijñānas] are evolved, and thus there take place various views of existence and a revolving cycle of birth and death (873)."

To be exact, the Citta is more than the mind as the

[1] P. 48, g. 116.

[2] Pp. 224, 19 (g. 433).

psychologist understands it: it has more of a metaphysical connotation; it is not merely an empirical mind. The Citta when it is understood in its absolute aspect is transcendental; it denotes something at the back of the mind of the psychologist, who, depending on his scientific methods, may fail to reach. It implies more than the sum-total of the Citta, Manas, Manovijñāna, and the Vijñānas. When the *Laṅkāvatāra* speaks of the "Mind-only," therefore, its foundation lies much deeper than the ordinary form of idealism. Otherwise intuition into the truth of Cittamātra cannot result in the spiritual emancipation which is the object of Mahayana discipline.

The "Sagāthakam" (g. 459) gives the following as synonyms of Citta:

Cittaṁ vikalpo vijñaptir mano vijñānam eva ca,
Ālayaṁ tribhavaśceshṭā ete cittasya paryapāḥ.[1]

Except Ālayavijñāna, the rest should be regarded as quite different from what the Citta is, unless we take them to mean that all these functions of the mind issue from the Citta, or that originally they lie quiescent in the Citta. In the gāthā following this, another puzzling statement is made. "Life, warmth, Vijñāna, Ālaya, life-force, Manas and Manovijñāna—they are synonyms of discrimination."[2] This is a grand mixing-up. When the two verses are put together and examined to draw something conclusive and definite about Citta, we get completely lost in the maze thus created. The only way to understand them intelligently will be to regard Citta as the container of all things, contradictory or otherwise. For is it not said that there is "Mind itself" (*citta-mātra*)? But coming down to the ordinary plane of reasoning, why did the writer of these verses in the "Sagāthakam" specially refer to such ideas as *vikalpa, vijñapti,*

[1] Citta, discrimination, representation, manas, and the vijñāna, ālaya, the wish for the triple existence,—these are citta's other names.

[2] *Āyurushmātha vijñānam ālayo jīvitendriyam, manaś ca manovijñānaṁ vikalpasya viśeshaṇam* (g. 460).

jīvitendriya, and *tribhavaśceshṭā* in connection with Citta? No doubt the *Laṅkāvatāra* has been found very difficult to understand systematically by all scholars, not only literally but philosophically.

Whatever this may be, the Citta is considered to be pure and immaculate (*pariśuddhi*) in its essential nature[1] in the *Laṅkāvatāra*, i.e., it is good and free from evil flowings (*kuśala-anāsrava*).[2] "The Citta is not separated from habit-energy (*vāsanā*), nor is the Citta together with habit-energy though it is enwrapped with the latter; there are no marks in it of differentiation. Habit-energy being with the Mano-vijñāna is soiled, and the Citta which is like a robe that is perfectly white does not shine out on account of habit-energy. As it is declared by me that the sky is neither a reality nor a non-reality, so is the Ālaya in the body[3] not limited by [the dualism] of being and non-being. When a revulsion (*vyāvṛitti*, generally *parāvṛitti*) takes place, the Citta is disengaged from turbidity; as it understands all existence, I state that the Citta is the Buddha."[4] Being pure or good does not always mean morally pure and good, it means rather logically pure, that is, absolutely free from the dualistic way of reasoning. Therefore, the sutra never tires of repeating that in order to realise the fact of the "Mind-only" the realm of dualities which is the product of false discrimination (*vikalpa*) must be transcended. False discrimination is the principle of turbidity which hides the truth from being clearly perceived. Buddhahood consists in removing this turbidity of discrimination, for the removing is emancipation and the restoring of the Citta to its original purity. This is known in the *Laṅkāvatāra* as inner realisation (*pratyātmādhigama*).

[1] P. 221, l. 1; 222, l. 16; etc.

[2] P. 235, l. 5.

[3] *Kāya*; this is missing in the T'ang translation; the addition does not seem to clarify the context.

[4] P. 296, gg. 236–239; cf. also p. 358, gg. 750–756.

The Citta and the Ālayavijñāna and the Ātman

Along with the conception of Citta there was that of the Vijñāna system, and also the deepening of the ego-idea. Early Buddhists denied the reality of an ego-substance, which was in accordance with their psychology, but the idea of ego was not necessarily the same as the assertion of self-will or egotism; even when self-will was destroyed, the idea remained. What was destroyed was the lower self and not the higher self, the smaller self and not the larger self; for the annihilation of the lower and smaller self was only possible through the assertion of the higher and larger one. Buddhists never thought of putting an end to whatever might go under the name of self. The idea of ego-substance (*ātman*) was inimical to the development of the higher centre of the individual, nor was it in harmony with the experience of their religious life. How is the question of the higher life to be solved, then? Where is it to be placed in the system of the Vijñānas? With this question an absolute Citta came to be separated from the empirical ego, and this absolute Citta to be identified with the Ālaya, which was now made the foundation of the whole Vijñāna group. So we have "*cittam-ālayavijñānam*"[1] and this then furnishes the reason of the inner realisation as taking place in the Tathāgata-garbha.[2] The philosophers take the Tathāgata-garbha, or the Ālayavijñāna[3] for the ego, that is, the lower, narrower, empirical ego, which is, however, far from the teaching of the Buddha. The real immaculate ego, *śuddhisatyātman,* going beyond the grasp of relative knowledge, cannot so easily be understood and so readily be asserted as is done by the ignorant. We thus read (gg. 757–771):

[1] P. 278, g. 102. [2] P. 357, g. 746.

[3] The following equations hold true: the transcendental Citta = Ālayavijñāna = Tathāgata-garbha (pp. 278, 235, 222, etc.). Ālaya is a psychological term belonging to the Vijñāna system; Tathāgata-garbha has a religious connotation; and Citta has been in use since the early days of Buddhism as denoting a certain function of the mind.

"Born or unborn, the Mind always remains pure: those who reason about the existence of an ego-substance—why do they not prove it by illustrations? (744).

"Those who vainly reason without understanding the truth are lost in the jungle of the Vijñānas, running about here and there and trying to justify their view of ego-substance (745).

"The self realised in your inmost consciousness appears in its purity, this is the Tathāgata-garbha which is not the realm of those given up to mere reasoning (746).

"When the Skandhas are analysed, there is that which apprehends and that which is apprehended; by understanding this aspect of relativity, true knowledge is born (747).

"The philosophers think that the Ālaya or where the Garbha is oriented, is the seat of thought and one with the self: but such are not the teachings declared [by the Buddhas] (748).

"When these are well discriminated, there is emancipation and seeing into the truth; by moral cultivation and intellectual training the evil passions are abandoned and made pure (749).

"The Citta, pure in its original nature and free from the category of finite and infinite is the undefiled Tathāgata-garbha, which is wrongly apprehended by sentient beings (750).

"As the beautiful colour of gold and the brilliancy of a [precious] stone are revealed by purification, so is the Ālaya which is hidden in the Skandhas revealed to sentient beings (751).

"The Buddha is neither an individual soul nor the Skandhas, he is the wisdom of non-outflowings (*jñānam-anāsravam*), and knowing that he is eternal quietude I take refuge in him (752).

"The Citta, pure in its original nature, is united with the minor impurities, Manas, and others, and with the ego—this is what is taught by the best of preachers (753).

"The Citta is in its original nature pure, but the Manas and others are not, and by them various karmas are accumulated, and as the result there are two sorts of impurities [or defilements] (754).

"On account of external defilements from the beginningless past the pure self is contaminated; it is like a soiled garment which can be cleansed (755).

"When the garment is unsoiled, or when gold is freed of its defects, they are restored and will not be destroyed; so it is with the self when remedied of its defects (756).

"As an unintelligent man seeks for the abode of sweet sound in the body of the lute, conch-shell, or kettle-drum, so does he look for a soul within the Skandhas (757).

"Like the gems in the treasure-house or like water under the ground, which are invisible though known to be there, so is the soul in the Skandhas (758).

"While the whole system of the Citta-activity with its proper functions is in union with the Skandhas, the unintelligent fail to comprehend it, so it is also with the soul in the Skandhas (759).

"Like the contents of the womb whose existence is known but invisible, so is with the soul in the Skandhas which is likewise not perceivable to the dull-minded (760).

"As the essence of medicinal herbs, as fire hidden in fuel, so the soul in the Skandhas is not perceived by the dull-minded (761).

"As the unwise fail to see that in all things existent there is the nature of eternity and emptiness, so they do not see the soul in the Skandhas (762).

"If no real self exists, there will be no stages [of Bodhisattvahood], no self-mastery, no psychic power, no anointment of the highest order, no excellent Samādhi (763).

"If the nihilist come and ask, 'If there be the self, show it to me,' the wise one's answer will be 'Show me your own discrimination' (764).

"Those who deny the self are the opponents of the

Buddhist teaching, their views are one-sided advocating either 'It is,' or 'It is not'; they are to be rejected by a general session of the Bhikshus (765).

"The doctrine of the self is illuminating, it releases one from the faults of the philosophers, it burns up the forest of selflessness like the fire arising at the end of the world (766).

"In sugar, sugar-cane, candy, honey, dadhi (curd), or tila-oil, there is its own taste; but one who has not tasted it does not comprehend it (767).

"In five different manners the ignorant may search for the self by lifting up the Skandhas, but they fail to see it, while the wise one sees it and is thereby released (768).

"Even by means of knowledge, illustrations, and other things, one is unable to gain an insight just into the Citta; how can one then gain an insight into the signification accumulated in it? (769).

"Not understanding that individuation is due to one mind (*citta*), the reasoning ones cling to the view that there is no cause, there is no evolving (770).

"The Yogin sees into the mind (*citta*) and the mind is not seen in the mind, the seeing is born of what is seen, and of what cause is the seen born? (771)."

These passages are to be carefully weighed, for if otherwise they dangerously verge on the doctrine of an individual ego-substance which is persistently denied by Buddhists, Mahayana as well as Hinayana. The main idea is that there is a principle of consciousness from which the whole Vijñāna system evolves and is set in operation, but which is not to be regarded as something individual residing in the five Skandhas. Ordinarily, this principle unknown, invisible, and beyond the grasp of the sense-vijñānas is taken for an ego, and unenlightened people try to locate it in the body just as they try to take hold of the pleasant notes that issue from the lute, or of the effective, curative agency that is hidden in a medicinal herb. Apart from the lute, the sound is non-existent; so with the curative quality, it does not exist outside the herb itself. The presence of the principle is to be realised inwardly by intuition and not by a process of analysis. This intuition, in other words, the "wisdom of non-outflowings" (*jñānam-anāsravam*), constitutes the original nature of the mind which is described in the above quotations as "originally pure" (*prakṛiti-prabhāsvaram*). If this is considered something concrete and individual, something separable from and capable of being picked out among objects of particularisation, saying, "Here it is!" this will be resorting to dualistic discrimination which is condemned so much in the *Laṅkāvatāra.* At all events it is evident that there was historically a close connection between the ego idea and the evolution of Ālayavijñāna.

The following noted stanza quoted whenever there is an allusion to the philosophy of the Yogācāra is taken from the Chinese *Sandhi-nirmocana-sūtra*:

"The Ādāna-vijñāna[1] is deep and subtle,
Where all the seeds are evolved like a stream;
I do not elucidate this for the ignorant,
For they are apt to imagine it an ego-substance."

When Citta among early Buddhist scholars came to denote "accumulation," Vijñāna, "discrimination," or "representation," and Manas, "deliberation" or "reflection," it was natural for the later psychologists to designate Citta as Ālaya or Ālayavijñāna as belonging to the general body of various Vijñānas. *Ālaya* means "storage" or "treasure-house," where all the results, called "seeds" (*bīja*), of one's mental and physical activities are hoarded, i.e., accumulated, and it does not stand outside the Vijñāna system: it is one of them though in the most fundamental sense of the expression. And for this reason the Ālaya is liable to be regarded as the ego-substance—the very idea against which Buddhism has been fighting ever since its inception. The *Laṅkāvatāra* is thus quite anxious to dispel this confusion.

[1] Ādāna is another name for the Ālayavijñāna, meaning "grasping" or "receiving."

In what follows the Buddha answers the question of Mahāmati as regards the identity of Ātman and Tathāgata-garbha which, as was mentioned before, is the same as Ālayavijñāna.

There is no doubt that this idea of Ālayavijñāna or Ādānavijñāna or Tathāgata-garbha or Citta caused confusion in the minds of some Mahayana Buddhists who have been brought up in the teaching of Anātman (non-ego). Hence the following question proposed by the Bodhisattva Mahāmati:[1] "The Tathāgata-garbha is mentioned in the text of a sutra and described as thoroughly pure and undefiled in its essential nature, as endowed with the thirty-two marks,[2] entering into the physical body of a sentient being, and enveloped within such matter as the Skandhas, Dhātus, and Āyatanas, and soiled with the dirt of greed, anger, folly, and discrimination, [but really] described by the Buddha as eternal, permanent, auspicious, and unchanged. If so, is not this Tathāgata-garbha something of the same order as the Ātman in the teaching of the philosophers? They teach the Ātman as eternal, creator, devoid of attributes, mighty, and imperishable."

To this question raised by Mahāmati and also cherished by most Bodhisattvas and scholars, the Buddha gives the following answer: "O Mahāmati, the doctrine of Ātman by the philosophers is not the same as my teaching of the Tathāgata-garbha. For what the Tathagatas teach is emptiness (*śūnyatā*), limit of reality (*bhūtakoṭi*), Nirvana, no-birth, no-appearance, no-desire (*apraṇihita*), and such other conceptions, with which the Tathāgata-garbha is characterised, and by which the ignorant are saved from the occasion of cherishing a sense of fear about the Buddhist teaching of non-ego, and they are thus finally led by the Tathagatas to the realm of no-discrimination and no-imagery, that is,

[1] P. 77 et seq.

[2] How did this notion of the Tathāgata-garbha being endowed with the thirty-two marks of a great personality get in here? It is all right in the case of a personal Buddha or Tathagata, but how can we make this an attribute of the Tathāgata-garbha itself?

to the entrance of the Tathāgata-garbha. O Mahāmati, Bodhisattvas-Mahāsattvas of the present and the future are warned not to entertain any idea of ego-substance here...."[1]

This explains how the Buddha came to talk about the Tathāgata-garbha and how it differs from the ordinary notion of the ego. With the philosophers the ego does not rise above the level of empiricism. The existence of the transcendental ego as maintaind by Buddhists, which apparently contradicts their traditional view of non-ego, is hard to understand for the ignorant as well as for those of the two Vehicles; for especially the latter are used to interpret existence in terms of transitoriness or momentariness. This leads to the question how the Ālaya or Tathāgata-garbha is to be conceived in relation to the doctrine of universal transitoriness. Is not the Tathāgata-garbha, however skilfully it may be expounded, after all a sort of ego-substance? It now becomes necessary for the *Laṅkāvatāra* to discuss the problem of momentariness in relation to the hypothesis of Tathāgata-garbha. This has partially been touched elsewhere, and let it suffice here to quote the following stanzas[2] which are by the way wrongly placed after the paragraph on the six Pāramitās instead of before it in all the texts of the *Laṅkāvatāra*.

"Existence (*saṁskṛita*) is discriminated by the ignorant as empty, transient, and momentary, and the nature of momentariness as they discriminate is illustrated by a stream, lamp-light, and seed (9).

"[But really] nothing is seen working at any moment, all is solitary, there is no [birth and] destruction, nothing is ever born—this is the Buddha's view of momentariness (10).

"Birth and death follow each other without interruption—this is not the teaching of the Buddha for the ignorant;

[1] For the continuation of this passage, see pp. 138–9 of the present work.

[2] Pp. 238–239.

[that birth and death] are uninterruptedly successive in all things is due to discrimination moving on in all the paths of existence (11).

"With ignorance as cause there is the evolving of all mental activities; [but] where do they get their anchoring while there is no birth of form (*rūpa*)? (12).

"An uninterrupted continuity breaks and there evolves another mind; while form has not yet been set up, depending on what will it [mind] be evolved? (13).

"As long as the mind is evolved depending on it, the cause is not the true one; not being sufficient in itself [as a cause] how can one know of anything that suffers destruction momentarily? (14).[1]

"The attainment of the Yogins, gold, the Buddha's relics (*śarīra*), and the mansions in Ābhāsvara Heaven,—these are indestructible from any worldly cause (15).

"Permanent are the truths attained and the knowledge realised by the Buddhas; [permanent is] the Bhikshu-nature and his attainment; how is momentariness seen here? (16).

"Visible objects (*rūpa*) are like the Gandharva's castle, māyā, and other [suchlike non-entities], and no momentariness is here: the elements are not realities, and how can we speak of their power to create? (17)."[2]

I have said that the Ālaya and the Tathāgata-garbha are one and the same thing, and that the one is more of psychological significance than the other, but the *Laṅkāvatāra* sometimes seems to distinguish one from the other, that is, to consider the Ālayavijñāna as presenting the impurity-phase of the Tathāgata-garbha. Read the following which also sheds a side-light on the question of the ego:

"Mahāmati asks: Tell me, O Blessed One, concerning

[1] The gāthās 13 and 14 are obscure, and the translation is after the T'ang which gives the best rendering.

[2] The definite meaning of the last gāthā is difficult to get at, and the translation is only tentative. It seems to mean that things existent and the so-called elements being like phantom creations as they have no reality in themselves, we cannot even speak of their momentary nature.

the evolution and disappearance of the Skandhas, Dhātus, and Āyatanas. If there is no Ātman, what is it that is evolved and disappears? The ignorant who, stationing themselves on things that are evolved and disappear, do not think of extinguishing pain, may not seek after Nirvana. [They must therefore be enlightened on the subject.] Whereupon the Buddha answers: The Tathāgata-garbha contains in itself causes both good and not-good, and from which are generated all the paths of existence.[1] . . . .

"When there takes place a revulsion [in the Ālaya-vijñā] by gradually ascending the steps of Bodhisattvahood, a man will no more be led astray by the methods and views of other philosophers. Then stationing himself on the stage of Bodhisattvahood known as the Immovable, he gains the passage leading to the bliss that accrues from the ten kinds of Samādhi. Supported by the Buddhas in Samādhi and reviewing the wonderful truths taught by the Buddhas as well as his own vows [which he made in the beginning of his career], he does not abide in the limit of reality (*bhūtakoṭi*) absorbed in the bliss of Samādhi; he has realised the supreme state in his own consciousness; and by the methods of discipline that do not belong to Śrāvakas and Pratyekabuddhas and philosophers, he gains the path belonging to the holy family of Bodhisattvas at the tenth stage, and also the will-body of knowledge which is above all [conscious] strivings after a Samādhi. For this reason let the Tathāgata-garbha known under the name of Ālayavijñāna be purified by those Bodhisattvas who are seeking after something distinctive.

"O Mahāmati, if there is no Tathāgata-garbha known under the name of Ālayavijñāna, no evolution, no disappearance will ever take place. But there is, both among the ignorant and the wise, evolution and disappearance. While abiding in the bliss that accrues from the enjoyment of the actual life and supreme state realised in their consciousness, the Yogins do not abandon their discipline and

[1] For the passage following, see p. 193 et seq. of this work.

hard labouring. O Mahāmati, this realm of Tathāgata-garbha-Ālayavijñāna is pure in its original nature indeed, but appears devoid of purity because of the false views and reasonings entertained by all Śrāvakas, Pratyekabuddhas, and philosophers, which defile the light by their external defilements. This is not the case with the Tathagatas. As to them, they see [the Tathāgata-garbha] as if it were an āmalaka fruit in their own palm.

"O Mahāmati, I inspired Queen Śrīmālā[1] and also other Bodhisattvas who are endowed with a fine, subtle, pure intelligence to expound in a text of discourse the meaning of the Tathāgata-garbha known under the name of Ālaya-vijñāna, so that the Śrāvakas, who are attached to the [Ālaya's] evolution with the seven Vijñānas, might see into the egolessness of things (*dharmanairātmya*). The realm of Tathagatahood which was elucidated by Queen Śrīmālā under the inspiration of the Buddha is not the domain of reasoning which belongs to Śrāvakas, Pratyekabuddhas, and philosophers. The realm of Tathagatahood indeed belongs to another realm where [the teaching that] the Tathāgata-garbha is the Ālayavijñāna is understood, and this is meant for the Bodhisattvas-Mahāsattvas who like yourself being endowed with a fine, subtle, penetrating intellect and understanding, know how to conform themselves to the meaning, and not for those other philosophers, Śrāvakas, and Pratyeka-buddhas, who are attached to words and texts of instruction. Therefore, O Mahāmati, may you and other Bodhisattvas-Mahāsattvas have a thorough understanding as to the realm of all Tathagatahood and [the teaching that] the Tathāgata-garbha is the Ālayavijñāna so that they may discipline themselves in this and not remain contented with mere listening [to the teaching]."[2]

[1]There is a sutra bearing her name in the Chinese Tripitaka, in which the doctrine of Tathāgatā-garbha is explained more fully. Prince Shōtoku wrote a fine commentary on it as early as A.D. 609.

[2] Pp. 221–223. The whole passage is concluded with the gāthās which appear on p. 195 of the present work.

False Discrimination, No-birth, and Causation

Enough has already been said about the *Laṅkāvatāra's* conception of habit-energy or memory (*vāsanā*) and the principle of individuation (*vishaya*). Let us now proceed to see what is meant by discrimination (*vikalpa*) and in what relation this stands to the doctrine of "Mind-only," and also to the Buddhist idea of no-birth (*anutpāda*) which is characteristic of the transcendental Citta. The following quotation may be illuminating.

"Inspired by the spiritual power of the Buddha, Mahāmati asked him again: What is the distinctive feature of the Buddhist doctrine of no-birth and no-annihilation? For do not all the philosophers teach also that the creative agents are neither born nor annihilated, which corresponds to the Buddhist teaching that Ākāśa, Apratisaṁkhyānirodha, and Nirvāṇa-dhātu[1] are not subject to birth, nor to annihilation? The philosophers too describe the world as having been produced by causation in the hands of creators, while the Buddha describes the world as being born depending upon ignorance, desire, karma, and discrimination. Whether creation by causation, or dependence, the difference is in names only. Thus both the Buddha and the philosophers proceed to teach the birth of external objects by external causation, and thus there is no distinction to be made between the Buddha's and the philosophers' theory. The philosophers assert that the nine substances containing such as atom (*aṇu*), Pradhāna, Iśvara, and Prajāpati are neither born nor annihilated, while according to the Buddha all existence is

[1] These are what is known as the three forms of Asaṁskrita, "things not-made" in contradistinction to Saṁskṛita, "things made." Ākāśa is space or vacuity; Apratisaṁkhyānirodha, literally meaning "annihilation effected without premeditated efforts," is a state of pure nothingness due to the want of proper conditions; while Nirvāṇa is an annihilation purposely effected by intellect and will, which is therefore Pratisaṁkhyānirodha.

subject neither to birth nor to annihilation, and neither being nor non-being is attainable. The elements again, according to the Buddha, are said to be indestructible, and their substance is neither born nor annihilated, while they circulate through the various paths of existence, they retain their self-nature. But this distinction concerning the elements and their transformations is also upheld by all the philosophers as well as by the Buddha himself. For this reason, the Buddhist doctrine has nothing distinctive. If there is anything distinctive, pray tell me this distinguishing point as unlike the doctrine held by the philosophers. If there is nothing distinctive in the Buddhist doctrine, the philosophers may also be said to belong to the group of Buddhas because of their doctrine of causes that are neither born nor annihilated. It was stated by the Buddha that not more than one Tathagata would appear in the world at one time and at one locality; but if what goes before obtains, there are Tathagatas more than one because[1] there is no distinctive point in the Buddha's own doctrine.''

To this answers the Buddha: ''O Mahāmati, my doctrine of no-birth and no-annihilation is not the same as that held by the philosophers, nor as the doctrine of birth and impermanence. For what reason? According to the philosophers, the theory of self-substance is upheld, and there really obtains something that is neither born nor transformed. But mine is above the category of being and non-being, and abandoning [the notion of] birth and destruction, I talk of that which is neither existent nor non-existent, that which has no more existence than the multitudinousness of things that appear like māyā or in a dream. What is meant by 'not existing'? It is meant that the self-nature [or self-substance] of things existent with individual marks

[1] The Sanskrit text has here, ''because of being-non-being-work-grasping,'' which is missing in T'ang and Sung. Wei has: ''Why? Because there is no difference according to the doctrine, as to the causes that are and those that are not, and there is no falsehood in what the Buddha teaches.''

and graspable [by the senses] has no reality (*bhāva*), because they are perceived and not perceived, they are grasped and not grasped. For this reason, all things existent are [really] neither existent nor non-existent. When, however, it is realised that what is presented to one's view is no more than the Mind itself, one knows how to establish oneself where discrimination ceases to rise, and the world stops its labouring. The ignorant make effort to discriminate, but the wise do not. [The ignorant] because of discrimination commit the error of taking non-existent things for realities. This world is like the Gandharva's castle or a magically-created person. It is like the case of a childish-minded person who, seeing magically-created people, a multitude of beings, and merchants going in and out of the Gandharva's castle, take them for realities, imagining, 'They are going in, they are coming out,' though in fact there is no going-in or coming-out whatever. This is indeed due to their discrimination which leads them to the erroneous viewing of existence; and so with the ignorant, their view of birth or of no-birth is an error. Whether things are created (*saṁskṛita*) or uncreated (*asaṁskṛita*), they are no more than magically-created figures, and of magically-created figures neither birth nor annihilation may be predicated, for no [category of] existence and non-existence is applicable to them. So with all things in the world (*sarvadharma*), they have nothing to do with birth and destruction. Only the ignorant cherishing the ideas grown out of falsehood imagine their birth and annihilation. It is not so with the wise. By falsehood (*vitatham*) it is meant that the self-nature of existence is not discriminated as it is in itself. It is no other than this. When it is discriminated in any other way [than *yathābhūtam*], there is an attachment to what is taken for the self-nature of existence, and one fails to see the Solitary (*vivikta*), and because of this failure there is no release from discrimination. For this reason, O Mahāmati, the view based on no-appearance (*animitta*) is superior to that of appearance, for the latter causes birth (*jamahetu*) and is not preferable. No-appearance means the ceasing of discrimination, and I state that Nirvana means no-birth. O Mahāmati, by Nirvana I mean the seeing into the abode where the meaning [of existence] is understood in its truthfulness, the abandoning of all discrimination which takes place in the mind and what belongs to it, and the realisation of the supreme wisdom which lies in the inmost consciousness of the Tathagata:—this I call Nirvana."[1]

Proofs for the "Mind-only"

So far no special efforts have been made to prove why there is Mind itself and no external realities. The *Laṅkāvatāra* is not a philosophical treatise and naturally does not profess to prove anything specifically in connection with the teaching or statement it propounds. But as we peruse the sutra, we cannot help coming across certain attempts at advancing proofs for its main thesis: *svacittadṛiśyamātram.* We will try to gather up these attempts already alluded to, though sporadically in previous pages, and present them in a more systematic way.

1. That things are not what they seem is proved from the analogy of a dream and magical creations.[2] When Rāvaṇa, king of Laṅkā, saw images of the Buddha all around him, which later disappeared, he thought, "Could this be a dream? or a magical phenomenon like the castle of the Gandharvas?" He reflected again, "This is no other than the projection of my own mental creations." As we do not truly understand things as they are, we separate the seen from the seer, thus producing a world of dualities. "Where there is no false discrimination, one really sees the Buddha." As long as we are in the dream, we do not realise that we are all dreaming, that we are slaves of false discrimination. For

[1] Pp. 197–200.

[2] Allusions to this analogy abound throughout the sutra, but see pp. 9, 56, 85, 90 110, 199, 214, etc.

it is only when we are awakened from it that we know where we have been. The analogy of dream is quite a strong argument against the reality of an external world, but it is not at all effective for them who are actually dreaming.

So it is with magical creations. The Indians have been noted for their skill in the art of conjuration, and there are no people among whom the use of mantrams and dharanis is so universal. Hence the frequent allusions to magic in the literature of Mahayana and Hinayana Buddhism. The magician is so wonderfully proficient in making the spectators see objects where there are none whatever. As long as they are under his spell, there is no way of making them realise that they are the victims of hypnotism.

The favourite analogies besides the dream and magic that are resorted to in the *Laṅkāvatāra* to show the unreality of objects seen externally and internally are:[1] (1) paintings, (2) a hair-circle to the dim-eyed, (3) a revolving fire-wheel, (4) a bubble looking like a sun, (5) reflected trees in water, (6) images in a mirror, (7) an echo, (8) *fata morgana*, (9) a mechanical man, (10) a floating cloud, and (11) lightning.

2. All things are relative and have no *svabhāva* (substance) which would eternally and absolutely distinguish one from another. Things are nothing but relations; analyse them into their component elements and there will be nothing left. And are not all relations the constructions of the mind? Thus the Citta seeing itself reflected is due to reflection and discrimination; so far no harm is done, for the mental constructions are perceived as such and there are no wrong judgments about them. The trouble begins at once when they are adhered to as externally real, having their own values independent of the valuing mind itself. This is why the sutra emphasises the importance of looking at things *yathābhūtam*, as they really are. When they are thus looked at *yathābhūtam*, they are no more than the mind

[1] P. 92 et seq.

itself. The principle of relativity creates a world of individuals, but when it is transcended, there is Mind itself.

3. Names and images are mere signs (*saṁketa*)[1] and have no reality whatever (*abhāva*) in themselves, for they belong to the imagination (*parikalpita*). Imagination is another name for false discrimination, which is the mischievous agency of creation. The fact of One Mind (*ekacittam*) is thus buried in the differentiation of individual existences.[2] Hence *jalpo hi traidhātukaduḥkha-yoniḥ.*[3] Again, "according to words they discriminate wrongfully and make statements concerning reality; and because of these statements they are burned in hell."[4] How much we owe in our daily intercourse to words! and yet what grave consequences, not only logically but spiritually, we suffer from words! The light of the mind is altogether beclouded in and with words. The mind has, indeed, created words, and now taking these words for realities independent of their creator, it gets entangled in them, and, as the sutra says, is swallowed up in the waves of transmigration.

"The ignorant take what is presented by the mind itself for objective realities which do not really exist, and because of this wrong representation, discrimination is falsified. This, however, is not the case with the wise. The latter know that names and signs and symbols are to be taken for what they are intended from the beginning, while the ignorant cling to them as if they were realities and let their minds blindly follow up this clinging. Thus, they get attached to a variety of forms and entertain the view that there are really 'I' and 'mine', and, by so doing, hold fast to appearances in their multiplicity. Because of these attachments, their higher wisdom is obstructed; greed, anger, and infatuation are stirred up, and all kinds of karma are com-

[1] P. 225.
[2] P. 770.
[3] Words are the source of pain in the triple world. P. 186, l. 9.
[4] P. 156, lines 3–4.

mitted. As these attachments are repeatedly committed, the ignorant find themselves hopelessly enwrapped within the cocoons woven out of their wrong discriminations. They are swallowed up in the waves of transmigration, and do not know how to go ahead in the work of emancipation for they turn round and round like the water-wheel. It is owing to their ignorance, indeed, that they fail to realise that all things, like māyā, the shining mote, or the moonlight on water, have no self-substance, that there is nothing in them to take hold of as 'me' and 'mine'; that all things are unreal (*abhūta*) born of wrong discrimination; that [ultimate reality] is above the dualism of marked and marking, and the course of birth, staying, and disappearance; that all that is manifested is due to the discriminating by one's own mind of what is presented to it. Imagining that [the world] is born of Iśvara, Time, Atom, or Universal Soul, the ignorant are addicted to names and forms thereby allowing themselves to be swayed by them."[1]

4. "[That which is unborn] has nothing to do with causation, there is no creator, all is nothing but the construction (*vyavasthāna*) of the mind, as I teach that which is unborn."[2] That there is no creator such as Iśvara or Pradhāna or Brahma is one of the principal theses of Mahayana Buddhism. According to the *Laṅkāvatāra,* the notion of a creator is due to discrimination, which always tends to lead the mind in a wrong direction. When it is seen that all is *cittamātra,* that which is unborn will present itself instead. Mahāmati was somewhat sceptical about this, wondering if the Master's teaching was not after all similar to that of the philosophers, as was quoted a few pages back,[3] and after this quotation the Buddha goes on to repeat more or less the same idea in the gāthās as usual:[4]

"In order to remove [the idea of] birth and to attain

[1] P. 225, after the sense.

[2] P. 201 g. 96.

[3] See supra, p. 264 et seq.

[4] Pp. 200–201.

[that of] no-birth, I teach the doctrine of no-cause which is not comprehended by the ignorant (86).

"That all is unborn does not mean that things do not exist, but that they are like the Gandharva's castle, like a dream, and māyā, and that their existence is without cause (87).

"Tell me how things are in their self-nature unborn and empty. When existence is freed from aggregations, no intelligence will take hold of it, and therefore I declare that it is empty, unborn, and without self-substance (88).

"Each individual aggregation is seen [as real], but it is no [real] existence as is maintained by the philosophers, for when analysed there is no aggregation (89).

"Dream, hair-circle, māyā, Gandharva's [castle], and mirage—they are seen without causal reality; so with the world of particulars (90).

"By suppressing cause-theory, the no-birth is accomplished; when the no-birth is accomplished, my eyes do not perish; when no-cause theory is announced, the philosophers are horrified (91).

"How, by what cause, why, and where is birth [to be regarded as] without cause? When existence (*saṁskṛita*) is regarded as neither causal nor non-causal, we turn away from the view of those who hold that there are [actual] birth and destruction (92).

"Do we speak of no-birth because of non-existence? or because it is to be regarded as mutually dependent? or because of existence being mere name with no reality [behind it]? Pray tell me (93).

"No-birth—not because of non-existence, nor because existence is to be regarded as mutually dependent, nor because there is a name for existence, nor because name has no reality [behind it] (94).

"That all is unborn does not belong to the realm of Śravakas, Pratyekabuddhas, or philosophers, or of those Bodhisattvas who are still on the seventh stage (95).

"I state that all is unborn, because [such predicates as] cause or dependence are inapplicable here, because no creatorship is to be assumed here; the no-birth is constructed on [the truth of] the 'Mind-only' (96)."

5. The logical necessity of reaching the ultimate notion of unity has made the author of the *Laṅkāvatāra* accept the doctrine of "Mind-only" instead of that of "matter-only." When no creator is recognised and all forms of dualism are set aside as not in accord with the real state of things, there remain two ways for achieving the unification of thought, realism and idealism; and as the *Laṅkāvatāra* denies the reality of an external world (*vishaya*), or outside objects[1] (*bāhyabhāva*) that are characterised with multitudinousness (*vicitratā*), the doctrine of "Mind-only" seems to be the natural conclusion. The philosophical thesis of the present sutra is thus an absolutely idealistic monism. "To take cognisance of the manifoldness of an objective world is relative knowledge (*vijñāna*), while to rise above this cognisance is transcendental knowledge (*jñāna* or *prajñā*)."[2] Again, this transcendental knowledge is not within the reach of the two Vehicles, as it, indeed, goes beyond the realm of beings; the knowledge of Śrāvakas moves by attaching itself to beings which they take for realities, while the pure transcendental knowledge of the Tathagata penetrates into the truth of the "Mind-only."[3]

Thus it is evident that as far as the *Laṅkāvatāra* is concerned the mind (*citta*) or self-mind (*svacitta*) is the principle of unity, while the objective world disturbs this unity and makes the mind, thus disturbed, perceive manifoldness within its own body. It then clings to these individualising disturbances as real, thus losing its original

[1] *Na ca bāhya-bhāva-lakshaṇa-vaicitrya-patitam anyatra svacittam eva* (p. 212, ll. 9–10). *Bāhya-bhāvā-'nabhyupagamāt tribhava-citta-mātro-'padeśād vicitra-lakshaṇā-'nupadeśāt* (p. 208, l. 13)......This idea appears throughout the sutra.

[2] *Asaṅgalakshaṇaṁ jñānaṁ vishaya-vaicitrya-saṅga-lakshaṇaṁ ca vijñānam* (p. 157, l. 14). [3] P. 158, g. 43.

purity or unity altogether in them. This is the source of spiritual tribulations.

6. The strongest of all the proofs that can be advanced for the statement that the world is Mind itself (*tribhavasvacittamātram*), is that of intuitive knowledge (*pratyaksha*). While this is what is final in all form of conviction, speculative or practical, the force is especially strongly felt in religious truths, which are not founded upon reasoning but upon immediate perception. So with the *Laṅkāvatāra,* its thesis is derived from its immediacy and not from its intellectual precision. Paramārtha, the ultimate principle of knowledge, is not dependent upon anything logically reasoned: it is "I see and I believe." Paramārtha[1] is what is realised within oneself by means of the supreme wisdom (*āryajñāna*) of the Tathagata, or rather it is the supreme wisdom itself, for the awakening of this wisdom means the grasping of the ultimate principle, which is the same thing as the realisation within one's inmost consciousness of the truth that there is nothing in the world but Mind. This truth is beyond the realm of discursive knowledge.[1] This special knowledge which may be called intuitive is variously referred to throughout the *Laṅkāvatāra.* To mention just a few: *parijñā,*[2] *abhisambodha,*[3] *svapratyātmabuddhi,*[4] *vicārāparapraṇeya,*[5] *adhigamāvabodha,*[6] *yāthātathya-mudrā,*[7] *nirābhāsabuddhi,*[8] *samatā-jñāna,*[9] etc., etc.; all go to describe the kind of knowledge which sees into the truth of the "Mind-only." "The wise do not cherish in that which is confused any thought either perverted or not perverted; O Mahāmati, if they form any notion at all about it, there will be no supreme wisdom (*āryajñāna*) taking hold

[1] *Paramārthas tu mahāmate āryajñāna-pratyātmā-gati-gamyo na vāgvikalpa-buddhi-gocaraḥ tena vikalpo nodbhāvayati paramārtham.* P. 87, ll. 12–13.

[2] P. 49, l. 7.

[3] P. 79, l. 5.

[4] P. 133, ll. 10–11.

[5] P. 133, l. 11.

[6] P. 133, l. 14.

[7] P. 166, l. 3.

[8] P. 123, l. 1.

[9] P. 135, l. 7.

of reality (*vastu*).'[1] By this we know that knowledge that takes hold of the ultimate cannot be brought into a system of categories; for if anything is to be said about it, it turns into an idea of it and the real thing is no more there, and what is left behind is nothing but confusion or delusion (*bhrānti*). "Attachment to realities as having self-substance is produced from not knowing (*anavabodha*) that there is nothing but that which is [projected and] perceived by one's own mind."[2] *Avabodha* is really "awakening"; something is awakened within the consciousness, and it is at once recognised that all is Mind. The awakening is above the dualism of "to be" (*sat*) and "not to be" (*asat*), the latter being due to false discrimination (*vikalpa*). The awakening is, therefore, the sight of the ultimate principle of existence as it is in itself and not determined by any form of confusion or otherness. This is what is meant by "to see *yathābhūtam*."

It is by this awakening which takes place in the inmost consciousness, not as the result of logical inference but as self-realisation, that the Buddha makes the following statement: "Between my enlightenment and my Nirvana I have not uttered a world. Indeed, not to say a word is the teaching of the Buddha."[3]

The *Laṅkāvatāra* goes on further to state that there is a twofold hidden meaning in the teaching of the Buddha, and when this is understood all is understood.[4] What are the two? Reality as realised in one's inmost consciousness (*pratyātmadharmatā*), and reality as abiding since eternity (*paurāṇasthitidharmatā*). These two realities are not two but one, which is to say, the truth subjectively perceived is the truth in objective existence; and the "Mind-only" is meant to designate this fundamental unity and purity of all things, uncontaminated by *bhrānti, vikalpa, viparyāsa* (perversion),[5] etc. In this unity and purity all the Buddhas are

[1] P. 107.
[2] P. 100, ll. 4–5.
[3] Pp. 144, 240.
[4] P. 143.
[5] See for instance p. 106, line 15.

one, and also all sentient beings if they are only enlightened and awakened to this fundamental truth.

The following from the *Laṅkāvatāra* is the most significant passage in this connection where the logic and the psychology of the present sutra are perfectly synthesised in the intuitive knowledge or the inner realisation of all the Tathagatas of the past, present, and future.[1]

"What is meant by reality as abiding since eternity? It is reality that is in me since eternity; it is like gold or silver or pearl that lies buried in a mine, O Mahāmati. Regardless of the appearance or the non-appearance of the Tathagata, the realm of the Dharma endures, the reality [or that which constitutes the essence] of all things endures, there is the continuity of the Dharma, there is the fixedness of the Dharma. It is, O Mahāmati, like unto a passage-way leading to an ancient city. O Mahāmati, suppose there is a man roaming about in the wilderness, who descries a perfect passage-way leading to an ancient city. He proceeds to go into that city, and entering there and resting there he enjoys all the pleasant doings that are going on in the city. Now do you think, O Mahāmati, that the passage-way leading to the city and its manifold affairs were constructed by that man? Said Mahāmati, No, sire, O Blessed One. And the Blessed One continued, Just so, O Mahāmati, the reality innerly attained by myself and the Tathagatas endures; it is the continuity of the Dharma, it is the fixedness of the Dharma, it is the so-ness (*tathatā*), real-ness (*bhūtatā*), and true-ness (*satyatā*), of things."

There is a reality (*dharmatā*) that endures, it is the realm beyond the ken of discrimination (*vikalpa*); it is the mind itself but freed from the entanglements of speculation and imagination; it reveals itself through our empirical consciousness when our empirical consciousness goes beyond itself, that is, when it transcends dualism. Dharmatā or reality, then, is no other than the supreme wisdom (*ārya-*

[1] Pp. 143–144.

jñāna) realised inwardly by and in oneself (*pratyātmādhigama*). When this realisation comes to one, no proofs are now needed for the doctrine of "Mind-only." As Zen declares, it is like drinking water yourself: you know without being told by others whether it is cold or warm.

Some Concluding Remarks

Having enumerated these considerations in the *Laṅkāvatāra* that lead to the thought of the "Mind-only," let us make this remark in the way of concluding this part of the present chapter. It is this: The *Laṅkāvatāra* was not written with the view of establishing a philosophical thesis to be called pure idealistic monism; its central motive was to make us realise that enlightenment comes when we are detached from the tyranny of language and discrimination, when we enter into the realm of *anāsrava* (non-leakage or non-outflowing),[1] when, going beyond all philosophical reasonings, we stand on the inner ground of consciousness and shine out in our own inner brightness. This being the case, as I have already remarked elsewhere, it would be unreasonable of us to expect anything systematically or logically thoroughgoing in the *Laṅkāvatāra*. Even when all the threads of logic are found in confusion, the *Laṅkāvatāra* will still insist on the doctrine of "Mind-only," saying that it is a fact of immediate perception and that enlightenment or spiritual freedom comes upon one after realising this fact within oneself. It will then be the business of the philosophers to

[1] *Āsrava* literally means "flowing out" or "discharge" or "leakage" according to the Chinese translators. It has a technical sense in Buddhism and denotes anything intellectual or affective that oozes out of one's mind having corrupted its purity. Where there are no such defiling outflows, the mind enjoys its native serenity and transcendental unity. This is the realm of the wise. When on the contrary there is a constant oozing of discrimination and attachment, one has no hope for emancipation. The object of the Buddhist life therefore is to dry up this source of evil filterings, which are generally enumerated as four: *kāma* (desire to have), *bhava* (will to live), *dṛishṭi* (intellection), and *avidyā* (ignorance).

logically demonstrate that fact and not to deny it or reject it. If we feel cold when it snows, the scientist will have to explain the fact and not reject it as being empirically impossible. The rejection or denial in such a case means intellectual suicide.

It is evident that the mind regarded here as the unitive principle of experience is not our empirical mind, and, naturally, it is variously designated by the author of the *Laṅkāvatāra* as it is observed from various points of reference. Besides those already mentioned such as *paramārtha, paurāṇasthitidharmatā, pratyātmadharmatā, Buddhatā,* etc., we give, below, some more synonyms and descriptive notions of the ultimate ground of existence:

1. *Vikalpa-vivikta-dharma,* truth that is detached from discrimination;[1]
2. *Pratyātmādhigama-viśesha-lakshaṇa,* an excellent state of consciousness attained inwardly by oneself;[2]
3. *Jñānaṁ subhaṁ. . . . .samudācāra-varjitam,* pure knowledge possessed by the Tathagata, which is free from all [consciousness of] action;[3]
4. *Svabhāvam ekaṁ deśemi tarka-vijñapti-varjitam,* I teach one self-nature that is beyond the ken of reasoning and representation.[4]
5. *Svayam evādhigata-yāthātathya-vivikta-dharma,* solitary truth of "thus-ness" realised by oneself.[5]
6. *Ārya-jñāna-svabhāva-vastu,* the supreme wisdom constituting the ultimate fact of existence.[6]
7. *Tathāgata-svapratyātma-āryajñāna-adhigama,* realisation by the Tathagata of supreme wisdom in his own inmost consciousness.[7]

[1] P. 215, l. 8.
[2] P. 148, l. 11.
[3] P. 158, ll. 9, 10.
[4] P. 267, l. 13.
[5] P. 165, l. 17.
[6] P. 165, l. 10.
[7] This phrase appears throughout the sutra. Very frequently it is not prefixed with *tathāgāta,* nor with *sva* (own), but simply *pratyātmāryajñāna.*

8. *Tattva*, "thatness," or *tathatā* or *tathātva*, "thusness" or "suchness."
9. *Yathābhūtārthasthānadarśana*, the view established on the truth of suchness.[1]
10. *Samyagjñā*, right knowledge which is one of the five categories (*dharma*).
11. *Nirābhāsa-gocara*, realm of no-shadows.[2]

I cannot conclude this study without referring, though casually, to the difference between the doctrine of Cittamātra and that of Vijñaptimātra (or Vijñānamātra), the latter being the thesis of the Yogācāra school of Buddhism which was founded principally by Asanga and Vasubandhu. In 1925, Professor Sylvain Lévi published Sthiramati's commentaries on the *Vijñapti-mātratāsiddhi* by Vasubandhu, which were discovered by him in Nepal; and we have at present two Japanese translations of it: one by Dr. Junjiro Takakusu and the other by Dr. Unrai Wogihara. Besides these two most important texts of the Yogācāra, Professor Lévi sometime ago (1907) published another Yogācāra text known as *Sūtrālaṁkāra* with his French translation. This is ascribed to Asanga. Thus furnished with the principal text-books of the Vijñānamātra doctrine of Mahayana Buddhism, scholars are now able to ask: How is the Cittamātra of the *Laṅkāvatāra* to be distinguished from the Vijñānamātra? Or are they the same, only differently designated? The following is given more to elucidate the *Laṅkāvatāra* position than to give a definite answer to the question. It is a most significant question deserving a fuller treatment than we may discuss here.[3]

The doctrine persistently maintained in the *Laṅkāvatāra* is Cittamātra or Cittadṛiśyamātra, and not Vijñāna- or Vijñapti-mātra, which, according to Asanga and Vasuban-

[1] P. 200, l. 6.

[2] P. 226, l. 13.

[3] The subject was cursorily touched upon elsewhere (pp. 181–182) in the present *Studies*.

dhu, is "*Idaṁ sarvaṁ vijñaptimātrakam,*"[1] meaning by *idam* that which is discriminated as "This is the self" and "That is an external reality," that is, this world where the subject is distinguished from the object, or, to use Buddhist terminology, the triple world including both *saṁskṛita* and *asaṁskṛita*. It is true that Citta is quite frequently identified with Vijñāna or Vijñapti as in the following gāthā, in which this identification is explicitly referred to:

"Mind (*citta*), discrimination, representation (*vijñapti*), the will (*manas*), consciousness (*vijñāna*), the storage (*ālaya*), that which makes the triple world,—all these are synonyms of mind (*citta*)."[2] But when the word "Cittamātra" is used, this Citta has a specific sense to be distinguished from the empirical mind which functions as Manas and Vijñāna. As I have repeatedly remarked, the Citta in the *Laṅkāvatāra* is the principle of mentality, and when it is said that there is the "Mind-only," this mind includes not only the empirical mind but that which constitutes the very basis of discrimination. The mind is what is left behind when all forms of discrimination are rejected as leading to spiritual bondage and defilement. It is thus something that has been here even prior to all discrimination, that is, even before the duality of subject and object had come to exist. The *Laṅkāvatāra* does not advocate nihilism pure and simple; it tries to take hold of somewhat beyond this world of particularisation. When one has actually taken hold of it by sheer act of intuition which is made possible by the working of non-discriminative wisdom (*avikalpa-jñāna*),[3] or supreme wisdom (*āryajñāna*),[4] or superior knowledge (*prajñā*) in the inmost recesses of consciousness (*pratyātmagocara*), the *Laṅkāvatāra* calls it the Mind (*citta*). And as there is nothing subjective or objective besides this Mind, the Cittamātra or "Mind-only" theory is now positively

[1] *Triṁśikāvijñapti-kārikāḥ*, verse 17.
[2] "Sagāthakam," g. 459.
[3] 無分別智 [4] 聖智

established. The philosophy, if there is any such thing in the *Laṅkāvatāra,* is ontology and not epistemology. Whereas the doctrine of Vijñaptimātra is epistemological.

The Yogācāra school is regarded as advocating indiscriminately the Vijñānamātra or the Vijñaptimātra, as if the two terms meant the same thing. Exactly stated, however, it seems to me that the Vijñaptimātra is not to be confused with the Vijñānamātra; for, in the first place, the *Triṁśikā-vijñapti-kārikā* which is the main text of the School, written by Vasubandhu, speaks of Vijñaptimātra and not of Vijñānamātra. In the Chinese translation 識 (*shih*) is often used for both *vijñapti* and *vijñāna,* which causes confusion. Both terms come from the same root *jñā*, to know, and *vijñapti* means "made known," "indicated," "named," "represented"; while *vijñāna* is "knowing," or "act of knowing," or "knowledge." Thus *vijñapti* is something marked, named, designated, represented, and one can most logically infer that "he who sees that all is 'name-only' sees that all is *vijñaptimātra.*"[1] In the Chinese *Laṅkāvatāra* (T'ang), the word is rendered as 說 (talk), 表示 (indication), 施設 (construction), 假名 (unreal or provisionary name), 假說 (provisionary talk), from which we can see that the Vijñaptimātra is not the Vijñānamātra. So we have in the *Triṁśika* (26), "So long as the Vijñāna does not abide in Vijñaptimātratva, there is no ceasing of the remorse [which arises from] the twofold grasping."[2] Again, "His mind abides in names because he then sees that all is name only; and as he abides in names, what is attained by means of representations (*vijñapti*) is cut off. Then he reaches the realm where there is no attainment as he goes on in his reflection; when he is [thus] liberated from all his hindrances, he attains supreme sovereignty."[3]

The main contention of the Vijñaptimātra theory is that

[1] *Sūtrālaṁkāra,* edited by Lévi, p. 67.
[2] That is, a dualistic view of existence.
[3] Quoted in *Triṁśika,* p. 42.

all that is thought of as reality, as having self-substance, is no more than name, that names are our own subjective creations and have no corresponding realities, that because we have so particularised and so named, or so "indicated," or so "labeled," or so "made known," we see all these particularised, individual objects, mental as well as physical, and yet we fail to realise this, imagining all the time that the world of particulars is final reality and worth while getting attached to and made the object of desperate longing. Verse 28 of the *Triṁśika,* therefore, declares that "when the Vijñāna takes no hold on an objective world[1] it abides in the Vijñaptimātratva, for when there is nothing to be grasped, there is no grasping." This is the gist of the theory of Vijñaptimātra as presented by Asanga and Vasubandhu.

In the *Laṅkāvatāra* no reference is made to the Vijñapti[2] except probably once, but rather to the Prajñaptimātra view of the world; and even in the latter case the reference is negligible, considering that the weight of the whole discourse in the *Laṅkāvatāra* falls on the Cittamātra and not on the Prajñaptimātra or Vijñaptimātra or Nāmamātra or Vikalpamātra.[3] The sutra does not linger long on the question of the world being merely a name or a representation, but it exhausts its powers of persuasion to convince the reader that the world is Mind itself, and that it is only by realising this truth in one's own inner consciousness that enlightenment ensues. The transcendental mind, or Mind itself, or "Mind-only" is thus made the chief subject of the text. In this it varies from the teaching of the Yogācāra: the latter emphasises the process of transformation which takes place in the Ālayavijñāna, and it naturally makes most of the

[1] Literally, "that which is taken hold of."

[2] Excepting the "Sagāthakam" which we have reason to suspect is a later production than the main text. In the "Sagāthakam" there are references to the Vijñaptimātra, for instance, in verses 44 and 77.

[3] *Vikalpamātraṁ tribhavam* (p. 186); *Vijñaptimātra-vyavasthānam* (p. 169); *prajñaptimātraṁ tribhavam* (p.168); *prajñaptimātraṁ katham* (pp. 26, 33). See also p. 181, of the present *Studies.*

aspect of existence which is to be considered merely ideational. It does not go further on to say that there is the "Mind-only" as the principle of unification in which all representations (*vijñapti*), cogitations (*manana*), discriminations (*vikalpa*), and a world of particulars (*vishaya*), leave no traces. According to Sthiramati's commentary, the *Triṁśika* is regarded as written for those who do not understand truthfully (*yathābhūtam*) what is meant by Cittamātram, but this does not mean that the Cittamātra is the Vijñaptimātra. The former may be based on the latter, or we can say that when the Cittamātra is declared as a fact of intuitive knowledge, the doctrine of Vijñaptimātra logically follows from this realisation. The *Triṁśika* may thus form a part of the *Laṅkāvatāra's* philosophical foundation, but we must not overlook the fact that there is a conceptual difference between the theme of the *Laṅkāvatāra* and the Yogācāra's psychological or rather epistemological interpretation of existence.

The natural course of procedure here on the part of the writer would be now to write about the relation between the *Laṅkāvatāra* and *The Awakening of Faith in the Mahāyāna,* which is usually ascribed to Aśvaghosha, as the latter almost seems an attempt at systematising the philosophy of the *Laṅkāvatāra.* But as the writer expects to publish a second revised English translation of this most important Mahayana text-book, he passes by the opportunity of touching upon the subject in this chapter.

2. THE CONCEPTION OF NO-BIRTH (*anutpāda*)

The Prajñāpāramitā and the Laṅkāvatāra

The *Prajñāpāramitā-sūtra* (*ashṭasāhasrikā*) opens with a chapter on the life of the Bodhisattva, which is based on the realisation of transcendental knowledge (*prajñā*), and a gist of it reads something like this:

Subhūti is asked by the Buddha to teach the Bodhisattva how to attain the perfection of Prajñā, to which Subhūti answers: There is no such being as a Bodhisattva on whom a man can lay his hand, nor is there anything to be known as Prajñā (transcendental knowledge); hence to talk about the attainment of its perfection is meaningless. In fact, to think or imagine that there is something doing or going on is against the true notion of Mind (*citta*) which is pure, that is, absolutely beyond all forms of functioning. That which is known as mind in discursive reasoning is no-mind (*acitta*), though without this, Mind cannot be reached. In any event there is Mind that is no-mind, and that is neither being nor non-being, neither to be perceived nor to be grasped.

Further, the Bodhisattva, so called, has no abiding place; therefore when Prajñā is realised by him he is not abiding anywhere, not in any of the five Skandhas, that is, he is not to be located in a world of matter and form, nor in a world of consciousness. Again, there is nothing in Prajñā that gives one a clue to its being grasped. When we say that a Bodhisattva has realised Prajñā we may imagine that there is a Bodhisattva, that there is Prajñā, and that the latter has entered into the consciousness of the former; and, further, that he takes hold of it as if a mother is tenderly cherishing her baby. But this altogether misses the mark. For the Bodhisattva is now in a Samādhi called sometimes Sarvadharmāparigrihīta (i.e., Samādhi of not grasping anything), sometimes Sarvadharmānupādāna (i.e., Samādhi of not getting attached to anything). Here he has gone far beyond the five Skandhas and has no consciousness whatever of doing or not doing anything, because he is not at all conscious even of the Samādhi itself, because such Samādhi is non-existent (*avidyamānatva*), does not present itself to his consciousness. Why? Because in his no-mind-ness (*acittatva*) he has no cravings, cherishes no attachments of any sort. In his mind, which is no-mind, that is, when he is abiding in his transcendental consciousness, he is not conscious of a world of particulars where things are always conceived in opposites.

Further, Subhūti goes on, the Bodhisattva while disciplining himself to attain an enlightened mind, an all-knowing mind, a mind with no outflowings (*āsrava*), an incomparable mind, and a mind which is beyond the attainments of Śrāvakas and Pratyekabuddhas, knows no such mind to cling to as one that is to be grasped by him. Why? Because an all-knowing mind has no outflowings, because what is known as an all-knowing mind is indeed without outflowings and is beyond the reach of one's grasping. Therefore, in this mind there is no possibility of being grasped. Why? Because there is what may be termed no-mind-ness (*acittatā*) in which mind and no-mind are merged as one, and which cannot be designated as either being nor non-being, and which is thus altogether beyond our perception and apprehension.

When these statements are read for the first time by those who have not been initiated into the Buddhist way of thinking, they may appear as the climax of absurdity. Think of a man who is a no-man seeking after a mind which is a no-mind, and, further, think of him as not knowing of anything being grasped by him when for all we can guess he seems to be in the midst of so-called enlightenment itself. What could be more nonsensical than this? And we are asked not to get alarmed (*uttrāsita*) nor terrified (*saṁtrāsita*). The Mahayana teaching according to the *Prajñā-*

pāramitā seems to be navigating over a stormy ocean where the boat has lost her compass and all her sailing paraphernalia. Can this really be the case with Mahayana Buddhism?

The one most important thing that students of Buddhism have to realise at the very outset of their study is that Buddhism is not a system of philosophy, has nothing to do with speculations as such, has no intention to present a logically-coherent formula of thought. What the Buddhist teaching professes to do is to get us truthfully (*yathābhūtam*) acquainted with the ultimate facts of existence. It requires us firmly to grasp facts based on personal experience, for when this is attained all the rest, including intellection, theorisation, or philosophising, will follow by itself according to the requirements of a mind in which the experience takes place. It will, therefore, be a great mistake to take the Mahayana sutras, such as the *Prajñāpāramitā* or the *Laṅkāvatāra* for a series of "Discourses on the Metaphysics of the Mahāyāna School of Buddhism" as Rājendralāla Mitra puts it. The Madhyamika school or the Yogācāra may have their own "metaphysics" in their sutras, but as far as the Mahayana sutras are concerned, perhaps excepting a very few, they have nothing to do with metaphysics or epistemology; what they contain are plain statements of facts experienced by the Indian Buddhist minds, that is, they are most direct statements based upon the intuitive knowledge these minds have gained regarding the religious life. Their statements may be logically untenable or impossible, but they have not lost sight of the facts or experiences that have flashed through their minds. All their paradoxes, contradictions, incomprehensibilities, and even all their apparently nonsensical utterances must be reduced first of all to their intuitions. Buddhist students are, therefore, requested to dig patiently down to the bedrock which forms the basis of these utterances if they desire to make them reveal their inmost secrets wrapped up in these uncouth or "terror-inspiring" (*saṁtrāsamāpta*) phrases and propositions of the *Prajñāpāramitā*.

It will be interesting to see how this Acittatā (no-mindness) view of the religious experience in the *Prajñāpāramitā* turns into the Cittamātra (mind-only) theory, so called, of the *Laṅkāvatāra*. Both start from the untenability or unknowability (*anupalabhyamānatva*) of ultimate reality which is beyond the dualism of being and non-being, of birth and death; and while the one ends in a form of negativism, the other comes to an affirmation, saying that there is nothing but Mind, that the mind alone is the last word one can say about the world. At the bottom of these two propositions, however, there is but one experience, for both aim at the realisation of one and the same fundamental truth. As we have already treated of the *Laṅkāvatāra* view of Cittamātra, let us proceed to see what the sutra has to say about what may be termed the no-birth view of existence (*sarvadharmānām anutpāda*). This will clear up not only the position of the *Prajñāpāramitā* but also of the general Mahayana attitude towards the problems of ontology.

While in the *Prajñāpāramitā* we are impressed with the idea of emptiness (*śūnyatā*), the *Laṅkāvatāra* does not make so frequent references to it. True, there are statements concerning existence being like māyā with no reality or substance, but one can trace in the latter sutra a more manifest effort to bring out the self-realisation which will reveal to us a realm of no-birth-and-death, or, rather according to the sutra, of no-birth. "When there is no actual perception (*pratyaksha*) of the truth, no actual seeing of the origin of things, all these philosophical views end in nihilism."[1] "All these views" include such notions as "continuity, birth, work, destruction, existence, Nirvana, path, fruit of action, truth, etc." This being the case we must be always in touch with the Buddhist experience itself when what seems to be a philosophical theory such as

[1] Pp. 40–41.

the subject of this chapter, the no-birth view of existence, is being discussed.

What is meant by no-birth (anutpāda)?

It is one of the most fundamental ideas of Mahayana Buddhism, and is closely associated and almost interchangeable with such terms as emptiness (*śūnyatā*), no-self-substance (*asvabhāva*), non-duality (*advaita*), ultimate limit (*bhūtakoṭi*), Nirvana, no-form (*animitta*), no-yearning (*apraṇihita*), etc. In the *Laṅkāvatāra* it is frequently mentioned together with the first three of these terms. Because of emptiness there is no-birth, and as there is no-birth there is no world of particulars in which the notion of self-substance obtains, and also that of duality or opposition or pairs of opposites; and when this is realised one has what is technically known as "compliance with reality not born" (*anutpattikādharmakshānti*). This already has been treated in one of the previous chapters of the present work.[1] The following quotation from the *Laṅkāvatāra*[2] may help us to understand the close relation existing between the four terms, *śūnyatā, anutpāda, advaya, niḥsvabhāva*:

"At that time the Bodhisattva Mahāmati asked the Buddha saying: Pray tell me concerning the four characteristic features of existence. When they are understood by myself and other Bodhisattvas, we shall speedily abandon the discriminating of being and non-being and attain the realisation of the highest knowledge (*anuttara-samyaksaṁbodhi*).

"Then the Blessed One said: Listen, O Mahāmati, to what I tell you. The idea of Śūnyatā belongs to the domain of imaginative contrivance (*parikalpita*), and as people are apt to cling to the terminology of this domain, we have the doctrines of Śūnyatā, Anutpāda, Advaya, and Niḥsvabhāva [i.e., with the view of freeing them from the clinging].

[1] See pp. 125 f. and 226 f.

[2] Pp. 73 ff.

"Briefly, there are seven sorts of Emptiness (*śūnyatā*): (1) Emptiness of Appearance (*lakshaṇa*), (2) Emptiness of Self-substance (*bhāvasvabhāva*), (3) Emptiness of Non-action (*apracarita*), (4) Emptiness of Action (*pracarita*), (5) Emptiness by which is meant the Unnamability of Existence (*sarvadharma-nirabhilāpya*), (6) Emptiness of the highest degree, by which is meant Ultimate Reality (*paramārtha*), i.e., Supreme Wisdom (*āryajñāna*), (7) Emptiness of Reciprocity (*itaretara*).

"What is meant by Emptiness of Appearance? Existence is characterised by mutual dependence; individuality and generality are empty when one is regarded apart from the other; when things are analysed to the last degree, they are to be comprehended as not existent; there are, after all, no aspects of individuation such as 'this,' 'that,' or 'both'; there are no ultimate irreducible marks of differentiation. For this reason, it is said that self-appearance is empty. [By this is meant that appearance is not a final fact.]

"What is meant by Emptiness of Self-substance? It is because there is no birth of self-substance by itself. [That is to say, individualisation is the construction of our own mind; to think that there are in reality individual objects as such, is an illusion; they have no self-substance, therefore they are said to be empty.]

"What is meant by Emptiness of Non-action? It means that harboured in all the Skandhas there is, from the first, Nirvana which betrays no sign of activity. [That is, their activities as perceivd by our senses are not real, they are in their nature quiet and not-doing]. Therefore, we speak of the non-acting of the Skandhas, which is characterised as emptiness.

"What is meant by the Emptiness of Action? It means that the Skandhas are free of selfhood and all that belongs to selfhood, and that whatever activities are manifested by them are due to the combination of causes and conditions. [That is, they are not by themselves independent creating agencies, they have nothing which they can claim as belonging to their 'self' (*ātman*), and their karmic activities are generated by the conjunction of many causes or accidents.] For which reason there is what we designate the Emptiness of Action.

"What is meant by the Emptiness of the Unnamability of All Things? As this existence is dependent upon our imaginative contrivance (*parikalpita*), there is no self-substance in it which can be named and described by the phraseology of our relative knowledge. This unnamability is designated here as a form of emptiness.

"What is meant by Great Emptiness of Ultimate Reality, which is Supreme Wisdom. When the supreme wisdom is realised in our inner consciousness, it will then be found that all the theories, wrong ideas, and all the traces of beginningless memory (*vāsanā*) are altogether wiped out and perfectly empty. This is another form of emptiness.

"What is meant by Emptiness of Reciprocity? When whatever quality possessed by one thing is lacking in another, this absence is designated as emptiness. For instance, in the house of Ṣrigālamātṛi there are no elephants, no cattle, no sheep, etc., and I call this house empty. This does not mean that there are no Bhikshus here. The Bhikshus are Bhikshus, the house is a house, each retaining its own characteristics. As to elephants, horses, cattle, etc., they will be found where they properly belong, only they are absent in a place which is properly occupied by somebody else. In this manner, each object has its special features by which it is distinguished from another, as they are not found in the latter. This absence is called Emptiness of Reciprocity.

"O Mahāmati, these are the seven forms of Emptiness, and of these the last-mentioned one is the lowest kind and is to be avoided by thee.

"Further, O Mahāmati, there is no-birth by itself, nor

are things said to be unborn, except when a man is abiding in a Samādhi. Therefore, we say that there are no-births.

"O Mahāmati, when we say that there are no self-substances, it means no-birth, according to the deeper sense of the word. All things have no self-substance, seeing that there is only an instantaneous uninterrupted continuation, and that changes from one state to another are observed throughout existence. [If there is self-substance which does not yield itself to changes and transformations, this universal flow of becoming will never take place.] This is what is meant by the non-existence of self-substance.

"What is the meaning, O Mahāmati, when we say that there is no duality? All things exist in pairs like light and shade, long and short, black and white; the one cannot be separated from the other. So are all things like Saṁsāra and Nirvāṇa, they are not two. It does not mean that where there is Nirvāṅa, there is Saṁśāra also, or that where there is Saṁsāra there is Nirvāṇa; for they issue from different causes. Yet they are not two, and so are all things, like Saṁsāra and Parinirvāṇa. [Duality is only possible by postulating something that is not dualistic. Nirvāṇa and Saṁsāra are evidently two, they are not to be merged indiscriminately, but so long as we cling to this dualistic thought we are unable to reach the unifying centre of thought where is the realisation of the Buddhist life. This transcending the duality of existence is called here non-duality.] For this reason, O Mahāmati, thou shouldst discipline thyself in Emptiness, Birthlessness, Non-duality, and Non-substantiality of Self.

"This was then expressed by the Blessed One in the gāthās.

"I have always been preaching Emptiness which is above eternality and extirpation; Saṁsāra is like a dream, like māyā, and yet there is no disappearance of karma.

"So are the sky and Nirvāṇa which are two forms of Nirodha (annihilation); the ignorant wrongly discriminate where there is no action, but the wise go beyond being and non-being.

"At that time the Blessed One said to Mahāmati: O Mahāmati, Emptiness, Birthlessness, Non-duality, and Non-substantiality of Self—this is what is taught by all the Buddhas in all the sutras, indeed there are no sutras in which this teaching is not to be met with. But, O Mahāmati, what is expressed in the sutras is in accordance with the way of thinking cherished by all beings. It deviates from the right path, it is not the talk directly established in the truth of suchness. For example, O Mahāmati, the thirsty deer taking the mirage for water and abiding by it, does not realise that there is no water here. In like manner, the teaching of all the sutras is an appeal to the discriminating habit of mind on the part of sentient beings. It is not the talk on the truth of suchness as established by supreme wisdom. Therefore, O Mahāmati, conform thyself to the inner meaning and do not allow thyself to be engrossed in words of teaching."[1]

From this quotation we can see that these four terms, *śūnyatā, anutpāda, niḥsvabhāva,* and *advaya* mean the same thing, or rather express so many aspects of the same fact. When it is said that all things are empty, it does not mean that all is void, but that particular objects as such have no ultimate reality. Particularisation is the construction of mind, it has no birth in the objective world, that is to say, nothing has been created in this world which can claim to be absolutely real, that is, to be in possession of self-substance. For existence is forever becoming, there is nothing in the world of particulars that retains its self-substantiality or self-identity or unchangeable and unchanging selfhood throughout eternity. The idea of becoming presupposes relativity, that is, duality, and as long as this duality or multiplicity is adhered to as final reality, this solid, hard-shelled world will resist the penetration of our intuition.

[1] Abstract, pp. 73–77.

As the result there will be no fusion of subject and object, this and that, self and not self, which means an eternal quarrel between the two, and consequently eternal unrest. When emptiness, no-birth, and non-substantiality are accepted, non-duality or non-multiplicity must be recognised as true also. All these are related ideas.

In the "Sagāthakam" we have:[1]

"No-birth and Suchness, Ultimate Limit of Reality and Emptiness—all these are different names for one thing[2], do not wrongly discriminate and regard them as non-existent.

"As in the world *hasti* (hand) is also called *kara*, and Indra is also called Śakra or Purandara, so with all things there are many names [for one and the same thing]. Do not wrongly discriminate and regard them as non-existent.

"Form (*rūpa*) and emptiness are not different, nor does no-birth differ. Do not wrongly discriminate; all erroneous views arise from asserting difference."

"Suchness means no-birth."[3]

The Buddhist conception of Immortality

Relatively speaking, no-birth implies no-death, and when the Mahayana philosopher declares that existence has the nature of no-birth, does he mean that the world as it stands is immortal and not subject to the law of causation? How does this view vary from that of the other Indian philosophers who uphold the hypothesis of a creator and his immortality? In short, in what respect does Buddhist immortality differ from other forms of immortality? This was the question proposed by Mahāmati who puts it in the following form:

"The doctrine of immortality (*anirodhānutpāda*) advocated by the Blessed One seems to me not different in any way from that of all the philosophers. For the latter

[1] Gg. 683–685.

[2] The Sanskrit text has here *rūpasya,* to which T'ang has nothing corresponding, while Wei has 法 (*fa*) which equals *dharma* or *bhāva.*

[3] G. 675.

too talk about the immortality of the causal agencies as much as the Blessed One himself who affirms the immortality of space, Apratisaṁkhya-Nirodha, and Nirvana. The philosophers explain the rise of the world from a creator and the law of causality, while the Blessed One too explains it as caused by ignorance, desire, and karma, Both uphold causality, the difference being in name only. This also applies to external objects which are conditioned externally. Seeing this, there is no difference between the views held by the Blessed One and those of the philosophers. The latter have atoms, primary germ, Iśvara, Lord of Creation, etc., and assume the immortality of these nine objects; whereas the Blessed One says that all things are neither born nor pass away, to which the categories of being and non-being do not apply. And then the elements are not destructible; their self-nature is neither born nor passes away; moving through the various paths of existence they retain their self-identity. Though the discrimination upheld by thee is somewhat different, all is recognised by the philosophers. For this reason, thou hast shown no deviation from the doctrine of the philosophers. If there is anything in thy doctrine distinguishing it from theirs, pray tell me. As far as the conception of immortality is concerned, thine and theirs do not betray any dissimilitude. According to the Buddha, many Tathagatas do not appear in the world at one time and at one place. If the philosophers make the same assertions as the Buddha himself, we must say that there are [more than one Tathagata]."

This was the way Mahāmati presented his doubt as to the sameness of the Buddhist position with that of their opponents. In the following the Buddha attempts to define his doctrine against the so-called philosophers' as regards the problem of immortality or that of "no-birth" and "no-passing-away."

"O Mahāmati, my view is not the same as that of the philosophers, not only as regards immortality, but as regards birth and impermanency. Why? According to them, there is a self-substance about which they assert immortality and unchangeability. My position is not that, for it does not fall into the categories of being and non-being. It goes beyond the categories of being and non-being, of birth and disappearance; it is not existence nor is it non-existence. How is it not non-existent? Because it is like unto a diversity of forms appearing in a dream or māyā. How is it not existent? Because the self-substance of forms is not to be asserted as existent. We see them as appearances which are not realities, we grasp (*grahaṇa*) them as before us yet they are not really graspable. For this reason, all existences are to be regarded neither as existent nor as non-existent. If we know that what we see before us is no more than the manifestation of our own mind and abide within ourselves where no dualistic discrimination takes place, we see that there is nothing astir in the world. The ignorant assert themselves in their doings, discriminate therein, but the wise do not.

"O Mahāmati, this is due to the discrimination of unrealities whereby the ignorant get altogether confused in their judgments. It is like the Gandharvas' palace or magically-created figures. O Mahāmati, it is like the child's observing the various magic-created trades-people who appear going into the Gandharvas' palace and again coming out of it; he imagines in his confused mind that all this is real and asserts to that effect. So it is with the ignorant who are confused in the judgment of birth and no-birth, and of the created and of the uncreated; there is really no appearance, no disappearance of the magical figures, of which we can assert either as born or as passed, because they are unpredicable as being or as non-being. The ignorant falsely assume birth and disappearance, but the wise do not.

"O Mahāmati, by being untruthful it is meant that the self-nature of things is not truthfully discerned as it is in itself. When however an untrue view prevails, there is an attachment to the self-substance of things, failing to see them in their solitary quietude, and as long as this quietude fails to be seen, there will be no disappearance of wrongful discrimination. Therefore, O Mahāmati, a view based on formlessness of things is superior to that based on form, because form is the cause of birth. When there is formlessness, it puts a stop to the rise of discrimination, and there is a state of immortality, which is Nirvana. O Mahāmati, one finds Nirvana where one sees the abode of reality in its truthful signification and abandons the discrimination of all that is mind and all that belongs to mind. Then there is the realisation of supreme wisdom which lies in the inmost consciousness of the Tathagata: this I call the Solitary (*vivikta*) and Nirvana.''[1]

No-birth Means Transcending Relativity

As is manifest throughout the *Laṅkāvatāra,* one of its main contests is that ignorance and consequently the state of always being in bondage is due to discrimination wrongfully made concerning the self-nature of existence. That is to say, because we are so addicted to the categories of being and non-being, birth and disappearance, creation and destruction, etc., which are the products of discrimination, we cannot look into the truth and reality of things; we must disentangle ourselves from this bondage of the so-called logical necessity of opposites and return to the primary experience if there be any such and see and interpret things from the knowledge revealed therein and thereby. By this primary experience which is not logical but issues from a discipline, existence is taken in its truthful signification, all the intellectual scaffoldings and constructions are thus done away with, and what is known as non-discriminative knowledge

[1] Pp. 197–200, according to the T'ang. For an abridgment see above, pp. 124 f; and for a translation from the Sanskrit see under the ''Mind-only,'' pp. 264–267, of these *Studies.*

(*avikalpajñāna*) in Mahayana terminology shines out, and as a result we see that all things are unborn, uncreated, and never pass away, and that all appearances are like magically-created figures, or like a dream, like shadows reflected on a screen of eternal solitude and tranquillity. The Mahayanist eye is always gazing at the screen itself, but it will be conscious of the screen as long as it is discriminated from the shadows which in turn are themselves discriminations. This is not yet perfect attainment, the *Laṅkāvatāra* wants to go on further declaring that the screen of eternity too must be abolished, for it is only thus that ignorance is forever dispelled leaving us perfectly free and unhampered in all our seeings and doings. When we come to this culmination of intellectual perspicuity we realise what is meant by all things being unborn and conform ourselves to the Anutpattika-dharma-kshānti.

When the following gāthās[1] are seen in this light, the doctrine of no-birth, no-causality, etc., will grow quite intelligible, and, as the *Prajñāpāramitā* warns, will not frighten us any longer.

97. "That all things are causelessly evolved, as they are not to be described in terms of relativity, such as being and non-being, discriminating and discriminated—this is what I call no-birth.

98. "The mind disengaged from objectivity and free from the twofold Svabhāva,[2] the mind that is obtained by a revulsion (*parāvṛitti*) at the basis of consciousness—this is what I call no-birth.

99. "It is no external existence, no non-existence,

[1] Pp. 200–204, freely translated. For gg. 86–96, see above, pp. 270–272. I may add that this whole series of gāthās 86–117 is repeated bodily in the "Sagāthakam" with some variations. See pp. 337–341, gg. 581–613. The reappearance of so many gāthās in the "Sagāthakam" properly belonging to the main text is provocative of interesting problems concerning the textual composition of the *Laṅkāvatāra*.

[2] The *Parikalpita* and the *Paratantra* view of existence.

indeed, it is beyond the grasp of the mind and transcends all philosophical views—this is what is characterised as no-birth.

100. "All such terms as 'empty,' 'having no self-substance,' etc., are to be thus understood. We talk of being empty not because of emptiness but because of no-birth."

The idea is that the Buddhist doctrine of emptiness is not absolute annihilation but the denial of a relative world as final reality where birth and death actually take place. This, however, does not mean that there is behind this world of appearance something which contrasts with the former and which is what is really real as distinguished or discriminated from the phenomenal. According to the Mahayana, the outside world of form-and-name and the inner world of thought and feeling are both no more than the construction of mind, and when the mind ceases, the weaving-out of a world of particulars is stopped. This stopping is called emptiness or no-birth, but it is not the wiping out of existence, it is on the contrary viewing it truthfully unhampered by discriminative categories. Buddhism, therefore, upholds causation on the ground that things actually come into view and pass out of view, only it rejects the view that causation has its first term, has started from a primary cause or causal agent which is a fixed final reality. The following is to be interpreted in this light.

101. "There is a concatenation of causal chains (*kalāpaḥ pratyayānām*), whereby things come into existence and pass out of it. If this linking is loosened, there will be no birth, no disappearance.

102. "As soon as there is any loosening at all in the chain mutually conditioning, there will be no existence; oneness and separateness are the ideas by which the philosophers discriminate [causation].

103. "There is nothing really born—being, non-being, and the negation of both; there is only a concatenation in which one sees things coming into existence and passing out of it.

104. "It is only owing to conventional ideas that we speak of a mutually-linked chain of causation. When a dislocation takes place in the chain there is no birth, so called, whatever.

105. "As there is absence of birth, we call it no-birth, in fact there is nothing but a continuity of chain; and thus we avoid the faults of the philosophers. The ignorant do not understand it.

106. "Apart from concatenation there is nothing to be regarded as born; if one says there is, he commits a sin against the doctrine of causation; he is the destroyer of the causal chain.

107. "If the causation-chain is [something external to things subject to it], like a lamp shining on a variety of things, there must be something somewhere [which is known as chain, but] altogether different from what it [truly] is.

108. "[Such things, if there be any, have] no self-substance, are unborn, and are by nature like the sky; such chains are realities that are different from true reality, they are what is cherished by the unwise.

109. "There is another kind of birthlessness which is the truth itself realised by the wise; they abide in conformity with this unborn truth whose birth is [what really constitutes] no-birth.

111. "Ignorance, hankering, working, etc., are internal causation-chains; the tree, lump of clay, utensil, wheel, seeds, elements, and suchlike constitute an external chain.

112. "If there is born anywhere anything outside these and yet determined by causation-chain, this goes against the view which upholds causation-only, and is not in accord with the right teaching.

113. "If birth, so called, is really non-existent, whose intelligence is there that is chained to concatenation? [But as far as our conventional senses go] there is mutual-conditioning and birth, and this is the reason for our maintaining the doctrine of causation-chain.

114. "Such categories as heat, fluidity, motion, solidity, etc., are discriminated by the ignorant; such are concatenations; they cannot be designated as categories, hence they have no self-substance."[1]

No-birth, Transcendental Truth, and Eternity Unthinkable

We know that there are two positions usually taken up by the Mahayana thinker who attacks problems of ontology. Unless we know which of the two positions is being upheld by him at the moment, we shall find him quite frequently contradicting himself. The one is that of conventionalism, and the other if we put it so is a highly metaphysical one. If we designate the first as a relative position, we may call the latter the absolute one. From the relative or conventional point of view the Mahayana admits that there is causation and the world moves on from one state to another in conformity with the law, but it refuses to give this continuance an absolute value, for it is real only as far as our senses are concerned. Conventionalism or naïve realism does not after all give real satisfaction to the deeper demands of the religious consciousness. So the Buddhists ask us to go beyond this world of appearance where supposedly all births and deaths are objectively real. A realm beyond the senses, however, must be opened from within ourselves. When we pursue our objective course they would say we come to no end, one chain leads to another, the concatenation has no beginning and no conclusion. We now make a retreat and dig deeper and deeper down into the very foundation-rock of consciousness. When we do this, as the *Laṅkāvatāra* says, there finally takes place a revulsion (*parāvṛitti*) apparently within our own minds. There opens up a new vista where we never expected anything religiously or spiritually convincing. In the beginning we supposed that we could not get down deep enough to come in touch with anything tran-

[1] Pp. 200–204.

scendental. But the new experience now inspires us with a conviction hitherto altogether unknown. This is the new position super-sensual and absolute, this is the supreme wisdom (*āryajñāna*), the realisation of which within ourselves is so emphatically reiterated in the sutra. And it is from this point of view that the world is now describable as unborn, with no self-substance, and unconditionally empty and not at all limited by causation. Birthlessness (*anutpāda*) or emptiness does not belong to the domain of our relative consciousness. The sutra in this respect is quite explicit lest the unwary should slip at this point. The development and definite assertion later in the Madhyamika school of the conception of twofold truth, Saṁvṛitti and Paramārtha, or worldly and transcendental, is the natural consequence of the positions taken up by the *Laṅkāvatāra*.

In order to show, though somewhat over-repeatedly, that the birthlessness of all things (*sarvadharmānām-anutpādam*) refers to a world not filled with sense-data, I quote the following:[1]

"Again, O Mahāmati, it is taught by the Tathagatas of the past, future, and present that all things are unborn. Why? All things[2] are unborn because they are the manifestations of our own mind and have no reality of their own, of which one can say that they are existent or non-existent, or that they are born. O Mahāmati, all things are like the horns of a hare or a horse or an ass or a camel. As they are discriminated erroneously owing to the wrong judgments that are cherished by the ignorant and confused, they seem to exist but in fact they are unborn. That all things are never born in their nature—this is realised only by supreme wisdom deeply buried in the inner part of consciousness, and is not to be grasped by the discriminative and dualistic intelligence of the ignorant and confused. The realms of

[1] P. 62.

[2] Throughout the text, sometimes *sarvabhāva,* sometimes *sarvadharma.*

supreme wisdom and relative knowledge are not on the same plane. The world in which our bodies are nourished, works of utility are carried on, and where we have our habitation—this world so characterised rises from the Ālaya-vijñāna when the latter divides itself into that which is grasped and that which grasps; whereby the ignorant are attached to the dualistic view of things, thinking that there is birth, abiding, and final passing away, and further they imagine that there really is the birth of all things to be subsumed under the categories of being and non-being. Therefore, O Mahāmati, in this thou hast to discipline thyself assiduously.''

The reference to the hare's horns requires some explanation. As our common-sense experience tells us, the hare has no horns, and this supplies one of the well-known analogies or illustrations for the Indian philosophers and logicians to their reasoning on non-existence and emptiness. Thus the *Laṅkāvatāra* makes frequent allusions to this illustration when the discourse turns on the problem of no-birth and other kindred subjects. What the sutra contends about this is that the doctrine of no-birth must not be understood in the same sense as the absence of horns on a hare's head. In the latter case the absence belongs to the field of relative knowledge, while the no-birth is one of the utterances directly issuing from the highest religious experience in the Buddha's life, and it naturally transcends a world of mere sense-data. That the hare has no horns gains its meaning when it is contrasted with a cow which is adorned with a pair of horns. Therefore, this kind of non-existence or birthlessness is a relative one and no analogy exists between it and the Buddhist doctrine of no-birth. There is another sense in which this analogy fails to illustrate the no-birth: for the notion that the cow has horns is a product of illusive discrimination, as such horns have no reality like other objects in this world of particulars. When that with which a thing is contrasted no more exists, the contrast itself loses its sense. There is still another aspect to this analogy which makes it irrelevant to the proper comprehension of the Buddhist doctrine of no-birth. That is to say, when the hare alone is considered in its absolute aspect, with no reference whatever to anything outside, we cannot make any statement whether affirmative or negative as to its horns. This is what the *Laṅkāvatāra-sūtra* means when it says that the absolute truth transcends the relative categories of being and non-being as in the case of the hare's horns. Not only the absence of horns on the hare is a relative assertion, but the idea itself is a result of discrimination. When the hare alone all by itself with no reference to anything is set before us, what argument, what inference, what relationship, and what discourse can we advance on it? Here is, indeed, the birthlessness of all things as maintained by the Mahayanists.[1]

When this idea of no-birth or birthlessness (*anutpāda*) is expressed in a more positive form it is eternity unthinkable (*nityam acintyam*). The truth being above the category of causation and not subject to birth and disappearance, it has no other way to be described but as eternity, and as this eternity is an absolute one and not contrasted to impermanence or transiency, it may most fittingly be qualified as unthinkable. So we have here the "nityam-acintyam" as the realm of supreme wisdom realised in one's innermost consciousness, as of the ultimate signification stamped with the seal of suchness (*yāthātathyamudrā*).[2] In what sense this is will be shown in the following pages.

Mahāmati wants to know what difference there is between the Buddha's own view of what is "unthinkably eternal," and that of the philosophers who also talk about the makers (*kāraṇa*) or creative agents being such. To this the Buddha answers: "What is so regarded by the philosophers, cannot be established as such because their idea of

[1] This is an abstract of the argument concerning the hare's horns (*śaśavishāna*) as somewhat subtly made out on pp. 51–53 ff.

[2] P. 59 ff, and p. 166.

a cause is not sufficient, because their causer has no reason in itself to be established as eternal. What is considered by them as eternal is in its nature something not eternal. Their view is based upon an irrelevant analogy: for their eternity is contrasted to things not eternal, that is, transient things of a relative world. Their eternity is a conditioned one, and not the unthinkable or transcendental. Theirs has no value of reality. It is like the hare's horns. It is only talked about; it exists in our language it is true, but with no corresponding reality. The philosophers fail to comprehend the meaning of *svahetulakshaṇa* (self-cause-character) by which the Buddha makes his assertion about eternity unthinkable. This is a state realised by all the Tathagatas in their inmost consciousness and aimed at by all the Bodhisattvas as the finality of a life of the usual discipline. Depending on this experience which is not conditioned by the logical categories of being and non-being but which is a self-realisation requiring no external proofs, the Buddha's position is unassailable. It is quite unlike the philosophers' conception of a maker; it is something un-made and unmaking, [we may say something un-born], it is like space, Nirvana, and Nirodha, and therefore it can most becomingly be designated as eternity unthinkable (*nityācintyatā*).''[1]

This something, ''eternity unthinkable,'' is also known as the truth such as it is, or supreme wisdom realised in the inmost consciousness of the Tathagatas. *Nityācintaiveyaṁ tathāgatānāṁ pratyātmāryajñānādhigamatathatā.*[2] The unborn has a positive connotation which is comprehensible through an experience only. But as our everyday life is so encumbered and warped by moral and intellectual prejudices, the *Laṅkāvatāra* makes desperate attempts to relieve us of this fatal inconvenience. Hence its untiring reiteration concerning the significance of transcending every form of dualism,—and this by experience and not by intellectualism.

[1] Abstract, pp. 59–61.
[2] P. 60, ll. 8–9.

Why? Because the latter is another name for discrimination (*vikalpa*), and discrimination is the builder of a world of particulars. As long as a man is thus in fetters, there is no hope of liberation for him.

The Positive Conception in No-birth

"Why are all things unborn?

"Because they are unpredicable as made or making, because they have no creator.

"Why have they no self-substance?

"Because when they are reviewed with the interior intelligence (*svabuddhi*),[1] the categories such as individuality and generality are inapplicable to them.

"Why are all things neither departing nor coming?

"Because though they are characterised with the marks of individuality and generality, these marks, coming and departing, neither come nor depart.

"Why do all things never cease to exist?

"Because their not having self-substance makes it impossible to take hold of them.

"Why are all things impermanent?

"Because as soon as they take forms [or appear with individualised marks] they assume the nature of impermanence.

"Why are all things permanent?

"Because though they take forms [or appear with individualised marks], they take [really] no such forms, and in reality there is nothing born, nothing passing away."[2]

When it is declared that there is no birth of anything,

[1] Also called "*pratyātmādhigatabuddhi,*" p. 166, line 4.

[2] Pp. 115–116. Cf. p. 166, where the Buddha refutes the proposition, "All things are unborn" as established by the philosophers, because the latter try to ground it on the logic of discrimination. The Buddha makes the same assertion, but in his case it grows out of his own experience, being an intuitive knowledge not determinable by discursive reasoning. Besides, no Buddhist knowledge is stained with egotistic motives.

that all is empty and has no self-substance, we are apt to come to an erroneous conclusion which is this: If this be the case what is the use of our disciplining ourselves for the cleansing of defiling passions and the realisation of supreme wisdom? Is not all a dream, a magically-created phenomenon, with no reality underneath? For this way of reasoning, Buddhism, especially Mahayana Buddhism, has been censured. But as we have stated over and over again, those who take this view are still under the bondage of wrong judgments and discriminations. The main thesis of the *Laṅkāvatāra,* aside from its practical message of self-realisation, may be said to dispel this form of erroneous inference. Therefore, announces the Buddha,[1] the doctrine of non-existence (*abhāva*) is, in fact, a means by which the ignorant rid themselves of erroneous imagination (*parikalpita*) and discrimination (*vikalpa*) ; and when they are ridded of these and get into the society of the wise (*ārya*), they would realise that there is indeed something really subsisting and endowed with self-substance. The eye that sees into the truth is an eye of wisdom (*prajñācakshus*).[2]

This something unborn and now so positively asserted is Tathatā, Suchness, as was above referred to, but Tathatā has still an intellective odour. If it is preferred, here is one with an ontological connotation, by which I mean the expression, *āryajñāna-svabhāva-vastu,* or *ārya-vastu-svabhāva.*[3] *Vastu* generally means "a really existing thing" or "essence of a thing," but in Buddhism it quite frequently denotes an individual object in the world of individuals and is not necessarily understood in a metaphysical sense. This is especially important because Buddhism being a form of idealism does not itself take kindly to terms savouring of a realistic interpretation of existence. Whatever this is, the

[1] P. 163 et seq.

[2] See also p. 40, l. 4.

[3] P. 165; see also p. 50, where Mahāmati asks the Buddha to discourse on *ārya-jñāna-vastu* which is the basis of distinguishing the one hundred and eight terms.

existence of a Vastu is affirmed by the *Laṅkāvatāra,* whose self-substance is supreme wisdom as residing in the depths of our consciousness.

Vastu is generally rendered as 事 (*shih*) in the Chinese texts, and this is what the Sung has here; but the Wei adopts 本有 (*pên-yu*) meaning "original being, or existence," and the T'ang 妙物 (*miao-wu*) "mysterious thing," in the translation of the following gāthā,[1] manifestly showing that *vastu* has here a special connotation:

"Being and non-being—between these two limits the mind moves; with the disappearance of this field the mind properly ceases to operate (9).

"When an objective world is no more grasped, there is neither disappearance nor non-being [as all these belong to a realm of relativity], except something absolute known as Suchness (*tathatāvastu*),[2] which realm belongs to the wise (10)."

Viewing the world from this point of view, i.e., from the point of Eternal Suchness unthinkable (*acintya*) and unattainable (*anupalabdhya*), it is quiet and unborn, cannot be characterised either as being or as non-being, it is above coming and going; and in this sense it is empty like the hare's horns, like a dream, like the barren woman's child, and like magical creations. From the idealistic understanding of existence, there is Mind itself (*cittamātra*), which when asserted divides itself into subject and object, and therefrom issues an eternal concatenation of causal chains. The philosophers take these transformations (*pariṇāma*) for

[1] P. 147.

[2] These two gāthās with the others on this page (147) are repeated in the "Sagāthakam," p. 288, gg. 176–177, g. 180; p. 290, gg. 194–196, with slight variations; for instance, instead of *tathatāvastu,* it reads here *tathatāvasthā,* "abode of suchness." The gāthā (g. 175) immediately preceding these in the "Sagāthakam" is illuminating to read in connection with them: "Words belong to the realm of thought (*citta*), they are misleading; Prajñā is truth and non-discriminative; thought falls into dualism, hence Prajñā is not of discrimination."

reality and cling to them with egotistical motives and evil designs. Nine transformations are recognised by the philosophers, as regards form (*saṁsthāna*), appearance (*lakshaṇa*), cause (*hetu*), combination (*yukti*), opinion (*dṛishṭi*), birth (*utpāda*), existence (*bhāva*), manifested condition (*pratyayābhivyakti*), and manifested work (*kriyābhivyakti*).[1]

Whatever one may say about the phenomenal world given to our senses, the *Laṅkāvatāra* insists that all things are unborn because they are found so and for no other reason. Here we return to the position from which we made our start, that is, that all the metaphysical and epistemological statements made ın this sutra are finally resolvable into self-realisation (*pratyātma-vedya-gati-dharma*).

[1] Pp. 158–159. Except the transformation of form (*saṁsthāna*), no explanation is given here of the other eight.

3. THE TRIPLE BODY OF THE BUDDHA

The Doctrine Outlined

The dogma of the Triple Body (*trikāya*) as now accepted by all Mahayana schools of Buddhism in China and Japan is a late development in the history of Mahayana. The dogma, before it was fully formulated, was only adumbrated here and there in the earlier Mahayana sutras. It was, probably, not until the Yogācāra philosophy began to be crystallised into a system by Asanga and his predecessors that the conception of the Triple Body came to form a part of their programme.

According to the Yogācāra philosophy, the Triple Body is Dharmakāya (法身, *fa-shên*), Saṁbhogakāya (報身, *pao-shên*), and Nirmāṇakāya (化身, *hua-shên*). *Dharma* here may be understood in either way as "reality," or as "law-giving principle," or simply as "law." *Kāya* means "body," or "system." The combination, *dharmakāya,* is then literally a body or person that exists as principle, and it has now come to mean the highest reality from which all things derive their being and lawfulness, but which in itself transcends all limiting conditions. But Dharmakāya is not a mere philosophical word, as is indicated by the term "kāya," which suggests the idea of personality, especially as it relates to Buddhahood. It belongs to the Buddha, it is what inwardly and essentially constitutes Buddhahood, for without it a Buddha loses altogether his being. We may regard the Dharmakāya as corresponding to the Christian idea of Godhead. The Dharmakāya is also known as Svabhāvakāya, meaning "self-nature-body" (自性身, *tzŭ-hsing-shên*), for it abides in itself, it remains as such retaining its self-nature. It is in this sense the absolute aspect of the Buddha, in whom perfect tranquillity prevails.

The second Body is the Saṁbhogakāya, which is ordinarily translated as Body of Recompense, or Enjoyment.

Literally, "enjoyment" is a better word for *saṁbhoga,* for it comes originally from the root, *bhuj,* "to eat," "to enjoy," to which the prefix *sam,* meaning "together" is added. Thus Saṁbhogakāya is often done into the Chinese 共用身 (*kung-yung-shên*), 受用身 (*shou-yung-shên*), or 食身 (*chih-shên*). When we have 報身, Recompense or Reward Body for it, the Chinese seem to point to another Sanskrit original, or else it is not quite a literal rendering, but given according to its derivative sense. For this Body of Enjoyment is attained as the result of or as the reward for a series of spiritual discipline carried on through so many kalpas. The Body thus realised is the Saṁbhogakāya, Body of Recompense, which is enjoyed by the well-deserving one, i.e., Bodhisattva-Mahāsattva.

The Buddha as the Body of Enjoyment is generally represented as a figure enveloped in all the glory of Buddhahood; for in him incarnated there is everything good and beautiful and holy accruing from the perfection of the spiritual life. The particular features of each such Buddha may vary according to his original vows; for instance, his environment, his name, his form, his country, and his activity may not be the same; Amitābha Buddha has his Pure Land in the West with all the accommodations as he desired in the beginning of his career as Bodhisattva; and so with Akshobhya as described in the sutra bearing his name.

This second Body of the Trinity is sometimes known in Chinese as Ying-shên (應身), instead of Pao-shên (報身). The original Sanskrit term for *ying* might not have been the same as the one for *pao. Ying* means "to respond" and it is at present quite difficult to ascertain what its original was, for we have not yet recovered, if this were possible, any Sanskrit sutra in which this term is used. From *saṁbhoga* or *saṁbhogya.*[1] 應 (*ying*) cannot be deduced, while the

[1] In Asanga's *Mahāyāna Sūtrālamkāra* edited by Sylvain Lévi, IX, 60.

chapter on "The Trikāya" in the *Suvarṇa-prabhāsa* is missing in the Sanskrit text in our possession, evidently this being a later addition. The two Chinese translations of the *Suvarṇa-prabhāsa,* one by I-tsing (義淨) and the other by Paramārtha contain this Trikāya chapter where both translators have *ying-shên* for the second Body. As to the original of *pao-shên* reference will be found later on.

The third Body is the Nirmāṇakāya, usually translated as *hua-shên* (化身), which means "Body of Transformation," or simply "Assumed Body." The Dharmakāya is too exalted a body for ordinary mortals to come into any conscious contact with. As it transcends all forms of limitation, it cannot become an object of sense or intellect. We ordinary mortals can perceive and have communion with this absolute body only through its transformed forms. And we perceive them only according to our capacities, moral and spiritual. They do not appear to us in the same form. We thus read in the *Saddharma-puṇḍarīka* that the Bodhisattva Avalokiteśvara[1] transforms himself into so many different forms according to the kind of beings whose salvation he has in view at the moment. The *Kshitigarbha-sūtra* also mentions that the Bodhisattva Kshitigarbha takes upon himself a variety of forms in order to respond to the requirements of his worshippers. The conception of the Nirmāṇakāya is significant, seeing that this world of relativity stands contrasted with the absolute value of Suchness which can be reached only by means of the knowledge of Suchness (*tathatājñā*). The essence of Buddhahood is the Dharmakāya, but as long as the Buddha remains such, there is no hope for the salvation of a world of particulars. The Buddha has to abandon his original abode, and must take upon himself such forms as are conceivable and acceptable to the inhabitants of this earth. The Holy Spirit emanates, as it were, from Absolute Buddhahood and is seen by those who are prepared by their previous karma to see him.

[1] Chapter XXIV. Kern's English translation p. 406 et seq.

Nirmāṇa comes from the root *mā,* "to measure," to "form," "to display," to which *nir,* meaning "out of," is prefixed; and the whole term, Nirmāṇakāya, is generally rendered as Body of Transformation (化身, *hua-shên*) in most sutras and śāstras. Sometimes, however, Ying-shên (應身), Response Body, is used for this third member of the Trinity, causing confusion with the second member, which is occasionally also designated as Ying-shên. It is suspected that Ying-shên as the third Body is not Nirmāṇakāya in Sanskrit, perhaps it is Saṁvṛiti, as can be gathered from Tibetan sources. Saṁvṛiti is contrasted with Paramārtha when truth is regarded as having a double aspect, one as absolute truth, and the other as relative (*paramārthasatya* and *saṁvṛitisatya*), in concession to or in response to the worldly way of thinking. The Saṁvṛiti-kāya, therefore, may mean the Body of the Buddha which he assumes in response to the requirements of his followers. In this the Buddha appears transformed and not in his original aspect as he is in himself.

The Suvarṇa-prabhāsa on the Triple Body

There is a chapter, as was stated above, in the Chinese *Suvarṇa-prabhāsa*[1] devoted to the exposition of the Trikāya dogma. It is entitled "The Trikāya Distinguished." The following is an extract from it. The Buddha addressing the Bodhisattva Ākāśagarbha said, "O son of a good family, the Tathagata has a triple body, Hua-shên, Ying-shên, and Fa-shên. When the Triple Body is attained, unparalleled supreme enlightenment is attained. How does a Bodhisattva understand Hua-shên (*Nirmāṇakāya*)? O son of a good family, when the Tathagata was of old disciplining himself, he practised all kinds of virtues for the sake of

[1] I-tsing (634–713) translated the sutra after his return from India in 695. Paramārtha's translation came out in the first year of Ch'êng-shêng (552). The earliest translation is by Dharmaraksha of the Northern Liang (397–439) and does not contain the Trikāya chapter.

sentient beings. The discipline reached its perfection, and by virtue of the discipline he attained the state of freedom; and because of this freedom he knows how to follow up the minds of all beings, how to be in accord with their conduct, and how to enter into their worlds. He understands all the multifarious ways in which they are living, and for this reason he appears to them in a variety of forms precisely when and where it is most opportune for them to come into his presence. He never makes mistakes in this respect, not only in time and space, but in conduct and discourse. The Body he there assumes in such multiple forms is called the Body of Transformation (*hua-shên*).

"O son of a good family, all the Buddhas and Tathagatas preach the ultimate truth to the Bodhisattvas in order to make them thoroughly conversant with [the nature of things], to make them see into the oneness of Nirvāṇa and Saṁsāra, to make the hearts of sentient beings rejoice by wiping them clear from all fears arising from the thought of an ego, to lay down the foundations for the teachings and doings of the Buddhas, which must have no boundaries to be truly in accordance with the Suchness of things, as well as with the knowledge of Suchness and also with their original vows. The Body of the Tathagata appears bearing the thirty-two marks of a great personality, accompanied by the eighty minor marks of excellence, and enveloped in a light around the shoulders and back. That body is the Ying-shên—the Body of Response.

"O son of a good family, in order to clear away all the possible hindrances arising from the evil passions and other things, and to conserve all good things, there is nothing but the Suchness of things and the knowledge of Suchness: this is known as the Dharmakāya (*fa-shên*).

"The first two Bodies are temporarily discriminated, while the third one is true reality being the root of the first two. For when severed from the Suchness of things and from the knowledge of non-discrimination, all the Bud-

The Various Designations of the Trikāya as Found in the Different Texts:

Texts and Translators		*Suvarṇaprabhāsa* (I-tsing)	*Awakening of Faith in the Mahāyāna* (Paramārtha)	*Awakening of Faith in the Mahāyāna* (Śikshānanda)	*Sūtrālaṁkāra* (Prabhākaramitra)	*Mahāyānasaṁparīgraha-śāstra* Paramārtha	*Mahāyānasaṁparīgraha-śāstra* Buddhaśanta	*Mahāyānasaṁparīgraha-śāstra* Dharmagupta	*Mahāyānasaṁparīgraha-śāstra* Hsüan-chuang
Trikāya	The First Body	法身 (fa-shên)	法身 (fa-shên)	法身 (fa-shên)	Svabhāva-, or Dharma-kāya (自性身 or 法身)	自性身 (tsŭ-hsing-shên)	眞身 (chên-shên)	自性身 (tsŭ-hsing-shên)	自性身 (tsŭ-hsing-shên)
	The Second Body	應身 (ying-shên)	報身 (pao-shên)	報身 (pao-shên) 受用身 (shou-yung-shên)	Sambhoga-kāya (食身)	應身 (ying-shên)	報身 (pao-shên)	共用身 (hung-yung-shên)	受用身 (shou-yung-shên)
	The Third Body	化身 (hua-shên)	應身 (ying-shên)	化身 (hua-shên)	Nairmā-nikakāya (變化身 or 化身)	化身 (hua-shên)	應身 (ying-shên)	化身 (hua-shên)	變化身 (pien-hua-shên)

The Laṅkāvatāra has the following names corresponding to the Trikāya:

For Dharmakāya,	Dharma-buddha, Dharmatā-buddha, Mūlatathāgata, Tathatājñāna-buddha;
„ Sambhogakāya,	Nisyanda-(nishyanda-)buddha, Dharmatā-nishyanda-buddha;
„ Nirmāṇakāya,	Nirmāṇa-buddha.

dhas cease to have virtues of their own. For the state of immaculate Buddhahood is attained only when the knowledge that constitutes the essence of all the Buddhas is realised and thereby putting an end ultimately to all evil passions. Therefore, the Suchness of things and the knowledge of Suchness contain in it all that makes up Buddhahood."

The Dharmakāya in the Laṅkāvatāra

The idea that great men are immortal seems to be innate with us human beings. We do not wish to think that our earthly death is the end of all that there is in us. We feel that there must be a spirit or soul or shadow that lives forever. The cult of ancestor-worship is no mere superstition, for its psychology is deep-seated in human nature. It was quite natural for the followers of the Buddha to conceive the idea of him as the Dharmakāya, abiding forever among them and eternally preaching the Dharma on the Mount of the Holy Vulture, although his Nirvana had taken place after eighty years of his fleshly life.

Thus we read in the *Saddharma-puṇḍarīka* XV: "An inconceivable number of thousands of kotis of kalpas (eons) is it since I attained supreme enlightenment, and I have never ceased to preach the Dharma(1). I have converted a great number of Bodhisattvas and established them in Buddha-wisdom; during many kotis of kalpas I have brought myriads of kotis of sentient beings into maturity(2). In order to discipline beings, I show them the stage of Nirvana, I make use of skilful means; but I have never entered into Nirvana, for I have been preaching the Dharma at this place (3)."[1]

In this light the following lines from the *Suvarṇaprabhāsa* ("On the Life of the Tathagata") are to be under-

[1] In the Chinese translations of the *Suvarṇaprabhāsa* by I-tsing and also by Jñānagupta, there is a stanza repeating exactly the sentiment herein expressed: "I am always at the Holy Vulture and preaching this sutra-treasure; my showing Nirvana is meant for the maturing

stood: "The Buddha does not pass away, the Dharma does not decline; it is for the purpose of ripening sentient beings that the Buddha appears to have passed away. Inconceivable is the Blessed One, the Buddha; the Tathagata is the body of permanence; in order to benefit sentient beings he shows a variety of works in fine array."[1]

When the Buddha was giving his farewell address, he said something to this effect that "Those who see the Dharma see me even after my passing." The statement may be regarded as confirming the common psychology of immortality. No wonder, then, that the doctrine of a dual body came to be propounded soon after the Nirvana, the one as Rūpakāya (material body) and the other as Dharmakāya, (the Body of Truth). So we read further in the *Suvarṇaprabhāsa* that the body of the Buddha is as solid as a diamond and what is manifested of him is his Body of Transformation,[2] and that the Dharmakāya is indeed Enlightenment, and the Dharmadhātu is the Tathāgata.[3] These two notions, Dharmakāya, unchangeable like a diamond, constituting the substance of enlightenment, and a body subject to change and transformation, must have been in the minds of early Buddhists, though it does not follow that they were conscious of the two notions as distinctly separable as we see them in the *Suvarṇaprabhāsa* and other sutras. They were probably only vaguely conscious of the difference between the Buddha that had passed away and the Buddha whose presence with them they could not somehow ignore, before these two Buddhas came to be conceived in terms of Body

of sentient beings. As the ignorant refuse to believe me owing to their erroneous views, I show my Nirvana in order to bring them to a state of maturity." Chapter II, "On the Life of the Tathagata." This passage is lacking in the Sanskrit text.

[1] *Na buddhaḥ parinirvāti na dharmaḥ parihīyate,*
Sattvānāṁ paripākāya parinirvāṇaṁ nidarśayate.
Acintyo bhagavān buddho nityakāyas tathāgataḥ,
Deśeti vividhān vyūhān sattvānāṁ hitakāraṇāt.

[2] *Vajrasaṁhatanakāyo nirmitaṁ kāyaṁ darśayet.*

[3] *Dharmakāyo hi saṁbuddho dharmadhātus-tathāgataḥ.*

(*kāya*) and regarded as at least two aspects of it, eternal and temporal.

So with the doctrine of the Triple Body (*trikāya*). Early Mahayana Buddhists thought of Dharmatābuddha and Mūlatathāgata, and Vipākabuddha and Nirmāṇabuddha as distinguishable; but in the earlier Mahayana sutras such as the *Laṇkāvatāra,* in which we are at present chiefly interested, no Kāya doctrine appears. Buddhas, indeed, are variously spoken of, but not as belonging to the Kāya system; for the Nirmāṇabuddha is not the same as the Nirmāṇakāya, nor is the Dharmatābuddha the same as the Dharmakāya. To determine the qualification of a Buddha in terms of Kāya is further advanced in thought than merely designating a Buddha as the Nairmāṇika or otherwise. Even Nāgārjuna is confusing in his discrimination of different Buddhas as belonging to the different Kāyas. He mentions two kinds of Kāyas, but the distinction is not quite clear, and besides they are variously designated. The clear-cut conception of the Kāya seems to have started with the Yogācāra school headed by Asanga and his predecessors.

Dharmakāya is often referred to in the *Laṅkāvatāra* and other early sutras but not as one of the members of the Trikāya. The *Laṅkāvatāra* speaks of the "Tathagata's Dharmakāya," of the "inconceivable Dharmakāya," and of the "Dharmakāya as will-body," but in all these cases there is no reference whatever to the conception of the Trikāya or any Kāya, except that it means something substantially constituting Tathagatahood or Buddhahood. The passages in the *Laṅkāvatāra* where the term "Dharmakāya" is found are as follows:

1. Where the attainment of the Tathāgatakāya in the heavens is spoken of as the result of the understanding of the highest spiritual truths belonging to Mahayana Buddhism,[1] Dharmakāya is used in apposition with Tathagata as something that transcends the nature of the five Dharmas,

[1] P. 51.

being furnished with things issuing from the highest knowledge (*prajñā*), and itself abiding in the realm of magical appearances (*māyāvishaya*). Here we may consider all these terms synonymous, Dharmakāya, Tathāgatakāya, and Tathāgata.

2. Tathāgatakāya is referred to also when the Bodhisattva attains to a certain form of meditation whereby he finds himself in accord with the suchness of things and its transformations. The Tathāgatakāya is realised when all his mental activities conditionally working are extinguished and there takes place a radical revolution in his consciousness. The Kāya is no less than the Dharmakāya.[1]

3. When the Bodhisattva is described as being anointed like a great sovereign by all the Buddhas as he goes beyond the final stage of Bodhisattvaship, mention is made of Dharmakāya which he will finally realise.[2] This Kāya is characterised as *vaśavartin* and made synonymous with Tathāgata. In Buddhism *vaśavartin* is used in the sense of supreme sovereignty whose will is deed since there is nothing standing in the way of its rulership. The Dharmakāya may here be identified with Sambhogakāya, the second member of the Trikāya. Here the Bodhisattva is sitting in the Lotus Palace decorated with gems of all sorts, surrounded by Bodhisattvas of similar qualifications and also by all the Buddhas whose hands are extended to receive the Bodhisattva here. It goes without saying that the Bodhisattva here described has comprehended the Mahayana truth that there is no self-substance in objects external or internal, and that he is abiding in the full realisation of the truth most inwardly revealed to his consciousness.

4. Dharmakāya is found again[3] in connection with the moral provisions obtainable in a realm of pure spirituality. The term is now coupled with *acintya*, inconceivable, as well as with *vaśavartita*.

[1] Pp. 42, 43, 51, 70.
[2] P. 70. [3] P. 134.

5. Where all the Buddhas are spoken of as of the same character (*Samatā*) in four ways,[1] the sameness of the body (*kāyasamatā*) is regarded as one of them. All the Buddhas who are Tathagatas, the Enlightened Ones, and the Arhats, share in the nature of sameness as regards the Dharmakāya and their material body (*rūpakāya*) with the thirty-two marks and the eighty minor ones, except when they assume different forms in different worlds to keep all beings in good discipline. In the light of the later developed theory of the Trikāya, all the three bodies are traceable in this passage of the *Laṅkāvatāra*. Besides the Dharmakāya expressly referred to, we have also Sambhogakāya solemnised with all the physical features of a superior man; and also the Nirmāṇakāya, the Body of Transformation, in response to the needs of sentient beings who are inhabiting each in his own realm of existence.

6. Anutpāda (no-birth) is said to be another name for the Tathagata's Manomaya-dharmakāya.[2] *Manomaya* is "will-made" and as is explained elsewhere[3] a Bodhisattva is able to assume a variety of forms according to his wishes just as easily as one can in thought pass through or over all kinds of physical obstructions. Does then the "Dharmakāya will-made" mean, not the Dharmakāya in itself, but the Dharmakāya in its relation to a world of multitudinousness where it may take any forms it likes according to conditions? In this case the Dharmakāya thus qualified is no other than the Nirmāṇakāya. So we read further that the Tathagata's other names are a legion in this world only that sentient beings fail to recognise them even when they hear them.[4]

7. The Tathagata's Dharmakāya is compared to the indestructibility of the sands of the Ganges which remain ever the same when they are put in the fire.[5] Further down, the T'ang translation speaks of the Dharmakāya (*fa-shên*)

[1] Pp. 141 ff. [2] P. 192. [3] Pp. 81, 136.
[4] See below pp. 353–355, of these *Studies*. [5] P. 232.

having no body whatever, and for that reason it is never subject to destruction. In the Sanskrit text the corresponding term is *śarīra* or *śarīravat,* and not Dharmakāya, but from the context we can judge that *śarīra* is here used synonymously with Dharmakāya. In fact, the Wei and the Sung translation also have 法身 (*fa-shên*), that is, Dharmakāya, here. In Buddhism *śarīra* is something solid and indestructible that is left behind when the dead body is consumed in fire, and it was thought that only holy men leave such indestructible substance behind. This conception is probably after an analogy of Dharmakāya forever living and constituting the spiritual substance of Buddhahood.

8. In the gāthā concluding this paragraph on the sands of the Ganges, the Buddha's Buddhahood (*buddhasya buddhatāḥ*) instead of Dharmakāya is made the subject of comparison to the sands which are free from all possible faults inherent in things relative. There is no doubt that the Buddhatā too means the Dharmakāya of the Tathagata, only differently designated.

From these references we can see that the idea of Dharmakāya is not wanting in the *Laṅkāvatāra,* and that it is used not in the sense of the Dharmakāya of the Triple Body dogma. No doubt the underlying notion of it is here, which contributed later to the formulation of the fully-developed dogma. In the following pages the different forms of the Buddhas as they are mentioned in the *Laṅkāvatāra* will be examined with the view of ascertaining how far the *Laṅkāvatāra* has paved the way to the Triple Body doctrine.

No Triple Body yet, but a Buddha Trinity

When different Buddha-personalities are distinguished in the *Laṅkāvatāra,* it is done so in terms of Buddha and not in terms of Kāya. The Buddhas are different as Buddhas and not as belonging to any one of the Trinity. This distinction is important, I think, in tracing the development of the Trikāya theory which did not formulate itself until sometime after Nāgārjuna. As was stated before, when the term Dharmakāya is used in the *Laṅkāvatāra* it is not as one of the Trikāya, but simply in contrast to the physical and therefore destructible aspect of Buddhahood. The Dharmakāya, therefore, means the Buddha-personality when it is perfectly identified with the Dharma, or the absolute truth itself making up the essence of Buddhism.

What corresponds in the *Laṅkāvatāra* to the idea of Dharmakāya as a member of the trinity is found in that of Dharmatābuddha, which is also designated as Tathāgata-jñāna-Buddha or as Mūla-tathāgata. Dharmatā-Buddha is sometimes shortened into Dharma-Buddha, but they both mean practically the same thing. ***Dharmatā*** is translated in Chinese as *fa-hsing* (法性), the nature of things, and, therefore, Dharmatā-Buddha means the Buddha whose nature is reality itself, and from whom all other Buddha-personalities flow. In the following passage the *Laṅkāvatāra* way of treating different Buddhas is clearly delineated.[1]

"And again, O Mahāmati, all things come into existence when we distinguish between individuality and generality as we are bound by habit-energy to see things projected outside our own minds. And owing to this false discrimination to which we are attached thinking it to be real, we have a variety of illusory beings and scenes; while we cling to them as real they are not at all attainable [as such]; this is what is preached by the Buddha who flows out of the Ultimate Essence (*dharmatā*).

"And again, O Mahāmati, the evolution of false discrimination takes place from clinging to relative knowledge [as final]. It is like a man skilled in magical art, who, depending upon grass, trees, shrubs, or creepers, projects all kinds of beings and forms. When a magically-created man takes a form like a substantial being, it is variously perceived and falsely judged [by the onlookers]. Being thus

[1] P. 56 f.

perceived, O Mahāmati, there is yet nothing substantial here; even so, O Mahāmati, depending on relative knowledge there is false discrimination whereby the mind discriminates variously and perceives particular forms. False discrimination, O Mahāmati, arises from habit-energy which makes one cling to the particularising aspect of existence, and we then have what is known as false discrimination. Such, O Mahāmati, is the discourse by the Buddha who flows out [of Ultimate Essence].

"Further, O Mahāmati, the Dharmatā-Buddha defines the extent of self-realisation which has nothing to do with modes of mentation.

"Further, O Mahāmati, the Nirmāṇa-Buddha who suffers transformation defines functions and fields differently allotted to Charity, Moral Conduct, Meditation (*dhyāna*), Tranquillisation (*samādhi*), various kinds of Wisdom (*prajñā*), and Knowledge(*jñāna*), Aggregates(*skandha*), Dhātus, Āyatanas, Emancipations, and Vijñānas, showing how these things in their nature far surpass the materialistic views of the philosophers.

"Further, O Mahāmati, the Dharmatā-Buddha is free of support; he is self-sufficing, disengaged from all doings, senses, measurements, and appearances; he is not within reach of the stupid-minded, Śrāvakas, Pratyekabuddhas, and philosophers, who are engrossed in clinging to the notion of an ego-substance.

"For this reason, O Mahāmati, you ought to devote yourself to bring about the excellent state of self-realisation and be disengaged from the views which regard your own mental projections [as objectively real]."[1]

The three kinds of Buddha here distinguished as the Dharmatā, the Nishyanda (or Dharmatā-nishyanda), and the Nirmāṇa (or Nirmita) apparently correspond to the trinity of Dharmakāya, Sambhogakāya, and Nirmāṇakāya. The Dharmatā is the absolute essence of the Buddhahood, which

[1] P. 56 ff.

is beyond all forms of limitation and of which nothing is the be predicable. It is realised only within mind (*abhisamaya*).[1] Whereas the Nishyanda which flows out from the Dharmatā, owing to the habit-energy or memory (*vāsanā*) accumulated in it from time immemorial, manifests a world of particulars where, by such categories as individuality and generality, relative knowledge (*paratantra*) is generated, and depending on this knowledge false discrimination (*parikalpita*) is made possible, which makes erroneous judgments on things only magically existing. That is to say, the conception of the Nishyanda means the beginning of a world of individual objects.

Nishyanda or *Nisyanda,* from the root *syand,* literally means "flowing down," or "flowing out," and the Buddha thus prefixed is sometimes translated in the Wei and the T'ang text as 報佛, *Pao-fo,* or Recompence Buddha; while in the Sung it is 依佛, *I-fo,* Depending Buddha. Not only is there no connection in sense between *nishyanda* and *sambhoga,* which means "enjoyment," but the definition given in the *Laṅkāvatāra* to the Nishyanda Buddha as to his functions seems to be quite different from the nature of the Sambhogakāya as we ordinarily have it. It is strange that the two Chinese texts have 報 (*pao*) occasionally for *nishyanda,* and at the same time for *vipāka* also,[2] where Vipākasthā-Buddha and Vipākaja-Buddha are rendered equally by 報佛 (*pao-fo*). *Vipāka* means "maturing," or "cooking," and may be translated as "reward," or "compensating," but how did *nishyanda* come to be *pao* as much as *vipāka*? And how did the Nishyanda-Buddha and the Vipāka-Buddha come to be considered as corresponding to the second member of the Kāya Trinity? Or is there really a correspondence between the three ideas? The reason why *nishyanda* and *vipāka* came to be rendered *pao* by the Chinese translators is perhaps this. They both belong to the category of cause and effect. In Buddhist philosophy five kinds of effects

[1] P. 242. [2] Pp. 28, 34.

(*phala*) are enumerated against six kinds of causes (*hetu*), and Vipāka and Nishyanda are two of the five effects, the others being Purushakāra, Adhipati, and Visaṁyoga.[1] By Vipāka-effect is meant that the nature of an effect is not the same as the nature of the cause. When a man does something good he is rewarded with something enjoyable. Pleasure and goodness are not of the same character, but there is an intimate relationship between them as cause and effect. In the case of the Nishyanda, however, cause and effect are of a similar nature. An act of goodness tends to produce the disposition to do more good; an effect of the same quality flows out of its cause. As thus the Nishyanda and the Vipāka are considered as expressing different forms of effect, or reward, or something that flows out of a cause, they came to be designated as 報 (*pao*), result, though somewhat indiscriminately. With all that we can say about it, however, it does not seem to be quite correct to regard *nishyanda* as meaning *pao*; for the idea explicitly expressed in the *Laṅkāvatāra* is that of flowing out, or depending on, and not of being rewarded. The teaching of the Nishyanda-Buddha, which concerns with the individualising phase of existence, is derived or flows out of the nature of reality, as we plainly read in the phrase, "*dharmatā-nishyanda.*"

That there is no idea of enjoyment (*sambhoga*) in the make-up of the Nishyanda-Buddha is evident, but there is something in the *Laṅkāvatāra* remotely suggesting the idea where the Nishyanda-Buddha is spoken of as being in the Akanishṭha Heaven. Read the following:[2]

"It is like the Ālayavijñāna, O Mahāmati, which makes manifest instantly a world of corporeality (*deha*), homestead

[1] The Purushakāra (man-working) effect takes place when the farmer cultivates the ground to make it yield a harvest of rice or wheat; the Adhipati is the effect of an efficient cause; and the Visaṁyoga is the outcome of Nirvana whereby one is released from all bondage.

[2] P. 56.

(*pratishṭha*), and utility (*ābhoga*), which is the projection of one's own mind; even so with the Nishyanda-Buddha, O Mahāmati, maturing the conditions of all beings, he directs the disciplining of his devotees at his abode which is in a mansion in Akanishṭha Heaven. It is, O Mahāmati, like the Dharmatā-Buddha being illumined instantly by the rays issuing from the Nishyanda and from the Nirmāna; even so, O Mahāmati, with the realisation of the truth in one's inmost consciousnsss, it instantly shines forth turning itself away from the false views of being and non-being."

In this quotation we gather that the Nishyanda-Buddha has his abode in Akanishṭha Heaven which is the highest of all the worlds that are designated as having a form (*rūpa*), and that he emits rays of light like the Nirmāṇa-Buddha which are reflected on the Dharmatā-Buddha. That the Akanishṭha is resplendent with light is seen from the verse 3, of the chapter on "Abhisamaya," *Akanishṭho virājate,* and that the Bodhisattva attains perfect enlightenment after passing beyond the tenth stage of Bodhisattvahood and becomes a full-fledged Buddha in Akanishṭha Heaven is referred to at several places[1] in the *Laṅkāvatāra.* Evidently this Heaven is the abode of all the Nishyanda-Buddhas, that is, Buddhas of Sambhogakāya, or Buddhas who are "enjoying" the state of supreme blessedness as the result of their long and arduous spiritual training. While this is the natural outcome of spirituality, it is no doubt also the outflow of the highest truth, depending on which all things exist. Was it then for this reason that the Nishyanda-Buddha came to be translated as 報佛 (*pao-fo*) as well as 依佛 (*i-fo*), and again more literally as 所流佛 (*so-liu-fo*)?

As regards the Vipāka-Buddha, or Vipākasthā-Buddha, as corresponding to the second of the Kāya Trinity, bare mention is made of it in the "One Hundred and Eight Questions," and in the "Sagāthakam" which may be said

[1] Pp. 28, 34, 51, 56, 215, 269, 361, etc.

not to belong to the *Laṅkāvatāra* proper. In the first place we have, "What are the Nirmāṇika-Buddhas? What are the Vipākaja-Buddhas? And what are the Tathatā-jñāna-Buddhas? Pray tell me."[1] A few pages down[2] we read, "You have asked me what are the Nirmāṇika- and the Vipākasthā-Buddhas, and the Tathatā-jñāna-Buddhas." The following is from the "Sagāthakam"[3]: "The Vaipākika Buddhas, the Nairmāṇika Buddhas, all beings, Bodhisattvas, and all countries in the ten quarters (140), the Nishyanda, the Dharma, and the Nirmāṇa-nairmāṇika,—they all issue from Amitābha's Land of Happiness(141). What is told by the Nairmāṇika-[Buddhas] and what is told by the Vipākaja-[Buddhas],—both are the doctrine expounded in sutras of the Vaipulya class. You should understand its esoteric meaning (142). What is told by sons of the Buddha is what the leaders also announce. But the speech of the Nairmāṇika is not [delivered] by the Vaipākika Buddhas (143)."

In order to show the relation between the Sanskrit originals for the various names of the Buddhas and their Chinese equivalents variously given in the different translations, they are tabulated on the following page.

The Nishyanda and the Nirmāṇa Buddha

As I said before, the distinction between the Mūla-Tathagata (or Dharmatā-Buddha), and the Nishyanda-Buddha (or Vipāka-Buddha) or Nirmāṇa-Buddha is quite well defined: for the first is the transcendental substance of all the Buddhas and Bodhisattvas, without which nothing can exist, nothing can come into existence; for "the Nirmita-Buddhas are not karma-created (*karmaprabhava*), and the Tathagata is not in them, nor is he anywhere else than with them."[4] Not only that the Nirmāṇa-Buddha derives its raison d'être from the Dharmatā, but that the Nishyanda

[1] P. 28. [2] P. 34.
[3] P. 283. [4] P. 242.

I. The Buddha in His Absolute Essence

Sanskrit	Dharmatā-Buddha[1]	Dharma-Buddha[2]	Tathāgata-jñāna-Buddha[3]	Maula-tathāgata[4]
Guṇabhadra	法佛	法佛	如如佛，智慧佛 平等智慧佛	眞如來
Bodhiruci	法佛	法佛	如智佛	根本如來
Śikshānanda	法性佛	法佛	眞如智慧佛	根本佛

II. The Buddha in His Derivative Form

Sanskrit	Dharmatā-nishyanda-Buddha[5]	Nishyanda-Buddha[6]	Vipākaja-Buddha[7]	Vipāka-sthā-Buddha[8]	Vaipākika-Buddha[9]
Guṇabhadra	法依佛	依佛	報生佛	報佛	(wanting)
Bodhiruci	法佛報佛	報佛（報相佛）	報佛	報佛	報佛
Śikshānanda	法性所流佛	報佛	報佛	報佛	報佛

III. The Buddha in His Transformations

Sanskrit	Nirmāṇa-Buddha[10]	Nirmāṇika-(Nairmāṇika-)Buddha[11]	Nirmita(-Nirmāṇa, -Nairmāṇika)-Buddha[12]
Guṇabhadra	化佛	化佛	化佛
Bodhiruci	化佛	化佛	應化化佛（應化佛）
Śikshānanda	變化佛（化佛）	變化佛（化佛）	變化如來（化佛）

[1] P. 56, line 10, 14; p. 57, line 8, 13; p. 93, line 10; p. 241, line 7.

[2] P. 283, line 6; p. 313, gg. 381 and 382.

[3] P. 28, line 6; p. 34, line 3.

[4] P. 16, line 14; p. 242, line 7, 8. Mauna-tathāgata in the Sanskrit edition.

[5] P. 56, line 14. Sometimes *nisyanda*.

[6] P. 56, line 8, 11, 14; p. 57, line 8; p. 283, line 6; p. 320, line 1.

[7] P. 28, line 5; p. 283, g. 142.

[8] P. 34, line 2.

[9] P. 283, gg. 140 and 143.

[10] P. 56, line 11; p. 283, line 6; p. 241, line 7 (-kāya); p. 320, line 2.

[11] P. 28, line 5; p. 283, line 6; p. 93, lines 9–10; p. 34, line 2; p. 283, line 4, 6, 8.

[12] P. 16, line 13; p. 57, line 10; p. 242, line 12, 6; p. 314, line 2 (pañca-); p. 320, line 1.

also is depending upon the Dharmatā has already been mentioned. But as to the differentia of the Nirmāṇa, there is some confusion between the latter and the Nishyanda; for it is manifestly the work of both Buddhas to discourse on the categories of individuality and generality; they both belong to the world of relativity.[1] What most definitely distinguishes the Nirmāṇa-Buddha from any other kinds of Buddhahood is his coming in direct contact with the world of suffering beings and listening to their fears and anxieties. Though it may not be one of his functions to reveal to us directly the secrets of the inner realisation, he helps us ignorant beings to know where to look for the ultimate seat of enlightenment and emancipation. This then we may regard as characteristic of the Nirmāṇa-Buddha. "This teaching [by the Nairmāṇika-Buddha] is occupied with the views entertained in the minds of the simple-minded and does not reveal to them any truth whose nature may go against [their understanding], the supreme wisdom whereby the realisation of the inner thing is made possible, or the blissful enjoyment of a Samādhi."[2]

That the Buddha assumes a variety of forms, so transformed as to bring all beings into maturity and shine in glory like the moon in water,[3] or like the sacrificial fire,[4] can be gathered from several passages scattered in the *Laṅkāvatāra*.[5]

In the "Sagāthakam," however, quite explicit references are made to the Nirmāṇa-Buddha. "Akanishṭha Heaven, where no sins prevail, is inhabited by those who are always in the practice of non-discrimination, detached from the mind and its workings (38). They are in possession of the Powers, Psychic Knowledge, and Self-mastery, and perfect in the attainment of the Samādhi; and there they are awakened into full enlightenment, and here perceived

[1] Pp. 56, 93. [2] P. 93. [3] P. 22 f. [4] P. 215.

[5] See, for instance, besides those already mentioned, pp. 72, 142, 196, etc.

as the Nirmita-[Buddha] (39). There are millions of the Nirmāṇa [forms] of the Buddhas, they are, indeed, immeasurable, and they are manifested everywhere. The simple-minded following them listen to the truth (*dharma*) (40)."

Further on we have this: "There is a land and there are the Nirmāṇa-Buddhas [teaching the doctrine of] the One Vehicle and Triple Vehicle; I never enter into Nirvana, [for] the Buddhas know that all is empty and has nothing to do with birth [and death] (g. 379). The Buddhas are classified under thirty-six, each of which is divided into ten; in accordance with the mentalities of all beings, they are manifested in all lands (g. 380). While in the world of discrimination there is multitudinousness, but in fact no multitudinousness exists. Even so it is with the Dharma-Buddha in this world (g. 381). The Dharma-Buddha is the [true] Buddha, and the rest are his transformations (*nirmitāḥ*); in accordance with the original nature of beings they are seen appearing as Buddhas (g. 382). Discrimination takes place because of being misled by delusive appearances; discrimination [however] is no other than suchness; the appearances do not discriminate [by themselves] (g. 383). The Self-nature-[Buddha, *svābhāvika*], the Enjoyment-[Buddha, *sambhoga*], the Transformation-[Buddha, *nirmita*], the Further-transformed-[Buddha, *pañcanirmita*], and the thirty-six groups of Buddha,—they are the Self-nature-Buddhas (g. 384)."

In these quotations we are able to trace the evolution from the Dharmatā-Buddha of the Nishyanda- and the Nirmāṇa-Buddhas, but as regards the distinctive characteristics of the Nishyanda- and the Nirmāṇa-Buddhas, we are still kept in the dark. A great deal is spoken of the Nirmāṇa Buddha in the sutra, perhaps from his deep interest in the affairs of mortal beings. We can almost safely dispense with the Nishyanda-Buddha as far as we mortals are concerned. This Buddha is evidently enjoying his blissful existence up in Akanishṭha Heaven, and enveloped in the light of supernatural character he does not seem to be very anxious to enter into human affairs. But it is possible that he takes upon himself a form of the Nirmāṇa-Buddha when we look up to him wishing that the Exalted One might cast his pitying eye on us who are in nature not altogether different from his former self? Perhaps this is the reason why the number of the Nirmāṇa-Buddhas is beyond measurement, and why they appear to us in the form in which we conceive them to be though each of us does this according to the light of his understanding.

This being the case in all likelihood, we may not wonder how the Nishyanda-Buddha came to be designated as above quoted as the Buddha of Enjoyment.[1] And at the same time we can conclude that the conception of the Triple Body has not attained its full development in the *Laṅkāvatāra*. Inasmuch as the Nishyanda or the Vipāka does not come out clearly delineated, while the significance of the Nirmāṇa is definitely emphasised to arrest our attention in the perusal of the sutra, the *Laṅkāvatāra* must be said to belong to the earlier period of Mahayana Buddhism. That the "Sagāthakam" is a later addition to the main text can also be inferred in this connection, as it describes the relations of the different Buddhas in a more detailed and organised manner, and further as it introduces the idea of the Sambhoga-Buddha which has not at all been made a subject of reference in the sutra proper.

There is another verse(434) in the "Sagāthakam" whose meaning is hard to get at but which points to the relationship existing between the three Buddhas: in the Sanskrit text it reads as follows:

Deśanā-dharma-nishyando yac-ca nishyanda-nirmitam,
Buddhā hyete bhavet paurāḥ śeshā nirmāṇa-vigrahāḥ.

This is translated in the T'ang version thus: "Depending

[1] "The Sagāthakam," g. 384.

on the Dharmakāya (*fa-shên*) there is the Nishyanda (*pao*), and from the Nishyanda there rises the Nirmāṇakāya (*hui-shên*). This is [or these are] the fundamental Buddha (*kên-pên-fo*), and the rest are all transformed manifestations." The first part of the Wei translation is unintelligible, while the latter part fully coincides with the T'ang; the unintelligible part reads: **說是眞法習，所有集作化.**

The Vipāka-Buddha

The nature of a Vipāka-Buddha is that of a Nishyanda-Buddha when this is understood in the sense of a result flowing from an antecedent cause, that is, as one of the five effects (*pañcaphala*), and not in the sense of something secondary which issues out of a more primary substance; and the idea is closely connected with the theory of Karma. This is not difficult to see, for the theory of Karma always requires something resulting from a cause; that is, according to it, no act can perish without leaving its effect in one way or another. The theory of Karma is another name for the law of causation. A deed, whether moral or psychological, therefore, once committed in the inner consciousness, or by the physical body, will never fail to bring, not only on the doer or thinker himself, but upon those intimately related to him some result some day, whose value will somehow correspond with the antecedent. Buddhism, thus, has developed an elaborate science treating of the law of causation in the moral world. This was the case especially with the earlier followers of the Buddha before the Mahayana began to develop to its full strength. The Jātaka tales are compiled wholly with the view of acquainting us with practical narratives illustrating the theory of Karma.

One of the forms in which the theory of Karma has impressed its marks in Mahayana Buddhism is the conception of the Vipāka, or the Nishyanda Buddha. The result of the moral discipline known as the six or ten Perfections (*pāramitā*) which every aspirant for Buddhahood is required to observe, must be visible in some way on the being of the Bodhisattva. And as long as a world of individual forms (*rūpaloka*) is to be accepted even as an inevitable outcome of discrimination (*vikalpa*), the result of the Buddhist devotion must be told, also, under this limitation. Then the Bodhisattva ascends to Akanishṭha Heaven where his coarser body is transformed into a shining one with all the marks of an ideally perfect personality. He is then no more a Bodhisattva endowed with the coarse physical corporeality like ourselves, but an immortal god or Buddha endowed with a will-made body (*manomayakāya*) to which the *Laṅkāvatāra* makes frequent allusions.

There is, however, another conception here entering into the make-up of a shining Buddha, which comes from our inmost religious yearnings. By this I mean the deep human longing for a body of transfiguration. We are not satisfied with our corporeal existence, we are all the time oppressed by the feeling of imprisonment, our spirit soars away from this world of physical limitations, we long forever for a manomayakāya (will-body). This physical body does not fully express the meaning of the spirit, it deranges, it tyrannises. In fact all the religious struggles and aspirations we experience in this life are centered on the control of this body. Theosophists, Swedenborgians, and the Taoists, and the Indian philosophers—they all have the idea of an immaterial body which we can assume when we are favoured by a divine gift, or when our moral discipline reaches its culmination. This is in one sense our longing for immortality. We immortalise all the great historical characters, for we cannot be reconciled to the idea that their physical ending means the end of all that has entered into their being.

The Buddhas' entrance into Nirvana by no means indicated the passing of all that belonged to him. His disciples could never make themselves believe that their Master was no more with them. The dogma of the Dharmakāya was the inevitable outcome of their psychology as well as of their logic. But the Dharmakāya was still too abstract and could not give full satisfaction to their deep-seated religious longings. These longings so innate to the human heart were combined in the case of the Buddhist with the doctrine of Karma, and as the result the Vipāka or the Nishyanda Buddha, or Pao-shên (報身), came into existence in his ideal glorification. Amitābha Buddha, the Lord of Infinite Light, who is one of these Pao-shên Buddhas sits now securely in his Land of Bliss and Purity, surrounded by his worshippers and inviting us poor earthly struggling mortals to join him there.

Between the Vipāka-Buddha and the Nirmāṇa-Buddha it will take some more research to ascertain the historic priority of the one or the other, whatever we may say about the self-enjoyment of the Bodhisattva or Buddha, he could not be a Buddha if he would not manifest himself in every possible form for the spiritual benefit of all beings. His original vow (*pūrvapraṇidhāna*) was to save his fellow-beings when he attained enlightenment; now that he has achieved that end, how can he stay quietly in Akanishṭha Heaven absorbed in a Samādhi of the highest order and enwrapped in the glow of supernatural nature? Even if he does not leave his lotus mansion (*padmavimāna*), he ought to despatch, at least, one of his transformation-bodies wherever and whenever that is desired by sentient beings. Or, to state the case in terms of suffering souls, they must be able to approach the Buddha in some way. If the Buddha himself is so transcendental and detached from a world of individual objects, suffering souls must be allowed to come into intimate relationship with his shadow or Transformation-Body, transformed (*nirmita-nirmāṇa*) for the sake of unregenerate mortals. This is why Avalokiteśvara has his thirty-three bodies, and why Kshitigarbha his innumerable representations.

Thus, the existence of the Nirmāṇa-Buddha can be

understood in two ways: one from the standpoint of the Buddha himself, whose loving heart cannot help resorting to every possible means of salvation, and the other from the standpoint of sinful mortals who desire every possible help from a power higher than themselves. This mutuality has filled the world with Nirmita-nairmāṇika Buddhas. Wherever we turn we come across one of these transformations, and if we are earnest and sincere and longing from the depths of the heart, we can see even the real Buddha himself in and through them. This is an idea pregnant with results both good and bad. When it is not judiciously handled, religion becomes a mass of superstition and idolatory grows rampant.

The relation of the three Buddhas to one another may be understood in the analogy of an individual person. That there is something ultimate making up the reason of this individual existence is to be granted, because the very conception of individuality is impossible without postulating something behind it. This something is variously designated in philosophy and religion, and also variously interpreted and speculated on. Even the denying of the existence of this something is in truth asserting it, for both denial and assertion are based on the same principle. We cannot escape this, and what makes it thus inevitable for us either to assert or deny it is the principle of individuality. This corresponds to the conception of the Dharmatā, or when personified, to the Dhamatā-Buddha.

Now this individual person stands in every possible manner of relationship to his fellow-beings, human or otherwise. As Chuang-tzŭ says, a woman may be regarded by her companions as the most beautiful person and as such admired and adored and loved. But when she comes near a pond and reflects her shadow on water, all the aquatic inhabitants will flee away from her as a most dangerous enemy. What is one man's poison is another's elixir of life. The same individual is not the same at all times to all others. Even a table standing in this room does not look alike to all spectators. As it is observed from different angles and with different frames of mind the object before them is not only physically not of the same size and colour, but psychologically not at all of the same value and significance. In the case of a living person this variability, temporal and constant, reaches its limits. The person himself has not apparently changed but he assumes or seems to assume different forms to his neighbours. May not this aspect of his being be called his Nirmāna value? In spite of all these external and relational mutations, the individual has not at all changed to his own consciousness. That he is himself he at all times knows and he enjoys his personality. This corresponds to the Vipāka-Buddha, or Sambhogakāya.[1]

Every conscious being may thus figuratively or rather metaphysically be said to be the owner of the Triple Body. In the case of the Buddha, the doctrine is filled with religious significance and it has played a most important rôle in the development of Mahayana Buddhism. One thing we have to notice here is the replacing of the Buddha-trinity by that of the Body (*kāya*). That Buddhist philosophers have come to talk of the Trikāya instead of Buddhatraya. It is not a matter of mere change of terminology, it involves a deeper meaning. The reason is that Kāya has a more synthesising value, while Buddha suggests more of individuality. The three different kinds of Buddhahood make one think of three different, separate individuals, but the Trikāya means one personality with three aspects. In the conception of the Triple Body we trace a systematising thought. The *Laṅkāvatāra,* therefore, marks a step toward this systematisation.

[1] The conception of the Body of Enjoyment is interesting from the point of view of karma, for the Mahayana has not ignored the effect of karma on the individual life though it teaches in the doctrine of Pariṇidhāna (vows) and Pariṇāmanā (transfering of merit) that there is a power transcending karma and working towards universal enlightenment and salvation.

The Triple Body in the Awakening of Faith in the Mahayana

With the author of the *Awakening of Faith in the Mahāyāna,* the theory of the Triple Body assumes a more finished form. The following deals with the subject.

"And again by the functions of Suchness (*tathatā*) is meant that all the Buddha-Tathagatas while they were still on the stage of self-discipline awakened great love and compassion, practised all the virtues of perfection, and embraced all beings making great vows, in which they expressed the desire to emancipate the entire world of beings without distinction and exception, nor have they set any limit to the number of ages, for their vows reach the furthest end of time. They regard all beings as if the latter were themselves. Yet they do not assume the form of a [particular] being. Why is this so? Because they really (*yathābhūtam*) know that all beings and themselves are of Suchness; that they both are of the same nature (*samatā*), without any distinguishing marks. As they have such great Upāyajñāna,[1] dispelling ignorance, they see the Dharmakāya in its original essence, and without being conscious of it, perform wonderful deeds, a variety of activities. They are indeed like Suchness itself manifesting themselves all over the universe, and yet they leave no marks whereby their activities can be traced. Why? Because the substance of all the Buddha-Tathagatas is no other than the Dharmakāya in its pure form of intelligence. There are no parts in Absolute Truth that correspond to worldly truths, it has nothing to do with [the constraints of] achievement. It, nevertheless, benefits all beings, as they catch glimpses of it through their senses, and thus we speak of its functionings.

[1] Literally, *upāyajñāna* means, "knowledge of means," which is generally contrasted with "knowledge of reality" (*tattvajñāna*). The latter sees into suchness of things, whereas the former goes out to a world of particulars. The Buddha is provided with both kinds of knowledge.

"Of these functionings we distinguish two kinds. What are they? The one is dependent on the Individualising Mind (*vastuprativikalpavijñāna*) and is perceived by the minds of the two-vehicle followers. It is known as Responding Body (*ying shên*).[1] As they do not know that this is projected by their Evolving Mind (*Pravṛittivijñāna*), they take it for something external to themselves, and making it assume a corporeal form, fail to have a thorough knowledge of its nature.

"The second one is dependent on the Karma-consciousness,[2] that is, it appears to the minds of those Bodhisattvas who have just entered upon the path of Bodhisattvahood as well as of those who have reached the highest stage. This is known as the Recompense Body, 報身 (*pao-shên*).[3] The Body is visible in infinite forms, each form has infinite marks, and each mark is excellent in infinite ways, and the world in which the Body has its abode is also embellished in manners infinitely varying. As the [Body] is manifested everywhere, it has no limitations whatever, it can never be exhausted, it goes beyond all the conditions of determination. According to the needs [of all beings] it becomes visible and is always held by [by them], it is neither destroyed nor lost sight of. All such characteristics [of the Body] are the perfuming (*vāsanā*) effect of the immaculate deeds such as the virtues of perfection and also the work of the mysterious perfuming [innate in the Tathāgata-garbha]. As it is thus in possession of immeasurably blissful qualities, it is called Recompense Body (*pao-shên*).[4] Those

[1] This corresponds to the Nirmāṇakāya, or the Nirmāṇa-Buddha of the *Laṅkāvatāra*. Śikshānanda has Hua-shên (化身).

[2] By Karma-consciousness is meant the first awakening of consciousness whereby all kinds of activities, psychical, logical, and physical, are stirred up.

[3] Śikshānanda has here 受用身 (*shou-yung-shên, sambhogakāya*). His text evidently differed from that of Paramārtha.

[4] Śikshānanda has here, "It is also known as Pao-shên." This also is significant, seeing that it was first called Shou-yung-shên.

which are visible to ordinary mortals are of coarser corporeality, appearing differently according to which one of the six paths of existence a man lives in. These different forms conceived by different beings are not of blissful character. Therefore, they are known as the Responding Body (*ying shên*).[1]

"And again, as the Bodhisattva who has first entered upon the path of Bodhisattvaship has a firm faith in the truth of Suchness, he is granted to have a partial glimpse [of the Recompense Body]. He knows that the forms, characteristic marks, embellishments, etc., belong to [the Recompense Body], are in their nature neither coming nor going, are beyond the categories of determination, that they are only visible depending upon the mind and not detached from Suchness. But in [the mind of] this Bodhisattva there is still individualisation as he has not yet entered upon the rank of Dharmakāya. When, however, his heart is thoroughly purified, he can see things of finer quality, and his activity will be more excellent than ever. At the culminating stage of Bodhisattvahood, his vision reaches its height[2]; and when the Karma-consciousness is no more, there is nothing for him to see; for the Dharmakāya of all the Buddhas has no forms, no marks whatever, of which there is any possibility of mutual perception.

"If the Dharmakāya of all the Buddhas has nothing to do with forms and marks, how is it possible for it to manifest itself in forms and marks?

"Because the Dharmakāya is the substance of all forms, it manifests itself in forms. From the very beginning, indeed, mind and form are not two, the essence of form is knowledge. Because the substance of form is not material, it is known as the Knowledge-body (*jñānakāya*); and be-

[1] Hua-shên, by Śikshānanda.

[2] Śikshānanda has this inserted here: "This subtle activity is the Enjoyment Body; as there is Karma-consciousness, the Enjoyment Body is visible."

cause the essence of knowledge is form, it is known as the Dharma-kāya,[1] which is omnipresent and whose visible forms have no limiting conditions. They appear according to the mind. In the ten quarters of the world there are innumerable Bodhisattvas, inumerable Bodies of Recompense,[2] innumerable embellishments; they are all distinct one from another, and yet they are not subject to limiting conditions, nor are they mutually exclusive. This is beyond the discrimination of a discerning mind, for it is due to the absolute activity of Suchness."[3]

[1] In this case, Dharma is evidently understood in the sense of form (*rūpa*) and not in the sense of truth or law. It stands constrasted to jñāna which belongs to the mind. The duality of jñāna and dharma, of mind and form, disappears when it is understood that they are after all one, as is stated most emphatically in the *Prajñāpāramitā*: *Iha śāriputra rūpaṁ śūnyatā, śūnyataiva rūpaṁ, rūpanna pṛithak śūnyatā, śūnyatāyā na pṛithagrūpaṁ, yadrūpaṁ sā śūnyatā, yā śūnyatā tadrūpaṁ.*

[2] Shou-yung-shên, according to Śikshānanda.

[3] This is from Paramārtha's Chinese translation. The other by Śikshānanda differs somewhat as has been noticed above. The author's translation of the *Awakening of Faith in the Mahāyāna* was published in 1900 by the Open Court Publishing Co., Chicago, which has, however, been out of print for some time. The author is contemplating the issue of a revised translation before long.

4. THE TATHAGATA

The *Laṅkāvatāra-Sūtra* being one of the principal Mahayana texts treating of the inner truth realised by the Tathagata (*pratyātma-vedya-gati-dharmaṁ tathāgatānām*), it behoves us to have some knowledge of the Tathagata himself, as far as it is given us in the sutra. In fact we already know something of him when we have investigated what this inner truth is, for it constitutes the very essence of Tathagatahood, who would not be himself if he had it not. Not only that, his whole life is regarded as to be given up to the propagation of Pratyātmadharma. The identification of the Tathagata with Pratyātmadharma does not require any specific proofs as this, indeed, composes the contents of the *Laṅkāvatāra* itself. But the Pratyātmadharma alone of itself does not make up the whole being of the Tathagata who requires something more to move among the ignorant and confused and who desires to lead all beings up to the same elevation where he himself is. The realm where he moves along with his inner revelations(*pratyātmagatigocara*) is, indeed, beyond that of the philosophers and the Śrāvakas and Pratyekabuddhas, as we are repeatedly reminded in the *Laṅkāvatāra,* but this self-enjoyment of the blissful Samādhi is not what we expect of the Tathagata. He must show something more, he must be more than himself, go beyond his inner revelations. This means that he must be a personality.

As was elsewhere noted,[1] a great compassionate heart (*kṛipā* or *karuṇā*), is to be awakened in the wise men who have seen *yathābhūtam* into the inner truth of things,[2] for this is what makes all great souls really living. To be a person means among other things to be a living being, to have a feeling heart, to live among the ignorant and confused, and not to remain isolated in his own intellectual transcendentalism. So all the Tathagatas of the past, present, and

[1] Pp. 35–36, 214–216, of the present work.

[2] P. 22.

future must be endowed with this affection for the world. The supreme wisdom (*āryajñāna*) by which they are able to realise in themselves the inner truth of things must not be merely intellectual; there must be an element of affection. This is, indeed, what distinguishes the Mahayana from the Hinayana. The reason why the *Laṅkāvatāra* is persistent in dwelling upon the mental attitude (*gocara*) of the Tathagata toward the world as in such contrast with that of the Śrāvakas and the Pratyekabuddhas and also the philosophers (*tīrthakara*) is that the Tathagata's (or the Bodhisattva's) comprises this tenderness for others in spite of his enlightenment which transcends the categories of being and non-being, of coming into existence and passing out of it. The supreme wisdom then distinguishes itself by three marks.[1] The first is the Nirābhāsa, meaning "free from all false appearances," "beyond semblance," "shadowless," or "imageless"; the second is the Buddha's own will and power; and the third is the realisation of the inner truth. When these three aspects or characteristics of supreme wisdom (*ārya jñāna*) are in perfect combination and operate harmoniously, a Bodhisattva is said to draw near Buddhahood. So we can say that supreme wisdom which is the essence of Tathagatahood is composed of the will of the Tathagata plus this nondualistic understanding. Aryajñāna is Prajñā supported by Praṇidhāna that is, by "the ten inexhaustible vows," while the unsupported Prajñā is designated as a lame donkey (*khañjagardabha*).[2] When this plase of Buddhist teaching is comprehended, we have mastered more than half of its secrets.

What is the meaning of Tathagata? This has been much discussed by scholars but so far nothing conclusive has been reached. *Tathā* means "thus," but the question is whether to divide *tathāgata* into *tathā* and *gata,* or into *tathā* and *āgata*: In the first case, *gata* is "gone" or

[1] Pp. 49–50. [2] P. 50.

"departed," and in the second case, if it is *āgata,* it means "is come" or "is arrived." The Chinese translators have adopted the second reading as they have rendered *tathāgata* by 如來 (*ju-lai*), but the Tibetans have དེ་བཞིན་གཤེགས་པ for it. In point of fact it does not matter whether the Tathagata is the "One thus come," or the "One thus gone." When his appearance in the world is made the centre of interest, he is the "One who has thus come"; on the other hand if we think more of his disappearance from among us, he is the "One who has thus departed."[1] The main question, however, with the Mahayanists is this,—Why is he designated "thus"? What does this "thus" mean? This is what we wish to know.

There is no doubt the *tathā* is connected with the Mahayana conception of the ultimate truth as *tathatā* (suchness or thusness) and also with the idea of seeing into the nature of things *yathābhūtam.* When the Tathagata's coming into existence and his passing away from it is considered from the *yathābhūtam* point of view, that is, as neither coming nor departing, as not subject to the category of being and non-being, his being and his doings may well be characterised as having the quality of "thusness." There is no other good way of describing them. Hence the appellation, the "One who has the nature of thusness in his coming and going," that is, the Tathagata.

In the *Diamond Sutra*[2] we have: "But if, O Subhūti, there is a man who would say, 'The Tathagata goes, he comes, he stands, he sits, or he lies,' that man understands not the meaning of what I say. Why? Because the Tathagata is he who goes nowhere and who comes from nowhere. Therefore, he is called the Tathagata, Arhat, Fully-enlightened One (29)."

[1] The Buddha is also called, Sugata (善逝) "one who has gone well."

[2] S.B.E., Vol. XLIX, p. 142.

The interpretation of Tathagata as the thusness of things (*sarvadharmatathatā*) is given in the *Ashṭaśahasrikā-prajñāpāramitā-sūtra* in a most characteristic manner as follows:

"At that time the Venerable Subhūti spoke to the Blessed One thus: This truth is preached by thee that all things are beyond the grasp of the understanding. This truth knows no obstruction whatever; there are no signs of obstruction in it; being like space no traces are left in it; it allows no similitude because of its having no companionship; it has no equal because of its standing above all opponents; it leaves no footsteps because of its never having assumed itself; it has never been born because of its being above birth and death; it has no tracks to follow because of no tracks ever being traced here; [it allows of no idle speculation because of its having nothing to do with words and discrimination. The Blessed One said to Subhūti: So it is, so it is, just as you say.[2]]

"Sakra, chief of the gods, Brahman, lord of the world, and the gods belonging to the world of Desire and that of Form, said to the Blessed One: Subhūti, the noble Śrāvaka and the Elder, is truly the one who is born after the Buddha.[3] Why? Because the truth which he declares, he declares indeed in accordance with the doctrine of Emptiness (*śūnyatā*).

"Then the Venerable Subhūti said to Sakra and the other gods: As to what the gods say about Subhūti the Elder's being born after the Buddha, he is indeed such because of his having never been born. Subhūti the Elder is born after the thusness [or suchness] of the Tathagata, that is, one who is thus come. As the Tathagata's thusness neither comes nor passes away, so does Subhūti's thusness neither come nor pass away. So, indeed, Subhūti's thusness neither

[1] Rājendralāla Mitra's edition, pp. 306–309.

[2] Added from Hsüan-chuang's Chinese translation.

[3] *Anujāta*, meaning "a younger brother."

comes nor passes away. So, indeed, is Subhūti the Elder born after the Tathagata in accordance with the thusness of the Tathagata; indeed from the first is Subhūti born after the Tathagata in accordance with the thusness of the Tathagata. Why? What is the thusness of the Tathagata that is the thusness of all things; and what is the thusness of the Tathagata as well as the thusness of all things, that is the thusness of Subhūti the Elder? Subhūti the Elder is born after this thusness, therefore he is the one who is born after the Tathagata. And this thusness is no-thusness, and after this thusness is Subhūti born. So indeed is Subhūti the Elder the one who is born after the Tathagata. What the Tathagata's permanency is, that is the permanency of thusness, and by this permanency Subhūti the Elder is the one who is born after the Tathagata.

"As the Tathagata's thusness is changeless, free from change, not discriminating, free from discrimination,[1] so is indeed Subhūti's thusness changeless, free from change, not discriminating, free from discrimination. So indeed Subhūti the Elder, who is by this thusness changeless, free from change, not-discriminating, free from discrimination, is the one born after the Tathagata. And as the Tathagata's thusness is changeless, free from change, not-discriminating, free from discrimination, nowhere obstructed; so is the thusness of all things changeless, free from change, not-discriminating, free from discrimination, and is nowhere obstructed. Why? What is the Tathagata's thusness and what is the thusness of all things, that is just one thusness; this thusness is not two, is not a duality, it is not a twofold thusness; this thusness is nowhere, is from nowhere, and belongs to nobody. As this thusness belongs to nobody, so it is not two, it is not a duality, it is not a twofold thusness. Even so is Subhūti the Elder born after the Tathagata's uncreated thusness. What is uncreated thusness, that is in

[1] Hsüan-chuang's Chinese translation has one more qualification: "moves universally in all things."

no time no thusness.[1] Since it is thusness that is not thusness in no time, this thusness is not two, is not a duality, is not a twofold thusness. So indeed is Subhūti the Elder born after the Tathagata. As the Tathagata's thusness is everywhere in all things without discrimination, free from discrimination, even so is the thusness of Subhūti everywhere in all things without discrimination, free from discrimination. So is Subhūti transformed by the thusness of the Tathagata, and yet there is no splitting into duality, it is not split into two, splitting is not obtainable. So indeed is Subhūti the Elder's thusness not different from the thusness of all things. What is not different from the thusness of all things, that is nowhere not thusness, it is just that thusness, the thusness of all things. It is admitted that Subhūti the Elder in accordance with the same thusness follows that thusness, it is not admitted that his following is somewhere somehow. So indeed is Subhūti the Elder born after the Tathagata.

"As the Tathagata's thusness belongs neither to the past, nor to the future, nor to the present, so indeed does the thusness of all things not belong to the past, nor to the future, nor to the present. Just so is Subhūti the Elder born after this thusness, he is said to be born after the Tathagata. Following thusness indeed by the thusness of the Tathagata, he follows thusness of the past by the thusness of the Tathagata. He follows the Tathagata's thusness by thusness of the past. By the Tathagata's thusness he follows thusness of the future. By thusness of the future he follows the Tathagata's thusness. By the Tathagata's thusness he follows thusness of the present. By thusness of the present he follows the Tathagata's thusness. By the Tathagata's thusness he follows thusness of the past, future, and present. By thusness of the past, future, and present,

[1] The sense is: This uncreated and uncreating thusness remains so all the time, never losing its absolute identity in spite of its presence and activity in all things.

he follows the Tathagata's thusness. Thus indeed Subhūti's thusness and thusness of the past, future, and present, and the Tathagata's thusness—the thusness indeed is not two, it is not a duality; so the thusness of all things and Subhūti's thusness is not two, it is not a duality. What is the thusness of the Blessed One and of one who is becoming a Bodhisattva, that is the thusness of the Blessed One who is fully awakened in the highest perfect enlightenment. This thusness by which the Bodhisattva-Mahāsattva is fully awakened in the highest perfect enlightenment is designated by the name of 'Tathāgata.'

"Now when this discourse on the thusness of the Tathagata was going on, the great earth shook in six different ways with eighteen great signs: is swayed, trembled, rattled, writhed, thundered, just as it did at the time when the Tathagata was awakened to the highest perfect enlightenment."

One of the ways of determining the conception of the Tathagata is to know what are the essential constituents of Bodhisattvaship, not only after his attainment of an ideal Buddhist life but while he is perfecting himself for such life. A Bodhisattva is a sentient being whose inherent possession is Bodhi, or who is disciplining himself for the realisation of Bodhi or enlightenment. He is thus far from being a Tathagata, but the difference is that between potentiality and actuality, that is, between one who is to be and one who is. When we know what the one is aiming at, we can guess what the other is after arriving at the goal.

What are the constituents of Bodhisattvahood? What are the essential qualities of the Bodhisattva? According to the *Laṅkāvatāra,*[1] he is the one who endeavours:

1. To get rid of all the perverted views of existence (*prapañca-darśana*) which he has been cherishing since the very beginning of time;

[1] Pp. 42–43; see also pp. 97 ff and pp. 213 ff, of these *Studies*, where the Bodhisattva is described.

2. Thereby to liberate himself from the conditions of discrimination (*vikalpapratyaya*), and to rise above the net of phraseology woven by erroneous imagination (*parikalpita-abhidhāna*);

3. And further to realise that an external world so called of particulars is no more than the construction of the Ālayavijñāna;

4. To attain a mental attitude by which he views Nirvāṇa and Saṁsāra as two aspects of one and the same fact (*samatā*);

5. To be furnished with (*a*) great compassionate heart (*mahākaruṇā*), and (*b*) skilful means (*upāyakauśalya*);

6. To perform effortless deeds (*anābhogocaryā*), to walk the road of formlessness (*animittapatha*), to enter upon a mental state of non-semblance (*cittanirābhāsa*);

7. To attain the perfection of Samādhi in which things are viewed as above all forms of perturbation and as unborn;

8. To be in the perfection of Prajñā, whereby to live always in the thusness of things (*tathatā*);

9. To manifest finally the Buddha-body which, now being endowed with the ten Powers, the six Psychic Faculties, and the tenfold Self-mastery, is able to assume any form at will to visit all the Buddha-lands, and to lead all beings to the perception of the truth of the "Mind-only."

When these are achieved, a Bodhisattva or in fact any being is regarded as having reached Tathagatahood. Aside from the question, what the Buddha-body or the Tathagata-body really is—this has partly been discussed in the previous chapter entitled "The Trikāya"—we may mention that the full attainment of this body takes place in the Akanishṭha heaven which is the highest of the Rūpadhātu (world of form).[1] According to this, as long as we are staying in this world of desire where we mortals are not able to escape the bondage of coarser matter, we cannot attain to the per-

[1] This is referred to in several places, for instance, pp. 51, 33, 56, 215, 269, etc.

fection of the Tathāgatakāya, which is evidently a kind of spiritual body able to take on any form as desired either by oneself or by others. Hence the conception of the Sambhogakāya and the Nirmāṇakāya.

The treatment of the Tathagata in the *Laṅkāvatāra* may be divided under two heads: (1) the Tathagata as he is, and (2) the Tathagata in his relation to sentient beings. As to the first head much has already been said, and in fact, the previous chapter on the relation of Zen Buddhism to the *Laṅkāvatāra* may be regarded in a way as an exposition of the inner consciousness of the Tathagata. The following quotations which are concerned with the essence of Tathagatahood[1] are more or less repetitions confirming the views already expounded.

"[The essence of enlightenment] goes beyond all logical measurement and the senses; it is neither effect nor cause; it is not intellective, nor is it to be reached by reason; it is not qualifying, nor is it to be qualified (79).

"The Skandhas, causation, and enlightenment—these are not seen by anybody anywhere. How can anyone anywhere make any assertion [or discrimination] about that which is not seen? (80).

"It is not something made, nor something unmade; it is not an effect nor a cause: it is not the Skandhas, nor no-Skandhas; nor is it any other composition (81).

"It is not to be discriminated as something existing, it is not so seen; this something unseen is not to be known as nothing, for it is that which constitutes the essence of all things (82).

"Something first in being, and there is non-being; nothing yet in being, and there is being; therefore, non-being is not to be attained, and being is not to be discriminated (83).

"Those who do not comprehend what is ego and what

[1] Cf. "The Essence of Buddhahood," p. 133 et seq., of the present work.

is non-ego, get themselves attached to words only. They drown themselves in dualism; they are ruined themselves and ruin the ignorant (84).

"When they see my doctrine which is liberated from all error, they see truthfully, they do not harm the Leader (85)."[1]

When Mahāmati asked what constituted Tathagatahood, the Buddha answered:[2] They are Tathagatas and Buddhas, who understand the twofold egolessness, descard the twofold hindrance (*āvaraṇa*), keep themselves away from the two forms of death (*cyuti*), and from the two classes of evil desires (*kleśa*). Whether they be Śrāvakas or Pratyekabuddhas, they are equally Tathagatas if they thus qualify themselves, and in this respect, the Buddha says that he teaches only one vehicle impartially carrying all classes of sentient beings. The twofold hindrance to the realisation of the inmost truth is the hindrance of evil desires and the hindrance of knowledge; we may say, the conative hindrance and the intellectual hindrance. The two kinds of death are death of discontinuity, and death of mysterious transformation (*acintyapariṇāma*). The first is that which takes place on a corporal plane and the second is a form of subtile transformation proceeding in the consciousness of a higher being. By the two kinds of evil desires are meant, (1) those that are stirred in us by the agency of ignorance, and (2) those that follow from this fundamental evil.

One of the significant teachings of the *Laṅkāvatāra* concerning the discourse of the Tathagata on the truth of Buddhism, is its insistence on the distinction between the truth itself and an exposition of it. This follows from the Mahayanistic attitude toward the use of language in Buddhism, which is this, that meaning is to be seperated from words, for the latter by no means exhaust the former and there

[1] Pp. 190–191.
[2] P. 140.

is always something that is escaping which can never be adequately expressed in words. Of course we must use words when something has to be transmitted from one person to another, but words are mere indication and not the thing itself. As the sutra says, we have to resort to the word-lamp of discrimination to enter into the inner truth of experience which goes beyond words and thoughts.[1] But it is perfect folly to imagine that this lamp is everything.[2] The *Laṅkāvatāra* is quite positive about this, for it says: "By merely following words and making discriminating attempts to formulate a proposition concerning the truth as it is, a man falls straightway into the bottom of hell on account of this very proposition."[3] Again "when the ignorant not comprehending the secret meaning (*saṁdhi*) endeavour to take hold of the knowledge of existence with words, they find themselves hopelessly, like the silk-worm, in a cocoon spun by their own false discrimination."[4] Thus Mahāmati in this sutra is always anxious to ask the Buddha concerning the relationship between the truth itself and its expression in words; for he is convinced that when this relationship is made clear, the Bodhisattvas including himself will have advanced many steps ahead toward the attainment of supreme enlightenment (*anuttara-samyak-sambodhi*).

This relationship is known in the *Laṅkāvatāra* as that between *siddhānta* and *deśanā,* that is, between realisation and instruction in words. "This most excellent realisation goes beyond words and letters of discrimination, for it belongs to the realm of non-outflowings (*anasravadhātu*), and is characterised with the inwardness of perception whereby one enters upon the stage [of Tathagatahood]. By destroying all the philosophers' erroneous views and evil ways of thinking, one shines forth in the light of inner truth. As to

[1] *Vāg-vikalpa-ruta-pradīpena bodhisattvā mahāsattvā vāg-vikalpa-rahitāḥ svapratyātmā-'ryagatim anupraviśanti* (p. 155).

[2] See also also p. 105 ff, of the present work.

[3] P. 156, g. 34.

[4] P. 163, g. 87.

the Tathagata's instruction in words, it is expressed in the nine divisions in which is given the doctrine of non-dualism transcending the categories of oneness and otherness, of being and non-being, but the main thing in them is to lead sentient beings by skilful means to the end after which their own believing hearts are striving.

"There are the truth of realisation and its instruction in words, the inner perception and its preaching; those who see well into the distinction will not be influenced by mere intellection (15).

"In the truth itself there are no such discriminations as are cherished by the ignorant. In non-being there is emancipation, indeed! Why do they not seek it there—they that are addicted to reasoning (16)?

"When we survey this world of things made, we see nothing but a continuation of birth and death; and [the ignorant] are nourishing their dualistic views and because of their perversion they fail to see [the truth] (17).

"This one alone is the truth; Nirvana is not to be taken hold of by thinking. The world as subject to discrimination is like the stem of a plantain tree, it is māyā, a shadow (18).

"There is no greed, no wrath, no folly, nor even a person; from desire, indeed, there rise the Skandhas, they are all like objects seen in a dream (19)."[1]

This distinction between realisation (*siddhānta*) and discoursing (*deśanā*) is repeated further below[2] in the sutra in almost identical words. The latter is meant for the ignorant, and the former for those who earnestly discipline themselves in it. The statement that the Tathagata uttered not a word since his enlightenment[3] refers to the truth of realisation.

Reference has been already made once (and will be made again later—this time more in detail) to the Buddha's teach-

[1] Freely rendered, pp. 148–149; these gāthās are repeated in the "Sagāthakam."

[2] Pp. 171–172.

[3] Pp. 143, 144, 240, 194.

ing of One Vehicle (*ekayāna*), in which all the Buddhists who see into the truth inwardly realisable are carried, no matter to which of the Triple Vehicle they may belong. Because of one universal Vehicle, all the Buddhas, Tathagatas, and Arhats are now said to be of one nature (*samatā*), and even that they are all one, i.e., of one substance. In the Mahayana sutras allusions are frequently made to Buddhas of the past, present, and future, and they are an immense number even at present abiding each in his Buddha-land, which fills the universes seen and unseen. Though the *Laṅkāvatāra* does not make any positive affirmation, we can quite reasonably infer that all these Buddhas are really one Buddha, revealing himself in time and space and thus mysteriously multiplying himself infinitely, altogether beyond the possibilities of our limited thinking. This is the conclusion we naturally come to when the idea of Samatā (oneness or sameness) is pursued logically.[1]

"Mahāmati asked the Blessed One, in what secret sense speakest thou in the assembly of thy being all the Buddhas of the past? and also in thy former births of thy having been King Māndhātṛi, or the elephant, the parrot, Indra, Vyāsa, or Sunetra, on such and such occasions?

"Said the Buddha: We talk of this in the assembly because of the secret teaching of fourfold sameness (*samatā*), that I was in ancient days the Buddha Krakucchanda, Kanakamuni, or Kāśyapa. What are these four? (1) Sameness in letters (*akshara*), (2) sameness in words (*vāc*), (3) sameness in the body (*kāyā*), (4) sameness in the truth (*dharma*) attained.

"(1) By 'sameness in letters' is meant that the title Buddha is equally given to all the Tathagatas, no distinction being made among them as far as these letters, B-U-D-DH-A, go.

"(2) By 'sameness in words' is meant that all the Tathagatas speak in sixty-four different notes or sounds with

[1] Pp. 141–142.

which the language of Brahma is pronounced, and that their language sounding like the notes of the Kalavinka bird is common to all the Tathagatas.

"(3) By 'sameness in the body' is meant that all the Tathagatas show no distinction as far as their Dharmakāya, their corporal features (*rūpalakshaṇa*) and their secondary marks of excellence are concerned. They differ, however, when they are seen by a variety of beings whom they have the special design to control and discipline.

"(4) By 'sameness in the truth' is meant that all the Tathagatas attain to the same realisation by means of the thirty-seven divisions of enlightenment."

That all the Tathagatas are one in the truth they have inwardly realised (*pratyātmadharmatā*)[1] is readily understood, but how are they one in their bodily form? This is an important teaching in the *Laṅkāvatāra*. The conception of an originally-abiding-essence-of-things (*pauraṇa-sthiti-dharmatā*)[2] may help us in this and also of that of the Tathāgata-garbha. The identification of this Dharmatā idea and the Tathāgata-garbha has not been effected in any explicit manner in the *Laṅkāvatāra*. The relation between the thus-identified-somewhat and the Dharmakāya is not also determined to such extent as to permit us to say definitely that the Buddha's Dharmakāya is in each one of us, that we are manifestations of Dharmakāya, and, therefore, that we are Buddhas even as we are, and, finally, that Mind, Buddha, and all sentient beings—these are of one essence and nature and substance. The *Laṅkāvatāra* is not a systematised treatise devoted to the exposition of a definite set of doctrines, but a mine containing all sorts of metals still in the state of ore requiring analysis and synthesis. It is full of suggestive thoughts which must have been fermenting at the time in the Mahayana thinkers' brains and hearts. The two great schools of Mahayana Buddhism, the Madhyamika and

[1] See also p. 143.
[2] P. 143.

the Yogācāra lie here in an incipient stage of development and differentiation.

While all the Tathagatas are one in the Dharmakāya, they may be variously known to various classes of beings, who imagine their object of worship to be exclusively their own. Indeed, there are so many synonyms for the name Tathagata that we cannot begin to enumerate them all. The wise know this well, but the ignorant may refuse to acquiesce in this way of understanding even after they have been instructed. Hence the following remarks in the *Laṅkāvatāra*:

"Said the Buddha, O Mahāmati, listen to what I tell thee. The Tathagata is not the non-existent (*abhāva*), he is not the holder of all that is unborn and undying in all things, he is not one who waits for conditions; I declare him to be the Unborn One, whose synonym is the Dharmakāya who manifests itself as it will. This is beyond the understanding of all the philosophers, Śrāvakas, Pratyekabuddhas, and those Bodhisattvas who have not yet passed the seventh stage.

"It is like Indra who is known as Śakra and Puraṁdara (city-destroyer); it is like the word *hasta* (hand), for synonyms of which there are *kara* and *paṇi*; it is again like *tanu, deha, śarīra,* meaning the body; like *pṛithivī, bhūmi, vasuṁdhara,* meaning the earth; and also like *kha, ākāśa, gagana,* meaning the sky. Any object may thus be known under several names though they are not to be adhered to as designating several different objects, each with its own irreducible characteristics. No false judgment must be formed here.

"I come into the hearing range of the ignorant in this Sahaloka world in hundreds of thousands of three asaṁkhyeyas of names, and they talk to me under these names, yet they fail to recognise that they are all my own appellations. There are some who call me the Self-existing One (*svayambhuva*), the Leader (*nāyaka*), the Remover-of-obstacles (*vināyaka*), the Guiding One (*pariṇāyaka*), Buddha, Rishi, Bull-king, Brahma, Vishnu, Iśvara, the Originator (*pradhāna*), Kapila, the Destroyer (*bhūtānta*), the Imperishable (*arishṭa*), Nemina, Soma, Fire, Rāma, Vyāsa, Śuka, Indra, the Strong One, or Varuṇa; there are others who know me as Immortality (*anirodhānutpāda*), Emptiness, Suchness, Truth (*satyatā*), Reality (*bhūtatā*), Real Limit (*bhūtakoṭi*), Dharmadhātu, Nirvāṇa, Eternity (*nitya*), Sameness (*samatā*), Non-duality (*advaya*), the Imperishable (*anirodha*), Formless (*animitta*), Causality (*pratyaya*), Teaching the Cause of Buddhahood (*buddha-hetūpadeśa*), Emancipation (*vimoksha*), Truth-paths (*mārgasatyam*), the All-knowing (*sarvajñā*), the Conquering One (*jina*), or the Will-body (*manomayakāya*).

"While I am thus known in hundreds of thousands of three-asaṁkhyeyas of titles, not only in this world, but in other worlds, my names are not exhausted; I am like the moon casting its shadow on water, I am neither in it nor out of it. Those who know me will recognise me everywhere, but the ignorant who cannot rise above dualism will not know me.

"They pay respect and make me offerings, but they do not understand well the meaning of words, do not distinguish ideas, the true from the false; they do not recognise the truth itself; clinging to words of teaching they erroneously discriminate that the unborn and undying means a non-existence. They are thus unable to comprehend that one Tathagata may be known in many different names and titles."[1]

This infinite multiplicity of names in which the Tathagata is known to all beings, though they do not themselves realise the fact, betrays the pantheistic tendency running through all the Mahayana schools of Buddhism, and at the same time leads us to the conception of the Transformation-body of the Buddha. There is no mystery in the Trikāya

[1] Pp. 192–193.

doctrine of Buddhism. If the Buddha is compassionate enough to see suffering beings, there is no other way to satisfy his heart's desire than that of the dividing himself into so many different forms and approaching sufferers. The latter, however, may think that they have what they want exclusively in the form revealed to their minds. In fact the Tathagata is not at all dividing himself; if it seems so, it is due to the discrimination of his devotees. The Transformation-body is thus a creation on their part, it is not an emanation of the Tathagata. I have said that he had to divide himself to satisfy his heart, but this is no more than a conventional and human way of speaking. Therefore, the sutra compares the activity of the Tathagata to the moon reflected in water. The moon is divided into thousands of reflections, as many indeed as there are dipperfuls of water. This is due to the presence and working of the original vows in the hearts of all the Buddhas, and the working is altogether effortless and without any designs; and yet how purposeful it all appears! This is one of the principal messages communicated in the *Laṅkāvatāra*. We now see that the Transformation-body is most intimately connected with the Praṇidhāna of the Buddha, and this Praṇidhāna is the spiritual echo or response to the suffering of beings. When sentient beings begin to be conscious of the contradictions within themselves, they have an intense desire (*āśaya*) awakened for some sort of unity or harmonisation, which may be called emancipation, or enlightenment, or salvation, according to the point of view taken of the situation. This intense desire thus awakened in the hearts of sentient beings cannot remain without calling forth some response somewhere, because the feeling is the cry that issues forth from life itself, and if there is anything living in the Dharmakāya of the Buddha he can never remain in the quiet of Samādhi: he must move out of his lotus-seat. This moving-out is, in the terminology of Mahayana Buddhism, his Praṇidhāna or vow. The *Laṅkāvatāra,* as one of the Mahayana literature, does not forget to touch on this subject. Properly, the sutra is devoted to the elucidation of the inner truth to be realised within oneself, but to neglect the mentioning of the Praṇidhāna would be a grievous fault on the part of the writer.

The whole significance of the idea of the Praṇidhāna is in short this: "The Bodhisattva also realises the inner truth as attained by the Śrāvakas, but because of his compassionate regard for all sentient beings and of his original vows which are now astir in him, he has no heart for the bliss of cessation (*nirodha-sukha*) and for the bliss of self-absorption (*samāpatti-sukha*)."[1] The *Laṅkāvatāra* alludes occasionally to the ten vows of a Bodhisattva[2] which he has made in the beginning of his career. They are principally concerned with the Bodhisattva and not with the Tathagata; but they may be taken at least in their principle as concerned with the life of the Tathagata as well. Amitābha's forty-eight vows mentioned in one of the Chinese versions of the *Sukhāvatīvyūha-sūtra*, Akshobhya's vows in the *Sutra of the Land of Akshobhya*, Kshitigarbha's ten vows in the *Sutra of the Vows of Kshitigarbha*, Bhaishajya-guru-vaiḍurya-prabhāsa-tathāgata's twelve vows in the sutra bearing his name, Avalokiteśvara's vows in one of the chapters in the *Saddharmapuṇḍarīka*, etc., are all so many developments of this idea of Praṇidhāna.

As regards such subjects as the Buddha's power being added to his devotees (*adhishṭhāna*) or its moving them from within and enabling them to act in this way or that way (*prabhāva* or *anubhāva*), they have been treated although somewhat briefly in the previous part of this work, that is, pp. 202–205.

[1] P. 58. Cf. also pp. 49, 66, 89, 123, etc., and for further exposition of the subject see pp. 220–235 of the present *Studies*.

[2] Pp. 277, 214, 161, 123, etc.

5. OTHER MINOR SUBJECTS

Among other subjects which are treated more or less briefly and in a detached way in the *Laṅkāvatāra*, the following have been selected as important. With these I hope the sutra has been explaind somewhat thoroughly as far as the main ideas making up the grand fabric of Mahayana Buddhism are concerned. I have purposely neglected making reference to the Sāṁkhya and Lokāyatika views refuted by the author of the *Laṅkāvatāra*. These are valuable when the historical position of the sutra is to be determined, which will be attempted later when a complete English translation of it is published. I have confined myself in this book to the study of such Mahayana thoughts as have engaged the attention of the writer of the sutra. He has by no means exhausted all the Mahayana doctrines, perhaps the sutra was compiled too early for that; one thing, however, I may mention at this juncture is that one of the ideas most distinctive as Mahayanistic has not received the slightest attention in the *Laṅkāvatāra*, not even bare mention of the term. By this I mean the doctrine of turning over individual merit towards attaining enlightenment, or towards helping others to do the same thing. That is known as Pariṇāmana, transferring of merit.

Pariṇāmana follows from the conception of Pariṇidhāna. In fact, Pariṇidhāna (vowing), Mahākaruṇā (great love), Upāyakauśalya (skilful means), and Adhishṭhana (power added and sustaining) are all most intimately related ideas; when any one of them is awakened and set to work out its own consequences, the rest inevitably follow it. The *Prajñā-pāramitā-sūtras* considered to be one of the earliest Mahayana literature constantly refer to Pariṇāmana, and also in the *Avataṁsaka* and in the *Sukhāvatīvyūha* it is one of the characteristic terms. Seeing this, it is strange that the *Laṅkāvatāra* is altogether silent about it.

The subjects to be mentioned below are (1) One Vehicle

and Triple Vehicle, (2) The Five Fatal Sins, (3) The Six Pāramitās, (4) Four Dhyānas, and (5) Meat-eating.

1. *Ekayāna* (pp. 133 ff)

The Buddha is often compared to a great physician who can cure every sort of illness by skilful treatment.[1] As far as the science of medicine goes, there is just one principle which, however, in the hands of an experienced doctor finds a variety of applications. The teaching of the Buddha does not vary in time and space, it has a universal application; but as its recipients differ in disposition and training and heredity they variously understand it and are thereby cured each of his own spiritual illness. This one principle universally and infinitely applicable is known as One Vehicle (*ekayāna*), or Great Vehicle (*mahāyāna*). "My teaching is not divided, it remains always one and the same, but because of the desires and faculties of beings that are infinitely varied, it is capable also of infinite variation. There is One Vehicle only, and refreshing is the Eightfold Path of Righteousness."[2]

Mahāyāna and Ekayāna are used synonymously in all the Mahayana texts. The idea of likening the Buddha's teaching into an instrument of conveyance was doubtless suggested by that of crossing the stream of Saṁsāra and reaching the other side of Nirvana. The Mahayana stands contrasted to the Hinayana, and the Ekayāna to the Dviyāna (twofold vehicle). The Dviyāna comprises Śrāvakas and Pratyekabuddhas, whereas the Ekayāna is meant for Bodhisattvas. The readers of the *Laṅkāvatāra* are naturally Mahayanists who have a penetrating insight into the nature of all things, know well the distinction between words and their meaning, and lead others to share also properly in the bliss of No-form (*animitta-sukha*).[3] Those of the two Yānas are

[1] P. 204.
[2] Based on p. 204, g. 117.
[3] P. 195.

indeed free from the thought of an ego-substance known as Satkāyadṛishṭi, have no doubt (*vicikitsa*) as to what they have realised within themselves, and do not wish for any external rewards accruing from their observance of morality (*śīla-vrata-parāmarśa*); but they have not yet reached the realm of the inconceivable wisdom which belongs to the inner life of the Tathagata;[1] and for this reason they have no desire to benefit others or to sacrifice themselves for the sake of others. They rest in the enjoyment of their Samādhi, for in them a great compassionate heart has not been stirred up as is the case of the Mahayana Bodhisattva. The latter is a follower of the Ekayāna.

Besides this Ekayāna and Dviyāna, the Mahayana sutras generally speak of Triyāna, which consists of the Śrāvaka-yāna, Pratyekabuddha-yāna, and Bodhisattva-yāna. But we must remember that the Ekayāna has really nothing to do with the number of Yānas though *eka* means "one"; *eka* in this case rather means "oneness," and Ekayāna is the designation of the doctrine teaching the transcendental oneness of things, by which all beings inclusive of the Hinayanists and Mahayanists are saved from the bondage of existence. So we have:

"My Mahāyāna is not a vehicle, or a voice, or letters; nor is it what may be termed truth, or emancipation, or realm of no-shadows.

"Yet when one is taken into the Mahāyāna one enjoys the sense of perfect freedom issuing from the Samādhi, and one can transform oneself into any form one may wish and, adorned with flowers, become absolute master of all things."[2]

This is the positive view of Mahāyāna or Ekayāna, and from another point of view which has been designated transcendental, these assertions concerning the Yāna are surely conventional, they are for the benefit of the ignorant.

"I preach the Triple Vehicle, the One Vehicle, and no-

[2] *Tathāgatācintya-gati-vishaya-gocara.* p. 117 ff.

[3] P. 137, gg. 1–2.

Vehicle, but they are all meant for the ignorant, the little-witted, and for the wise who are addicted to the enjoyment of quietude.

"The gate of the ultimate truth is beyond the dualism of cognition (*vijñapti*); when it is abiding in the realm of no-shadows, how can there be the establishment of the Triple Vehicle?"[1]

Further we have:

"The Vehicle for the Gods, the Brahma-Vehicle, the Vehicle for Śrāvakas, one for Tathagatas, and one for Pratyekabuddhas—these Vehicles I preach.

"As long as mind evolves, these vehicles cannot be done away with; when it experiences a revulsion (*parāvṛitti*), there is neither vehicle nor driver.

"I speak of a variety of vehicles, but there is no real establishment of them; I speak of a variety of vehicles in order to induce the ignorant.

"There are three forms of emancipation; realisation that there is no self-substance in anything, knowledge of sameness, and the liberation from evil desires.

"Like a piece of wood drifting in the ocean, tossed about by the waves, the Śrāvaka, weak in wisdom, is tossed about by appearances.

"[The Śrāvakas] are indeed disjoined from these outstanding evil passions, but still under bondage to the passions arising from memory (*vāsanā*); drunk with the liquor of Samādhi, they tarry in the world of non-outflowings.

"For them there is as yet no reaching the utmost limits of that world, nor is there any more sliding-back. For him who is thoroughly absorbed in Samādhi there is no hope even unto eternity for his awakening therefrom.

"Like a drunken man who is awakened only after the effect of the liquor has disappeared, the Śrāvakas will realise, when they are awakened, my body known as the Buddha-dharma."[2]

[1] P. 65, gg. 131–132. [2] Pp. 134–145.

Lastly, what is the path of the Ekayāna? How does one realise it?

"The way to realise the path of the Ekayāna is to understand that the process of perception is due to discrimination; when this discrimination no longer takes place, and when one abides in the suchness of things, there is the realisation of the Vehicle of Oneness. This Vehicle has never been realised by anybody, by the Śrāvakas, Pratyekabuddhas, or the Brahmans, except indeed by myself. Therefore, it is called the Vehicle of Oneness."[1]

Why does the Buddha speak of the Triple Vehicle, and not of the Vehicle of Oneness? This is asked by Mahāmati. Answers the Buddha: "There is no truth of Parinirvāṇa to be realised by the Śrāvakas and Pratyekabuddhas all by themselves; therefore, I do not preach them the Vehicle of Oneness. Their emancipation is made possible only by means of the Tathagata's guidance, discretion, discipline, and direction; it does not take place by them alone. They have not yet made themselves free from the hindrance of knowledge (*jñeyāvaraṅa*) and the working of memory; they have not yet realised the truth that there is no self-substance in anything, nor have they attained the inconceivable transformation-death (*acintyapariṅāmacyuti*). For these reasons I do not preach the Vehicle of Oneness. I preach the Triple Vehicle to the Śrāvakas. When their evil habit of memory is all purgated, when they have an insight into the nature of all things that have no self-substance, and when they are awakened from the intoxicating result of Samādhi which comes from the evil habit of memory, they rise from the state of non-outflowings. When they are thus awakened, they will supply themselves with all the moral provisions on a plane which surpasses the state of non-outflowings where they have hitherto remained."[2]

[1] Pp. 133–134.
[2] P. 134.

2. *The Five Deadly Sins*[1]

The following five deeds are regarded by Buddhism as the worst offences to be committed by its followers: (1) murder of the mother, (2) of the father, (3) of the Arhat; (4) disturbing the peace of the Brotherhood; and (5) making the Buddha bleed with an evil motive. They are called the "five immediate or uninterrupted sins"[2] because the offender is to be subjected to an uninterrupted series of tortures in hell. The *Laṅkāvatāra* gives this its opposite interpretation as follows: "Who is the mother of all beings? Thirst (or Desire, *tṛishṇā*) which is regenerative and, accompanied by pleasure and greediness, is the nursing mother. The fatherly quality of ignorance (*avidyā*) causes one to be born in the community (or hamlet) of the six houses (*āyatana-grāma*). When the root of these two is cut off it is called the slaying of father and mother. To extirpate completely the passions that pursue a man like a deadly enemy and excite him furiously like a poisoned rat—this is the slaying of the Arhat. What is the breaking-up of the Brotherhood? To destroy completely the root of mutuality and solidarity that holds together the five Skandhas—this is the breaking-up of the Brotherhood. O Mahāmati, to destroy completely the system of eight[3] Vijñānas which perceives an external world as constructed on the principles of individuality and universality altogether independent of mind, and to do this by means of a discrimination which is injurious [to the working of the Vijñāna system] but which is productive of a triple emancipation devoid of the

[1] P. 138 et seq. [2] *Pañcānantarāṇi.*

[3] It is significant that Sung has here "seven" instead of "eight." The eighth Vijñāna is the Ālaya where a revulsion (*parāvṛitti*) takes place and consequently a complete change of one's spiritual outlook. When the Mahayanists refer to the doctrine of mind-only, this mind ultimately means the Ālaya, or eighth Vijñāna; for it is here that memory (*vāsanā*), since the beginningless past, is stored up from which the whole external world evolves.

outflowings (*anāsrava*),—this is called an "Immediate' (*ānantaryaka*), because it causes the bleeding of the Buddha-body of the Vijñānas with an evil motive.

"O Mahāmati, these are the inner five "Immediates." For those who commit these deeds, be they sons or daughters of a good family, there is an immediate realisation of the truth.

"Again, O Mahāmati, I will tell you about the external 'Immediates,' so that you and other Bodhisattvas may not in the future harbour any doubt about them. By the external 'Immediates' I mean those mentioned in the sutras. Those who commit those deeds will never have any sort of realisation of the triple emancipation (*vimokshatraya*), except those who attain to the realisation by the superadded power (*adhishṭhāna*) of the Transformation-Buddha. When the Śrāvaka supported by the power of a Bodhisattva or by that of a Tathagata sees others committing deeds of the 'Immediate' nature, and, wishing to make them abandon their evil deeds, so that they will be free from the yoke of their errors, is moved to wake them up, he is supported by the supernatural power of the Transformation-Buddha[1] and will attain realisation. But there is no such realisation for those who are simply addicted to the 'Immediate' deeds. But he will have realisation (*abhisamaya*) who, understanding the doctrine that all things are no more than the manifestations of mind, abandons the view that there really is a world of particulars where the body, property, and the abode, are distinguished, cuts himself off from the idea of an ego-

[1] The theory of Transformation-Buddha is also illustrated in the following classification of the Arhats. "There are three kinds, (1) those who are single-mindedly intent on walking the path of quietude, (2)) those who, disciplining themselves in a life of enlightenment, lay up a store of merit, and (3) those who are forms of the Transformation-Buddha. The class one is of Srāvakas, but the other two are of Bodhisattvas and the transformations of the Buddha who manifest themselves in consequence of skilful means derived from their original vows and also in order to adorn the assembly of the Buddhas." (P. 120.)

substance and what belongs to it, befriends good companions whenever and wherever they are met who will induce him to another world, and is able to release himself from the faults of self-discrimination. It is thus said:

"Thirst is indeed the mother, and ignorance is the father, when from the understanding of an objective world there rises Buddha-knowledge.

"The passions are the Arhat, and the five Skandha-aggregates are the Brotherhood; as these and no other 'Immediates' are to be destroyed, here is indeed a set of deeds called 'Immediate'."

In this quotation I wish to draw the reader's attention to the reference to *nirmita-adhishṭhāna*. The term is somewhat casually introduced here, but the idea indicated here is an important one; for it shows that there has been since the early days of Buddhism a notion that not only the Tathagata but even a Bodhisattva when he reaches a higher state of spirituality is able to manifest himself in a variety of forms if necessary for the welfare and salvation of all beings. If a Bodhisattva wishes to save a wretched drunkard, for instance, he may turn himself into one of his companions if he thinks that is the best way to approach him and awaken him from the wretchedness of his position. For when the Bodhisattva remains in his original purity and saintliness, the drunkard may not come within the range of his moral influence; like seeks like, and consequently drunkards find it easier to associate with one another, they hate a mixed society, especially with him who is decidedly opposed to them and openly anxious to save their souls. So in Buddhism, the Bodhisattva in his apparent transformation puts on the garb of a drunkard himself and mixing himself with his bacchanalian friends he awaits a chance. Perhaps he may show that he has been regenerated and raised to a higher plane of spirituality. His friends may now wonder how a drunkard could be so reformed, and so on. When this wonderment is once grafted into the consciousness of his drunkard-friend, the Bodhisattva will redouble his efforts, and, making use of his "skilful means" (*upāya*), see to it that the grafted idea at first occupying only an obscure corner of the intoxicated consciousness, a former friend of the Bodhisattva, strike root gradually, steadily grow, and finally cause a sudden awakening (*parāvṛitti*) in the soul that was hitherto in a most wretched state of spirituality, or rather of non-spirituality. This Bodhisattva who in this case has proved to be an instrument of salvation is said to be a transformation-body of the Tathagata led by his supernatural power (*adhishṭhāna*). The skilful means he has resorted to here is technically known as *samānārthata* (同事 in Chinese), engaging in the same work, which is a kind of proletarian morality. The aristocracy of saintship cannot penetrate into the depths of an ordinary soul, and to understand this a Bodhisattva has to become an ordinary character himself. The doctrine of Upāya-kauśalya ("skilful means") is an interesting one in the evolution of Mahayana Buddhism. The thought is organically and intimately connected with the great compassionate heart that constitutes the centre of existence.[1]

3. *The Six Pāramitās* (p. 236 ff)

This is one of the marks most characteristically distinguishing the Mahayana from the Hinayana. In most Mahayana sutras the six Pāramitās are stated specifically as meant for Bodhisattvas. All the virtues that are meant for Bodhisattvahood are included herein, and, indeed, it was as the result of the six Pāramitās that the Buddha was able to gain the grand enlightenment about two thousand and five hundred years ago. If he did not practise all these virtues to their utmost in his past lives he would never have gained an insight into the truth of existence. *Pāramitā*

[1] See also the *Saddharmapuṇḍarīka*, Kern's English Translation, p. 410 et seq., where the Bodhisattva Avalokiteśvara and his transformations are described.

may mean either "reaching the other shore," or "perfection." In the Chinese sutras it is in most cases left untranslated as 波羅蜜 (*pa-lo-mi*).

The six Pāramitās are: (1) charity (*dāna*), (2) morality (*śīla*), (3) patience or humility (*kshānti*), (4) energy, or strenuosity (*vīrya*), (5) meditation (*dhyāna*), (6) wisdom, or intuitive understanding of the ultimate truth of things (*prajñā*).

The *Laṅkāvatāra* gives three kinds of Pāramitās: (1) worldly, (2) super-worldly, and (3) super-worldly in its highest degree. The worldly kind is practised by worldly people who cling to the idea of an ego and what belongs to it; they are unable to shake themselves off the fetters of dualism such as being and non-being, and all the virtues they would practice are based on the idea of gaining something material as a reward. They may gain certain psychic powers and after death be born in the heaven of Brahma. The super-worldly kind is practised by Śrāvakas and Pratyekabuddhas who, clinging to the idea of Nirvana, are determined to attain it at all costs; they are like the worldly people who are attached to the enjoyment of egotism. The Pāramitās that are super-worldly in the highest sense are practised by a Bodhisattva who understands that the world is dualistically conceived, because of the discriminating mind, and who is detached from erroneous imaginations and wrong attachments of all kinds, such as mind, form, characters, etc. He would practise the virtue of charity solely to benefit all sentient beings and to lead them to a blissful state of mind. To practise morality without forming any attachment to the condition in which he binds himself—this is his Śīla-pāramitā. Knowing the distinction between subject and object, and yet quietly to accept it without waking any sense of attachment or detachment, this is the Bodhisattva's Kshānti-pāramitā. To exercise himself most intently throughout the night, to conform himself to all the requirements of discipline, and not to evoke and discriminating mind—this is his Vīrya-pāramitā. Not to cling to the philosopher's view of Nirvana and to be free from discrimination—this is Dhyāna-pāramitā. As to Prajñā-pāramitā, it is not to evoke a discriminating mind within oneself, nor to review the world with any kind of analytical understanding, not to fall into dualism, but to cause a turning at the basis of consciousness. It is not to destroy the working of a past karma, but to exert oneself in the exercise of bringing about a state of self-realisation. This is Prajñā-pāramitā.

4. *The Four Dhyānas* (pp. 97 f)

The classification of Dhyāna under four heads has been treated previously in my *Essays in Zen Buddhism*,[1] and I will not repeat it here except to quote the gāthās which appear after the prose.

"There is (1) Dhyāna that surveys the meaning, (2) Dhyāna practised by the ignorant, (3) Dhyāna depending on suchness, and (4) the Tathagatas' pure Dhyāna.

"The practiser (*yogin*) may see [while in meditation] something in the shape of the sun or moon, something like a lotus-flower, or like the lowest region; he may see something resembling the sky, or fire, or a picture, or something heaped up (*pūñjān?*).

"All these forms, a variety of things, but lead the yogin to the path of the philosophers, and make him fall into the realm of Śrāvakas and Pratyekabuddhas.

"When all these are abandoned and he is in the state of no-shadows, all the Buddhas will come together from their lands and with their shining hands anoint the head of the blessed with unguents; his [mental] state is in full conformity with suchness (*tathatā*)."[2]

Further down there is another statement concerning the attainment of the Dhyānas:

[1] Series I, p. 81 et seq.
[2] P. 98.

"All the Dhyānas, Apramāṇas,, Ārūpas, Samādhis, the Cessation of Thought,—all these are mental constructions, nothing of the sort is really attainable.

"The fruit resulting from the life of a Srotāpanna, of a Sakṛidāgāmin, or of an Anāgāmin, or of an Arhat—all this is mental confusion.

"The Dhyāna practised, Dhyāna itself, and the subject of Dhyāna, the abandonment, the seeing of the truth,—all this is discrimination; he who understands is released."[1]

5. *On Meat-eating* (p. 244 et seq.)

The motive for having this chapter appended to the *Laṅkāvatāra,* when it has no organic connection with the text proper, seems to lie in a passage towards the end. According to it, the Buddha evidently dislikes the idea of being thought of as the one who has permitted meat-eating among his followers. He says, there may be some unenlightened followers of mine after my death, who, not knowing the spirit of my teaching and training, may wrongly conclude that I allowed them to eat meat and that I myself ate it. This would be disastrous. For how can those who are abiding in a merciful heart, disciplining themselves in asceticism, and trying to follow the path of Mahayana, tell others to eat animal food? Indeed, I have elsewhere given rules as to the eating and not eating of meat; ten rules for avoiding and three rules for accepting it. But in this *Laṅkāvatāra* as well as in the *Hastikakshya, Mahāmegha, Nirvāṇa,* and *Aṅgulimālika* sutras, meat-eating is absolutely forbidden. Not only in the past, but in the future and now, all my followers are to shun animal food no matter how it has been prepared. If there is any one who would accuse me of eating meat myself and allowing others to eat it, he will surely be born in an undesirable region. Holy people refuse to eat even the food of ordinary people, how much more so with meat-eating! Their food is the food of truth

[1] P. 121.

(*dharmāhāra*), the Tathagata's Dharmakāya is supported by that.[1]

According to this, there must have been the accepting of meat-food among the followers of Buddhism in the time when the *Laṅkāvatāra* was compiled. Evidently, the Buddha did not object to their eating it if the animal was not especially killed for them. This caused unfavourable comments among the other religions, for instance, the Lokāyatas,[2] and the Buddhists naturally did not like them, and this must have started the new effort to prohibit meat-eating altogether among the Mahayana advocates.

The following are the reasons for not eating animal food as recounted in this sutra:

(1) All sentient beings are constantly going through a cycle of transmigration and stand to one another in every possible form of relationship. Some of these are living at present even as the lower animals. While they so differ from us now, they all are of the same kind as ourselves. To take their lives and eat their flesh is like eating our own. Human feelings cannot stand this unless one is quite callous. When this fact is realised even the Rakshasas may cease from eating meat. The Bodhisattva who regards all beings as if they were his only child cannot indulge in flesh-eating.

(2) The essence of Bodhisattvaship is a great compassionate heart, for without this the Bodhisattva looses his being. Therefore, he who regards others as if they were himself (*sarva-bhūtātmabhūta*), and whose pitying thought (*kṛipātma*) is to benefit others as well as himself, ought not to eat meat. He is willing for the sake of the truth to sacrifice himself, his body, his life, his property; he has no greed for anything; and full of compassion towards all sentient beings and ready to store up good merit, pure and free from wrong discrimination, how can he have any longing for meat? How can he be affected by the evil habits of the carnivorous races?

[1] Pp. 254–256. [2] Cf. p. 244.

(3) This cruel habit of eating meat causes an entire transformation in the features of a Bodhisattva, whose skin emits an offensive and poisonous odour. The animals are keen enough to sense the approach of such a person, a person who is like a Rakshasa himself, and would be frightened and run away from him. He who walks in compassion (*maitrī-vihāri*), therefore, ought not to eat meat.

(4) The mission of a Bodhisattva is to create among his fellow-beings a kindly heart and friendly regard for Buddhist teaching. If they see him eating meat and causing terror among animals, their hearts will naturally turn away from him and from the teaching he professes. They will then lose faith in Buddhism.

(5) If a Bodhisattva eats meat, he cannot attain the end he wishes; for he will be alienated by the Devas, the heavenly beings who are his spiritual sympathisers and protectors. His mouth will smell bad; he may not sleep soundly; when he awakes he is not refreshed; his dreams are filled with inauspicious omens; when he is in a deserted place, all alone in the woods, he will be haunted by evil spirits; he will be nervous, excitable at least provocations; he will be sickly, have no proper taste, digestion, nor assimilation; the course of his spiritual discipline will be constantly interrupted. Therefore, he who is intent on benefitting himself and others in their spiritual progress, ought not to think of partaking of animal flesh.

(6) Animal food is filthy, not at all clean as a nourishing agency for the Bodhisattva. It readily decays, putrifies, and taints. It is filled with pollutions, and the odour of it when burned is enough to injure anybody with refined taste for things spiritual.

(7) The eater of meat shares in this pollution, spiritually. Once King Simhasaudāsa who was fond of eating meat began to eat human flesh, and this alienated the affections of his people. He was thrown out of his own kingdom. Sakrendra, a celestial being, once turned himself

into a hawk and chased a dove because of his past taint as a meat-eater. Meat-eating not only thus pollutes the life of the individual concerned, but also his descendants.

(8) The proper food of a Bodhisattva, as was adopted by all the previous saintly followers of truth, is rice, barley, wheat, all kinds of beans, clarified butter, oil, honey, molasses, and sugar prepared in various ways. Where no meat is eaten, there will be no butchers taking the lives of living creatures, and no unsympathetic deeds (*gataghṛiṇā*) will be committed in the world.

A SANSKRIT-CHINESE-ENGLISH GLOSSARY

In the following Glossary, the figures after each Sanskrit term refer to pages in the present work; the figures in parentheses to pages and lines in the Sanskrit text of the *Laṅkāvatāra*, thus: 28—7, 8 means p. 28, lines 7 and 8, of the Sanskrit text; the figures accompanying "The Sagāthakam" refer to the verses. T = the T'ang translation, W = the Wei, and S = the Sung.

A SANSKRIT-CHINESE-ENGLISH GLOSSARY

Akanishṭha(-bhavana), 208, 324, 327, 329, 331, 332, 346, 色究竟天 阿迦膩吒天; *Akanishṭha* literally means "not the least" or "not the smallest," and the heaven so designated is regarded as situated at the highest end of the Rūpadhātu or Rūpaloka, the world of Form. According to Dr. Unrai Wogihara (*Mahāvyutpatti*, "Notes," p. 306), *aka* must have been originally *agha*, and *agha* ordinarily means "evil" or "pain," but Buddhists understood it in the sense of form, perhaps because pain is an inevitable accompaniment of form. Hence the Chinese 色究竟, that is, the limit or end of form. In the *Laṅkāvatāra* (28—7, 8), we have: Kāmadhātau kathaṁ kena na vibuddho vadāhi me, akanishṭhe kim arthaṁ tu vītarāgeshu budhyase. 云何於欲界，不成等正覺，何故色究竟，離染得菩提(T). The idea that the Bodhisattva attains his supreme enlightenment when he is reborn in the Akanishṭha Heaven and not while he is on earth, i.e., in the world of Desire (*kāmadhātu*), recurs throughout the *Laṅkāvatāra*. Kāmadhātau tathārūpye na vai buddho vibudhyate, rūpadhātvakanishṭheshu vītarāgeshu budhyate ("Sagāthakam," 774), 欲界及無色，不於彼成佛，色界究竟天，離欲得菩提(T). So long as we have desire (*rāga*) based on egoistic impulses, we are barred from really spiritual realisation; and when we have it, we are no more in this world of Desire where existence is too deeply tinged with individuality. The Saṁbhogakāya, therefore, belongs to the heaven where form or individuality reaches its utmost end as the spirits here are no more bound by the mutually exclusive sense of a bodily existence. Does the belief in the attainment of Supreme Enlightenment upon one's being reborn in the Pure Land come from this notion of the Akanishṭha Heaven? For references in the *Laṅkāvatāra* see pp. 28—7, 8; 33—15, 16; 51—8; 56—9; 215—14; 269—4; 361—6. Akanishṭho virājate, 324, 色究竟熾然, That this Heaven is filled with brightness is natural, seeing that form obstracts and excludes while light intermingles, and the Akanishṭha is the abode of Shining Buddhas and Bodhisattvas.

Akshara, 109, 文字, word, letter, syllable. Tattvaṁ hy aksharavarjitam (48—12), 眞實離文字(T), "The truth is detached from letters." Niraksharatvāt tattvasya (190—6), 眞實之法離文字故(T), "because of the truth being detached from letters." Na ca mahāmate tathāgatā aksharapatitaṁ dharmaṁ deśayanti (194—3), 大慧如來不説墮文字法(T), "The Tathāgatas do not preach the doctrine that has degenerated into mere words." Aksharasamatā, 351, 字平等, sameness of letters.

Acalā, 78, 225, 262, 不動地, immovable, the eighth of the ten stages of Bodhisattvahood. When the Bodhisattva reaches here, he gets rid of discrimination and has a thorough understanding of the nature of existence, realising why it is like māyā, etc., how discrimination starts from our innate longing to see existence divided into subject and object, and how the mind and what belongs to it are stirred up; he would then practise all that pertains to the life of a good Buddhist, leading to the path of truth all those who have not yet come to it. This is the Bodhisattva's Nirvana which is not extinction. See above, p. 215.

Acitta, 201, 283, 非心, no-mind, beyond mentation; Acittatā or acittatva, 284, 286, 非心, no-mind-ness. Such abstract terms as these are frequently met with in the sutras belonging to the Prajñāpāramitā class of Mahayana literature.

Acintya, 146, 201, 317, 不思議, beyond mentation; Acintyajñāna, 208, 不思議智, knowledge or wisdom that is beyond the understanding, that is, 不思議諸佛如來智慧境界,

(*acintyajñānajinagocaravishaya*); Acintyapariṇāmacyuti, 212, 348, 361, 不思議變易死, death of mysterious transformation or inconceivable transformation-death. This has nothing to do with corporeal existence. It happens only to such spiritual beings as Bodhisattvas; Acintyavāsanāpariṇāma, 178, 不思議薰變, mysterious transformation that takes place within the mind (*citta*), making it comprehend an external world of particular objects.

Ajāta, 227, 不生, not born.

Ajñānakarmatṛishṇā, 167n, 無明·業·愛, ignorance, karma, and desire—the three motive powers that keep the present world a-going. Ajñānatṛishṇākarmādiḥ saṁkalādhyātmiko bhavet (203—14), 無明與愛業是則內鉤鎖 (T'ang). "Ignorance, desire, karma, etc. are the inner fetters." (See also 68—11, 177—18). Bhagavān apyajñānatṛishṇākarmavikalpapratyayebhyo jagata utpattiṁ varṇayati (197—14, 15), 世尊亦說無明愛業妄想爲緣生諸世間 (Sung). "According to the Buddha, too, the world rises from such causal combinations as ignorance, desire, karma, and discrimination."

Atyantaprakṛitipariśuddhi, 180n, 畢竟自清淨; Tathāgatagarbhaḥ prakṛitiprabhāsvaraviśuddhaḥ (77—15), 如來藏本性明亮清淨. That the original essence of the Garbha is pure and transparent, means that it is absolutely neutral and transcends all the logical categories that are derived from the dualism of subject and object. This is Suchness, the state of being unborn.

Advaya, 123n, 354, 無二 or 不二, non-duality; Advaita, 166, 287, 不二 or 無二, non-duality.

Adhigamāvabodha, 273, 證知, realisation.

Adhipatiphala, 323, 增上果, one of the Pañcaphalāni; see under *Phala*.

Adhishthāna, 79, 203 ff, 356, 363, 365, 加持力, or 威神力, the spiritual power of the Buddha which is added to a Bodhisattva and sustains him through his course of discipline. This is one of the conceptions peculiar to Mahayana Buddhism. Amitāyushas tathāgatasya pūrvapraṇidhānādhishṭhanena (*Sukhāvatīvyūha,* 55—14), 無量壽佛威神力故, 本願力故 (Saṁghavarman). "Owing to the sustaining power of the original vows made by the Tathāgata Amitāyus." Aśraushīd rāvaṇo.......tathāgatādhishṭhānāt (2—10), 羅婆那以佛神力聞佛語 (T).

Anāgāmin, 268, 阿那含 (不還), one who returns not. Anāgāmiphala, 148, 阿那含果 (不還果), the state of not-returning. One of the four "fruits" of the Buddhist ascetic life (沙門 *śramaṇa*), which are: 1. Srotaāpanna, 須陀洹 (預流), he who has entered upon the stream; 2. Sakṛidāgāmin, 斯陀含 (一來), he who returns once to this life; 3. Anāgāmin, 阿那含 (不還), he who never returns; and 4. Arhat 羅漢, he who has attained the highest end of the Buddhist life.

Anabhinirvṛitti, 227, 無起, not rising.

Anavabodha, 274, 不覺, not knowing. Vastusvabhāvābhiniveśaḥ svacittadṛiśyamātrānavabodhāt pravartate (100—4, 5), 事自性相計著者, 從不覺自心現分齊生 (S); 何者執着世事體相, 謂不如實知唯是自心見外境界故 (W); 執着諸法自性相者不覺自心所現故起 (T). "One's attachment to the self-nature of realities takes place owing to one's not knowing the truth that what is presented [as an external world] is no more than the mind itself." Observe how variously *vastusvabhāva* here is translated by the Chinese translators.

Anābhāsa, sometimes Nirābhāsa, 168, 無影像, 無影, 無相, See also *Nirābhāsa*.

Anābhoga, 43, 無功用, 無開發 (Sung), effortless, purposeless, not being aware of conscious strivings. Anābhogapūrvapraṇidhānaviśvarūpamaṇisadṛiśavishayānantalakshaṇapracāram (89—6, 7), 以無功用本願力故, 如如意寶普現一切無邊境界 (T); 依本願力, 如如意寶, 無量境界修行之相自然行故 (W); 無開發本願, 譬如衆色摩尼, 境

界無邊相行(S). "Owing to the original vows which have no purposeful motives, he manifests himself like a many-coloured gem in all possible conditions and with infinitely varied signs." Anābhogacandrasūryamaṇimahābhūtacaryā gatigamāḥ (161—1, 2). 無方便行，猶日月摩尼四大(S)；譬如四大日月摩尼，自然而行 (W)；以無功用，種種變化，光明照曜，如日月摩尼地水火風 (T). "Their course of life is purposeless like the moon, the sun, the gem, and the four elements." Anābhogacaryā, 99, 216, 222, 346, 無功用行，無開發行, purposeless deeds, a life free from conscious strivings. One of the very significant conceptions of Mahayana Buddhism.

Anāsrava, 276, 無漏, non-flowing. Āsrava (有漏) is something which oozes or flows out of the mind and spoils generally the upward career of the Buddhist life; to get rid of this is the aim of the ascetic discipline. The four principal poisonous outflows are: lust (*kāma*), clinging to life (*bhāva*), speculation (*dṛishṭi*), and ignorance (*avidyā*). Anāsrava is a state free from these impurities. Anāsravadhātu, 349, 360. 無漏界, realm of non-outflowings.

Animitta, 97, 259, 287, 954, 無相, formless, no-form, devoid of appearances. It is generally used in connection with *śūnyatā* and *apraṇihitam*. Animitta = nirābhāsa. Animittapatha (or animittādhishṭhāna), 346, 無相道，無相處, path or abode of formlessness; Animittasukha, 358, 無相樂, bliss of formlessness. Svātmānaṁ ca samyaganimittasukhena prīṇayanti parāṁśca samyaṅmahāyāne pratishṭhāpayanti (195—7, 9), 彼則能以正無相樂，而自娛樂，平等大乘建立衆生(S)；爾時自身於無相法樂而受樂，安住大乘中，令衆生知 (W)； 則能令自身受無相樂亦能令他安住大乘 (T). "They will thus make themselves properly enjoy the bliss of formlessness and also make others properly abide in the Mahāyāna."

Anirodha, 354, 不滅, not subject to destruction; Anirodhānutpāda, 292 ff, 354, 不滅不生, immortality, being above birth and death.

Anishṭhita, 227, 無盡, not extinguished.

Anujāta, 342n, 隨生, born after. Yathā tathāgatatathatā 'nāgatā 'gatā evaṁ hi subhūtitathatā 'nāgatā 'gatā, evaṁ hi subhūtiḥ sthavirastathāgatatathatām anujātaḥ (*Praj.* p. 307—1, 2); 如來眞如無來無去，本性不生，善現眞如亦無來無去，本性不生，故善現隨如來生 (Hsüan-chuang); 如如來如不來不去，須菩提如，從本已來，亦不來不去，是故須菩提隨如來生 (Kumārajīva). For the English translation see *The Studies,* pp. 242 f.

Anuttara-samyak-saṁbodhi, 206, 287, 349, 阿耨多羅三藐三菩提，無上正等正覺, the supreme enlightenment realised by the Buddha.

Anutpatti, 141, 不生, no-birth.

Anutpattikadharma, 228n, 法不生, the eight. The eight ways in which the conception of no-birth is established are as follows: ādau tattve 'nyatve avalakshaṇe svayamathānyathābhāve, saṁkleśe 'tha viśeshe kshāntir anutpattidharmoktā (*Sūtrālaṁkāra,* xi, 52), 本來及眞實，異相及自相，自然及無異，染汙差別八, (Prabhākaramitra). (1) Things (*dharmas*) have never been born because the idea of birth-and-death does not obtain in reality. (2) From that which precedes there is that which follows, and there is no difference between antecedents and consequents, and no absolute beginning can be assigned to anything. (3) If anything is already here nothing else can take its place unless we assume an independent origin, which is impossible. (4) The notion of self-substance comes from the imagination which is not based on reality. (5) Because of relative dependence (*paratantra*) we assume natural origin, but in reality there is nothing that can be called self-substance. (6) The absolute oneness of perfect knowledge (*parinishpanna*) excludes the idea of otherness. (7) When the knowledge of complete destruction (*kshaya-*

jñāna) is realised there is never again the assertion of evil passions. (8) In the Dharmakāya of all Buddhas there is perfect unity, and no differentiating individuation. When this eightfold notion of no-birth is realised one attains the recognition of the birthlessness of all things.

Anutpattikadharmakshānti, 75, 107, 125, 126n, 211, 226, 227f, 287, 298, 無生法忍. This is the recognition that nothing has been born or created in this world, that when things are seen *yathābhūtam* from the point of view of absolute knowledge, they are Nirvana itself, are not at all subject to birth-and-death. In this connection Kshānti seems to be somewhat differently understood from when it is used in opposition to Jñāna as in the *Abhidharmakośa*. The Mahayana Kshānti is an independent notion, and final as far as its spiritual value is concerned, for when one gains Anutpattikadharmakshānti one has realised the ultimate truth of Buddhism. The attainment of this Kshānti is *adhigama*, realisation (12—10).

Anutpanna, 166, 227, 無生, unborn. Anutpannasvabhāvaḥ, 122, 自性不生. If there is anything to be called self-substance, it cannot be subject to birth-and-death.

Anutpāda, 34, 43, 94n, 96, 123n, 168, 239, 283 ff, 不生, no-birth. Anutpādaṁ sarvadharmānām, 諸法不生. Anutpādo nirvāṇam, 295, 涅槃者不生, Nirvana means no-birth. (Anything that is subject to birth and death is not Nirvana.)

Anupalabdhya, 306, 不可得, unattainable, unknowable; Anupalabhyamānatva, 286, 不可得, unknowability. Bhāvasvabhāvalakshaṇāsattvāt sarvadharmā nopalabhyante (115—16, 17), 謂一切法無性相故，不可得故 (T), "All things are beyond the reach of knowledge because there are no such things as self-substance and its outward signs." Cittamātravinirmuktaṁ brahmādir nopalabhyate (210—1), 若離於心者，一切(梵天等)不可得 (T), "Apart from the Mind-only such notions as Brahma, etc. are not to be known.''

Anubhāva, 203, 356, 威神力, 神力' 威力, Buddhānubhāvena utthāyāsanāt (22—2, 3), 承佛神力從座而起, "Having risen from his seat through the power of the Buddha.''

Anulomikikshānti, 126n, 柔順忍, Kshānti of obedience.

Anuvyañjana, 352, (八十)隨好, secondary marks of excellence which are reckoned eighty. For detail see the *Mahāvyutpatti*, xviii.

Anyonyahetuka, 191, 互爲因 mutuality; Dve 'pyete 'bhinnalakshaṇe 'nyonyahetuke (37—18), 此二識無異相互爲因. "These two have no differentiating marks, they condition one another.''

Aparapraṇeya, 73, 202, 不由於他, not depending upon another. Svapratyātmabuddhyā vicārayatyaparapraṇeyaḥ (133—10, 11), 自覺觀察不由於他 (S). "Not depending upon another he reflects with his own intelligence.''

Apavāda. 157, 165, 180, 247, 誹謗, controversy, refutation. Kudṛishṭisamāropasyānupalabdhipravicayābhāvād apavādo bhavati (71—6, 7), 於諸惡見所建立法, 求不可得, 不善觀察, 遂生誹謗(T). "A controversy takes place when the impossible nature of a proposition based on wrong views is not clearly comprehended.''

Apracarita (-śūnyatā), 288, 無行 (空), Emptiness of non-action, one of the seven Emptinesses.

Apratishṭhita, 95, 無所住, not-abiding. This idea of not abiding anywhere is more in evidence in the *Prajñāpāramitā Sūtra* than in the *Laṅkāvatāra*. =anabhinivishṭa, =anābhoga, =apraṇihita, etc.

Apratisaṁkhyānirodha, 264, 293, 非擇滅, annihilation taking place without premeditated efforts. One of the three Asaṁskṛitas(無爲).

Apraṇihita, 138, 141, 259, 287, 無願, being without constrained efforts. One of the three Vimokshas.

Apramāṇa, 39, 148, 368, 無量, immeasurable. Apramāṇāni, 126n, 四無量心; the "four virtues of infinite greatness'' are (1) *maitrī* 慈, (2) *karuṇā* 悲, (3) *muditā* 喜, and (4) *upekshā* 捨.

Apravishṭam, 110, 不入, not entered. Udakacandra ivāpravishṭanirgatam (193—5), 如水中月不入不出 (T), "like the moon on water, which is neither in it nor out of it."

Apravṛitti, 127, 227, 無轉, not changing, not taking place.

Apsarā, 69, 70, 采女.

Abhāva, 103, 269, 305, 353, 非有, non-reality. Abhāvasvabhāva, 227, lacking in self-substance. 無性爲性, (Sikshānanda), 無所有性, (Kumārajīva).

Abhijñā, 39, 66, 97, 150, 210, 六神通, six supernatural faculties. In the *Laṅkāvatāra* these are generally found together with the tenfold self-control (*vaśita*) and the ten powers (*bala*) as possessed by a full-fledged Bodhisattva. The six Abhijñās are. 1. *Divyaṁ cakshus*, divine sight, 天眼通; 2. *Divyaṁ śrotra*, divine hearing, 天耳通; 3. *Paracittajñāna*, the faculty of reading others' thoughts, 他心通; 4. *Pūrvanivāsānusmṛitijñāna*, the faculty of remembering one's former abodes or lives, 宿命通; 5. *Ṛiddhividhijñāna*, the knowledge that transforms one's modes of life at will, 如意通; 6. *Āsravakshayajñāna*, the knowledge that destroys the evil outflows (impurities), 漏盡通

Abhidhāṇa, 133, 語言, naming. Abhidhānavinirmuktam abhidheyaṁ na lakshyate (187—2), 若離於語言，其義不可得 (T), 若離於言說, 亦無有所說 (S), 離於言語法, 可說不可得(W).

Abhidheya, 133, 義, meaning.

Abhidheyavikalpa, 111, 所說分別, wrong discrimination regarding what is described; one of the twelve subjects of wrong discrimination (*vikalpa*).

Abhinirhāra, 79, 行, (引發).

Abhiniveśa, 105, 128, 200, 執着, attachment. Abhiniveśasaṁdhi, 113, 密執, close attachment. Aparimito mahāmate sarvadharmānāṁ yathārutārthābhiniveśasaṁdhiḥ (161—10-11), 大慧, 於一切法, 如言取義, 執着深密其數無量

(T); 無量一切諸法，如所說義，計著相續 (S); 一切諸法，相續不相續相者....(W). "Innumerable, O Mahāmati, are signs of close attachment to the world by taking letters as exactly corresponding to meaning." The Sutra enumerates a few of them as typical.

Abhinnalakshaṇa, 191, 異相, differentiating marks.

Abhilashaṇa, 200, earnestly desiring, 専求 (T), 樂修 (W), 善樂(S). The Sanskrit text has *abhilakshaṇa* instead of *abhilashaṇa,* but the Chinese translations seem to have read it differently. Svapratyātmāryajñānādhigamābhilashanatayā, 専求自證聖智故 (T); "By earnestly seeking for the realisation of the supreme wisdom which is in one's inmost consciousness" (80—1, 2).

Abhilāpavikalpa, 111 f, 言說分別, wrong discrimination concerning sounds and expressions; one of the twelve Vikalpas. Vicitrasvaragītamādhuryābhiniveśaḥ (128—9, 10), 執著種種美妙音詞，是名言說分別 (T); "getting attached to various pleasant sounds and songs—this is *abhilāpavikalpa.*"

Abhisheka, 78, 灌頂, anointed. When the Bodhisattva reaches his last stage (*dharmamegha*) of self-discipline, he is anointed by the Buddhas with their own hands and formally inaugurated as one of them. Dharmameghābhishekābhishiktās tathāgatapratyātmabhūmim adhigamya... (123—6, 7), 至法雲地而受灌頂入於佛地 (T).

Abhisamaya, 321, 363, 現證, inner realisation. This is more than an intellectual understanding of the truth, it is spiritual. Buddhism abounds in terms of this order.

Abhisambodha, 273, 證, being fully awake.

Abhūtaparikalpa, 190, 虛妄分別, false judgment. Arthavividhavaicitryābhūtaparikalpābhiniveśān mahāmate vikalpaḥ pravartamānaḥ pravartate (150—9, 10), 種種義，種種不實妄想，計著妄想生(S); 於種種境...計能所，取虛妄執着，起諸分別 (T); 執着不實虛妄想者從見種種虛妄法生 (W). "As a variety of false judgments is given to objects conceived in their multiplicity, there takes place a strong clinging [to the external world]; O Mahāmati, this is the way discrimination goes on asserting itself.''

Amitābha-Buddha, 325, 無量光佛, often 無量壽佛.

Ayāna, 148, 非乘, triyānam ekayānaṁ ca ayānaṁ ca vadāmy aham (65—11), 我所立三乘, 一乘及非乘(T).

Arishṭa, 354, 無盡者, the imperishable.

Arūpyacārin, 39, 無色行, formless deeds. What this exactly means is difficult to know. Does it refer to the life in the world of no-form? or is it to be regarded as synonymous with *anābhogacaryā*? The mention of *arūpya* (*-drishṭi*) in connection with *tīrthyadrishṭi* confirms the first interpretation.

Artha, 108 ff, 義, or 境, or 財, meaning, or object, or wealth. When the term is used in the first sense, it stands contrasted to words or letters, and the latter are thought inadequate to fully describe the former. When it means objects in general it is almost equivalent to the external world, which is, however, better expressed by Vishaya. Vishaya seems to have a more collective sense than Artha when both refer to the objective world.

Arthapravicayam, 367, 觀察義禪, one of the four Dhyānas mentioned on p. 97, which consists in examining the meaning of a proposition or theory.

Arthavikalpa, 111 f, 財分別, one of the twelve Vikalpas (128—5). Suvarṇarūpyavividharatnārthavishayābhilāpaḥ, 謂取著種種金銀等寶而起言說, (T); ''To get attached to gold, silver, and other various treasures and to the talking about them—this is discriminating about wealth (*artha*).

Arhat, 363n, 368, 阿羅漢, one who has realised the highest fruit of the ascetic life, the ideal saint of Hinayana Buddhism. The Mahayana ideal is the Bodhisattva and not the Arhat, for the Bodhisattva does not enter into Nirvana like the Arhat, but stays in this world as long as there is even one of his fellow-beings left unsaved. Arhattva, 148,

羅漢, the state of being an Arhat.

Alakshaṇa, 227, 無相, without marks or recognisable signs.

Alabdha, 173n, 不可得. *Pu-k'o tê* (不可得) is frequently used for *na lakshyate* as well as for *na vidyate,* and in these cases it simply means "not existing." But when Tattvam is spoken of as *pu-k'o-tê* (*alabdha*), it refers to its transcending the reach of relative knowledge or discursive understanding. Tattvaṁ bhūtaṁ niścayo nishṭhā prakṛtiḥ svabhāvo 'nupalabdhiḥ tat tathālakshaṇam (228—12, 13), 眞實,(不虛),決定,究竟,根本,自性,(不)可得,是如如相 (T). "Truth, reality, certitude, limit, origin, self-nature, unattainability, incomprehensibility—these are the marks of Suchness." See also under *Anupalabdhya*.

Alātacakra 96, 旋火輪, fire-circle, one of the several comparisons adopted by the *Laṅkāvatāra* to illustrate the illusive nature of existence. A real wheel or circle comes into view when a fire brand is rapidly turned round, but in reality there is no wheel, being a mere vision.

Avalokiteśvara, 332, 觀自在菩薩.

Avastu, 119, 非物, non-reality; Sā ca na vastu nāvastu (108—9), 非即是物, 亦非非物(T).

Avikalpa, 106, 無分別, non-discriminating; Avikalpajñāna, 279, 296, 無分別智, non-discriminative wisdom; Avikalpapracāra, 72, realm of non-discrimination; Avikalpapracārasthitāsya (9—12), 住無分別 (T); 不住於分別心中(W).

Avidyā, 74, 81, 362, 無明, ignorance.

Avidyamānatva, 284, 無所有, not existing. Avidyamānatvena tasya samādhes taṁ samādhim na jānāti na saṁjānīte (*Ashṭasāhasrika,* 24—8, 9), 如是諸空無所有故, 於如是空無解無想 (玄奘譯, 大般若第五百三十八卷, 縮刷, 八十二丁, 六行).

Avināśa, 159, 不壞, not to be destroyed; Avināśita, 227, 無壞, not dissolved. Samyagjñānaṁ tathatā ca mahāmate avināśatvāt svabhāvaḥ parinishpanno veditavyaḥ (227—15-17),

正智如如，不可壞故，圓成性(T). "As Right Knowledge and Suchness are indestructible, they are to be regarded as Perfect Knowledge, of the three Svabhāvas."

Ashṭottaraṁ padaśatam, 40 f, 百八句, the 108 clauses; Ashṭottaraṁ praśnaśatam, 38, 百八問, the 108 questions.

Asaṁbhūta, 227, 無成, not combined.

Asaṁskṛita, 119, 264n, 279, 無爲. The Hinayana philosophers divide existence into two main groups, Saṁskṛita (有爲法) and Asaṁskṛita (無爲法). The Saṁskṛita comprises such dharmas as are tied to chains of causation and capable of producing effects, while the Asaṁskṛita exists unconditioned. The three dharmas belong to this head: space (*ākāśa*), Nirvana, and a negative state due to the absence of proper conditions.

Astināsti, 112, 116, 有無, being and non-being.

Asvabhāva, 287, 無自性, being without self-nature; asvabhāva=śūnya=nairātma=anutpanna. Asvabhāvatva, 39, 無自性, the state of being without self-nature.

Ākāśa, 137, 264, 293, 303, 353, 虛空, sky, space.

Āgata, 340, 來, come, arrived.

Āgantukleśa, 186, 客塵. *Kleśa* literally means "pain," "external dust," "affliction," or "something tormenting" and is translated as 煩惱. As there is nothing so tormenting spiritually as selfish evil desires and passions, *kleśa* has come to be understood chiefly in its derivative sense. In the present work the term is rendered "evil passion" arising from egotistic impulses, that is, from the conception of a permanent individual soul-substance. Here both the T'ang and the Wei have 客塵, "external dust," for *āgantu-kleśa*, while the Wei has 煩惱 besides 客塵, as if the latter were not sufficient. For further account see under *Kleśa*.

Ātman, 94, 130, 169, 289, 我, ego-soul; ātman=svabhāva=pudgala. Ātmakatva, 134, 體性, self-substance. Ātman means anything substantially conceived that remains eternally one, unchanged, and free. When an ego-soul (*pudgala*) is thought as such, that constitutes the *ātmadrishṭi* (我見). When the reality of an individual object (*dharma*) as such is denied, this is what is meant by *dharmanairātmya* (法無我).

Ātmavāda, 138, theory of ego. Tīrthakātmavādopadeśatulyas tathāgatagarbhopadeśo na bhavati (78—18, 79—1), 我說如來藏，不同外道所說之我 (T). "The tathāgatagarbha of which I speak is not like the doctrine of the ego maintained by the philosophers."

Ātmasukha, 141, 自樂, self-enjoyment. Yathaiva bālā ātmasukhanirvāṇābhilāshiṇaḥ (237—10), 如愚癡凡夫爲於自身求涅槃樂 (W). "Like those ignorant people who seek after Nirvana for their self-enjoyment." Ātmahitam, 214, 自利, benefitting oneself.

Ādarśavimba (or prativimba), 188, 鏡中像, mirror-image. Ādarśavimbadarśanavat (44—10), 譬如明鏡現衆色像 (T); like a mirror reflecting images.

Ādānavijñāna, 258, 阿陀那識, or 執持識.

Ānantarya, 363, 無間(業), the five most sinful deeds that result in the offender's being subjected to an "uninterrupted" series of tortures in hell.

Ābhāsvaravimāna, 261, 光音宮 or 極光淨天, a heaven, belonging to the world of Form (*rūpaloka*), where no sounds are heard according to a commentator; when the inhabitants wish to talk, a ray of pure light comes out of the mouth, which serves as speech.

Āyatanagrāma, 362, 六處聚落, hamlet of six houses.

Ārūpya, 148, 368, 無色定. There are four Samāpattis (等至 = coming together = mental collectedness) belonging to the world of No-form (*arūpaloka*): 1. *Ākāśānantya-āyatanam* 空無邊處. When the mind, separated from the realm of form and matter, is exclusively directed towards infinite space, it is said to be abiding in this form of concentration.

2. *Vijñānānantya°* 識無邊處. When the mind going beyond infinite space is concentrated on the infinitude of consciousness it is said to be abiding in this Samāpatti. 3. *Ākiṁcanya°* 無所有處. When the mind going even beyond the realm of consciousness finds no special resting abode, it acquires the concentration called "knowing nowhere to be." 4. *Naivasaṁjñānāsaṁjña°* 非想非非想處. The first three Samāpattis are designated from the disciplinary point of view of the yogin himself, while the fourth gains its title in regard to the nature of the concentration which is neither in the sphere of mental activities nor out of it.

Ārya, 143n, 305, 聖人, or 賢聖, the wise as distinguished from the ignorant 無智 (*avidvat*), the simple-minded 愚夫 (*bāla*), the confused 迷者 (*bhrānta*), and also from the philosophers 外道 (*tīrthaka*).

Āryajñāna, 38, 81, 102, 119, 128, 140, 141, 143, 147, 279, 288, 340, 聖智, supreme wisdom whereby one is enabled to look into the deepest recesses of consciousness in order to grasp the inmost truth hidden away from the sight of ordinary understanding. Āryajñāna=prajñā. In the *Laṅkāvatāra,* it is generally found in such combinations as *svapratyātmāryajñāna* or *āryapratyātmajñāna.* Āryajñānacakshus, 114, 聖智眼, the eye of supreme wisdom, also called *prajñānacakshus* (慧眼); Āryajñānasvabhāvavastu, 277, 305, 聖智自性事, supreme wisdom as constituting the ultimate fact of existence. Kim idaṁ....viviktadharmopadeśābhāvaśca kriyata āryajñānasvabhāvavastudeśanayā (165—9, 10), 何以故, 不說寂靜空無之法, 而說聖智自性事 (T); 何故說空法非性而說聖智自性事 (S); 何以故以言諸法寂靜無相聖智法體如是無相故 (W). "How is it, O Blessed one, that thou deniest the truth of negation by upholding the existence of a reality which makes up the substance of supreme wisdom?"

Āryavastusvabhāva (=āryajñānasvabhāvavastu), 305, 聖事自 [性.

Ālambana, 183, 192, 所緣 or 攀緣 resting or depending upon. Tad hetvālambanatvāt.....saptānāṁ vijñānānāṁ pravṛittir bhavati (126—17, 18), 以彼爲因及所緣故七識得生 (T); 彼因及彼攀緣故七識不生 (S); 以依彼念觀有故轉識滅七識亦滅(W). Observe how widely the three translations differ from one another. T'ang agrees with the Sanskrit, Wei gives no sense, while Sung adds an unnecessary 不, which altogether changes the meaning of the context. Ālambālambya, 241, 能緣所緣, mutual dependence, subject and object; Ālambavigata, 144, 遠離(一切)所緣, free from all conditions.

Ālayavijñāna, 3, 38, 67, 81, 97, 99, 103, 108, 167, 171 ff, 125 ff, 178 ff, 180, 182 ff, 186 ff, 192, 195 ff, 208, 281, 299, 阿賴耶識, or 藏識, 阿梨耶識(W), the all-conserving mind; Ālayavijñānodadhi, 67, 藏識大海; Ālayaugha, 171, 藏識海.

Āvaraṇa, 348, 障 or 礙, that which hinders the realisation of the truth; Āvaraṇadvaya, 132. The two hindrances are conative and intellectual, *kleśāvaraṇa* (煩惱障) and *jñeyāvaraṇa* (所知障). The latter is easier to destroy than the former, for the will to live or the egoistic impulses are the last thing a man can bring under complete control.

Āśraya, 158, 183, 所依, that which constitutes the basis of the various Vijñānas, that is, the Ālayavijñāna; Āśrayaparāvṛitti, 184, 轉依, revulsion or turning-over which takes place at the basis of consciousness, whereby we are enabled to grasp the inmost truth of all existence, liberating us from the fetters of discrimination. All the Buddhist discipline aims at this catastrophe without which there is no permanent conversion. ....svacittadṛiśyabāhyārthaparijñānād vikalpasyāśrayaparāvṛittir moksho na nāśaḥ (233—15, 16), 了知外境自心所現分別轉依名爲解脫非滅壞也(T); 自心現知外義, 妄想身轉, 解脫不滅(S); 如實能知唯自心見, 外所分別心廻轉故, 是故我說名爲解脫, 言解脫者非是滅法 (W). As is seen here, Wei is generally clumsy and not quite to the point, while Sung is too brief tending to obscurity. T'ang agrees with the Sanskrit text. "When it is thoroughly comprehended that the external world is no more than the manifestation of one's own mind, there is a revulsion at the basis of discrimination, which is emancipation and not destruction." Parāvṛittaṁ hi tathatā vihāraḥ kalpavarjitaḥ ("Sagāthakam," verse 151). 所住離分別，轉依卽眞如(T)；轉彼卽眞如，離分別是行(W). "The revulsion is Suchness; the abode is free from discrimination."

Āśrasya parāvṛittim anutpādaṁ vadāmyaham (202—3), 296. The first line of this gāthā reads: Cittaṁ dṛiśyavinirmuktaṁ svabhāvadvayavarjitam. 唯心無所見，亦離於二性，如是轉所依，我說是無生(T)；心離於見法及離二法體，轉身依正相，我說名無生(W)；唯有微(?)心住，想所想俱離，其身隨轉變，我說是無生(S).

Āśaya, 355, 意樂, desire.

Āsrava, 276n, 284, 漏, impure outflows of the mind, which are also known as Kleśa (煩惱). The three impurities are *kāma* (欲, desire to possess), *bhava* (有, will to live), and *avidyā* (無明, ignorance). When *drishṭi* (見, wrong view) is added, we have the four impurities. See also under *Anāsrava*.

Icchantika, 219n, 一闡提迦，無佛性, those who are destitute of the Buddha-nature.

Itaretara, 288, 彼彼空, reciprocity, one of the seven kinds of Emptiness.

Indra, 354, 因陀羅.

Uccheda, 73, 123n, 斷, cutting off, destruction; Uccheda-śāśvata, 128, 斷常. See also *Śāsvata*.

Ucchedadarśana, or Ucchedavāda, 120, 215, 斷見, negativism or nihilism opposed to eternalism; the philosophical school which teaches that the world is destined to come to a total extinction when the law of causation works no more.

Uttrāsita, 284, 驚, alarmed. Bodhisattvā mahāsattvā imaṁ nideśaṁ śrutvā nottrasishyanti na saṁtrasishyanti na saṁtrāsam āpatsyante.'' (*Ashṭasāhasrikā,* p. 17, etc.). This is one of the sentences most frequently met with in the *Prajñāpāramitā Sūtra,* 菩薩摩訶薩聞是說無驚怖退沒 (Kumārajīva). In the *Laṅkāvatāra* this is referred to on p. 64—15-17..... acintyavishayadeśyamāne nottrasati na saṁtrasati na saṁtrāsam āpadyate veditavyamayaṁ tathāgatayānābhisamayagotraka iti, 若有聞說.... 不思議境不驚不怖不畏, 當知此是如來性 (T). ''He who is not frightened, alarmed, betrays no sense of fear even when this realm beyond comprehension is shown to him—he is to be known as belonging to the family of the Tathāgata-yāna.''

Utpāda, 127, 183, 307, 生, 起, birth; Utpādanirodha, 116, 生滅, birth and extinction; Utpādapadam anutpādapadam, etc., 41, 生句非生句, ''what is termed birth is not birth.'' Utpādavikalpa, 111 f, 生分別, discrimination regarding birth, one of the twelve wrong judgments arising from imagination (*parikalpitasvabhāva,* 妄計自性).

Udakacandra, 96, 110, 水月 or 水中月, moon in water. This comparison is used to illustrate the illusive nature of existence which is beyond all predicates. The moon in water is not the real one as it is a reflection, but its appearance there is not to be denied. So we have also the following: Tad yathā mahāmate jalāntargatā vṛikshacchāyā khyāyate sā ca na cchāyā nācchāyā vṛikshasaṁsthānāsaṁsthānataḥ (93—13 f), 大慧, 譬如水中, 有樹影現, 彼非影非非影, 非樹形非非樹形 (T). More similes such as a mirror-image, an echo, a mirage are given in the same vein of thought.

Udadhitaraṅgālayavijñānagocaraṁ tathāgatānugītaṁ dharmakāyaṁ prabhāśasva, 188, 說如來所歎海浪藏識境界法身 (S). ''Pray tell us concerning the nature of the Ālaya-vijñāna compared to the ocean and its waves [and also] concerning the Dharmakāya praised by the Tathagatas.''

Upaklishṭa, 186, (客塵)所染, contaminated (by external dirt).

Upalakshaṇa, 200, seeing clearly, 善知 (T), 觀 (S), 善解 (W). Bāhyabhāvābhāvopalakshaṇatayā, 善知外法無性故 (T), 觀外性非性 (S), 善解外 (法) 有無故 (W); "by well understanding the unreal nature of the external objects" (80—1).

Upāya, 34, 88, 91, 97, 99, 132, 138, 314, 365, 方便 means, expediency, method, contrivance; Upāyakauśalya, 19, 346, 357, 善巧方便, skilful means; Upāyajñāna, 335, 方便智. The idea of "skilful means" is an important one in Mahayana Buddhism and inseparable from that of a great compassionate heart moving the whole being of Buddhahood. It is not enough for the Bodhisattva to have Āryajñāna or Prajñā fully awakened, for he must also be supplied with Upāyajñāna whereby he is enabled to put the whole salvation machinery in practice according to the needs of beings.

Ubhaya-anubhaya, 112, or Ubhaya-nobhaya, 116, 俱不俱, bothness and not-bothness.

Ṛiddhipāda, 39, 如意足 or 神足, miraculous psychic powers attained by means of Samādhi. There are four ways of realising the Samādhi through (1) the will-power (*chanda*, 欲), (2) thought-power (*citta*, 心), (3) strenuous efforts (*vīrya*, 精進), and (4) deep thinking (*mīmāṁsā*, 觀).

Ṛishi, 354, 仙, hermit-philosopher.

Ekacittam, 269, 一心, one mind.

Ekatva-anyatva, 112, 一異, oneness and otherness.

Ekam api aksharaṁ nodāhṛitam na pravyāhṛitam, 213, 不說一字, "not a word has been said nor declared." The Zen masters' favourite utterance, 四十九年一字不說, comes from this statement.

Ekayāna, 52, 148, 328, 351, 358 ff, 一乘, One Vehicle or

Vehicle of Oneness. This is identified with Mahāyāna. Ekayānāvabodha, 361, realisation of the One Vehicle. Yathābhūtāvasthānād apravṛitter vikalpasya....(133—16), 如實處不生妄想, 是名一乘覺(S); 離(能取所取)分別如實而住(T). "[The realisation means] the extinction of wrong discrimination by abiding in Suchness."

Ekāgra, 85, 121, 一緣, oneness.

Kara, 292, 353, 手, the hand.

Karuṇā, 101, 339, 悲, love, a compassionate heart.

Kartṛi, 130, 139, 作者, creator.

Karma, 182, 186, 業, act. Nakarmaprabhava, 145n, 325, 不從業生, not karma-created. Sarve hi nirmitabuddhā na karmaprabhavāḥ (242—12), 一切化佛不從業生 (T); Karmabīja, 197, 業種子, karma-seed; Karmāvaraṇa, 212, 業障, hindrance to the attainment of Bodhi, which rises from the past karma; Karmavijñāna, 187, 業識.

Kalāpaḥ pratyayānām (ca pravartate nivartate, 202—9), 297, 因緣共集會是故有生滅(T). "Because of a concatenation of causal chains there is birth, there is disappearance."

Kāmadhātu, 79, 欲界, world of Desire, one of the triple world (*triloka*, 三界), the other two being the world of Form (色界) and the world of No-form (無色界).

Kāma-bhava-drishṭi-avidyā, 276n, 欲·有·見·無明, which make up the contents of Āsrava (漏, evil outflow).

Kāya, 308, 身, system, body, Kāyasamatā, 318, 352, 身平等, [All the Tathāgatas are] the same as regards the body, [because aham ca tathāgatā....dharmakāyena ca rūpalakshaṇānuvyañjanakāyena ca samā nirviśishtāḥ (142—6 f)], 我與諸佛, 法身, 色相, 及隨形好等, 無差別(T).

Kāraṇa, 122, 146, 188, 302, 作者, creator, deity.

Kāshtha, 360, a piece of wood. Yathā hi kāshṭham udadhau.... (135—8), 譬如海中木(T).

Kuśalānāsrava, 198, 253, 善無漏法, good virtues free from

evil flowings, enjoyed by the wise when they are deeply drunk in the bliss of the Samādhi and abiding in the bliss of existence as it is.

Kuśalamūla, 72, 93 f, 善根, stock of merit.

Kṛitaka-akṛitaka, 116, 作非作, made and not-made, or done and not-done.

Kṛipā, 339, 悲, pity, compassion; Kṛipātma, 369, pitying thought. Māṁsaṁ sarvam abhakshyaṁ kṛipātmano bodhisattvasya (245—8), 菩薩當生悲愍不應噉一切肉 (T'ang). "The Bodhisattva with a pitying heart ought not to eat any meat whatever."

Kṛiyā, 193, 行, action; Kṛiyābhivyakti, 307, 所作明了 (轉變), manifested work.

Klishṭamanas, 178, 染污意, Manas contaminated.

Kleśa, 186, 224, 256, 348, 煩惱; Kleśakshaya, 130, 煩惱斷, the extinction of the evil desires; Kleśadvaya, 132, 二煩惱, two kinds of evil passions, primary and secondary; Kleśa-jñeya, 35, 36, 37, that is *kleśāvaraṇa* and *jñeyāvaraṇa*, hindrances caused by the evil passions and by intellection, 煩惱障及所知障; Kleśakhyāvivarjita, 360, 離諸煩惱, liberated from the evil passions so called; Kleśāvaraṇa, 177, 煩惱障, hindrance of the Kleśa. Kleśa is generally divided into two groups, primary and secondary. The primary comprise such evil impulses that lie at the foundation of every tormenting thought and desire. They are six in number: 1. *rāga* 貪 (desire to have), 2. *pratigha* 瞋 (anger), 3. *mūḍhaya* 癡 (folly or ignorance), 4. *māna* 慢 (self-conceit), 5. *dṛishṭi* 見 (false views), and 6. *vicikitsā* 疑 (doubt). Sometimes, 1. *ātmadṛishṭi* (我見, the belief in the existence of an ego-substance), 2. *ātmamoha* (我痴, ignorance about the ego), 3. *ātmamāna* (我慢, conceit about the ego), and 4. *ātmasukha* (我愛, self-love)—these four are regarded as the fundamental evil passions originating from the view that there is really an eternal substance known as ego-soul. The secondary Kleśa are sometimes twenty, sometimes twenty-four, sometimes only nineteen, according to the different schools. Vasubandhu's *Triṃśikā* gives twenty-four: 1. impatience (念, *krodha*), 2. hatred (恨, *upanāha*), 3. hypocrisy (覆, mraksha), 4. stinging talk (惱, *pradāśa*), 5. envy (嫉, *īrshyā*), 6. stinginess (慳, *mātsarya*), 7. deceit (誑, *māyā*), 8. duplicity (諂, *śāṭhya*), 9. arrogance (憍, *mada*), 10. hurting others (害, *vihiṁsa*), 11. shamelessness (無慚, *ahrī*), 12. recklessness (無愧, *atrapā*), 13. torpidity (惛忱, *styānam*), 14. restlessness (掉擧, *uddhava*), 15. unbelief (不信, *aśraddha*), 16. indolence (懈怠 *kauśīdya*), 17. thoughtlessness (放逸, *pramāda*), 18. senselessness (失念, *mushitasmṛititā*), 19. uncollected state (or unsteadiness) of mind (散亂, *vikshepa*), 20. inaccuracy of knowledge (不正見, *aśaṁprajanya*), 21. evil doing (惡作, *kaukṛitya*), 22. drowsiness (睡眠, *middha*), 23. investigation (尋, *vitarka*), 24. reflection (伺, *vicāra*).

Kshaṇikam, 194, 剎那, momentariness.

Kshānti, 126, 忍, generally translated "patience," or "resignation," or "humility," when it is one of the six or ten Pāramitās. But "acceptance," or "recognition," or "submission" will be better when it occurs in connection with the dharma that is unborn. In the *Abhidharmakośa*, Chapter VII, Kshānti is used in a way contrasted to Jñāna. According to it, Kshānti is not knowledge of certainty which Jñāna is, for in Kshānti doubt has not yet been entirely uprooted. Its characteristic is to enquire, to investigate, to examine so that an intellectual understanding may turn into intuitive certainty whereby errors are totally destroyed, never to assert themselves again. In this case, jñāna = parijñā = prajñā = adhigama = abhisamaya = svasiddhānta = pratyātmāryajñāna, while Kshānti is an intelligent recognition of a theory or doctrine. For the ten kinds of Kshānti, see p. 126 f.

Kshitigarbha, 332, 地藏尊.

Kha, 353, 虛空, sky.

Khacitavigraha, 84, 壁上彩畫, a painted figure on the wall (*bhitti*).

Khañjagardabha, 340, a lame donkey.....iva cittaprajñājñānalakshaṇaṁ hitvā (50—1), 捨跛驢智慧心相 (T'ang), "throwing away such thought, wisdom, knowledge as resembles the character of a lame donkey."

Khyātivijñāna, 189 ff, 現識, which almost corresponds to perception.

Gagana, 353, 虛空, sky.

Gata, 340, 去, gone, departed; Gataghṛiṇa, 371, 無慈愍, unsympathetic.

Garbha, 177, 藏, or 胎, womb.

Garbhakośadhātu, 177, 胎藏界. The dualism of the Garbhakośa and the Vajra is the attempt by Shingon philosophers to describe the constitution and development of the spiritual world. The Garbhakośa conceives the world as a stage on which Vairocanabuddha residing in the inmost heart of every being develops his inherent possibilities, whereas the Vajra depicts the Buddha in his own manifestations. The pictures illustrating the scheme and process of these developments are called Maṇḍala (曼陀羅).

Guṇa, 74, 130, 求那, 德, virtues or attributes.

Gocara, 104, 340, 境界, 所行, experience, mental attitude. *Gocara*, literally meaning "range for cattle," or "pasturage," is a field for action and an object of sense. In the *Laṅkāvatāra* it is frequently more than that, for it points to a general mental attitude one assumes towards the external world, or better a spiritual atmosphere in which one's being is enveloped. *Artha* which is also translated as 境 is an object of sense, while *Vishaya* also meaning 境 has a more general connotation since it designates a world of particulars as objects of mental activity. (Tārkikāṇām avishayaṁ śrāvakāṇāṁ na caiva hi,) yaṁ deśayanti vai nāthāḥ pratyātmagatigocaram (49—4, 5), 174. 世間依怙者，證智所行處，外道非境界，聲聞亦復然(T). "The world-leaders teach the state of consciousness realised by their inner perception, which is beyond the realm of the philosophers and the Śrāvakas."

Grāhaka, 195, 能取, seizing, one who seizes or perceives; Grāhaṇa, 127, 294, 能取, seizing, perceiving; Grāhya, 195, 所取, seized, that which is perceived; Grāhyagrāhaka, 97, 116, 201, 所取能取, that which is perceived or apprehended, and that which perceives or apprehends.

Ghoshānugakshānti, 126n, 音響忍, Kshānti in sounds. This is understood to mean the ready, willing response which is made characteristically by the devout follower to the verbal instruction of his teacher.

Cakshurvijñāna, 178, 188, 眼識, the sense of vision.

Catushkoṭikā, 116, 122, 132, 134, 135, 165, 四句(有句，無句，非有非無句，亦有亦無句), the four propositions.

Citta, defined, 176; as the whole system of vijñānas, 180 ff; originally pure, 174; 心, mind. *Citta* is generally translated as "thought," but in the *Laṅkāvatāra* as in other Mahayana sutras may better be rendered "mind." When it is defined as "accumulation" or as a "store-house" where karma-seeds are deposited, it is not mere thought, it has an ontological signification. Cittaṁ vikalpo vijñaptir mano vijñānam eva ca, ālayaṁ tribhavaśceshṭā ete cittasya paryapāḥ ("Sag." 459), 252. 心意及與識，分別與表示，本識作三有，皆心之異名(T)；心分別及識，意及於意識，阿梨耶三有，思惟心異名(W)；Tad hetukaṁ tad ālambya manogatisamāśrayam, hetuṁ dadāti cittasya vijñānaṁ ca samāśritam (127—10, 11), 250. 意識爲心因，心爲意境界，因及所緣故，諸識依止生 (T)； 彼因彼攀緣，意趣等成身，(—?)，爲識之所依(S)；依彼因及念，意趣諸境界，識與心作因，爲識之所依 (W)； 依彼因及觀，共意取境界，依於識種子，能作於心因(W in "Sagāthakam").

Cittam avyākṛitaṁ nityam, 249, 心常爲無記 (T); 心常無記法 (W); mind eternally quiescent, or neutral, or undivided. The whole verse ("Sagāthakam" 103) runs thus: Cittamavyākṛitaṁ nityaṁ mano hyubhayasaṁcaram, vartamānaṁ hi vijñānaṁ kuśalākuśalam hi tat. 心常爲無記，意具二種行，現在識通具，善與不善等 (T); 心常無記法，意二邊取相，取現法是識，彼是善不善 (W). "The Mind remains eternally neutral; Manas moves in two ways; the Vijñāna taking in what is presented is either good or not-good."

Cittaṁ manaś ca vijñānam, 39, etc., 心·意·意識. These three are found in combination throughout the *Laṅkāvatāra* meaning the whole machinery of mentation. When Citta is thus coupled, it corresponds to the empirical consciousness, i.e. Citta in its relative aspect and therefore together with false discrimination ....cittamanomanovijñānavikalpasaṁjñāvigamāt.... (215—5), ... 離心意意識妄分別想....(此是菩薩所得涅槃)(T).

Cittaṁ vishayasaṁbandham, (jñānaṁ tarke pravartate, 130—7), 179, 心爲境所縛，覺想智隨轉 (T). "The mind is bound up by an external world, speculation puts Jñāna in operation." Jñāna in this case is the reasoning faculty and stands contrasted to Prajñā which is the intuitive faculty meant for grasping the transcendental truth.

Cittaṁ hi traidhātukayoniḥ, 243, 三界由心生 (T). "The mind is the origin of the triple world."

Cittaṁ hi sarvaṁ (sarvatra sarvadeheshu vartate vicitraṁ gṛihyate 'śabdhiś cittamātraṁ hy alakshaṇam, 282—7, 8), 243. 心遍一切處，一切處皆心，以心不善觀，心性無諸相 (W); 心起一切法，一切處及身，心性實無相，無智取種種 (T). "All is mind, mind pervades in all places, in all the bodies. The ignorant perceive multiplicity, but there is nothing predicable in Mind-only."

Cittam utpādayitavyam, na kvacit pratishṭhitam, 95, 應無所住而生其心 (Kumārajīva). "[A Bodhisattva] should have his thoughts awakened without abiding in anything whatever.''

Cittakalāpa, 192, 心聚 (T, S), mentation-system. Cittakalāpaḥ pravartate 'nyonyahetukaḥ (127—3, 4), 生種種心，猶如束竹迭共爲因(W), 心聚生起展轉爲因(T). ''The whole mental system is evolved mutually conditioning [like a bundle of bamboo-sticks].''

Cittanirābhāsa, 346, 心無相, the mind that has no form.

Cittabāhyādarśana (42—10, 11), 243, 離心無得 (T); 心外無所見 (S); 自心見外境界故 (W). W was evidently a different text.

Cittamanādimatisaṁcitam, 176n. The complete line reads: Avidyāhetukaṁ cittam anādimatisaṁcitam (368—15). 無始所積集，無明爲心因 (T). ''Ignorance accumulated over and over again owing to imperfect intellection since the infinite past is the origin of the mind.''

Cittamanomanovijñāna, or cittaṁ manaś ca vijñānam, 73, 98, 119, 132, 150, 168, 172, 211, 221, 226, 246, 心，意，意識.

Cittamātra, 唯心, Mind-only, or Mind-itself; Cittamātraṁ lokam, 243, 世間唯是心, the world is Mind-only. Bāhyabhāvānabhyupagamāt tribhavacittamātropadeśād vicitralakshaṇānupadeśāt (208—13, 14), (何以故)，不取外法故，三界唯心故，不說諸相故 (T); (所以者何) 謂外法不決定故，唯說三有微心，不說種種相 (S); (何以故) 我不說外境界有故，我說三界但是自心，不說種種諸相是有 (W). ''Why? Because I do not admit the existence of an external world, but I teach that the triple world is Mind-only and do not teach about signs of multiplicity.'' Cittamātraṁ yadā lokaṁ prapaśyanti jinātmajāḥ, tadā nairmāṇikaṁ kāyaṁ kriyāsaṁskāravarjitam.... (73—8,9). 佛子能觀見，世間唯是心，示現種種身，所作無障礙.... (T); 心量世間，佛子觀察種類之身，離所作行....(S); 佛子見世間，惟心無諸法，種類非身作....(W). ''When the world is seen by those born of the Buddha as no more than mind, they assume a variety of bodies which are free from [constrained] activities and conditionalities."

Cittamātradṛiśya, 123, etc., 唯心所現, or simply, cittamātra, 唯心, is one of the principal phrases recurring in the *Laṅkāvatāra*. Ye grāhyagrāhakābhinivishṭāḥ svacittadṛiśyamātraṁ nāvabudhyante....(104—8, 9). 若不了諸法唯心所現，計有能取及以所取....(T). "Those who are attached to the notion of duality (object and subject) fail to understand that there is only what is seen of the Mind."

Cittamātravinirmuktaṁ nopalabhyate, 180, 離心不可得. "Apart from mind nothing is attainable, that is, comprehensible"; in other words, Dṛiśyacittaparijñānād vikalpo na pravartate (343—17), 了境唯是心，分別則不起 (T). "When what is seen [or an external world] is penetratingly understood as Mind [-itself], discrimination never takes place." "Unattainability" or "incomprehensibility" means that the thing is altogether beyond the reach of analytical, relative knowledge. See also under *Anupalabdhya*.

Cittavikalpalakshaṇa, 179, 心分別相. Svacittavaicitryavikalpakalpitatvāt...vaicitryabhāvalakshaṇābhiniveśāt...(152—2, 3). 分別自心種種諸法，著種種相.....(T). "Since one's own mind is discriminated under various forms of discrimination and since one gets attached to a variety of signs of existence"....

Cittasvabhāva, 68, 心自性, the self-nature of mind, mind as it is, mind in itself.

Cittena cīyate karma, 176n, 249, 採集業爲心 (T, S) (觀察法爲智, T; 不採集爲智, S); 識能集諸業.... (智能了分別 W). The whole line runs: ....jñānena ca vidhīyate (158—3). "Karma is accumulated by mind, and arranged in order by Jñāna, [analytical knowledge in contradistinction to Prajñā, which is transcendental, intuitive knowledge]." Sung evidently had a different text as it reads 不採集 instead of 觀察 or 分別; 不採集 is perhaps for *vicīyate* as in the "Sagāthakam," verse 285, where this line is repeated.

Cittodadhi, 188, 心海, mind-ocean. Vishayapavanacittodadhitaraṅgā acyucchinna.... (44—11), 心海亦爾, 境界風吹, 起諸識浪, 相續不絕(T); "the waves of the mind-ocean are uninterruptedly [stirred by] the wind of objectivity."

Citra, manifold; Vaicitrya, citratā, manifoldness; 133, 161, 242, 種種.

Cintāmaṇi, 98, 如意寶珠, 摩尼寶珠, wish-gem. Viśvarūpacintāmaṇisadṛisā (72—15), 如摩尼隨心現色 (T), "it is like mani-gem which takes all colours as wished."

Cīyate, 190, 積集, accumulated, from √*ci* meaning "to accumulate."

Cyuti, 211 f, 348, 死, death. There are two kinds of death, one of the physical body and the other of the superphysical, which is a sort of *sūkshmaśarīra* 微細身, assumed by a Bodhisattva. See also *Acintyapariṇāmacyuti.*

Chindati, 250, 了 or 分別, to discriminate or distinguish, from √*chid*, "to split," "to separate." This word appears in the following connection: Cittena dhāryate kāyo mano mayati vai sadā, vijñānaṁ cittavishayaṁ vijñānaiḥ saha chindati (323—4, 5). 心住持於身, 意常覺諸法, 識自心境界, 共於識分別 (W); 心能持於身, 意恒審思慮, 意識諸識俱, 了自心境界 (T). "Mind (*citta*) sustains the body, Manas always reflects, the [Mano-]vijñāna together with the [sense-]vijñānas discriminates a world of particulars created by Citta."

Janmahetu, 267, 生因, birth-cause. Animittadarśanam eva śreyo, na nimittadarśanam, nimittaṁ punar janmahetutvād aśreyaḥ (200—3, 3). 無相見勝, 非相見, 相者受生因, 故不勝 (S); 無相見勝, 非是相見, 相是生動(T); 見寂靜者名爲勝相, 非見諸相名爲勝相, 以不能斷生因相故(W); 生因 means that when the reality of a phenomenal world is asserted and adhered to as such, one is led to accept the doctrine of birth, i.e. of causation even beyond the realm of relativity.

Jalacandra, 110, 水中月 water-moon. Sa (tathāgatabhūmiṁ) pratilabhya sattvaparipācanatayā vicitrair nirmāṇakiraṇair virājate jalacandravat (227—3,4). 得如來地已，種種變化，圓照示現，成熟衆生，如水中月 (S)；入如來地已，爲教化衆生，現種種光明，應莊嚴身，如水中月 (W)；成如來地已，爲衆生故，如水中月，普現其身 (T). "Attaining Tathagatahood, he manifests himself, in order to bring beings into maturity, in various transformations shinning like the moon in water."

Jalpo hi traidhātukaduḥkhayaniḥ, 269, 言說三界(苦)因(T)；言語三(界)苦本(S). To complete the line: . . .tattvaṁ hi duḥkhasya vināśahetuḥ (186—9). 眞實滅苦因 (T). "The truth is the destructive cause of pain."

Jāti, 186, is generally rendered as 生, but here means the genuine state of a thing as it is in itself, 眞.

Jāmbūnada, 93, 贍部捺陀金, gold from the Jambū river.

Jina, 354, 勝者, victor, an epithet of the Buddha; Jinadhātu, 261, 佛舍利, Buddha's relics, hard substance left after the cremation of the body, same as *śarīra* which see; Jinaputra, 38n, 勝者子，佛子, sons of the Victorious One, meaning Bodhisattvas.

Jīva, 130, 壽, life, or vitality regarded as a principle.

Jñāna, 84, 139, 160, 272, 智. Jñāna is a very flexible term, as it means sometimes ordinary worldly knowledge, knowledge of relativity, which does not penetrate into the truth of existence, and also sometimes transcendental knowledge in which case being synonymous with Prajñā or Āryajñāna. See the *Laṅkāvatāra*, pp. 157-8, where the distinction between Jñāna as transcendental knowledge and Vijñāna as relative knowledge is fully distinguished. Asaṅgalakshaṇaṁ jñānaṁ vishayavaicitryasaṅgalakshaṇaṁ ca vijñānam (157—14, 15), 272, 著境界相是識，不著境界是智 (T)；智者無障礙相，識者識彼諸境界相 (W)；無礙

相是智，境界種種礙相是識 (S). "Jñāna is non-attachment, Vijñāna is attached to an external world of particulars." Jñānakāya, 338, 智身, knowledge-body, =Dharmakāya, =Tathāgatakāya.

Jñānaṁ lokottaram, 139, 出世間智, super-worldly knowledge; Jñānaṁ lokottaratam, 139, 出世間上上智, supreme supra-worldly knowledge; Jñānaṁ laukikam, 139, 世間智, worldly knowledge; Jñānaṁ śubham...., śānte kshāntiviśeshe vai jñānaṁ tāthāgataṁ śubham, saṁjāyate viśeshārthaṁ samudācāravarjitam (158—9, 10), 277. 寂滅殊勝忍，如來清淨智，生於善勝義，遠離諸所行 (S, W, T). "The immaculate Tathāgata-knowledge is obtained in the Kshānti [acknowledgment or assertion], tranquil and most excellent, and it gives birth to the most excellent meaning which transcends all doings"; Jñānam anāsrava, 225, 258, 無漏智, pure knowledge, which is free from the taint of egotism.

Jñeyāvaraṇa, 117, 212, 361, 所知障, hindrance of knowledge, generally coupled with Kleśāvaraṇa, hindrance of passions, 煩惱障.

Tattvam, 106, 109, 114, 126, 131, 146, 150, 173, 195, 278, 眞實, truth. Tathā hi aksharasaṁsaktās tattvaṁ na vetti māmakam (224—1). 計著文字者，不見吾眞實 (T). "Likewise, my truth is not known to those who are tied to letters." Tattvaṁ aksharavarjitam (48—12), 眞實離文字 (T). "The truth is detached from letters." Tattvaṁ pratyātmagatikaṁ (kalpyakalpena varjitam, 48—14), 174, 眞實自證處，能所分別離 (T). Tattvaṁ duḥkhasya vināśahetuḥ, 133, 如實智滅苦, truth is the destroyer of sorrow. See also under *Jalpa*.

Tattvajñāna, 335, 眞實智, knowledge of absolute truth which is contrasted to Upāyajñāna, 方便智, knowledge of means, or of particulars.

Tathatā, 26, 38, 99, 107, 114, 118, 120, 127, 146, 155 f, 161,

173n, 212, 275, 278, 334, 341, 342 f, 346, 355, 367, 如如 (五法者所謂相・名・分別・如如・正智, T), 眞如 (名相・分別・二自性相, 正智・眞如, 是圓成性, T), 眞理; Tathatājñāna, 106, 310, 眞如智慧; °buddha, 38, 眞如智慧佛; Tathatālambanam, 367, 緣眞如禪. This is the third of the four Dhyānas described in the *Laṅkāvatāra*, p. 97. The object of the discipline is to realise the suchness of truth by keeping thoughts above the dualism of being and non-being and also above the twofold notion of egolessness. It is the Dhyāna "depending upon suchness." Tathatāvastu, 有事悉如如 (S); 如眞如本有 (W); 有眞如妙物 (T). See under *Vastu*. Tathatāvasthāna, 306n, 住眞如 (W), 住如如 (T), abode of suchness.

Tathā, 340, 如, thus; Tathātva, or tathatva, 278, 如如, thusness, or suchness.

Tathāgata, 339 ff, 如來. This term may be divided into either of the following formulas: tathā + gata, or tathā + āgata. In the former case, it is 如去, and in the latter 如來.

Tathāgatapūrvapraṇihitatva, 150, 如來本願 (T), Tathagata's original vow. °āt sarvasukhasamāpattiparipūryā sattvānāṁ na kalpayanti na vikalpayanti (231—13). 如來本願以三昧樂安衆生故無有惱亂 (S); . . . 無有愛憎, 無有分別 (T).

Tathāgatasvapratyātmāryajñānādhigamaṁ nirvāṇam (200—7, 8), 295, 獲如來內證聖智, 我說此是寂滅涅槃 (T). See also under *Nirvāṇa*.

Tathāgatakāya, 97 f, 141, 317, 如來身, 佛身, Buddha-body.

Tathāgatagarbha, 3, 73, 85, 103, 105, 121, 137 ff, 176, 177, 179 f, 182, 185, 193, 194, 198, 201, 如來藏, the womb where the Tathagata is conceived and nourished and matured; = the Ālayavijñāna fully purified of its habit-energy 習氣 (*vāsanā*) and evil tendencies (*daushṭhulya*); Tathāgatagarbho mahāmate kuśalākuśalahetukah (sarvajanmagatikartā, 220—9,10), 180n, 大慧, 如來藏是善不善因, 能徧興起一切趣生 (T); . . . . . 能與 (興?) 六道作生死因緣 (W).

"The Tathāgatagarbha which is the cause of goods as well as evils creates the various paths of existence"; Tathāgatagarbhahṛidayam, esha mahāmate parinishpannasvabhāvaḥ (68—1), 159. 大慧, 此是圓成自性, 如來藏心 (T).

Tathāgatācintyagativishayagocara, 359, 如來不可思議智慧(所行)境界 (T); 如來不可思議境界修行 (W); 諸如來不思議究竟境界(S). *Vishaya* is *gocara*, and *gocara vishaya*, both being properly rendered as 境界. In the present work I have generally "realm" or "subjective attitude," for *gocara*, and for *vishaya* "objectivity" or "the objective world."

Tathāgatayāna, 148, 360, 如來乘, the Tathagata-vehicle.

Tathāgatasvapratyātmāryajñānādhigama, 277, 如來所獲自證聖智. See *Pratyātmāryajñāna.*

Tanu, 353, 身, body.

Taraṅga, 193, 波浪, waves.

Tarka, 38, 102, 132, 計度, speculation, or imagination.

Tāthāgatam (dhyāna), 367, 如來禪, one of the four Dhyānas (p. 97). This is the highest kind of Dhyāna practised by the Mahayana believers of Buddhism. The yogin has realised the inner truth deeply hidden in the consciousness, yet he does not remain intoxicated with the bliss thereby attained, he goes out into the world performing wonderful deeds of salvation for the sake of his fellow-beings.

Timira, 161, 瞖, cataract of the eye. Bālā grihṇanti jāyanataṁ timiraṁ taimirā yathā (95—13). 如瞖者所見, 愚夫生執着 (T). "The ignorant grasp the created as a person with bedimmed eyes grasps his own darkness."

Tīrthakara, 34, etc., 外道, the philosophers not belonging to Buddhism. Tīrthakara is generally found in combination with Śrāvakas (hearers) and Pratyekabuddhas (solitary Buddhas), to all of whom the ideals of Bodhisattvahood are not known.

Tīrthya, same as *tīrthakara,* 102.

Tṛishṇā, 168, 362, 愛, *lit.*, thirst, will-to-live. Together with *avidyā* (ignorance, 無明) and *karma* (deeds, 業), *tṛishṇā* is the inner agent of the world-creation. Tṛishṇā hi mātā ity uktā avidyā ca pitā tathā (140—5), 364, 貪愛名爲母, 無明則是父 (T). "The will-to-live is mother and ignorance is father." Tṛishṇāyā hy uditāḥ skandhāḥ (149—11), 350, 從愛生諸蘊 (T). "The Aggregates are produced by the will-to-live."

Tair ācitāni karmāṇi (358—14), 176n, 彼所積集業 (T). "All kinds of karma are accumulated by them (i.e. the Ālaya and Manas)."

Trikāya, 142 ff, 308 ff, 355, 三身, the triple body of the Buddha.

Tribhavasvacittamātram, 243, 273, 三界唯心 (T); 三界唯是自心 (W); 三有微 (唯?) 心 (S).

Triyāna, 148, 328, 358 ff, 三乘; the triple vehicle is the Śrāvaka, the Pratyekabuddha, and the Bodhisattva.

Trisaṁtati, 73, 三相續, the triple continuation. What these three are I have not so far been able to find out. The Pali Dictionary (by Rhys Davids and Stede) gives *citta-santati* (心相續), *dhamma*° (法), *rūpa*° (色), and *san-khāra*° (行).

Traidhātuka, 245, 三界; the triple world is *Kāma*° (欲界), *Rūpa*° (色界), and *Arūpa*° (無色界).

Darpaṇa, 84, 鏡, mirror.

Daśanishṭhāpāda, 231n, 十無盡句 (S, W), or 十無盡願 (T); sometimes simply, (*daśa-*)*nishṭhāpāda*, 十盡句. The reference is to the Ten Inexhaustible Vows (*daśanishṭha-praṇidhāna*) to be made by the Bodhisattva at the stage of Joy (*pramuditā*), which is the first of the ten stages (*daśa-bhūmi*) of Bodhisattvahood. The Vows are called "inexhaustible" because their objectives are of such nature. The ten objects towards which the Bodhisattva's vows are directed are: 1. *Sattvadhātu* (無生界, world of beings); 2. *Lokadhātu* (世界, this world); 3. *Ākāśadhātu*

(虛空界, space); 4. *Dharmadhātu* (法界, the world where the Dharma prevails); 5. *Nirvāṇadhātu* (涅槃界, Nirvana-world); 6. *Buddhotpādadhātu* (佛出現界, the world where the Buddha is born); 7. *Tathāgatajñānadhātu* (如來智界, the world of Tathagata-knowledge); 8. *Cittālaṁbanadhātu* (心所緣界, the world as the object of thought); 9. *Buddhavishayajñānadhātu* (佛智所入境界界, the world as the object of Buddha-knowledge); and 10. *Lokavartanī-dharmavartanī-jñānavartanī-dhātu* (世間轉法轉智轉界 the world where this worldly life, the Dharma, and the Buddha-knowledge are evolved). All these ten worlds will never come to an end, and as long as they continue to exist, the Bodhisattva will ever put forward his great vows with energy and determination. See Rahder, *Daśabhūmika,* p. 17, and Śikshānanda's *Avataṁsaka,* Vol. XXXIV.

Dāna, 366 f, 布施, one of the six virtues of perfection (六波羅蜜).

Dīpapradīpa, 85, 燈火, lamplight.

Dūraṁgamā, 223, 遠行地, the far-going, the seventh stage.

Dṛiśya, 251, 所現, what is presented to one's view.

Dṛishṭa, 165, 所見, seen; dṛishṭi, 307, 見, generally 妄見 a wrong view held by the Tīrthakara.

Dṛishṭānta, 40, 喻, illustration, example, a logical term. The hill is fiery (宗, *pratijñā,* proposition). Because it has smoke (因, *hetu,* reason). All that has smoke is fiery like a kitchen, and whatever is not fiery has no smoke like a lake (喻, *dṛishṭānta,* example).

Dṛishṭivikalpa, 111 f, 見分利, views based on the dualistic discrimination of existence such as held by the philosophers; one of the twelve Parikalpita notions (127 f).

Devayāna, 360, 天乘, Devayānaṁ brahmayānaṁ śrāvakīyaṁ tathaiva ca, tāthāgataṁ ca pratyekaṁ yānān etān vadāmy aham (134, 135). 天乘及梵乘, 聲聞緣覺乘, 諸佛如來乘, 諸乘吾所說 (T).

Deśanā(-nayalakshaṇa), 109, 349, 350, 言說法相, word-teaching contrasted with self-realisation (*siddhānta,* 宗趣, or *pratyātmadharma,* 自證法), Siddhāntaś ca nayaś cāpi pratyātmaśāsanaṁ ca vai, ye paśyanti vibhāgajñā na te tarkavaśaṁ gatāḥ (149—2, 3). 宗趣與言說，自證及敎法. 若能善知見，不隨他妄解(T). "Those who well understand the distinction between realisation and teaching, between inner knowledge and instruction, are kept away from the control of mere speculation."

Deśanāpāṭha, 77, 80, 149, 語言文字. Avalokya deśanāpāṭhābhiratānāṁ sattvānāṁ cittavibhramo bhavishyatīti (14—2). 觀察一切衆生心皆樂於名字說法，心迷生疑(W). Deśanāpāṭhakathām, 76, 名字章句 (W), teaching, recitation, and story. This stands here (12—16, 17) against Tathāgatapratyātmagatigocarakathām (說於內身修行境界，W) as elsewhere, showing that the whole purport of the *Laṅkāvatāra* is to emphasise the inner attainment of the truth realised by all the Tathagatas of the past, present, and future.

Deśanārutapāṭhābhiveśatam, na, 110, 莫執着文字, do not cling to words! Tathāgatagarbha ālayavijñānavishayas... bodhisattvānāṁ mahāsattvānām arthapratisaraṇānāṁ no tu yathārutadeśanāpāṭhābhinivishṭānām (223—6-9). 如來藏藏識(是佛)境界，菩薩摩訶薩，隨順義者所行之處，非是一切執着文字(外道二乘)之所行處 (T). "The realm of the Tathāgatagarbha which is the Ālayavijñāna belongs to those Bodhisattva-mahāsattvas who follow the course of truth, and not to those philosophers who cling to the letter, learning, and mere discourse."

Deha, 353, 身, the body.

Dehabhogapratishṭhāna, 97, 172, 175, 180, 242, 244, 247, 322 f, 363, 身·資·所住. This combination occurs quite frequently in the *Laṅkāvatāra* and refers to the material side of life. *Deha* is the physical body, *bhoga* is property belonging to the body and enjoyed by it, and *pratishṭhāna* is the material environment in which the body is found moving. They are however manifestations of the Ālaya. Dehabhogapratishṭhānam ālayaṁ khyāyate nṛiṇām (54—10). 自受用安立，識藏現衆生 (S)；內識衆生見，身資生住處 (W)；身資所住影(?)衆生藏識現 (T).

Daushṭhulya, 178, 200, 過惡, evil tendency, or error. Anādikālaprapañcadaushṭhulyavāsitaṁ vikalpavijñānam (94—12). 無始戲論惡習所薰 (T)；無始虛僞習氣所薰妄想計著 (S)；因無始來煩惱心薰習戲論分別 (W). "The discriminating consciousness that is found infested since beginningless time by the evil tendency or habit-energy inherent in the delusion." Na mahāmate māyā bhrāntikāraṇam adaushṭhulyadoshāvahatvāt (109—4, 5). 非諸幻事爲妄惑因，以幻不生諸過惡故 (T)；大慧非迷惑法生煩惱過 (W)；大慧非幻惑因，不起過故(S). "Mahāmati, māyā is not the cause of confusion, for it does not produce errors, [as errors come from wrong discrimination]."

Dravya, 74, 物, 陀羅驃 (S), substance. Bhūtaguṇāṇudravyasaṁsthānasaṁniveśaviśeshaṁ dṛishṭvā......(51—13). 見大種·求那·塵等諸物，形量·分位·各差別(T). "Seeing that the elements, qualities, atoms, and substances are all different as regards their form and position."

Dvaya, 195, 二, duality.

Dvayanairātmya, 175, 211, 二無我, the twofold egolessness, i.e. of *dharma* and *pudgala*.

Dvātriṁsadvaralakshaṇa, 75, 三十二相, the thirty-two marks of excellence as revealed in the body of the Buddha.

Dviyāna(?), 358 f, 二乘 (聲聞乘與緣覺乘), the two vehicles of Śrāvakahood and Pratyekabuddhahood.

Dvesha, 259, 瞋, anger, one of the three evil passions (三毒) known as poison (*visha*); the other two are *rāga* (貪, the desire to have) and *moha* (痴, stupidity).

Dharma, 173, 法, the truth, the law; for various shades of meaning attached to the term, see pp. 154 f; Dharma, aksharapatita-, 109, 法墮於文字, the truth in the bondage of letters. Rutaṁ mahāmate aksharapatitam, artho 'naksharapatitaḥ (194—1). 一切言說墮於文字, 義則不墮 (T). Dharmo naiva ca deśito bhagavatā pratyātmavedyo yataḥ, 110, 自證不可說, (引物說法性, Prabhākaramitra). Dharmādharma, 80, 120, 121, 155, 法非法, truth and untruth, any object and that which is not that object, A and not-A, a dualistic conception in any form such as *sat* and *asat*, being and non-being, Saṁsāra and Nirvāṇa, etc.

Dharmapañcakam, 39, 66, 五法, the "Five Categories," which is one of the important topics treated in the *Laṅkāvatāra*.

Dharmakāya, 36, 127, 141, 142 ff, 151, 154, 188, 212, 308 f, 352, 353, 355, 369, 法身, often translated as the Law-body, or Truth-body. 1. The truth conceived in the fashion of the physical body and standing in contrast to it, i.e. Rūpakāya (色身); 2. One of the Triple Body of the Buddha when he is identified with the Absolute; 3. = the Tathāgatakāya, Buddhakāya, Jñānakāya. Dharmakāyo hi saṁbuddho dharmadhātus tathāgataḥ, 315, 法身是正覺, 法界卽如來 (I-tsing).

Dharmakshānti, 127n, 法忍, same as 無生法忍, acceptance of the statement that all things are as they are, not being subject to the law of birth and death, which prevails only in the phenomenal world created by our wrong discrimination.

Dharmacakra, 154, 233, 法輪, the Wheel of the Law.

Dharmatā, 72, 83, 142, 185, 275, 320, 法性, 體性, the ultimate essence of things existing. Cittasya dharmatā śuddhā (298—9). 心性本淸淨(T). Dharmatānishyanda, 321, 法性所流; °buddha, 144, 法性所流佛, the Buddha conceived as flowing out of the ultimate essence of things, that is, a manifested form of the Absolute; Dharmatābuddha, 142 ff, 208 f, 316, 法性佛, the Buddha as Essence itself, i.e. the Dharmakāya in its absolute aspect.

Dharmadvaya, 80, 二法, duality.

Dharmadhātu, 152, 242, 275, 354, 法界. It may be rendered properly as "realm of ideas," as the term expresses the most comprehensive view of the universe, including not only this visible sense-world but all possibly conceivable ideal worlds.

Dharmaniyāmatā, 212, 275, 法位, orderliness or fixedness of things each in its own position, or *gesetzmässigkeit*.

Dharmanairātmya, 78, 138, 154, 194, 263, 360, 法無我. The idea that there is no self-substance or Ātman (ego) constituting the individuality of each object is insisted on by the followers of Mahayana Buddhism to be their exclusive property not shared by the Hinayana; but how far this is historically true may be contested. As the idea of Dharmanairātmya is closely connected with that of Śūnyatā and as the latter is one of the most distinguishing marks of the Mahayana it was natural for its scholars to give to the former a prominent position in their philosophy. Dharmanairātmyajñāna, 167f, 167n, 法無我智, the power of cognisance whereby the truth of Dharmanairātmya is accepted. Cittamanomanovijñānapañcadharmasvabhāvarahitān mahāmate sarvadharmān vibhāvayan bodhisattvo mahāsattvo dharmanairātmyakuśalo bhavati (69—11, 13). 觀察一切諸法，離心・意・意識・五法・自性，是名菩薩摩訶法無我智 (T). "When a Bodhisattva-mahāsattva recognises that all dharmas are free from Citta, Manas, and Manovijñāna, the Five Dharmas, and the Threefold Svabhāva, he is said to understand well the signification of Dharmanairātmya."

Dharmaparyāya, 154, 法門, doctrine, or system of teaching. Another name of the *Laṅkāvatāra* is "Cittamanomanovijñānapañcadharmasvabhāvalakshaṇadharmaparyāya"(43—14, 15), 心意意識五法自性相衆妙法門(T); and still another is "Āryajñānavastupravicayam" (50—14, 15) 聖智事自性法門. When the first one is shortened, it runs thus:

"Pañcadharmasvalakshaṇapravicayam" (68—6), 觀察五法自性相法門. Sung has 經 instead of 法門 for *dharmaparyāya*.

Dharmapūjā, 230, 232, 法供養, moral offerings

Dharmabuddha, 23, 法佛, evidently same as Dharmatābuddha.

Dharmameghā, 78, 204, 法雲地, literally, dharma-cloud, the last of the ten Bodhisattva stages.

Dharmavaram, 68, 最勝法, the highest truth.

Dharmavaśavartin, 於法自在者, one who has control over all things, or one who is perfectly acquainted with all truths. It depends upon how we understand *dharma* in this connection. Sarvadharmānābhogavaśavartitā dharma ityucyate (181—1); 於一切法悉得自在, 是名法利 (T); 於一切法無開發 (無功用, T) 自在, 是名爲法 (S). *Sarvadharma*, 諸法, or 一切法, means "all things," "existence generally," or "the world"; and the whole passage is to be understood thus: "to have full control over things worldly without any reference to egotistic purpose." To be master of oneself as well as the whole world—this is indeed the Dharma. Bhagavantaṁ sarvayogavaśavartinam (11—16), 世尊於觀自在 (T), "[I wish to see] the Blessed One who is perfect master of all disciplinary practices."

Dharmaviraja, 69, 清淨法, truth immaculate.

Dharmaś cāśarīraḥ, 151, 法身無有身 (T), the Dharma(-body) is without the body.

Dharmasamatā, 351, 法平等, the sameness of the truth taught by the Tathagatas; one of the fourfold sameness.

Dharmasthititā, 212, 275, 法住, continuity of existence.

Dharmasvabhāvānabodhamanomayakāya, 210, 覺法自性意成身, the will-body assumed when the self-nature of things is understood as having no self-nature.

Dharmāhāra, 369, 法食, food of truth. Dharmāhāra hi mahāmate mama śrāvakāḥ pratyekabuddhā bodhisattvāśca nāmishāhārāḥ prāg eva tathāgatāḥ(255—13, 14). 我諸聲聞緣覺菩薩唯法食（不食肉），豈況如來 (T). "Mahāmati, my Śrāvakas, Pratyekabuddhas, and Bodhisattvas feed themselves on truth, not on meat; how much more the Tathagatas!"

Dharmātmyalakshaṇa, 111, 法無我相, the belief that there is something substantial behind what is presented to one's view.

Dharmānāṁ dharmatā, 137, 諸法性, that which constitutes the reason of things.

Dhyāna, 38, 禪那, or shortly 禪, a concentrated state of mind. The classification of Dhyāna into four heads, 367 f, is characteristically Mahayanistic, and the *Laṅkāvatāra's* intimate relation to the teaching of Zen Buddhism may be gleaned from it. Na shaḍdhyānādidhyāyinā (10—11), 73, 不應住六定等中 (T). The author has not been able to ascertain what these are.

Naṭa, 195, 工技兒, dancer.

Nāyaka, 354, 導者, leader.

Nāgakanyā, 66 ff, 龍女, Nāga-maidens.

Nāma, 26, 155 f, 名, name, one of the Five Dharmas; Nāmamātra, 281, 唯名, name-only. Vijñaptir nāmamātreyaṁ lakshaṇena na vidyate (96—4), 唯假施設名，求相不可得 (T).

Nāstyasti, 291, 有無, being and non-being.

Niḥsvabhāva, 96, 166, 168, 287, 無自性, without self-nature. °lakshaṇa, 134n, 無自性相, signs indicating the absence of self-nature.

Nikāyasahajāsaṁskārakriyāmanomayakāya, 210, 種類俱生無作行意成身, the will-body acquired by penetrating into the inner realisation of the Buddha.

Nitya, 119, 146, 354, 常, eternal; °tā, 120, eternity; Nityam acintyam, 302, 常不思議, eternity unthinkable. Nityam acintyaṁ pratyātmāryagatigocaraṁ paramārthagocaraṁ ca (59—11, 12). 常不思議 自聖證智第一義境 (T). Nityānitya, 116, 常無常, eternal and not-eternal. Nityācintaiveyaṁ tathāgatānāṁ pratyātmāryajñānādhigamatathatā (60—11, 12), 此常不思議, 是諸如來自證聖智所行眞理 (T).

Nimitta, 26, 127, 155 ff, 相, appearance, one of the "Five Dharmas."

Nimittalakshaṇābhedatvāt, (106—16), 119, 相相不壞故 (S), 相不異故, (T), 以想差別故 (W).

Nirābhāsa, 40, 98, 138, 140, 141, 148, 160, 208, 247, 340, 360, 無影像 generally, or 無相, imageless, shadowless. Cittaṁ hi bhūmayaḥ sapta nirābhāsā tvihāshṭamī (215—11), 七地是有心, 八地無影像 (T); 七地爲心地, 無所有八地 (W); 心量地第七,無所有第八(S). "Up to the seventh stage there is still a trace of mindfulness, but at the eighth the state of imagelessness [i.e. no conscious strivings] obtains." Prajñayā ca nirābhāsaṁ prabhāvaṁ cādhigacchati (158—4). 慧能得無相, 及妙莊嚴境 (W); 慧能證無相及自在威光 (T); (觀察一切法), 通達無所有, 及得自在力, 是則名慧 (S). "It is by means of Prajñā that the Imageless and the supernatural glory are realised." Nirābhāsagocara, 97, 278, 無照現境, realm of no-shadows. Tathatāvyavasthitaś ca bodhisattvo mahāsattvo nirābhāsagocarapratilābhitvāt pramuditāṁ bodhisattvabhūmiṁ pratilabhate (226—12 f). 菩薩摩訶薩住如如者, 得無所有境界故, 得菩薩歡喜地 (S); 菩薩住眞如法者, 得入無相寂靜境界入已, 得入菩薩摩訶薩初歡喜地 (W); 菩薩摩訶薩住如如已, 得無照現境, 昇歡喜地 (T). "The Bodhisattva-mahāsattva who abides in the suchness of things, enters into the realm of no-shadows, and thereby reaches the stage of Bodhisattvahood known as Joy"; Nirābhāsabuddhi, 273, 無相智 (T), 無所有智 (S), 眞實智 (W), shadowless knowledge.

Nirālamba, 144, 非所攀緣, unsupported; Dharmatābuddhaḥ nirālambaḥ (57—13), 法性佛非所攀緣 (T).

Nirukti, 134, 辭句, terminological explanation.

Nirodha, 39, 127, 148, 183, 290, 303, 滅, cessation; Nirodha-samāpatti, 245, 滅盡定, mental tranquillity; Nirodha-sukha, 356, 寂滅樂, the bliss of cessation. Bodhisattvena ....nirodhasukhaṁ samāpattisukhaṁ ca sattvakriyāpekshayā pūrvasvapraṇidhānābhinirhṛitatayā ca na sākshāt-karaṇīyam (58—13-15). 菩薩不取寂滅空門樂，不取三摩跋提樂，此憐愍衆生故，起本願力行故 (W)；菩薩非滅門樂，正受樂，顧愍衆生及本願，不作證 (S)；以憐愍衆生故，本願所持故，不證寂滅門及三昧樂 (T). "Because of his compassion with which he regards all beings and because of his desire to fulfil his original vows, the Bodhisattva does not personally realise the bliss of cessation and that of tranquillity."

Nirgatam, 110, 不出, not out of (water). See *Apravishṭam*.

Nirmāṇa, or Nirmāṇika, 142, 311, 應化; Nirmānakāya, 212, 308 ff, 347, 化身, the transformation-body; Nirmāṇa-buddha, 23, 38, 142 ff, 208 f, 316, 化佛, the transformation-buddha; Nirmitādhishṭhāna, 363 f, 變化加持, being sustained by the power of the transformed one; Nirmita-nirmāṇa, 80, 應化化佛; Nirmitabuddha, 328, 化佛.

Nirvāṇa, 35 f, 41, 97, 100, 108, 127 ff, 168, 192, 193, 202, 218 ff, 293, 303, 312, 314 ff, 354 涅槃，滅度; Nirvāṇam āryajñānapratyātmagatigocaram (99—1), 涅槃者自證聖智所行境界. This is one definition of Nirvana in the *Laṅkāvatāra* which is significant in many ways. Nirvāṇaṁ manavarjitam (149—8), 350, 涅槃離心意. Na buddhaḥ parinirvāti na dharmaḥ parihīyate, sattvānāṁ paripākāya parinirvāṇaṁ nidarśayet. Acintyo bhagavān buddho nityakāyas tathāgataḥ, deśeti vividhān vyūhān sattvānāṁ hitakāraṇāt. P. 315. 佛不般涅槃，正法亦不滅，爲利衆生故，示現有滅盡，世尊不思議，妙體無異相，爲利衆生故，現種種莊嚴 (I-tsing). Nirvāṇam iti yathābhūtārthasthāna-darśanam (200—6), 296, 涅槃者見如實處 (T), "By Nirvana is meant to see into the abode of reality as it is";

Nirvāṇadhātu, 264, 涅槃界, the abode of Nirvana, one of the three Asaṁskṛitas (三無爲法).

Nirvikalpa, 106, 138, 無分別, non-discrimination. Nirvikalpanirābhāsagocaraṁ tathāgatagocaram (78—10), 無分別, 無影像處, 是如來藏門 (T). Nirvikalpācāra, 75, 無分別行, deeds of non-discrimination. Nirvikalpajñāna, 201, 無分別智, non-discriminative knowledge. Nirvikalpalokottarajñānam, 185, 無分別出世間智, non-discriminative transcendental knowledge.

Nirvṛitti, 185, 滅, disappearance.

Nishyanda, 322 f, 所流, 等流, flowing-out or -down; Nishyandabuddha, 23, 142 ff, 208 f, 所流佛, 等流佛.

Nemina, 354, 阿利吒尼彌 (W).

Nairātmyam, 39, 139, 無我, egoless; Nairātmyadvaya, 29 f, 35, 37, 66, 154, 166 ff, 二無我, the twofold egolessness, *pudgalanairātmya* (人無我) and *dharmanairātmya* (法無我).

Nairmāṇika, 142, 化, transformed; Nairmāṇikabuddha, 23, 化佛, Buddhas of transformation.

Padmavimāna, 332, 蓮華(微妙)宮殿 (T), the lotus-palace.

Pañcadharma, 26, 29 f, 141, 154 ff, 161, 162, 175, 194, 211, 316, 五法, the "five categories."

Pañcanirmitabuddha, 328, 五化佛, the five transformation-Buddhas, not yet identified.

Pañcaphala, 330, 五果, the five fruits (or effects); see *Phala*.

Pañcavijñānakāya, 189, 五識身, the system of the Vijñānas.

Paratantra, 158 ff, 161, 163 ff, 322, 依他起性, 緣起相, the knowledge of relativity.

Paramārtha, or paramārthasatya, 148, 160, 163 ff, 244, 273, 277, 288, 311, 第一義諦, sometimes distinguished from Saṁvṛitisatya, relative knowledge or worldly truth.

Parahita, 214, 利他, benefitting others. Bodhisattvāḥ.... parahitahetor anekarūpaveśadhāriṇo bhavanti (72—12-14). 菩薩爲衆生故, 作種種身 (T); 爲安(穩)衆生故, 作

ledge, one of the Three Svabhavas (三自性), corresponding to Right Knowledge (*samyagjñāna,* 正智), of the Five Dharmas.

Pariśuddhi, 253, 清浄, pure.

Pāṇi, 353, 手, hand.

Pāramitā, 39, 41, 126, 141, 143, 199, 365 ff, 波羅蜜 (*palomi*), perfection, or reaching the other shore. There are six (sometimes ten) Virtues of Perfection, which are regularly practised by the Bodhisattva. See also *Prajñā.*

Piśāca, 117, 毘舍闍, a goblin.

Puṇyāpuṇya, 130, 福非福, merit-demerit. Anye puṇyāpuṇyaparikshayāt (183—17). 或計福非福盡 (是涅槃, T). "Others [think Nirvana consists] in the extinction of both merit and demerit."

Pudgala, 130, 139, 256, 人, the individual soul; Pudgaladharmanairātmya, 140, 人法無我, the egolessness of both the individual soul and external objects; Pudgalanairātmyajñāna, 167, 人無我智, the knowledge that there is no ego-soul.

Puraṁdara, 353, 不蘭陀羅 (W), city-destroyer, epithet of Indra.

Purusha, 130, 人, 士夫, supreme spirit.

Purushakāra, 323, 士用果, one of the five "fruits" (*phala,* 果), literally, man-working. It is the effect produced by a human agent at work.

Pūñjān, 367, something heaped up(?)

Pūrvadharmasthititā, or Paurāṇasthitidharmatā, 212, 213, 274, 277, 352, 本住法, originally-abiding truth or reality.

Pūrvapraṇidhāna, 332, 本願, an original vow made by a Bodhisattva when he begins his career as a Mahayana follower of the Buddha.

Pṛithagjana, 143, 異生, generally coupled with *bāla,* 愚夫, meaning a man not yet illumined, i.e. ignorant.

Pṛithivī, 353, 大地, earth.

Posha, 130, 壽者, 養者, growth, nourishing or growing one;

found in combination (183—13, 1) with Ātma (我), Satta (衆生), Jīva (命), Posha (壽者), Purusha (士夫), Pudgala (人).

Prakṛiti, 130, 自性, nature, or original nature, contrasted to Purusha, supreme spirit; Prakṛitiprabhāsvaram, 255 f, 258 f, 268, 自性清淨, pure in its original essence. —— cittam upakleśair manādibhiḥ, ātmanā saha saṁyuktam (358—11). 本性清淨心, 隨煩惱意等, 及與我相應 (T). "The Citta, pure in its original essence, gives itself up to the influence of the secondary evil passions, Manas, etc., and the ego."

Pracārita(-śūnyatā), 288, 行空, emptiness of action, one of the seven Śūnyatās.

Prajñapti, 181, 假設, =vijñapti, representation, ideation, mental construction; Prajñaptināmamātreyam, 181, 唯假設名. This is the form in the "Sagāthakam" 23, but on p. 96, *vijñapti*. Evidently, *prajñapti* and *vijñapti* are convertible terms as far as the *Laṅkāvatāra* is concerned. Prajñaptimātra, 181, 281 f, 唯假設; Prajñaptimātraṁ katham (26—17), 181, 281n, 云何唯假設; Prajñaptimātraṁ tribhavaṁ (nāsti vastusvabhāvataḥ, 168—7), 181, 281n, 三有唯假名, 無有實法體 (T); Prajñaptisatya, 242, 假名 (T), 世諦 (S, W), worldly way of thinking. Prajñaptisatyato hy ātmā dravyasan na hi vidyate (153—10), 假名世諦我, (施設世諦我), 彼則無實事 (S, W); 施設假名我, 而實不可得 (T). "In accordance with the worldly way of thinking, there is an ego-substance, which, however, has really no existence."

Prajñā, 34, 35 f, 43, 52, 83, 101, 108, 127, 138, 160, 177, 200, 229, 272, 279, 283 ff, 306n, 366, 般若, 智慧, transcendental knowledge; Prajñācakshus, 115, 305, 慧眼, wisdom-eye; Prajñāpāramitā, 206, 般若波羅蜜多, one of the Pāramitās. The six or ten Virtues of Perfection (*pāramitā*) are enumerated; when they are ten, the following four are added to the six: 7. *Upāya,* 方便, means, 8. *Praṇidhāna,* 願,

vows, 9. *Bala,* 力, power, and 10. *Jñāna,* 智, knowledge. The last two are more or less repetitions of *Vīrya* and *Prajñā*. According to the Yogācāra philosophers all the four are regarded as the amplification of the sixth Pāramita, *Prajñā*. Prajñopāya, 227, 智慧方便, knowledge and means.

Pratītyasamutpāda, 121, 緣起, the theory of causation.

Pratibimba, 84, 97, 164, 影像, image.

Prativikalpa, 81, 分別, discrimination. *Kalpa* (20—3), *vikalpa, saṁkalpa* (總分別, 350—7), *parikalpa* (徧分別, 350—7), *pratikalpa*—they are more or less synonymous. See also under *Parikalpa*.

Pratiśrut, 85, 響, echo.

Pratishṭhāpikabuddhi, 165, 建立智, the intelligence whereby a proposition is set up.

Pratisaṁkhyanirodha, 264n, 擇滅, the annihilation of evil desires by means of the intellect and will, which is Nirvana attained by the Buddhists. One of the three Asaṁskṛitas (三無爲法).

Pratyaksha, 201, 273, 286, 現證, 現量, immediate perception. A good definition of *pratyaksha* is given in the *Mahāvyutpatti,* CCII, 1. Satsaṁprayoge purushasyendriyānāṁ buddhijanma pratyaksham. 遇有則人之諸根生覺, 謂之現前. "When an object appears before a sense-organ the latter perceives it and recognises it as something external." This is immediate knowledge forming the basis of all other forms of knowledge. =pratyātmāryajñāna.

Pratyaya, 139, 354, 緣, causation.

Pratyayābhivyakti, 307, 緣明了轉變, one of the nine Pariṇāmas, but what it means is not explained.

Pratyātmāryajñāna, 67, 68, 74, 85, 98, 100 f, 103, 109, 114, 127, 132, 140, 150, 153, 184, 193, 253, 273, 277, 307, 339, 自證(覺)聖智. *Pratyātma* (自證), *āryajñāna* (聖智), *gatigama* (所行), *adhigama* (所證), *gocara* (境界), *dharma* with its synonyms, and some other terms appear in the

Laṅkāvatāra in almost every possible combination. This is natural seeing that the object of the sutra is to elucidate the doctrine of Pratyātmajñāna. The following gives all the chief combinations to be found in it grouped under three heads: 1. Those containing *āryajñāna* as principal ideas; though they also frequently include such words as *gocara, lakshaṇa, gati, gatigama,* or *adhigama,* yet the main stress of the combination may be regarded as placed on *jñāna*; 2. Those phrases purporting to emphasise the experience-aspect of the realisation, i.e., those made up with such terms as *gocara, gotra, gati, gatigama,* or *adhigama,* and without any special reference to its intellectual significance; and 3. Those combinations more expressive of the metaphysical sense which is conveyed in terms such as *dharma, dharmatā, vastu, tathatā, tattvam,* or *bhūtakoṭi.*

1. *Pratyātmajñāna* (with or without *sva*), 2—7, 98—2, 228—4, 231—10; (with *gocara*), 13—13, 21—4, 35—7, 50—10, 231—1; (with *gatigocara*), 99—1, 67—17, 68—6, 62—12; (with *gatilakshaṇa*), 49—17, 50—6, 133—2, 13; (with *gatigama*), 89—3, 87—12; (with *adhigama*), 61—12, 75—8, 80—2, 93—1, 12, 194—18; (with *tathāgata-bhūmi* and *gata*), 93—4; (with *vastumukha*), 94—14, which is variously translated in the Chinese showing discrepancies in the original texts: 聖智自證法性門 (T), 聖人內身證智門 (W), 自住事門 (S). In one case *buddhi* is used for *jñāna,* 133—10; sometimes *āryajñāna* is not prefixed by *pratyātma,* for instance, 125—12, 77—10, 75—9, 165—10; sometimes we have *vedyā* substituted for *jñāna*, 88—13, 215—13; sometimes *vedyagati*, 3—12, 16.

2. *Pratyātmagati* (with or without *sva,* and sometimes with *tathāgata, ārya,* or *lakshaṇa*), 5—14, 6—2,8—12, 11—6, 18—12, 58—10, 11, 16, 17, 62—1, 123—8, 127—17, 155—12, 224—18, 238—6, 7; (with *gatigocara*), 4—16,

5—5, 7—8, 7—11, 11—16, 13—13, 23—16, 39—16, 49—5, 55—1, 57—9, 59—11, 155—2, 172—12, 242—15; (with *gatigama*), 43—8, 222—3; (with *adhigama*), 58—3, 4, 12, 60—4, 61—8, 148—11; (with *abhisamayagotra*), 64—12; (with *tathāgatabhūmi*), 224—10, 214—4, 10—15.

3. *Pratyātmadharma* (or *dharmatā*), 6—11, 8—1, 143—5, 144—12, 185—3, 226—18; (qualified with *vedyagati*), 3—12, 3—16, (with *nayalakshaṇa*), 15—3; (with *tattvam*), 48—14; (with *vastu*), 95—4; (with *tathatā*), 132—3; (with *bhūtakoṭi*), 88—13.

In the "Sagāthakam" we have the following combinations: *Pratyātma-vedyayāna,* 163, °*dharmatā,* 350, °*vedya,* 421, °*tathatā,* 545, °*gatigama,* 746, °*dṛishṭigatika,* 781, °*dṛishṭadharma,* 881.

Pratyekabuddha, 獨覺，緣覺, a solitary Buddha who has no desire to announce his truth to the world; Pratyekabuddhayāna, 360, 緣覺乘.

Pradhāna, 264, 勝者, Pradhānam īśvaraḥ kartā cittamātram vikalpyate (79—12), 勝自在作者，此但心分別 (T).

Praṇidhāna, 203, 205, 209 f, 340, 355 f, 357, 願, vow, prayer, earnest wish.

Prapañca, 137, 200, 201n, 戲論, vain talk, diffusive trivial reasoning; °darśana, 345, 虛妄見; °daushṭhulya, 190, 戲論過惡; Anādikālaprapañcadaushṭhulyavikalpavāsanāhetukam (43—7), 無始虛僞過惡妄想習氣因 (S). "Owing to the habit-energy accumulated since beginningless time by trivial erroneous discrimination."

Prabandha, 183, 相續, continuation.

Prabhāva, 203, 356, 威力，威神力, sovereign power, =anubhāva and adhishṭhāna.

Prabhedapracāra (ṁ vyavasthānayati, 57—12), 143, 分別觀察建立 (S), 建立差別行 (W).

Prabhedanayalakshaṇa (127—14), 110, (妄計自性) 差別相, the aspect of individuation arising from false imagination.

Pramāṇa, 134, 137, 量, logical survey. Naikatvānyatvobhayatvānubhayatvasaṁbaddhaṁ tat sarvapramāṇavinivṛitam (189—16). 非一非異,非俱非不俱,以是義故,超一切量(T). "That which is not bound by [such opposites as] oneness and otherness, bothness and not-bothness, is beyond all logical survey."

Pramuditā, 222, 歡喜地, the stage of Joy, the first of the ten Bodhisatvabhūmi.

Pravicayabuddhi, 165, 觀察智, the intellect that sees into the self-nature of existence which is beyond the fourfold proposition (*catushkoṭika,* 四句).

Pravṛitti, 182, 185, 生起, 轉, rising, appearance; °vijñāna, 186 ff, 198, 210, 336, 轉識, the Vijñāna in its dynamic aspect, i.e. as evolving in conjunction with the sense-organs.

Praśama, 85, 寂滅, tranquillity.

Prāyogikacaryā, 224, 加行, 有功用行, effortful life, opposed to *anābhoga,* 無功用.

Preta, 118, 餓鬼, hungry ghost.

Phala, 323 f, 果. There are five "fruits" or effects (*pañcaphalāni*): 1. *Vipākaphala,* 異熟果: when an evil deed is committed, the doer suffers pain; when a good is done, he enjoys pleasure. Pleasure and pain in themselves are unmoral and neutral as far as their karmaic character is concerned. Hence the name "differently ripening." 2. *Nishyanda*° 等流果: when an evil (or a good) deed is done, this tends to make the doer more easily disposed towards evils (or goods). As cause and effect are of the same nature, this *phala* is called "flowing in the same course." 3. *Purusha*° 士用果: vegetables or cereals grow abundantly from the earth owing to the will, intelligence, and labour of the farmer; as the harvest is the fruit brought about by a human agency, the name *purusha* is given to this form of effect. 4. *Adhipati*°, 增上果: that anything at all exists is due to the cooperation positive or negative of all other things; for if the latter interfere in any way, the former will cease to exist. When thus the co-existence of things is regarded as the result of universal mutuality, it is called "the helping." 5. *Visaṁyoga°* 離繫果: Nirvana is the fruit of spiritual discipline, and as it enables one to be released from the bondage of birth-and-death, it is called "freeing from bondage."

Bandhanaṁ cittasaṁbhavam, 179, (彼相即是過) 皆從心縛生(T), the bondage is mind-made, that is, this world of faulty appearances is the construction of the mind.

Bandhābandhavikalpa, 111 f, 縛解分別, discrimination as to bondage and release, one of the twelve Vikalpas.

Bala, 39, 66, 97, 142, 150, 209, 力. The ten powers of the Bodhisattva according to the *Avataṁsaka* (Sikshānanda, LVI) are: 1. *Āśayabala,* 深心力, having a mind strongly turned away from worldliness; 2. *Adhyāśaya°*, 增生深心力, having a belief growing ever stronger in Buddhism; 3. *Prayoga°*, 加行 or 方便力, the power of discipling himself in all the exercises of Bodhisattvahood; 4. *Prajñā°*, 智力, the intuitive power to understand the mentalities of all beings; 5. *Praṇidhāna°*, 願力, the power of making every prayer fulfilled; 6. *Caryā°*, 行力, the power of working till the end of time; 7. *Yāna°*, 乘力, the power of creating all kinds of conveyance (*yāna*) without ever giving up the Mahāyāna; 8. *Vikurvaṇa°*, 神變力, the power of making a world of immaculate purity in every pore of the skin; 9. *Bodhi°*, 菩提力, the power of awakening every being in enlightenment; 10. *Dharmacakra-pravartana°* 轉法輪力, the power of uttering one phrase which appeals uniformly to the hearts of all beings.

Bala-abhijñā-vaśita, 346, 327, 力, 神通, 自在, the powers-supernatural-faculties-self-mastery, generally found in triplet as the endowments of the Bodhisattva.

Balin, 354, 大力者, the strong one, an epithet of the Buddha.

Bālopacārikam, 367, 愚夫所行禪, one of the four Dhyānas mentioned in the *Laṅkāvatāra*, p. 97. Though he is regarded as ignorant or dull-witted (*bāla*) who practises this kind of Dhyāna, this is the ordinary form of meditation carried on by most people, some of whom are quite intelligent and sharp-witted. But the Mahayana goes beyond these meditations which are more or less relative and artificial and not of the highest sort; for meditating on impurities, the impermanence of things, sufferings of life, etc., is the first lesson for the beginners of Buddhism.

Bāhyamadhyātmaka, 116, 內外法, external and internal.

Bāhyabhāva, 132, 272, 外法, an external world. ——abhāvānabhinivesāt (184—16), 不取外境 (T), 不著外性 (S), 不取著外諸境界 (W); "By not clinging to the existence or non-existence of an external world."

Buddha, 35 f, 354, 佛, 佛陀, 覺者, the enlightened one. Deśanādharmanishyando vac ca nishyandanirmitam, buddhā hy ete bhavet paurāḥ śeshā nirmāṇavigrahāḥ (320—1, 2), 329. 依法身有報, 從報起化身, 此爲根本佛, 餘皆化所現 (T); 說是眞法習, 所有集作化, 是諸佛根本, 餘者應化佛 (W).

Buddhatā, 137, 277, 佛性, 佛體性, that which constitutes Buddhahood. ....kleśadvayaprahāṇāc ca mahāmate buddhānāṁ bhagavatāṁ buddhatā bhavati (140—12, 13), ...斷二煩惱是佛體性 (T). "The reason of Buddhahood consists in the destruction of the twofold Kleśa (evil passions), etc."

Buddhadharma, 152, 155, 360, 佛法, Aparapraṇeyā bhavishyanti buddhadharmeshu (133—5), 於佛法中不由他悟 (T), "In the teachings of the Buddha they establish themselves not depending upon anybody else." Buddhabuddhatā sarvapramāṇendriyavinivṛittā, 137, 正等覺者, 永離一切諸根境界(T), Buddhasya buddhatā, 153, 319, 佛體性. Vāhānukūlā nityāśca tathā buddhasya buddhatā (234—8), (譬如恒河沙, 悉離一切過), 而恒隨順流, 佛體亦如是 (T).

"As the sands of the Ganges which always arrange themselves along the stream, so does the essence of Buddhahood [conform itself to the stream of Nirvana].

Buddhahetūpadeśa, 354, 佛性....教導(T), one who teaches the reason of Buddhahood.

Buddhi, 27n, 152, 162, 164 ff, (two kinds of), 202, 智. The difference between *buddhi* and *jñāna* is sometimes difficult to point out definitively, for they both signify worldly relative knowledge as well as transcendental knowledge. *Prajñā* is distinctly the latter.

Buddhiboddhavya, 116, 覺, 所覺, knowing and knowable. ——rahitaṁ saṁyaksaṁbuddhatvam (190—7), 正等覺體(T), 離覺所覺.

Bodhi, or saṁbodhi, 38, 菩提, or 正覺, enlightenment; Bodhicittotpāda, 103, 206, 發菩提心, awakening the thought of enlightenment.

Bodhipakshya, the thirty-seven, 352, 三十七助道品, which is, fully stated, *saptatriṁśadbodhipākshikā dharmāḥ*, the thirty-seven items leading to enlightenment. They are:

I. The Four Smṛityupasthāna, 四念處, the four objects of meditation; 1. *kāya*°, 身, the body; 2. *vedanā*°, 受, sensations; 3. *citta*°, 心, thought; 4. *dharma*°, 法, the Doctrine. II. The Four Samyakprāhaṇa, 四正斷, the four right ways of cutting down evil desires and thoughts: 1. to keep down evils that have not yet been done; 2. to uproot evils that have already been put in action; 3. to do goods that have not yet been done; 4. to make goods already done grow ever stronger. III. The Four Ṛiddhipāda, 四如意足, four strong determinations to attain supernatural powers by means of concentration on: 1. *chanda*, 欲, desire; 2. *citta*, 心, thought; 3. *vīrya*, 精進, energy; 4. *mīmāṁsā*, 觀, reflection. IV. The Five Indriya, 五根, five controlling principles: 1. *śraddhā*°, 信, faith; 2. *vīrya*°, 精進, energy; 3. *smṛiti*°, 念, mindfulness; 4. *samādhi*°, 定, concentration; 5. *prajñā*°, 慧, wisdom. V. The Five Bala,

五力, the five powers which are the same as the five Indriyas; the one is conceived as a sort of principle by which the other is manifested. VI. The Seven Bodhyaṅga, 七覺支, the seven factors leading to enlightenment: 1. *smṛiti°*, 念, mindfulness; 2. *dharmapravicaya°*, 擇法, a discerning judgment for the right doctrine; 3. *vīrya°*, 精進, energy; 4. *prīti°*, 喜, joyfulness; 5. *praśrabdhi°*, 輕安 repose; 6. *samādhi°*, 定, concentration; 7. *upekshā°*, 捨, equanimity. VII. The Eight Aṅgikamārga, 八正道, the eight noble paths of righteousness: 1. *samyagdṛishṭi*, 正見, right view; 2. *°kalpa*, 正思惟, right thinking; 3. *°vāg*, 正語, right speech; 4. *°karmānta*, 正業, right conduct; 5. *°jīva*, 正命, right livelihood; 6. *°vyāyāma*, 正勤, right effort; 7. *°smṛiti*, 正念, right mindfulness; 8. *°samādhi*, 正定, mind hightly collected.

Bodhisattva, the meaning of, 345, 菩提薩埵, 菩薩, 覺有情, one who seeks enlightenment not only for himself but for others, another name for the Mahayana follower; Bodhisattvecchantiko 'tra mahāmate ādiparinirvṛitān sarvadharmān viditvātyantato na parinirvāti (66—11), 220, 大慧, 彼菩薩一闡提, 知一切法本來涅槃, 畢竟不入 (T). "Mahāmati, the Bodhisattva-icchantika knowing that all things are in Nirvana from the beginning refrains for ever from entering into Nirvana."

Bodhyaṅgas, 39, 菩提支, factors of enlightenment.

Brahma, 352, 梵.

Brahmayāna, 360, 梵乘.

Bhāva, 131, 193, 307, 法, 有, existence, being, sometimes =dharma, sometimes=lakshaṇa. In the following instances, =dharma: Astitvaṁ sarvabhāvānām (156—7), 見諸法實有(W); Abhāvāt sarvadharmānām (156—9), 一切法若無(W); Sarvabhāvā anutpannāniruddhāḥ (198—1), 一切諸法不生不滅(T). *Bhāva* is *lakshaṇa* in these examples: Bhūtāvināśac ca svalakshaṇaṁ notpadyate na nirudhyate (198—2), 大種不壞，以其自相不生不滅 (T); Bhūto bhūtasvabhāvaṁ na vijahāti (198—3), 大種不捨其自性 (T). Bhāvābhāva, 128, 有無, being and non-being.

Bhāvasvabhāva, 43, 124, 性自性 (S), 自性 (T), 諸法自性 (T), 法性 (T), reason, being, self-nature, that which constitutes the essential nature of a thing. Na mahāmate yathā bālaprithagjanair bhāvasvabhāvo vikalpyate tathā bhavati (163—16), 一切凡愚，分別諸法，而諸法性非如是有 (T). "The nature of existence is not, Mahāmati, as it is discriminated by the ignorant." Tatra vitatham iti mahāmate na tathā yathā bhāvasvabhāvaḥ kalpyate (199—16 f), 言虛妄者不如法性起顚倒見 (T). "By being 'false' it is meant not to discriminate things as they are in themselves." Bhāvasvabhāva(-śūnyatā), 288, 自性空, emptiness of self-nature, one of the seven Śūnyatās.

Bhāskara, 354, 火, an epithet of the Buddha.

Bhūta, 74, 實, reality, element (*mahābhūta*).

Bhūtakoṭi, 164, 259, 262, 287, 354 實際, the limit of reality.

Bhūtatā, 213, 275, 354, 法性 (? T), reality. Yanmayā.... adhigataṁ sthitaivaishā dharmatā....tathatā bhūtatā.... (144—4 f), 我所証眞如常住法性 (T). "What has been realised by me, that is the ever-abiding nature of things, suchness, reality, etc."

Bhūmi, 97, 地, stage; 353, 大地, earth. Bodhisattvabhūmi, 菩薩地, of which there are ten, grading the upward course of the Bodhisattva's spiritual development, which culminates in the realisation of Buddhahood. The *Daśabhūmika-sūtra* is specifically devoted to the treatment of the ten stages of Bodhisattvahood. See J. Rahder's edition, in which, however, the gātha portions are mostly omitted. In the *Laṅkāvatāra* (chapter on "Abhisamaya"), the distinction between the Bodhisattva and the two Vehicles is emphasised, as the latter are unable to go up further than the sixth stage where they enter into Nirvana. At the seventh stage, the Bodhisattva goes through an altogether new spiritual experience known as *anābhogacaryā,* which may be rendered "a purposeless life." But, supported by the majestic power of the Buddhas, which enters into the great vows first made by the Bodhisattva as he started in his career, the latter now devises various methods of salvation for the sake of his ignorant and confused fellow-beings. But, continues the *Laṅkāvatāra*, from the absolute point of view of the ultimate truth (*paramārtha*) attained by the Bodhisattva, there is no such graded course of spirituality in his life; for here is really no gradation (*krama*), no continuous ascension (*kramānusandhi* 相續), but the truth (*dharma,* 法) alone which is imageless (*nirābhāsa,* 無影像), and detached altogether from discrimination (*vikalpaviviktadharma*). The names of the ten stages are: 1. Pramuditā (歡喜地), 2. Vimalā (離垢), 3. Prabhākarī (發光), 4. Arcishmatī, 燄慧, 5. Sudurjayā, 極難勝, 6. Abhimukhī, 現前, 7. Dūraṁgamā, 遠行, 8. Acalā, 不動, 9. Sādhumatī, 善慧, and 10. Dharmameghā 法雲. For a tabular description of each stage, see Sylvain Lévi's French translation of the *Mahāyāna-sūtrālaṁkāra* by Asanga.

Bhrānti, 38, 40, 118, 200, 274, 妄法, roaming, error; Bhrāntis tattvam (107—3), 119, 妄法是眞實 (T), 迷惑法名之爲實 (W); 惑亂眞實 (S); Bhrāntiḥ śāśvatā, (106—16), 119, 妄法是常相 (T); 迷惑法常 (W); 惑亂常 (S).

Mattapurusha, 360, 昏醉人, drunken man. Yathā hi mattapurusho madyābhāvād vibudhyate (135—14), 譬如昏醉人, 酒消然後悟 (T). "Like unto a drunken man who grows conscious when the effect of liquor wears off."

Madhyamā, 163, 242, 中道, the middle way. Vinivṛittir vikalpasya pratipatsye ca madhyamā (311—2), 亦離妄分別, 此行契中道 (T). "When discrimination is done away with, the middle way is reached."

Manas, 84, 99, 171 ff, 177, 190, 195 ff, 282, 意, consciousness as the will-to-be.

Manomayakāya, 145, 208 ff, 331, 354, 意生(成)身, the will-body.

Manomayadharmakāya, 318, 如來意成法身, the Tathagata's Dharmakāya as a will-body.

Manovijñāna, 38, 84, 171 f, 177 f, 191 意識, consciousness more intellectually conceived; the world of particulars.

Mano hyubhayasaṁcaram, 250, 意具二種行 (T), Manas walks in two ways.

Manyati, 250, 思慮, to reflect.

Mahā-augha, 193, 暴流, great flood. Yathā kshīṇe mahā-aughe taraṅgānām asaṁbhavaḥ (127—12), 如大暴流盡波浪則不起(T). "It is like a great flood whose force being exhausted waves are no more stirred in it."

Mahākaruṇā, 34, 97, 152, 177, 223, 357, 大悲, 大悲心, great love, great compassionate heart. Bodhisattvāḥ....pūrva-praṇidhānakṛipākaruṇopetāḥ....(214—2, 3), 菩薩便憶念本願大悲(T). "Recalling their original vows growing out of a great compassionate heart, the Bodhisattvas...."

Mahāpraṇidhāna, 230, 大願, great vows made by the Bodhisattva in the beginning of his spiritual career.

Mahābhūta, 246, 大種, primary elements.

Mahāmati, 大慧, the principal interlocutor in the *Laṅkāvatāra*.

Mahāyāna, 358 f, 大乘, the great vehicle.

Mahāyānaprabhāna, 203, 大乘光明定, a samādhi.

Mahāyogayogin, 103n, 大修行者, he who exerts himself in the great discipline leading up to Buddhahood.

Mahāśūnyatā, 288, 大空, emptiness of the highest degree, that is, *paramārthāryajñāna*, 第一義聖智大空.

Māṁsacakshus, 114, 肉眼, human eye. Buddhyā na māṁsa-cakshā (13—3), 以慧眼觀, 非肉眼觀 (T).

Māṁsabhakshaṇa, 368 ff 肉食, meat-eating.

Māyā, 幻, magic; Māyāvishaya, 141, 317, 幻境, realm of māyā.

Māyopama, 97, 100, 168, etc., 如幻, māyā-like; Māyopama-samādhi, 209, 如幻三昧, the highest samādhi in the *Laṅkāvatāra*; Māyopamasamādhikāya, 140, 如幻三昧身, the body in which this samādhi is realised.

Mārga, 39, 道, path; Mārgam ashtāṅgikam, 358, 八支道, the eightfold path. See under *Bodhipakshya*; Mārgasatya, 354, 道諦.

Muni, 36 f, 牟尼.

Mūlatathāgata, 146, 316, 根本如來, the original Tathagata, =Dharmakāya, =Dharmatābuddha.

Mṛigatṛishṇā, 112, 陽炎, 鹿渴, deer-thirst, fata morgana.

Mṛitparamāṇu, 187, 泥微塵, clay-atom; °bhyo mṛitpiṇḍo na cānyo nānanyaḥ (38—9), 泥團與微塵, 非異不非異 (T), "A lump of clay is neither different nor not-different from its atoms."

Maitrīvihāri, 370, 安住慈心, those who abide in compassion.

Moksha, 38, 132 f, 解脫, emancipation.

Moha, 259, 痴, folly, one of the three poisonous desires.

Maunatathāgata, 80, the Tathāgata in silence, =mūlatathāgata. Nothing corresponding to this in the Chinese translations.

Maulatathāgata, 145n, 根本如來, the original Tathāgata.

Yathātathyadarśana, 73, 如實見, seeing into the truth as it is. Yathātathyamudrā, 302, 如實印, the seal of suchness. Vimokshatrayādhigatayāthātathyamudrāsumudritā bhāvasvabhāveshu pratyātmādhigatayā buddhyā pratyakshavihāriṇo bhavishyanti nāstyastitvavastudṛishṭivivarjitāḥ (166—3,5). 得三解脫, 如實印所印, 於性自性, 得緣自覺觀察住, 離有無事見相 (S); 得三解脫門, 得已以如實印善印諸法, 自身內證智慧觀察, 離有無見 (W); 悟三解脫門, 獲如實印, 見法自性, 了聖境界, 遠離有無一切諸著 (T). "Let all beings realise the triple emancipation, be well stamped with the seal of suchness, abide in the intuitive understanding of the self--nature of things, which is to be gained by the inner faculty of realisation, and cease from viewing things in their relative aspect."

Yathābhūtam, 105, 114, 115, 118, 119, 121, 122, 128, 132, 195, 197, 215, 268, 273, 274, 282, 285, 294, 335, 339, 341, 如實, truly, as it is.

Yathābhūtasvalakshaṇāvasthānāvasthitam, 123n, 如實相自相分齊住 (S); 住如實處 (T); 住於自相如實法中 (W); "abiding in the place where reality remains in its original identity."

Yathābhūtārthasthānadarśana, Tatra nirvāṇam iti mahāmate (200—6), 123; 大慧言涅槃者, 見如實處 (T);....如眞實義見 (S);....謂見諸法如實住處 (W). "Mahāmati, Nirvana means seeing into the abode of reality in its true signification." The abode of reality is where a thing stands by itself, and we have in the *Laṅkāvatāra* the following (178—15): avasthāne 'vatishṭhata iti na pravartata ity artho....自處住者, 是不起義 (T). "To abide in one's self-station means not to be astir, [i.e. to be eternally quiescent]."

Yathābhūtāvasthānadarśana, 123, 123n, 127, 278. °ṁ sarvadharmāṇāṁ yaduta svacittadṛiśyamātrāvatāraḥ (112—6), 如實處見一切法者, 謂起(超)自心現量 (S); 云何住如實見, 謂入自身見諸法故 (W); 見一切如實處者, 謂能了達唯心所現 (T). "By 'seeing into the abode of reality as it is' is meant 'to get into the understanding that there is only what is seen of one's own mind, [and no external world as such]'."

Yathārutārthābhinivishṭa, 77, 隨言取義 (T); 如說而取著 (W), "to cling to the letter as fully in accordance with the sense."

Yathārutārthābhiniveśasaṁdhau na prapatata (164—14), 110, 不墮如言取義深密執着 (T); 不墮如所說義計著相續 (S); 不墮執著諸法相續不相續相 (W). The Wei text seems to differ very much from both Sung and T'ang. But Wei and Sung agree in reading *saṁdhi* as 相續 (combination or continuation) while T'ang has 深密 (hidden meaning) for it. I follow the T'ang reading.

Yathālabdham (at the end of the Tibetan *Laṅkāvatāra*), 23, as far as accessible or available.

Yāna, 360, 乘, vehicle. The Buddhist doctrine that carries one from this side of birth-and-death to the other side of Nirvana has been compared to a vehicle of conveyance since the early days of Buddhism.

Yugāntāgni, 257, 劫火, fire at the end of the world.

Yukti, 132, 如實, truth; 307, 相應(轉變), combination, concordance, transformation; Yuktivikalpa, 111 f, 理分別, reasoning as to the existence of the ego, one of the twelve false discriminations.

Yoga, 103, 瑜伽, 修行, discipline; Yogin, 修行者, devotee.

Raṅga, 195, 觀伎衆(S, T), 伎兒(W), the stage, theatre. Naṭavan nṛityate cittaṁ mano vidūshasādṛiśam, vijñānaṁ pañcabhiḥ sārdhaṁ dṛiśyaṁ kalpeti raṅgavat (224—2, 3). 心如工伎兒, 意如和伎者, 五識爲伴侶, 妄心觀伎衆(S, T); 心如工伎兒, 意如狡猾者, 意識及五識, 虛妄取境界, 如伎兒和合, 誑惑於凡夫(W). For the English, see p. 125.

Rākshasa, 34, 羅刹, a class of demons living in Laṅkā under the leadership of Rāvaṇa.

Rāga, 194, 259, 貪, greed, desire to have.

Rāgadveshamoha, 269, 貪瞋痴, known as the three poisons (三毒).

Rāma, 354, 羅摩, name of a hero.

Ruta, 108 ff, 文字, 語, word. Kathaṁ ca bhagavan bodhisattvo mahāsattvo yathārutārthagrāhī na bhavati (154—9, 10), 世尊, 菩薩摩訶薩, 何故不應依語取義(T). "O Blessed One, how is it that a Bodhisattva-mahāsattva is not to grasp meaning according to words?"

Rutārtha, 113, 語與義, word and meaning. Rutārthakuśalo bodhisattvo mahāsattvo rutam arthād anyannānyad iti samanupaśyati, arthaṁ ca rutāt (155—5, 6), 菩薩摩訶薩善於語義, 知語與義, 不一不異, 義之與語, 亦復如是(T). "The Bodhisattva-mahāsattva who is well acquainted with word and meaning, recognises at once that word is neither different nor not-different from meaning, and vice versa."

Rūpa, 175, 292, 292n, 色, form, material existence; Rūpakāya, 315, 318, 色身, the physical body; Rūpadhātu, 346, 色界, world of form, material world; Rūpalakshaṇa, 352, 色相, corporeal features; Rūpaloka, 331, 色界, world of form; Rūpasvabhāva, 188, 色自相, the self-nature of the external world.

Lakshaṇa, 165, 182, 183, 186, 193, 288, 307, 相, aspect, sign, appearance. *Ābhāsa* and *Nimitta* are also translated 相, and it is often confusing in the Chinese sutras to distinguish one from another. *Lakshaṇa* generally means individual "signs" by which one object is marked off from another object; *nimitta* is "appearance" or "tangible form"; while *ābhāsa* is not used by itself in the *Laṅkāvatāra* but in its negative form, *anābhāsa* or *nirābhāsa*, meaning "imageless," or "shadowless," i.e. "beyond the reach of the senses." Lakshyalakshaṇa, 97, 116, 133, 所相能相, predicating and predicated. This kind of antithesis appears throughout the *Laṅkāvatāra*; Lakshaṇavikalpa, 111 f, 相分別, one of the twelve false discriminations; Lakshaṇaśūnyatā, 288, 相空, emptiness of appearance, one of the Śūnyatās.

Lokaṁ vijñaptimātraṁ (ca dṛishṭyaughaṁ dharmapudgalam, 270—1), 181, 如是諸世間,唯有假施設,諸見如暴流,行於人法中 (T); 但心如是見,我法如暴水 (W). "The world is no more than subjective construction; various views concerning it rage like a torrent, [assuming the reality of] an ego-soul and of an external world."

Vajragarbha, 226 f, 金剛藏, the chief speaker in the *Daśabhūmika-sūtra*, who, inspired by the Buddha, discourses with Vimukticandra (解脫月). That Vajragarbha is the only Bodhisattva referred to in the *Laṅkāvatāra* besides its chief interlocutor, Mahāmati, points to this sutra's connection in some way with the *Daśabhūmika* or the *Kegon* (*Avataṁsaka*) *sutra*.

Vajradhātu, 177, 金剛界, the universe viewed as the manifestation of Vairocana Buddha whose image is reflected in the heart of every being. See also *Garbhakośadhātu*.

Vajrapāṇi, 145n, 金剛手, literally, thunderbolt-handed, a Buddhist god who accompanies the Buddha and protects him all the time.

Vajravimbopama. 97, 金剛喩定 or 三昧 a samādhi. It is the highest samādhi attainable by the Buddhist yogin who by this destroys the subtilest form of the Kleśa as if he wielded a thunderbolt. (Cf. the *Abhidharmakośa*, Louis de la Vallée Poussin, Chapter VI, pp. 228 f.)

Vajrasaṁhatanakāyo nirmitakāyaṁ darśayet, 315, 世尊金剛體, 權現於化身 (I-tsing).

Varuṇa, 354, 如水者 (T), or 水神, river-god, one of the immunerable epithets of the Buddha whereby he is made accessible to immunerable classes of beings.

Vasuṁdharā, 353, 大地, the earth as wealth-container.

Vaśavartin, 317, 自在, holding command over things. The Buddha is regarded as *sarvayogavaśavartin* (11—16), 於觀自在; *acintyadharmakāyavaśavartin*, (154—14), 不思議自在法身; *sarvadharmānābhogavaśavartin* (181—1), 於一切法悉得自在 (T, in which 無功用 is omitted), etc.

Vaśita, 39, 66, 98, 150, 209, 自在, self-control. The tenfold mastery or self-control as described in the *Avataṃsaka* (Śikshānanda, XXXVIII and LV) is as follows: 1. *Āyurvaśita*, 命自在, mastery over the duration of life; 2. *Citta°*, 心自在, mastery over the mind which can enter into every possible form of self-concentration; 3. *Parishkāra°*, 資具 (or 財) 自在, power over an infinite variety of embellishment whereby the Bodhisattva enriches the worlds; 4. *Karma°*, 業自在, submitting himself to the working of karma as the case requires; 5. *Upapatti°*, 受生 (or 生)

自在, mastery over birth so that he can be born in any world; 6. *Adhimukti*°, 解自在, the power of seeing the Buddhas filling up the entire universe; 7. *Praṇidhāna*°, 願自在, the power of attaining enlightenment at any moment and in any place as he wills; 8. *Ṛiddhi*°, 神力 (or 如意)自在, the power of exhibiting all kinds of miraculous works; 9. *Dharma*°, 法自在, the ability of teaching Buddhism in all its possible aspects; and 10. *Jñāna*°, 智自在, the power of understanding whereby he reveals in every thought of his the Tathagata's wonderful powers and perfect serenity (*abhaya*) leading to the realisation of the Bodhi.

Vastu, 119, 274, 305 f, 306, 本有, 妙物, 事, 事物, fact, event, reality. *Vastu* is a flexible term, generally having 事 for it, but its variations are frequently met with. For example, for vidyate tathatāvastu (147—6), T'ang has 有眞如妙物, Wei 如眞本有, and Sung 有事悉如如. Citravastutva(108—8) is rendered 種種事物 in T'ang and 種種法體 in Wei; and na vastu nāvastu (108—9) is 非卽是物, 亦非非物 (T). Broadly speaking, however, *vastu* (事) means a particular object discriminated by the mind, but it may also designate ultimate reality conceived as an object of transcendental intuition.

Vastuprativikalpajñāna, 189 ff, 336, 事分別識, i.e. empirical mind or consciousness as the faculty of discriminating particular objects.

Vāksamatā, 351, 語平等, the sameness of all the Tathagatas as regards their power of commanding sounds and languages.

Vāgaksharasaṁyogavikalpa, 108, (云何爲語), 謂言字妄想和合(S), "false discrimination in union with [i.e. as expressed in] words and syllables."

Vāgvikalpabuddhigocara, 163n, 言語分別智境, Paramārthas tu mahāmate āryajñānapratyātmagatigamyo na vāgvikalpabuddhigocaraḥ tena vikalpo nodbhāvayati paramārtham (87—12, 13). 第一義者是聖智自內證境，非言語分別智境，言語分別不能顯示 (T). Sung mainly agrees with T'ang, but Wei as in other cases widely diverges: 第一義者，聖智內證，非言語法是境界，以言語能了彼境界(W). "The ultimate truth points to the realisation of supreme wisdom in the inmost consciousness, and does not belong to the realm of words and discriminative intellect; thus discrimination fails to reveal the ultimate truth." But the lamp of words is useful to illuminate the passage to final enlightenment. Vāgvikalparutapradīpena bodhisattvā vāgvikalparahitāḥ svapratyātmāryagatim anupraviśanti (155—11), 109, 菩薩因語言燈入離言說自證境界 (T).

Vāsanā, 98, 108, 119, 121, 128, 133, 152, 167, 176, 178 f, 183 ff, 199, 201, 206, 208, 習氣，薰習, perfuming impression, memory, habit-energy; Vāsanāvīja, 189, 薰習種子, memory-seed. Every act, mental and physical, leaves its seeds behind, which is planted in the Ālaya for future germination under favourable conditions. In the Vijñaptimātra school of Asanga and Vasubandhu, this notion plays an important rôle.

Vikalpa, 26, 72, 96, 108n, 155 ff, 200, 201n, 274, 分別, (false) discrimination. In the *Laṅkāvatāra* discrimination stands contrasted to intuitive understanding which goes beyond discrimination (*avikalpa*). In ordinary worldly life, Vikalpa, if properly dealt with, works to produce good effects, but it is unable to penetrate into the depths of consciousness, where the ultimate truth lies hidden. To awaken this from a deep slumber Vikalpa must be abandoned. Hence the *Laṅkā's* strong arguments against it. The following are regarded as synonyms of Vikalpa, by which it is meant that they are all productions of discrimination: Āyur ushmātha vijñānam ālayo jīvitendriyam, manaś ca manovijñānaṁ vikalpasya viśeshaṇam (323—2, 3), 252. 壽 (命 W) 及於煖識，阿賴 (梨，W) 耶命

根，意及與意識，皆分別異名 (T).

Vikalpapratyaya, 346, 分別緣, conditions of discrimination; °prapañca, 84, 分別戲論, discrimination and futile reasoning; °mātra, 281, 唯分別; °mātraṁ tribhavaṁ (bāhyam ārthaṁ na vidyate, 186—16), 281n, 三有唯分別 (外境悉無有), "the triple world is no more than [the product of] discrimination, there is no such thing as an external world"; °lakshaṇagrāhābhiniveśaprashṭhāpikā (-buddhi), 27n, 取相分別執着智, which makes one cling to signs of individuality and work out false discrimination. This Buddhi is contrasted to the Pravicaya (觀察智). (Nirābhāsa-) vikalpaviviktadharma, 277, 無所有妄想寂滅法, truth which is imageless and detached from discrimination. See also *Viviktadharma,* 寂滅之法, the solitary, the eternally serene.

Vikrīḍita, 66, 遊戲, literally, sportive. This is an important conception describing the life of a Bodhisattva, which is free from every form of constraint and restraint. It is like that of the fowls of the air and the lilies of the field, and yet there is in him a great compassionate heart functioning all the time freely and self-sufficiently. =Lalita.

Vicārāparapraṇeya, svapratyātmabuddhyā (133—11), 273, (自覺) 觀察不由於他 (S), to examine with one's own intelligence, not depending upon another.

Vicikitsā, 359, 疑, doubt.

Vicitratva, or vicitratā, 160, 272, 種種, multiplicity, manifoldness, multitudinousness.

Vicīyate, 190, 250, to divide, to put in order; but the Chinese translators read "to accumulate extensively." Manasā ca vicīyate (46—17). 意能廣積集 (T); 意名廣採集 (S); 意能觀集境 (W). On p. 302 we have "jñānena ca vicīyate," 智於中分別 (W); and on p. 158 "jñānena vidhīyate," 不採集爲智 (S); 智能了分別 (W); 觀察法爲智 (T). See also *Vidhīyate* and *Cittena cīyate karma.*

Vijānāti, 251, to distinguish, to recognise. Vijñānena

vijānāti dṛiśyaṁ kalpeti pañcabhiḥ (46—18), 了別故名識. 對現境說五 (T); 諸識識所識, 現等境說五(S); 識能了所識, 五識現分別(W). "Cognition goes on by the Vijñāna, whereas the discrimination of what is presented [as an external world] is done by the five [Vijñānas]."

Vijñapti, 181, 279, 280, 282, representation. Variously translated in the Chinese texts: 1. 說 or 識, na svabhāvo na vijñaptir na vastu na ca ālayaḥ (167—16), 無自性無說, 無事無依處 (T); —— 無相續(S); 無自體無識, 無阿梨耶識 (W). 2. 假名, 設言教, 施設名, nimittaṁ vastu vijñaptiṁ manovispanditaṁ ca tat (168—9), 相事設言教, 意亂極震掉 (S); 相事及假名, 心意所受用 (W); 假名諸事相, 動亂於心識(T). Vijñaptimātravyavasthānam (169—5), 是施設量建立 (S); 境界唯是假名 (T); 善知唯是內心 (? W deviates greatly and is hard to get at the original). 3. 表示, (T), Cittaṁ vikalpo vijñaptir mano vijñānam eva ca (323—17), 心意及與識, 分別與表示(T); 心分別及識, 意及於意識 (W). 4. 假施設, lokaṁ vijñaptimātram ("Sagāthakam" 44), 如是諸世間, 唯有假施設(T); 但心如是見 (W suggests a different text). 5. *Vijñapti* appears in other connections where the Chinese point to ceratin discrepancies: Vijñaptimātraṁ tribhavam ("Sagāthakam" 77), 三界唯是心 (T, W). Param ālayavijñānaṁ vijñaptir ālayaṁ punaḥ ("Sagāthakam" 59), 顯示阿賴耶, 殊勝之藏識 (T); 阿賴耶本識, 意及於意識 (W). Tarkavijñaptivarjitam (Sagā. 28), 離於妄計度 (T), 離於諸覺觀 (W). Dehaḥ pratishṭhā bhogaś ca grāhyavijñaptayas trayaḥ, manodgrahavijñaptivikalpo grāhakās trayaḥ (Sa. v. 72). 身資及所住, 此三爲所取, 意取及分別, 此三爲能取 (T). W has nothing corresponding to this, while T omits *vijñapti*; but the body, property, and abode, Manas, holding-on, and discrimination—these are evidently *vijñaptis*, i.e. ideas or representations. Vijñaptimātra, 181, 239n, 278 ff, 唯識 or 假施設, ideas only. °vyavasthānam (164—5), 181, 281n, 境界唯是假名 (T). Vijñaptidvayavarjita, 360, 遠離於二取(T, 敎S), free from dualistic recognition Dvāraṁ hi paramārthasya vijñaptidvayavarjitam, yānatrayavyavasthānaṁ nirābhāse kutaḥ (65—13, 14). 第一義法門, 遠離於二取(敎), 住於無境界(無所有), 何建立三乘(T, S); —— ——建立於三乘, 爲住寂靜處(W). Wei differs greatly in the translation of the second half verse, but Sung and Wei agree in having 敎 for what corresponds to *vijñapti*. I take *vijñapti* as meaning in this case "comprehension," i.e. "cognition." Vijñaptivishaya, 189, field of representations. Atha cānyonyābhinnalakshaṇasahitā pravartante vijñaptivishayaparicchede (44—18). This is one of the difficult sentences as it is seen from the various renderings given to it. 俱時而起, 無差別相, 各了自境(T); 而彼各各壞相俱轉, 分別境界分段差別(S); the sense of which is hard to make out; 而彼各各不異相, 俱現分別境界(W). Evidently, W and S have 分別 for *vijñapti* here.

Vijñāna, 42, 66, 67, 154, 169, 171 ff, 175n, 182 ff, 識, cognition, discrimination, consciousness, but as any one of these does not cover the whole sense contained in Vijñāna, the term has been left untranslated in this book; Vijñānamātra, 181, 239n, 276 f, 278, =vijñaptimātra, but in this case *vijñāna* may better be understood in the sense of knowledge dealing with the relative aspect of existence. Vijñānamātram will then mean that existence is merely relative; Vijñānataraṅga, 74, 188, 識浪, waves of mentation.

Vijñāna, 272, 識, relative knowledge. This is also rendered 識 by all the Chinese translators even when it is used as in the present case in contradistinction to *jñāna* in purely intellectual sense. Jñāna is transcendental knowledge dealing with such subjects as immortality, non-relativity, the unattained, etc., whereas Vijñāna is attached to duality of things.

Vitatham, 266, 虛妄(T), 不如實(S), 顚倒(W), falsehood.

Tatra vitatham iti mahāmate na tathā yathā bhāvasvabhāvaḥ kalpyate nāpyanyathā (199—17). 顚倒者如心分別，此法如是如是，而彼法不如是如是 (W)；不如實者不爾如性自性，妄想亦不異 (S)；虛妄者不如法性起顚倒見 (T).

Vitarka, 201n, 計度，臆度, speculation, supposition. In the *Abhidharmakośa*, it is generally translated as 尋 (reflection) and found coupled with *vicāra* (伺 investigation). Tathāgatā na vitarkayanti na vyavacārayanti (240—7), 如來無覺無觀 (T, W)；如來(常定故) 亦無慮亦無察 (S).

Vitarkadarśana, 186. Ayaṁ tathāgatagarbhālayavijñānagocaraḥ sarvaśrāvakapratyekabuddhatīrthyavitarkadarśanānāṁ prakṛitipariśuddho 'pi sannaśuddha ivāgantukleśopaklishṭatayā....(222—14 f). 此如來藏藏識 一切聲聞緣覺心想所見，雖自性淨，客塵所覆故猶見不淨 (S)；此如來心阿梨耶識如來藏諸境界，一切聲聞辟支佛諸外道皆不能分別，何以故，以如來藏是淸淨相，客塵煩惱，垢染不淨 (W)；此如來藏藏識，本性淸淨，客塵所染，而爲不淨，一切二乘及諸外道臆度起見，不能現證 (T). "This realm of the Tathāgatagarbha which is [another name for] the Ālayavijñāna, is beyond the views based on the imagination of the Śrāvakas and Pratyekabuddhas and philosophers; although its original nature is pure, it loses this purity by being contaminated as it were by external dirt."

Vidūsha, 195, jester; Mano vidūshasādṛiśam (224—2), 意如和伎者 (T)

Vidhīyate, 250, 觀察 (? T). 了分別 (W), 不採集 (? S), to arrange.

Vināyaka, 354, 勝導者 (T),廣導者 (S), 將者 (W), remover of obstacles.

Viparyāsa, 118, 274, 顚倒, confusion, perversion. Bhrāntir āryāṇāṁ viparyāsāviparyāsavarjitā (106—14, 15). 諸聖於此惑亂，不起顚倒覺，非不顚倒覺 (S)；諸聖人迷惑法中，不生顚倒心，亦不生實心 (W)；諸聖者於妄法中，不起顚

倒非顚倒覺(T). "To the wise, [what is to be ordinarily regarded as] an error, [that is, this world of particulars] appears neither perverted nor unperverted."

Vipāka, 206, 208, 251, 314, 322 f, 成就, 異熟, maturing, ripening. Vipākaja(-buddha), 142, 325, 報生佛; Vipākabuddha, 316, 324, 334, (異熟佛 ?) 報佛; Vipākastha-buddha, 142, 324, 報(住)佛, (異熟住佛 ?).

Vibhāvana, 200, 觀察 (T), 善分別 (S), 善知(W), penetrating comprehension. Svacittadriśyavibhāvanatayā (79—18), 觀察自心所現故 (T), "by thoroughly comprehending that the world is the manifestation of one's own mind."

Vimoksha, 39, 143, 354, 解脫, emancipation; °mukha, 解脫門, emancipation-entrance; °traya, 138, 166n, 362, 363, 三解脫, the three emancipations, which are: 1. *Śūnyatā* (空, emptiness), 2. *Animitta* (無相, having no-signs), and 3. *Apraṇihita* (無願, desirelessness); they are also called the three Samādhis.

Vivarjana, 200, 遠離, free from. Utpādasthitibhaṅgadrishṭivivarjanatayā (80—1), 遠離生住滅見故 "by freeing oneself from the view [that is based upon the reality] of birth, abiding, and disappearance."

Vivikta, 245, 260, 266, 寂滅(T), 寂靜(S, W), disjoined, solitary, alone, eternally serene; °dharma, 221, 226, 寂滅之法, that which is alone, the truth solitary. Na....paramārthe kramo na kramānusaṁdhir nirābhāsavikalpaviviktadharmopadeśāt (215—7, 8). 第一義中亦無次第, 無次第行, 諸法寂靜亦如虛空(W); 於第一義無次第相續說, 無所有妄想,寂滅法 (S); 第一義中, 無有次第, 亦相續, 遠一切境界分別, 此則名寂滅之法 (T). Viviktadharmamatibuddhi, 221, 寂滅慧 (T), 寂滅智慧覺 (S); 知覺諸法寂靜 (W).

Vivecya, 162, 觀察 (reality) discerned (from falsehood).

Viśuddhi, 38, 清淨, purity, or purification.

Vishaya, 171, 174, 180, 196, 264, 272, 282, 境界, individuation external world, world of particulars; generally distinguishable from *artha*, which means each particular sense-field or a particular sense-object; °pavana, 67, 188, 190, 境界風, wind of objectivity; °paricchedalakshaṇa, 110, 差別境相, the aspect of individuation.

Visaṁyoga, 323, 離繫果, release from bondage, one of the five "fruits" (*phala*), q.v.

Vīrya, 366 f, 精進 energy, one of the six virtues of perfection (*pāramitā*).

Vṛitti, 174, 轉, evolution, differentiation.

Vaipākika Buddha, 23, 325, 報佛.

Vyavasthānam, 175, 270, 建立, construction; 安立, a resting abode. Cittamātram vyavasthānaṁ kudṛishṭyā na prasīdati (54—16), 心量安立處, 惡見所不樂 (S); 唯心所安心, 惡見者不信 (T); 但心安住處, 惡見不能淨 (W); 說但是於心, 邪見不能淨 (W in the "Sagāthakam", 439). See also under *Vijñaptimātravyavasthānam*.

Vyavahāra, 163, 世俗, the worldly way of thinking. Na cotpādyaṁ na cotpannaḥ pratyayo 'pi na kiṁ ca na, saṁvidyante kvacit kecid vyavahāras tu kathyate (85—8, 9). 無能生所生, 亦復無因緣, 但隨世俗故, 而說有生滅 (T); 非已生當生, 亦復無因緣, 一切無所有, 斯皆無言說 (S); 如是等諸法, 自體是空無, 亦無有住處, 爲世間說有 (W). "Nothing is produced, nothing is producing, and even causality is nowhere, there exists nothing whatever anywhere, but in conformity to our worldly experience, it is talked of [them as if things were really existent]."

Vyāsa, 354, 毗耶娑 (W), a celebrated sage.

Vyāvṛitti, 253, 轉依, revulsion, turning-over. Manovijñāna-vyāvṛittaṁ cittaṁ kālushyavarjitam (296—11), 意識若轉依心則離濁亂 (T).

Śakra, 353, 帝釋天.

Śamathasukha, 78, 奢摩多樂, the bliss of tranquillisation. Śamatha is the practical art of keeping the mind serene and undisturbed by evil thoughts and passions; while Vipaśyanā (觀, or 毘鉢舍那) is meditation fixing one's mind upon a definite subject or proposition. When the mind is tranquillised by Śamatha, it is ready for intellectual activity of the higher sort. The *Laṅkāvatāra* is not, however, quite explicit on this point as is *The Awakening of Faith in the Mahāyāna.*

Śarīra, 92, 199, 319, 353, 舍利, 體, 身; Śarīravat, 319, 如舍利, Śarīra-like; solid, indestructible substance. Ato jñānātmakās tathāgatā jñānaśrīrāḥ (20—2, 3). 是故如來以智爲體, 以智爲身 (T); 如來爲智身智體 (W). Śarīravatāṁ hi mahāmate nāśo bhavati, nāśarīravatāṁ dharmaś cāśarīraḥ (232—14-16). For this, Sung has: 大慧,身法者有壞,如來法身非是身法; Wei: 大慧,一切有身皆是無常磨滅之法,非無身故,諸佛如來,唯法身故; T'ang: 大慧, 以有身故. 而有滅壞, 法身無身故無滅壞. While all these three Chinese translations have "dharmakāya" (法身), the Sanskrit has only "dharma." "Those that have the [material] body are subject to annihilation, but not those that have no body, and the Dharma has no body."

Śaśavishāṇa, 302n, 兎角, hare's horns. This generally goes in pair with *kūrmaropa,* 龜毛, the tortoise's hair. One of the favourite comparisons used by Buddhist scholars who by this attempt to illustrate the nature of existence as both real and unreal.

Śānti, 121, 寂靜, 寂滅, tranquillity.

Śāśvata, 119, 123n, 常, opposed to *uccheda* (斷); eternal, constant; Śāśvata-uccheda, 116, 常斷. Śāśvatocchedavarjaś ca lokaḥ (22—10), 世間遠離於斷常 (T). Śāśvatavāda, 120, 常見, the philosophical school that upholds the eternity of existence as it is.

Śīla, 366 f, 戒, morality, one of the six Pāramitās.

Śīlavrataparāmarśa, 359, 戒禁取, taking hold of the merit accruing from the observance of the rules of morality. One of the three knots (三結, *saṁyoga*) tying up the followers of the two Yānas. See also *Satkāyadṛishṭi* and *Vicikitsā.*

Śuka, 354, 戍迦, one of the Buddha's epithets; nothing corresponding to this in Sung and Wei. Also the name of Rāvaṇa's minister, 輸迦, 68.

Śuddhisatyātman, 254, real immaculate ego.

Śūnya, or śūnyatā, 38, 41, 43, 74, 94n, 101, 115, 116, 118, 123n, 126n, 128, 141, 166, 167n, 168, 170, 239, 259, 286, 354, 舜若多, 空, empty, emptiness, void. Mahayana Buddhism is popularly identified with Śūnyatā philosophy: this is right as far as it concerns the denial of the substance theory as held by the realistic schools of Buddhism, but we must remember that the Mahayana has its positive side which always goes along with its doctrine of Emptiness. The positive side is known as the doctrine of Suchness or Thusness (*tathatā*). The *Laṅkāvatāra* is always careful to balance Śūnyatā with Tathatā, or to insist that when the world is viewed as *śūnya,* empty, it is grasped in its suchness. Naturally, such a doctrine as this goes beyond the logical survey based on our discursive understanding as it belongs to the realm of intuition, which is, to use the *Laṅkā* terminology, the realisation of supreme wisdom in the inmost consciousness. Iha śāriputra rūpaṃ śūnyatā, śūnyataiva rūpaṃ, rūpān na pṛithak śūnyatā, śūnyatāyā na pṛithag rūpaṃ, yad rūpaṃ sā śūnyatā, yā śūnyatā tad rūpam (*Prajñāpāramitāhṛidaya*), 338n 舍利子, (色是空空是色) 色不異空, 空不異色, 色卽是空, 空卽是色. O Śāriputra, this phenomenal world (or form) is emptiness, and emptiness is truly the phenomenal world. Emptiness is not different from the phenomenal world, the phenomenal world is not different from emptiness. What is the phenomenal world that is emptiness, what is emptiness that is the phenomenal world.

Śūnyatānutpādaniḥsvabhāvādvaya, 291 f, 空, 無生, 無自性, 無二 (T), emptiness, no-birth, no-self-substance, no-duality. Deśayatu bhagavāñ chūnyatānutpādādvayaniḥsvabhāvalakshaṇaṁ sarvadharmāṇāṁ yena śūnyatānutpādadvayaniḥsvabhāvalakshaṇāvabodhenāhaṁ cānye ca bodhisattvā mahāsattvā nāstyastivikalpavarjitāḥ kshipram anuttarāṁ samyaksaṁbodhim abhisambudhyeram (73—12-16). 願爲我說一切空無生無二無自性相，我及諸菩薩悟此相故，離有無分別，疾得阿耨多羅三藐三菩提(T). "Pray tell us about the aspect of existence in which things are said to be empty, unborn, non-dual, and without self-substance; when I and other Bodhisattva-mahāsattvas have a thorough understanding as regards this aspect of existence we shall quickly come to the realisation of the supreme enlightenment."

Śrāvakayāna, 360, 聲聞乘, "class of hearers," generally referring to the Buddhists not belonging to the Mahayana.

Śrīvatsa, 76, 德字(卐), that is, swastika.

Śrotravijñāna, 178, 耳識, auditory sense.

Saṁvṛiti(-kāya), 311, 應身(?). The body assumed by the Buddha for the benefit of the masses.

Saṁvṛiti, or Saṁvṛitisatya, 160, 163 f. 311, 世俗, 世諦(W), 俗諦, relative, worldly knowledge, or truth. Saṁvṛitiḥ paramārthaś ca tṛitīyaṃ nāstihetukam, kalpitaṁ saṁvṛitir hy uktā tac chedād āryagocaram (131—2, 3). 世俗第一義第三無因生，妄計是世俗，斷則聖境界(T). Sarvaṁ vidyate saṁvṛityāṁ paramārthe na vidyate, dharmāṇāṁ niḥsvabhāvatvaṁ paramārthe 'pi dṛiśyate, upalabdhiniḥsvabhāve saṁvṛitis tena ucyate (280—8-10). 世諦一切有，第一義則無，諸法無性性，說爲第一義，於無自性中，而有物起者(?)，是名爲俗諦(T). "According to relative truth all things exist, but in absolute truth nothing is; in absolute truth one sees that all things are devoid of self-nature; there is, however, a perception where there is no self-nature, hence relative truth."

Saṁvṛityā deśanā, 38, 160, 隨俗說, relative teaching. ——katham (25—4, 33—5). 云何隨俗說(T). See also *Vyavahāra*.

Saṁsakta, 160, 計著, tied. Aṅgulyagraṁ yathā bālo na gṛihṇanti niśākaram, tathā hy aksharasaṁsaktās tattvaṁ na vetti māmakam (223–224): 如愚見指月，觀指不觀月，計著文字者，不見我眞實 (T).

Saṁsāra, 34, 97, 100, 116, 128, 129, 290, 312, 346, 生死, birth-and-death. Saṁsāranirvāṇasamatā (42—7). 生死涅槃平等. "The sameness of birth-and-death and Nirvana" is one of the spiritual attainments of the Bodhisattva, who, however, practises "effortless" deeds and "skilful means" born of a great compassionate heart.

Saṁskṛita, 260, 279 有爲 distinguished from 無爲, *asaṁskṛita*. Dharmas are grouped under the two heads, and those belonging to the first (*saṁskṛita*) are seventy-two and those of the second are three according to the *Abhidharmakośa*, whereas the Vijñaptimātra or Yogācāra school has ninety-four Saṁskṛita-dharmas and six Asaṁskṛita. It is not easy to give one English equivalent for *saṁskṛita*; it means anything that does something and productive of some effect, anything that can be brought under the law of causation and mutual dependence. 有爲 "doing something," (*yu-wei*) is a very good Chinese substitute for *saṁskṛita* and 無爲, "doing nothing," (*wu-wei*) for *asaṁskṛita*.

Saṁsthāna, 241, 307, 形, 處, form, position.

Sakṛidāgāmin, 368, 斯陀含, 一來, one who comes back once more to this earthly life before he is fully enlightened; the second of the four ascetic fruits (*phala*). See also under *Anāgāmin*.

Sakṛidāgāmiphala, 148, 斯陀含果, 一來果, the state of coming back once more.

Saṁketa, 156, 269, 假名, sign, provisionary symbol. Nāmasaṁjñāsaṁketābhiniveśena mahāmate bālāścittam anusaranti (225—6,7). 凡愚不知名是假立，心隨流動 (T); 愚夫計著俗數名相，隨心流散 (S); 一切凡夫計著名相，隨順生法 (W). "As they are attached to names, images, and signs, Mahāmati, the ignorant allow their minds to wander away.''

Saṁgha, 364, 僧伽, brotherhood, one of the three treasures (*ratna*): Buddha, Dharma, and Saṁgha.

Saṁcodana, 151, 令覺知 (W), inspiring, wakening. Apramāṇaḥ sattvaparipākasaṁcodanam upādāya (232—6), 欲爲成熟無量衆生 (T); 爲化衆生令覺知故(W); Pūrvakuśalamūlasaṁcoditasya (9—12, 13). 往昔所種善根力故 (T); 以過去世善根力故 (W). Both T and W here have no corresponding words for *saṁcodana*, 開發.

Saṁjnānirodha, 368, 想滅, cessation of thought.

Saṁdha, 213, 密意, 密語, secret meaning; Saṁdhi(-artha), sarvadharma°, 349, 一切法深密義, the secret meaning of existence.

Satkāyadṛishṭi, 359, 身見, thought of an ego, one of the ''Three Knots'' (三結, *trīṇi saṁyojanāni*). There are two ways in which one comes to conceive the real existence of an ego: the one is subjective imagination and the other the objective conception of relativity.

Sattva, 130, 有情, 衆生, being, sentient being.

Satya, 114, 163, 諦, truth; Satyatā, 212, 275, 354, 諦性, truth, true-ness.

Sadasat, 35, 112, 115, 117, 118, 121, 122, 133, 134, 139, 201, 215, 229, 有無, being and non-being.

Saddharma, 154, 正法, true teaching, right doctrine. Saddharmaparigrahācca mahāmate buddhavaṁśasyānupacchedaḥ krito bhavati (195—13, 14). 若能攝受正法則不斷佛種(T). ''When the right doctrine is comprehended, Mahāmati, there will be no discontinuation of the Buddha-family.''

Saṁtati, 139, 相續, continuity. Here (79—11) it is evidently one of the views held by the philosophers. In other places the ''triple continuity'' (*trisaṁtati*) is referred to, although its content is not known as far as the *Laṅkāvatāra* is concerned. See pp. 9—18 and 146—17.

Saṁtrāsamāpta, 286, 驚怖, terror-inspiring.

Saṁtrāsita, 284, 怖 terrified. Bālānāṁ nairātmyasaṁtrāsapadavivarjitārtham (78—9), 爲令愚夫離無我怖(T); 爲斷愚夫畏無我句故(S); 爲諸一切愚癡凡夫, 聞說無我生於驚怖(W). "In order to dispel the feeling of fright which is cherished by the ignorant as they listen to the doctrine of non-ego."

Samatā, 99, 310, 346, 354, 平等, sameness; Samatājñāna, 273, 360, 平等智, the knowledge that grasps the principle of sameness.

Samatikram, 224,超過, going beyond.

Samādhi, 39, 66, 85, 121, 132, 140, 148, 三昧, 定. Cittaṁ samādhīyate (58—8). 心得寂止 (S); 心住一境 (T); 得心三昧 (W); Samādhimada, 360, 三昧酒, liquor of samādhi; Samādhisukha, 75, 77, 78, 80, 三昧樂, the bliss arising from a concentrated state of mind. Those who have not yet been able to rise to the rank of Bodhisattvahood are too deeply drunk with the beatitude of a samādhi, forgetful of the outside world where so many unenlightened ones are waiting for emancipation. This class of self-complacent Buddhists is severely indicted by followers of the Mahayana; Samādhisukhasamāpattimanomayakāya, 210, 三昧樂正受意生身, one of the three will-bodies (*manomayakāya*).

Samāpatti, 39, 74, 75, 140, 150, 正受, 等持, 定, 三摩鉢底, 三摩跋提. Samāpatti, Samādhi, and Dhyāna are synonymously used in all the sutras except that each has its own usage and shade of meaning. They designate a concentrated state of mind in which the subject is completely identified with the object of meditation. Psychologically, it is a state of consciousness in perfect equillibrium, i.e. "tranquillised"; Samāpattisukha, 356, 正受樂, 三昧樂 =Samādhisukha.

Samāropa, 157, 165, 180, 247, 建立, assertion, or theory-making. *Samāropa* stands against *Apavāda* (refutation), that is, as 建立 versus 誹謗. *Samāropa* and *Apavāda* on p. 226—10 are however rendered by Śikshānanda (T'ang) as 損益 (loss and gain)—a unique instance in this translation. Samāropāpavādāntadvayakudṛishṭivivarjitam.... 遠離損益二邊惡見 (T); 以離有無邪見故 (W); 捨離二見建立及誹謗 (S).

Samānārthatā, 365, 同事, engaging in the same work. This is one of the four sympathetic deeds known as Catvārisaṁgrahavastūni (四攝法), which are: 1. *dāna,* 布施, charity; 2. *priyavacana,* 愛語, kindly talk; 3. *arthacaryā,* 利行, useful deeds; and 4. *samānārthatā,* 同事, engaging in the same work.

Samāhita, 174, 定, collected state of mind.

Saṁbandhavikalpa, 111 f, 相屬分別, discrimination as to dependence, one of the twelve Vikalpas.

Saṁbodhi, 104, 127, 覺, 正覺, enlightenment.

Saṁbhāra, 227, 361, 資糧, moral provisions, preparatory material.

Saṁbhogakāya, 308 ff, 347, 142, 應身, Body of Recompense; Saṁbhogabuddha, 328, 報身, 受用身, Recompense-Buddha.

Saṁyagjñā, or Saṁyagjñāna, 26 ff, 155 ff, 278, 正智, right knowledge, one of the five Dharmas.

Sarvakalpanāvirahitam, 118, 遠離一切諸分別, being free from all discrimination.

Sarvajña, 354, 一切智, all-knowing.

Sarvadharma, 123n, 168, 一切法, 諸法, all things, existence in general, the world; °tathatā, 342, 諸法如, 一切法眞如, the thusness of all things; °nirabhilāpya (-śūnyatā), 288, 一切法不可說空, emptiness as the unnamability of existence, one of the seven Emptinesses; °aparigṛihīta, 283, 於一切法無攝受定 (Hsüan-chuang), a samādhi; °śūnyatā, 154, 一切法空 the emptiness of all things; Sarvadharmānāṁ śūnyatā-anutpāda-advaya-niḥsvabhāvalakshaṇa, 215, 一切法空, 無生, 無二, 無自性相, the aspect of existence in which all things are to be regarded as empty, unborn, non-dual, and without self-substance; Sarvadharmāṇām anutpāda, 125, 286, 300. 一切法不生, all things are unborn; Sarvadharmā nirātmānaḥ, 135, 一切法無我, all things are egoless; Sarvadharmānupādāna, 283, 於一切法無執取定 (Hsüan-chuang), a samādhi; Sarvadharmā bhaṅgotpādavarjitaḥ (199—14, 15), 294, 一切諸法(亦爾), 離於生滅 (T), =sarvabhāvā anutpannā niruddhāḥ (198—1), 一切諸法不生不滅 (T); Sarvadharmavaśavartin, 77, (世尊)於法自在 (T), master of all the world.

Sarvapramāṇa(-indriyavinivṛittaḥ, 242—9), 146, (離)諸(根)量(T), beyond all senses and logical measurements.

Sarvabhāva, 124, 155, 200n, 諸法, same as Sarvadharma, both being used indiscriminately in the *Laṅkāvatāra*.

Sarvabhūtātmabhūta(-sya kṛipātmanaḥ sarvaṁ māṁsam abhakshyaṁ bodhisattvasya 248—15 f), 367, 菩薩慈念一切衆生猶如己身.... 不應食肉(T). "The Bodhisattva who regards all beings as himself ought not to eat meat."

Sarvābhogavigata, 224, 捨一切功用行 (Śikshānanda), discarding all effortful works.

Sarvarūpāvabhāsaṁ hi yadā cittaṁ pravartate (276—12), 244, 衆色由心起(T),現諸一切色, 心法如是生 (W).

Sahāloka, 353, 娑婆世界, a world of endurance, that is, this world.

Sādhumatī, 78, 善慧地, one of the Daśabhūmi (十地, ten stages of Bodhisattvaship).

Sāmānyalakshaṇa, 139, 共相, generality, or those marks that are common to all things conditioned, such as impermanence, pain, emptiness, and egolessness.

Siddhānta, 40, 109, 349, 350, 宗, proposition, intuitive truth, self-relisation. Dṛishṭāntahetubhir yuktaḥ siddhānto deśanā katham (30—11). 云何因譬喻, 相應成悉檀(T), 譬喻因相應, 力說法云何(W), 譬因成悉檀(S). The *Laṅkāvatāra* takes special care to make a sharp distinction between *ruta* (letter) and *artha* (meaning), p. 154, and between *deśanā* (teaching) and *siddhānta* (realisation), pp. 148, 172; for what comes through the letter and teaching does not in truth belong to one's self, and it is only that which comes out of one's own mind that destroys the fetters. So we read: Nayo hi dvividho mahyaṁ siddhānto deśanā ca vai, deśemi yā(?) bālānāṁ siddhāntaṁ yoginām aham (172—17, 18), 我說二種法，言敎及如實，敎法示凡夫，實爲修行者(T). "I teach the twofold truth: realisation and teaching. I teach the ignorant; realisation is for those who discipline themselves [in Buddhism]." Siddhāntaś ca nayaś cāpi pratyātmaśāsanaṁ ca vai, ye paśyanti vibhāgajñā na te tarkavaśaṁ gataḥ (149—2, 3). 宗趣與言說，自證及敎法，若能善知見，不隨他妄解(T). "Self-realisation and philosophy, inner perception and doctrinal teaching—those who see into their differences and understand well will not be influenced by mere speculation." Cf. the *Abhidharmakośa,* Chapter VIII, Louis de la Vallée Poussin's French translation, p. 218 f, where the Good Law of the Master is said to be of twofold nature: *āgama,* doctrinal teaching, and *adhigama,* realisation.

Siddhi, 160, 成就, valid, perfected.

Sugata, 68, 善逝, en epithet of the Buddha.

Sumeru, 77, 須彌山, a mythical mountain.

Sūkshmamati, 74, 妙慧(T), exquisite knowledge.

Sthiti, 182, 住, abiding, generally in this combination, *utpādasthitinirodha* (or *bangha*), 生住滅, birth-abiding-disappearance.

Srotaāpanna, 368, 須陀洹(預流), he who has entered the first of the four ascetic fruits. See under *Anāgāmin.*

Srotaāpattiphala, 148, 須陀洹果, the state of entering upon the stream.

Skandha, 39, 139, 347, 350, 陰，蘊, aggregate. According to Buddhist philosophy, each individual existence is composed of the five elements or aggregates, which are: 1.

rūpa, 色, material element; 2. *vedanā,* 受, sensation; 3. *saṁjñā,* 想, perception or ideation; 4. *saṁskāra,* 行, formative principle; and 5. *vijñāna,* 識, consciousness; Skandhatā, 242, 蘊性, the substance of a Skandha, that which makes the Skandha what it is. Skandhānāṁ skandhatā tadvat prajñaptyā na tu dravyataḥ (153—11). 諸蘊蘊假名, 亦皆無實事 (T). Skandha-dhātu-āyatana, 81, 98, 143, 167, 168, 194, 218, 259, 262, 321, 蘊, 界, 處. The combination sums up the individual and his world. The Skandhas are the constituents of an individual personality as mind and body, whereas the Dhātus and Āyatanas make up the objective world where the six Vijñānas take in each its own field of perception. The eighteen Dhātus (fields or spheres) and the twelve Āyatanas (seats or abodes) are distinguished, but they are rather two different ways of classifying the same objects. The twelve Āyatanas are inner and outer. The inner ones are: 1. *cakshurāyatana,* 眼處, 2. *śrotra°*, 耳處 3. *ghrāṇa°* 鼻處, 4. *jihva°* 舌處, 5. *kāya°* 身處, and 6. *mano°* 意處; the outer Āyatanas are: 1. *rūpāyatana,* 色處, 2. *śabda°* 聲處, 3. *gandha°* 香處, 4. *rasa°* 味處, 5. *sparshṭavya°*, 觸處, and 6. *dharma°* 法處. The eighteen Dhātus are the following six added to the twelve Āyatanas: 1. *cakshurvijñānadhātu,* 眼識界, 2. *śrotravijñāna°*, 耳識界, 3. *ghrāṇavijñāna°* 鼻識界, 4. *jihvavijñāna°*, 舌識界, 5. *kāyavijñāna°*, 身識界, and 6. *manovijñāna°*, 意識界.

Skandhebhyo nānyo nānanyas tathāgataḥ, (188—16), 136, 如來與蘊非異非不異 (T). "The Tathagata is neither different nor not-different from the Skandhas."

Svacitta, 272, 自心, self-mind. (Cittamanomanovijñānamātraṁ traidhātukaṁ samanupaśyati, ātmātmīyavigataṁ svacittavikalpodbhavaṁ) na ca bāhyabhāvalakshaṇavaicitryapatitam anyatra svacittam eva (212—7), 272, 菩薩摩訶薩, 見於三界但是自心, 心意意識離我我所法, 唯是自心分別, 不墮外法種種諸相 (W); 菩薩摩訶薩觀三界, 心意意識量, 離我我所, 自妄想修墮外性種種相 (S); 觀察三界一

切唯是心意意識自分別起離我我所,不見外法種種諸相(T). "The Bodhisattva-mahāsattva sees that the triple world is no more than [the creation of] the citta, manas, and manovijñāna, that it is brought forth by falsely discriminating one's own mind, that there are no signs of an external world where the principle of multiplicity rules, and [finally] that it is just one's own mind." Svacittamātraṁ traidhātukam, 243, 三界唯是自心. "The triple world is no more than one's own mind." Svacittadṛiśya, 180, 自心所現, manifestation of one's own mind. Svacittadṛiśyadhārāviśuddhi, 179, 205 ff, 淨自心現流. Kathaṁ bhagavan svacittadṛiśyadhārā viśudhyati yugapat kramavṛittyā vā (55—4). 世尊, 云何淨諸衆生自心現流, 爲漸淨, 爲頓淨耶(T). Svacittadṛiśyamātra, 72, 179, 267, 唯自心所現, no other than the manifestation of one's own mind.

Svapariṇidhānādhishṭhāna, 140. Pūrvabuddhasvapraṇidhānādhishṭhānataḥ pravartate (50—6). 由諸佛自本願力所加持故, 而得生起 (T).

Svabuddhabuddhatā, 134, 139, 自覺性, the essence of Buddhahood. Deśayatu me bhagavāṁs tathāgato 'rhansamyaksaṁbuddhaḥ svabuddhabuddhatāṁ yenāhaṁ cānye ca bodhisattvā mahāsattvās tathāgatasvakuśalā svamātmānaṁ parāṁś cāvabodhayeyuḥ (187—4-6). 世尊願爲我說, 如來應正等覺自覺性, 令我及諸菩薩摩訶薩, 而得善巧自悟悟他(T). "Blessed One, pray tell me about the nature of the inner enlightenment attained by the Tathagata, Arhat, Fully-enlightened One, whereby I and other Bodhisattva-mahāsattvas may get properly enlightened not only for ourselves but for others."

Svabuddhi, 108, 304, 自智. Svabuddhyā vāsanāśrayaparāvṛittipūrvakaḥ (155—2). 自智境界, 轉諸習氣(T). "By means of his own intelligence the Bodhisattva causes a revolution in his inmost abode where his former memory is stored."

Svabhāva, 73, 101, 111; and Ātman, 166, 268, 288, 自性,體性,

The term is used in the *Laṅkāvatāra* at least in two senses. When it means self-substance making up the substratum of the individual being, it is synonymous with Ātman and Pudgala. This may be seen from such phrases as "svabhāvaśūnyatā," 自性空, or "niḥsvabhāvāḥ," 一切法無自性. It also means the reason or suchness of existence, in which case it is identical with Tathatā. Svabhāvo 'nupalabdhiḥ tathatālakshaṇam(228—13), 自性不可得, 是如如相(T). "The self-nature unattainable is the mark of suchness." Further, *svabhāva* is used in the sense of "nature" or "what makes up the being of a thing." Rutam evārtha iti rutasvabhāvāparijñānāt (193—16), 是人不了言音自性, 謂言卽義. "It is owing to his not perfectly understanding the nature of words that he regards them as identical with the sense." Seven forms of Svabhāva are enumerated, but as no explanation is given of them, it is impossible to know what they really signify (39—9-12): 1. *samudayasvabhāva*, 集自性, collection or aggregate; 2. *bhāvasvabhāva*, 性自性, being, existence; 3. *lakshaṇasvabhāva*, 相自性 sign, symbol; 4. *mahābhūtasvabhāva*, 大種自性, the elements; 5. *hetusvabhāva*, 因自性 cause, reason; 6. *pratyayasvabhāva*, 緣自性, condition, causation; and 7. *nishpattisvabhāva*, 成自性, perfection. As regards the three Svabhāvas, see below. Svabhāvam ekaṁ deśemi tarkavijñaptivarjitam (.......svabhāvadvayavarjitam, 267—13, 14). 277. 我唯說一性, 離於妄計度, 自性無有二...(T). 我說一實法, 離於諸覺觀....離二法體相(W). Svabhāvatraya or svabhāvalakshaṇatraya, 29 f, 66, 154, 157, 161, 168, 194, 211, etc., 三自性(相). Svabhāvadvaya is also mentioned (pp. 99 f) as regards our attachment to words (*abhilāpa*, 言說) and things (*vastu*, 諸法) when they are imagined as having the signs of self-nature or reality. Generally, the two Svabhāvas in the *Laṅkāvatāra* refer to the first two of the three Svabhāvas, which are 妄計性, *parikalpita*, imagination, and 依他起性, *paratantra*, reality. Svabhāvavikalpa, 111 f, 自性分別 discrimination as regards self-nature; one of the twelve Vikalpas. Svabhāvabuddha, 328, 自性佛, the Buddha as he is.

Svayam evādhigatayāthātathyaviviktadharma, 277, 如實證寂靜 (T), 自得如實空法 (S), 自身如實證法 (W).

Svayaṁbhuva, 354, 無師者 (T), 自覺者 (S), 自在者 (W), self-existing one as one of the Buddha's epithets.

Svalakshaṇa (=svabhāva), 135, 139, 自相, individuality, or individual marks which distinguish one class of beings from another; for instance, matter has its own characteristics as distinguished from mind, and mind from matter, and so on. The following combinations are quite frequent, Svalakshaṇasāmānyalakshaṇa, 116, 自相與共相, Svasāmānyalakshaṇa, 168, 304, 140, 143, 158 f, 自共相.

Svasiddhānta, 98, 100, 自悉檀, self-realisation. Bodhisattvena mahāsattvena svaśiddhāntakuśalena bhavitavyam (43—12, 13). 菩薩摩訶薩於自悉檀應善修學 (T); 諸菩薩摩訶薩修行自內法故 (W).

Svahetulakshaṇa, 303, 因自性, self-cause-character, that is, reality. Vāgvikalpamātraṁ hi mahāmate śaśavishāṇaṁ svahetulakshaṇābhāvat (61—7). (外道常不思議) 唯是分別, 但有言說, 何故, 彼因同於兎角, 無自因相故 (S). "It is no more than mere verbal discrimination, Mahāmati, it is the hare's horn, there are no real signs of selfhood."

Hasta, 292, 353, 手, hand.

Hetu. 40, 165, 192, 307, 323, 因, cause, antecedent, condition; reason, principle. The combination, "hetupratyaya," meaning causation or causality, is frequently met with. Hetu and Pratyaya are really synonymous, though they are differently enumerated, that is, six Hetus and four Pratyayas. In this case, Hetu is regarded as a more intimate and efficient agency of causation than a Pratyaya. Other synonyms are *kāraṇa, nidāna,* and *nimitta*. The six causes (*hetu*) are: 1. *Kāraṇahetu,* 能作因, the reason that makes the existence of anything possible; 2. *Sahabhū°*, 俱有因, the law of mutuality, that is, the state of being mutually conditioned; 3. *Vipāka°*, 異熟因, the law of retribution, or fruition; 4. *Saṁprayukta°*, 相應因, the law of association; 5. *Sarvatraga°*, 徧行因, the law of generality, which is applicable to certain mental qualities making the common ground for others; and 6. *Sabhāga°*, 同類因, the law that like produces like. The *Laṅkāvatāra* gives another group of six Hetus, pp. 83 f: 1. *Bhavishyaddhetu*, 當有因, the possibility of anything becoming cause to others; 2. *Saṁbandha°*, 相屬因, mutual dependence; 3. *Lakshaṇa°*, 相因, uninterrupted continuity of signs; 4. *Kāraṇa°*, 能作因, a causal agency that wields supreme power like a great king; 5. *Vyañjana°*, 顯了因, the condition in which things are manifested as if illumined by a light; and 6. *Upekshā°*, 觀待因, the law of discontinuation.

Hetuvikalpa, 111 f, 因分別, one of the twelve wrong discriminations.

Hetupratyaya, 122, 因緣, causation; also one of the four secondary causes which are: 1. *Hetupratyaya*, 因緣, the general law of causation; 2. *Samanantara°*, 次第緣, (or 等無間緣), condition governing the succession of events; 3. *Ālambana°*, 所緣緣, condition of becoming an object of cognition; and 4. *Adhipati°*, 增上緣, =Kāraṇahetu, the "supreme" condition.

INDEX